Decentralized Futures

This book provides readers with a comprehensive grasp of blockchain technology by exploring its applications, security measures, and protocols along with the need for safe blockchain networks, and the incorporation of artificial intelligence (AI) improving blockchain performance.

Decentralized Futures: Navigating the Integration of Blockchain Technology with Artificial Intelligence seeks to provide readers with a thorough understanding of blockchain technology, delving into use cases, security, and the integration of AI. The book initially focuses on the characteristics of blockchain, along with different frameworks. The authors delve into machine learning techniques to identify suspicious and fraudulent transaction patterns, such as in behavior analysis, and examine AI-based clustering and classification techniques to break apart blockchain data for easier processing and more efficient analysis. In addition, this book also has a deep dive into the consensus mechanisms that makes blockchain more effective. The book contains case studies from real-world applications, and readers will learn by applying the take-home messages and guidance in these case studies to their works. The book explores the integration of AI with blockchain to make decentralized futures in an effective way. It will also give an explorative idea of opportunities and challenges of this integration.

This book targets a mixed audience of data scientists, engineers, researchers, academics, and students on different levels to share and contribute cutting-edge technologies, methodologies, frameworks, and practices in blockchain integrated with AI.

Decentralized Futures

Navigating the Integration of Blockchain Technology with Artificial Intelligence

Edited by
Amrutanshu Panigrahi, Abhilash Pati,
Prince Jain, and Haipeng Liu

CRC Press
Taylor & Francis Group
Boca Raton London New York

CRC Press is an imprint of the
Taylor & Francis Group, an **informa** business

Designed cover image: © Getty Images

First edition published 2027
by CRC Press
2385 NW Executive Center Drive, Suite 320, Boca Raton FL 33431

and by CRC Press
4 Park Square, Milton Park, Abingdon, Oxon, OX14 4RN

CRC Press is an imprint of Taylor & Francis Group, LLC

ISBN: 9781041111665 (hbk)
ISBN: 9781041111672 (pbk)
ISBN: 9781003658597 (ebk)

DOI: 10.1201/9781003658597

Typeset in Times
by KnowledgeWorks Global Ltd.

To our family, colleagues, and our beloved institutions for their unwavering support throughout the development of this work.

Contents

About the Editors

Dr. Amrutanshu Panigrahi is an accomplished academic and researcher, currently serving as Assistant Professor in the Department of Computer Science and Engineering at Siksha 'O' Anusandhan (Deemed to be University), Bhubaneswar, Odisha, India. Demonstrating a strong commitment to international research collaboration, Dr. Panigrahi is currently undertaking postdoctoral research at Lincoln University College, Malaysia. His core research interests lie at the intersection of blockchain technology, ML, DL, and cloud computing. Dr. Panigrahi has published more than 100 research articles in reputable SCIE, ESCI, Scopus-indexed journals, and international conferences. He is an editorial board member of *BMC Artificial Intelligence, Edelweiss Applied Science and Technology* journal, and *Discover Artificial Intelligence.* He also serves as a reviewer for several SCIE, ESCI, and Scopus-indexed journals.

Dr. Abhilash Pati is currently working as Assistant Professor in the Department of CSE, FET-ITER, Siksha 'O' Anusandhan (Deemed to be University), Bhubaneswar, India, and also a postdoctoral fellow at Lincoln University College in Malaysia. He qualified UGC-NET (Assistant Professor Only) in December 2019. His research interests include IoT, fog computing, ML, and DL, and he has more than 100 publications in SCIE, ESCI, and Scopus-indexed journals and/or conferences. He is an editorial board member of various journals, including *Discover Artificial Intelligence, Big Data and Computing Visions, BMC Artificial Intelligence*, and *Edelweiss Journal of Engineering and Technology.* He is also an active reviewer for various SCIE, ESCI, and Scopus-indexed international journals and has authored three textbooks.

Dr. Prince Jain is an accomplished academic, researcher, and innovator in machine learning, artificial intelligence, and advanced engineering. He currently serves as Assistant Professor (Research Cadre) at Parul Institute of Technology, Parul University, Vadodara. He earned his Ph.D. in Electronics Engineering from Punjab Engineering College, Chandigarh, where he developed a strong foundation in interdisciplinary research. Recognized among the world's top 2% scientists in 2025 by Elsevier–Stanford, Dr. Jain's work spans cutting-edge areas such as metamaterials, IoT-based healthcare systems, and biomedical signal processing. With prior academic experience at reputable institutions such as Chandigarh University, he is dedicated to advancing knowledge through research, teaching, and innovation. His contributions reflect a commitment to solving real-world problems using technology, while mentoring students and collaborating on impactful scientific developments across multiple domains.

Dr. Haipeng Liu is a researcher and academic professional specializing in wearable healthcare technologies, biomedical sensing, and intelligent monitoring systems. He is affiliated with Coventry University, where he actively contributes to research and postgraduate supervision, particularly on projects focused on cost-effective healthcare solutions using wearable sensors. His work centers on post-stroke rehabilitation monitoring, leveraging emerging technologies such as artificial intelligence, the Internet of Medical Things (IoMT), and cloud-based diagnostics to enable continuous, remote patient care. Dr. Liu has also contributed to scholarly publications, including reviews on advanced wearable sensor systems for healthcare applications. Beyond research, he mentors students and promotes diversity initiatives, including supporting female participation in STEM through international scholarship programs. His contributions reflect a commitment to advancing accessible, technology-driven healthcare and improving patient outcomes through innovative engineering solutions.

Contributors

Deepak Kumar Acharya
Department of CSE
Bhubaneswar Institute of Technology
Bhubaneswar, Odisha, India

Sathish Babu B
R.V. College of Engineering
Bangalore, India

Shubha Dattatreya Bahinipati
Department of Computer Science and Engineering
Siksha 'O' Anusandhan (Deemed to be) University
Bhubaneswar, Odisha, India

Sruthi Balammagary
School of Computer and Information System
University of the Cumberlands
KY, USA

Sujit Bebortta
Department of Computer Science
Ravenshaw University
Cuttack, Odisha, India

Vuppala Sindhu Bhargavi
Software Development Engineer Intern, Amazon
Bengaluru, Karnataka, India

Naga Bhavani Chakka
VIT-AP University
Amaravati, Andhra Pradesh, India

Pooja CS
Government Engineering College
Challakere, India

Ayushee Das
Department of Computer Science
Rama Devi Women's University
Bhubaneswar, Odisha, India

Gobinda Chandra Das
Department of Computer Science and Applications
KL Deemed to be University
Andhra Pradesh, India

Manmathnath Das
Department of CSE (Cyber Security, Data Science) and AIDS
VNRVJIET
Bachupally, Hyderabad, Telangana, India

Sukanta Das
Department of Data Science and Artificial Intelligence, Faculty of Science and Technology (IcfaiTech)
ICFAI Foundation for Higher Education
Hyderabad, India

Laxminarayan Dash
Department of Computer Science and Technology
GITA Autonomous College
Bhubaneswar, Odisha, India

Ahmed A. Elngar
Faculty of Computers and Artificial Intelligence
Beni-Suef University
Beni-Suef City, Egypt

Ashalatha Gali
Department of CSE (Cyber Security, Data Science) and AIDS
VNRVJIET
Bachupally, Hyderabad, Telangana, India

Irshed Hussain
Department of CSIT
Siksha 'O' Anusandhan
Bhubaneswar, Odisha, India

Debarun Joardar
Brainware University
Kolkata, West Bengal, India

Shashi Kant
Department of Management, College of Business and Economics
Bule Hora University
Ethiopia, Africa

Teklu Kassu
Ethiopian Civil Service University
Addis Ababa

Madhumita Mahapatra
Department of Computer Science and Engineering
Delhi Technical Campus
Gr. Noida, India

Sushanta Kumar Meher
Department of Computer Science and Engineering
Centurion University of Technology and Management
Bhubaneswar, Odisha, India

Janmejaya Mishra
Department of Information Technology
Capella University
Minneapolis, USA

Kush Dharmesh Modi
Department of CSE (Cyber Security)
VNRVJIET
Bachupally, Hyderabad, Telangana, India

Bijayini Mohanty
Department of Computer Science and Engineering
Centurion University of Technology and Management
Bhubaneswar, Odisha, India

Tanmay Mukherjee
Department of CSE
Siksha 'O' Anusandhan (Deemed to be) University
Bhubaneswar, Odisha, India

Dileep Kumar Murala
Department of Computer Science and Engineering, Faculty of Science and Technology (IcfaiTech)
ICFAI Foundation for Higher Education
Hyderabad, Telangana, India

Debasish Swapnesh Kumar Nayak
Department of Computer Science and Engineering
Centurion University of Technology and Management
Bhubaneswar, Odisha, India

Soumen Nayak
Department of Computer Science and Engineering, Institute of Technical Education and Research
Siksha 'O' Anusandhan Deemed to be University
Bhubaneswar, Odisha, India

Subrat Kumar Nayak
Department of Computer Science and Engineering
Siksha 'O' Anusandhan (Deemed to be University)
Bhubaneswar, Odisha, India

Bijayalaxmi Panda
Department of Computer Science and Technology
GITA Autonomous College
Bhubaneswar, Odisha, India

Manaswinee Madhumita Panda
Department of Computer Science and Technology
GITA Autonomous College
Bhubaneswar, Odisha, India

Sandeep Kumar Panda
Department of Data Science and Artificial Intelligence, Faculty of Science and Technology (IcfaiTech)
ICFAI Foundation for Higher Education
Hyderabad, India

Sucheta Panda
Department of CSE-AI/ML
GMR Institute of Technology
Rajam, Andhra Pradesh, India

Amrutanshu Panigrahi
Department of CSE
Siksha 'O' Anusandhan (Deemed to be University)
Bhubaneswar, Odisha, India

Sasmita Parida
Department of CSE
Siksha 'O' Anusandhan (Deemed to be) University
Bhubaneswar, Odisha, India

Abhilash Pati
Department of CSE
Siksha 'O' Anusandhan (Deemed to be University)
Bhubaneswar, Odisha, India

Swagat Patnaik
Department of Computer Science and Information Technology, Institute of Technical Education and Research
Siksha 'O' Anusandhan Deemed to be University
Bhubaneswar, Odisha, India

Prarthana Pattanaik
Department of Computer Science and Information Technology, Institute of Technical Education and Research
Siksha 'O' Anusandhan Deemed to be University
Bhubaneswar, Odisha, India

Sambit Ranjan Pattanayak
Center for Data Science
Siksha 'O' Anusandhan (Deemed to be University)
Bhubaneswar, Odisha, India

Sushree Bibhuprada B. Priyadarshini
Department of Computer Science and Information Technology, Institute of Technical Education and Research
Siksha 'O' Anusandhan Deemed to be University
Bhubaneswar, Odisha, India

Moumita Roy
Department of CSIT
Siksha 'O' Anusandhan
Bhubaneswar, Odisha, India

Shaiku Shahida Saheb
VIT-AP University
Amaravati, Andhra Pradesh, India

Bibhuprasad Sahu
Symbiosis Institute of Technology, Hyderabad Campus
Symbiosis International (Deemed University)
Pune, India

Karthik Salikanti
AI Software Engineer, UnPlatforms Technologies Private Limited
UnPlatforms Inc.
Hyderabad, Telangana, India

Saptarshi Kumar Sarkar
Brainware University
Kolkata, West Bengal, India

Vinutha Ragavaiah Sethupathy Sarma
Oral & Maxillofacial Pathologist & Cancer Researcher
Saveetha Dental College and Hospital
Chennai, India

Anupama Sen
Brainware University
Kolkata, West Bengal, India

Sudhir Kumar Senapati
College of IT and Management Education
Bhubaneswar, Odisha, India

Rachana Sharma
Department of Computer Science and Engineering
Delhi Technical Campus
Gr. Noida, India

Debabrata Singh
Department of Computer Application
ITER, SOA
India

Nrusingha Tripathy
Department of Computer Science and Engineering
Siksha 'O' Anusandhan (Deemed to be University)
Bhubaneswar, Odisha, India

Seema Verma
Department of Computer Science and Engineering
Delhi Technical Campus
Gr. Noida, India

Preface

The rapid evolution of the digital landscape has ushered in the era of Industry 5.0, where the seamless integration of human creativity with high-speed, automated systems defines the next frontier of global productivity. However, this hyper-connected ecosystem, driven by the Internet of Things (IoT), presents an unprecedented surface area for sophisticated cyber threats. As we transition from purely automated processes to human-centric industrial collaboration, traditional cybersecurity paradigms must be reimagined. This book, *Decentralized Futures: Navigating the Integration of Blockchain Technology with Artificial Intelligence*, serves as a comprehensive roadmap for navigating these complexities. By synthesizing cutting-edge research in blockchain technology and machine learning (ML). From securing smart grids and healthcare networks to implementing decentralized trust management in supply chains, the chapters herein bridge the gap between theoretical frameworks and practical, industrial applications. We explore how blockchain serves as the 'trust layer' for IoT, how AI-driven intrusion detection systems (IDS) provide proactive defense, and how the impending quantum era necessitates a shift in our cryptographic foundations.

Designed for a diverse audience of researchers, system architects, and graduate students, this work provides both the high-level strategy for policymakers and the technical depth required by researchers. We hope this book serves as a foundational text that inspires further innovation, helping secure a future in which technology empowers humanity without compromising the privacy or security of the individual.

As editors, we extend our deepest gratitude to the contributing authors, whose expertise and rigorous research form the backbone of this volume. We also thank the peer reviewers for their invaluable feedback, which ensured the highest academic and technical standards. Finally, we thank our families and the editorial team at CRC Press for their unwavering support in bringing this ambitious project to fruition.

The Editors
Dr. Amrutanshu Panigrahi
Dr. Abhilash Pati
Dr. Prince Jain
Dr. Haipeng Liu

Acknowledgments

The completion of this book, *Decentralized Futures: Navigating the Integration of Blockchain Technology with Artificial Intelligence*, is the result of a collaborative journey that spans several years of research, coordination, and dedication. As editors, we would like to express our deepest gratitude to the many individuals and organizations who contributed their expertise and support to this project.

First and foremost, we extend our sincere thanks to the **contributing authors**. Your rigorous research, timely submissions, and willingness to refine your work through multiple stages of review form the intellectual core of this volume. It has been a privilege to curate such high-quality contributions from experts across the global academic and industrial landscape.

We are deeply grateful to the **peer reviewers** who volunteered their time and critical insight. Their meticulous evaluations and constructive feedback significantly enhanced the technical depth and clarity of each chapter, ensuring that this work meets the prestigious standards of **CRC Press/Taylor & Francis Group**.

A special word of thanks goes to the editorial and production team at **CRC Press**. We appreciate their professional guidance, patience, and technical assistance throughout the publication process, from the initial proposal to the final manuscript preparation. Their commitment to excellence has been instrumental in bringing our vision to fruition.

On a more personal note, Dr. Amrutanshu Panigrahi and Dr. Abhilash Pati express their deepest gratitude to **Sikha 'O' Anusandhan (Deemed to be University), Bhubaneswar, India**, for providing the resources, environment, and intellectual freedom necessary to pursue this ambitious project. The support of our colleagues has been a constant source of inspiration throughout this endeavor.

1 Introduction to Blockchain Technology

A Revolutionary Paradigm Shift

Deepak Kumar Acharya, Sudhir Kumar Senapati, Bibhuprasad Sahu, and Shashi Kant

1.1 INTRODUCTION

Blockchain has emerged as one of the most revolutionary technologies of the 21st century and is fundamentally changing the way we manage trust, store data, and transfer value in the growing digital world. Blockchain is, in its most basic definition, a distributed and decentralized registry that records transactions across multiple computers in an objective, secure, transparent, and finalized manner. Unlike conventional (centralized) established systems, where a single authority (bank, government, corporate, etc.) can validate and process the data, blockchain is perceived as self-sovereign, where an individual creates trust through cryptographic proofs or consensus mechanisms instead of relying on intermediaries [1]. It is a paradigm shift in the institution of trust and is an example of algorithmic trust – enabling transactions to be safely, openly, and autonomously transacted on a worldwide scale. It was acknowledged in 2008, when the pseudonymous author, Satoshi Nakamoto, published a paper in which the idea of a completely peer-to-peer electronic cash system was presented – the Bitcoin whitepaper. Bitcoin's use case was one of the first instances of utility for a blockchain and, over the years, developed beyond mere digital currency to smart contracts, decentralized finance (DeFi), non-fungible tokens (NFTs), supply chain registries, and even decentralized autonomous organizations (DAOs) and other features of Web3. Blockchain technology is fast losing its recognition as merely a tool for technological advancement and gaining ever more credibility as a driver of fundamental change in industries, economies, and societies [2].

In traditional systems, data management depends on the core use of a central server and a trusted intermediary to rectify and authorize transactions. There are numerous challenges associated with this model that include single points of failure, the issue of data manipulation, breach of privacy, and inefficiencies created by overburdened bureaucracy. However, it has been a successful model since time immemorial. The blockchain does not overcome such challenges by spreading the

DOI: 10.1201/9781003658597-1

same copies of the ledger among thousands of nodes, which means that there is no certain entity that can modify the data without prior agreement. Using blockchain-based transactions is time-stamped, cryptographically secured, and associated with past records to form an unalterable history. This immutability makes blockchain a very trustworthy platform in situations where accuracy, transparency, and data integrity count the most. For example, currently, blockchain has the potential in sectors such as the finance industry, healthcare, supply chain management, and voting, among others. By providing functions that can initially enhance efficiency while also increasing the level of security and accountability, it provides a certain degree of trust and transparency that was previously impossible in a centralized context [3].

The solution to intermediaries is one of the most revolutionary factors about blockchain technology, which is capable of providing a method of direct and peer-to-peer interaction. Historically, banks, clearinghouses, or government institutions have been critical in the verification, authorization, and settlement of transactions. With blockchain, they no longer have to rely on each other as it shifts human-based trust to cryptographic trust, which allows individuals and entities to interact without the need for centralized control while maintaining an element of security and transparency. This decentralization has ushered in entirely new economic paradigms, with borderless transactions, tokenized assets, and programmable financial instruments forming the bedrock of DeFi. Yet a system like this restores power in the social fabric, allowing people to have better control of their property and data, as well as the potential to take power away from central systems and decentralize them and run them as ecosystems [4].

For Web3 or the next generation of the internet, built on the web's triad of decentralization, blockchain is used as the foundational infrastructure. This will enable decentralized applications (dApps) to run globally without centralized servers, autonomous smart contracts to run using standard rules without human intervention, and token-based economies that incentivize participation and innovation. In Web3, blockchain redefines how individuals create, share, and consume value online, transforming the internet from a corporate-controlled platform to a user-controlled ecosystem where individuals can freely exchange value across both the digital and the real world.

Blockchain has enabled end-to-end visibility in supply chains and can assure the authenticity and traceability of goods in their journeys, from their point of origin to their final destination. This could particularly be relevant in industries where provenance matters to retain quality and assure consumer confidence, just as in the case of pharmaceuticals, farming, and even luxury goods. Introducing blockchain into healthcare establishes patient data sovereignty, where computerized patients can gain absolute benefit unlike their past treatment, while authorized patients securely retrieve information without any complexity. Governments worldwide are expanding blockchain applications far beyond identity verification, online voting, and land registry to increase efficiency and transparency. Since records are immutable and traceable to previous years, corruption levels will decrease and citizen accountability and institutional trust will increase. These cross-industry applications have reflected a wide range of technologies and have demonstrated their potential to revolutionize society at micro- or macro-level [5].

Fear of scalability, energy consumption, interoperability, and uncertainty of the regulation are just a few issues that hamper the widespread adoption of blockchain. Relying on major blockchains, such as Bitcoin and Ethereum, reveals limits in both capacity and strict rules, which leads to network congestion, making both networks much slower and more expensive to use. Specifically, proof-of-work (PoW) has also been characterized as energy-intensive. This has prompted various debates on environmental sustainability and biased the development of an option that is more eco-friendly, such as proof-of-stake (PoS) options using Layer-2. Also, due to the fact that blockchain is not limited to specific nations, the absence of uniform international regulations in several nations poses a challenge to both the innovators and investors, as well as to the consumers themselves. Governments and policymakers around the world are yet to determine the balance between the two to maintain stability, as they continue to negotiate on issues of innovation and compliance, as well as consumer protection and stability on the financial front. These issues are, in fact, quite substantial, but these questions are being addressed continuously and ever better by technological and policy innovations, and in the future, blockchain will become a regular thing.

Revolutionize healthcare services and public administration with blockchain technology, which offers secure, reliable ways to manage digital information. In the area of health care, decentralized systems allow individuals to control access to their medical histories while enabling authorized professionals to retrieve the information they need. Governments are also looking at technology in domains such as electoral systems, land registries, and digital public services. Blockchain technology, a public digital ledger, ensures that any transaction is permanent and can be verified, thereby improving transparency and accountability. The adoption of this phenomenon in various domains demonstrates the potential of blockchain-based solutions to induce significant transformations in society and institutions. As digital transformation progresses, injecting itself into the age of digital ecosystems and open economies, blockchain is not just a technology but a seed in the redefinition of the forms that societies have. The chapter begins by describing the rise and emergence of the blockchain and how it works and proceeds to explain why it is indeed adequate to see it as a revolution of the world as we know it.

1.2 EVOLUTION OF BLOCKCHAIN

In distributed systems and cryptography research, we study how networked computers work together to maintain consistency and tolerate faults. Byzantine fault tolerance (BFT) and other theoretical frameworks demonstrate the way to overcome consensus problems in peer networks when some peers do not act in good faith. The early intelligentsia behind secure peer-to-peer communication and decentralized record-keeping were busy with interlocking ideas from these concepts, long time before the term blockchain was resurrected. In the past, researchers, such as Stuart Haber and W. Scott Stornetta, came up with cryptography-verified lists of blocks to verify time, which is a part of Blockchain v1.0. This is because their work described how tamper-evident records would come about through non-centralized creation, and that would one day culminate in decentralized digital ledger books.

1.2.1 Bitcoin and the Birth of Blockchain

It was not until 2008 and the issuance of the Bitcoin whitepaper by the pseudonymous Satoshi Nakamoto that the clear breakthrough of blockchain technology occurred. Bitcoin was the first proven decentralized digital currency, as well as the first open application of blockchain as a registry system. Nakamoto built upon preexisting ideas of cryptographic hashing, digital signatures, and distributed consensus and designed a new architecture that enabled a peer-to-peer network to authenticate and store transactions without the involvement of a third party, such as a bank. A key innovation was the introduction of a PoW consensus mechanism, which requires miners (players) to solve costly mathematical puzzles to add new blocks. This system ensured that no single party could correct records that had already been made by using enormous amounts of computer resources. All transactions with Bitcoin were publicly verifiable, immutable once documented, and protected with a decentralized structure made up of nodes. Furthermore, blockchain has solved the problem of multiple expenses in a digital currency by creating a transparent environment where a single coin cannot be spent twice [6].

1.2.2 Bitcoin to Ethereum

Despite demonstrating that digital money could be decentralized, Bitcoin's blockchain was narrow. It was created with peer-to-peer payments rather than broad computational services. In 2015, the next breakthrough was Ethereum, which extended blockchain utility beyond currency into programmable platforms. Ethereum brought the idea of a smart contract, a self-executing agreement with terms written into the software right at the bottom. These agreements enabled developers to create decentralized applications (dApps), which were independent of central servers (or trusted intermediaries). This has facilitated the introduction of innovations in the fields of DeFi, games, identity management, and supply chain tracking. Whereas Bitcoin executed a very niche feature, Ethereum has built a generic generational blockchain platform that appeals to a universe of developer/entrepreneurial users.

The period after the release of Ethereum witnessed an explosion of blockchain initiatives that ameliorated the issue of scalability, cross-centrality, and governance. Hyperledger Fabric has built more enterprise aspects by implementing permissioned blockchain in financial, medical, and logistics sectors. The other network that Polkadot and Cosmos focused on was interoperability, i.e., when different blockchains will be able to communicate with one another and share information without any problems. In the meantime, consensus mechanisms based on PoS have been proposed to replace energy-intensive PoW to offer greater efficiency and environment-friendly features. Governments and corporations explored the potential of this technology by investigating the storage of digital identity, land registry, and cross-border payments, in addition to cryptocurrencies.

1.2.3 Blockchain 1.0–3.0

It has been observed that the development of blockchain technology is a means of fishing through generational waves, each extending the range of utility of decentralized systems. Blockchain 1.0 represents the era of digital currency, led by Bitcoin. At this time, blockchain was designed as a safe, decentralized registry to execute value transfer. Its applications were limited, but revolutionary, and demonstrated that it was, in fact, possible to create a digital trust between people without any need for a central authority [7, 8].

With the growing use of Ethereum smart contracts, Blockchain 2.0 became the next step in its expansion beyond just transactions. This generation made money programmable, followed by decentralized uses capable of complex process automation, as well as the invention of economic models. It was smart contracts that made it easy to peer-lend, decentralize exchanges, issue NFTs, and much more, beyond digital cash. However, in this period, many recognized issues of low throughput of transactions, network congestion, and high cost of transactions became apparent.

The current wave is Blockchain 3.0, which attempts to fix the failures of the previous generations besides making the blockchain available to the masses. Some of the most important attributes of this generation are scalability, interoperability, sustainability, and ease of use. Solutions, such as the Lightning Network from the second layer, sharding solutions, and new forms of consensus (e.g., delegated PoS (DPoS), proof-of-authority (PoA)), are currently in development to scale up to millions of transactions per second, without compromising security or decentralization. Moreover, more modern and smart technologies, like artificial intelligence (AI), the Internet of Things (IoT), and edge computing, are also expected to be added to Blockchain 3.0 in order to allow smarter and connected ecosystems to emerge.

Blockchain 4.0 is a further advancement in the evolution of distributed ledger technology. It is unrelated to digital currency or decentralized applications. Rather, it is intricately connected to advanced technological domains such as AI, the IoT, and edge computing. Earlier generations primarily focused on decentralization, smart contracts, and scalability. However, the objective of Blockchain 4.0 is to enable industrial-scale adoption by emphasizing interoperability, automation, and real-time application processing. This leads to a greater emphasis on fine-grained government structures like decentralized organizations (DAOs), which are collectives that make decisions based on some set of rules implemented as smart contract code. The idea of cross-chain interaction is the key to Blockchain 4.0. The idea here is that with a few blockchains working together, we could end up with a network of digital, interwoven ecosystems, rather than separate ones. Blockchain 4.0 has the potential to become the backbone of a digital economy by integrating smart cities, automating supply chains, providing people with digital identities, and enabling machines to communicate with each other. Blockchain is capable of serving more than just financial transactions; it can even hide a nearby intelligent network system. Additional advances from Blockchain 2.0 through Blockchain 4.0 are depicted in Figure 1.1.

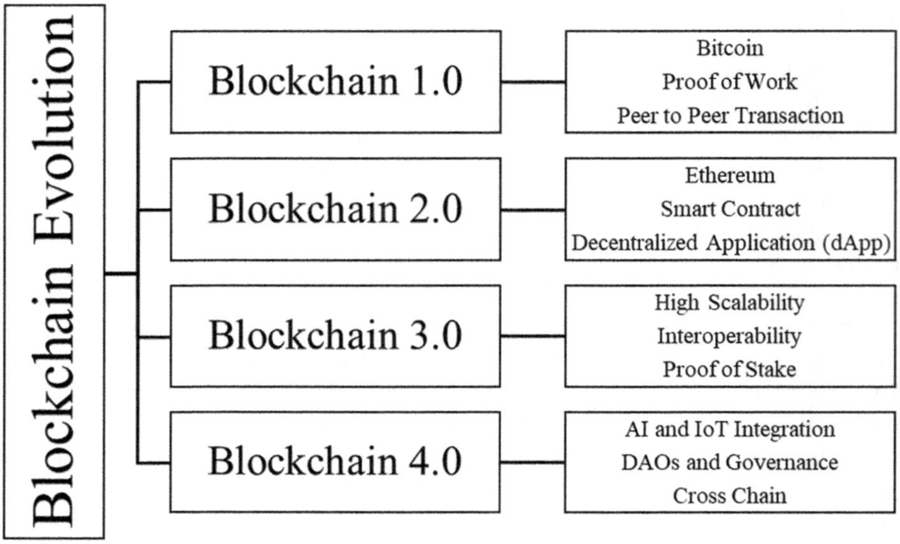

FIGURE 1.1 Evolution of Blockchain 1.0–4.0.

1.3 CORE CONCEPTS OF BLOCKCHAIN

The basis for autonomous development of reliable, open, and decentralized digital systems is blockchain technology. Blockchain technology combines elements that include distributed ledgers, consensus protocols, and encryption to empower users to store data in a decentralized manner. Understanding the three main parts of blockchain technology: blocks, transactions, and chains, is important before getting to an example of how it provides data security and immutability. While on-chain smart contracts make it easier to integrate programming into the blockchain, consensus mechanisms are equally important since they allow several parties to come to an agreement on how to organize the ledger's information. In terms of their use, governance, and accessibility, the current differences between public blockchains, private blockchains, and hybrid blockchains to date illustrate possible technical improvements. These basic concepts and how they function are covered in this section. Additionally, it helps make sense of the complex workings of blockchain technology and how it evolved into the backbone of decentralized digital systems [9].

1.3.1 Block, Transaction, and Chain

The core component of blockchain technology is the very concept of the block, which is a digital container of a set of verified transactions. Every transaction is an exchange of value or information over the network, e.g., sending cryptocurrency, transferring ownership of a piece of digital property, or recording supply chain information. Validated transactions are grouped in blocks so that only valid entries are added to the ledger. In general, a block is composed of three essential parts: metadata, the body, and a header. All block numbers, a date, the cryptographic hash of the last block, and the Merkle root that provides an overview of the transactions in the block are key bits of information in the block header. The real list of confirmed transactions is represented within the block body, and metadata usually contains additional useful information, such as the complexity of the mining operation or details about the block producer [10].

The reason blockchain records are tamper-proof and secure is because of the chaining principle applied. The blocks all point to the hash of the block they reference and consequently create one continuous and interconnected system that makes up the blockchain. This consists of a design that renders computer intrusion into the records of the past computationally infeasible. For example, if an attacker tries to edit a transaction in a previous block, the cryptographic hash of that block has changed, and there is no relationship to the new block. Therefore, the attacker would have to redo the PoW (or PoS) on every block that followed, which is extremely difficult to perform in a properly decentralized network. Openness, immutability, and verifiability independent of trust are three of blockchain's essential properties that are provided via these structures.

Another critical component is the length of the deal. Whenever a user requests a money transfer, the system notifies a network of nodes that check the request against predetermined standards. To do this, cryptocurrencies use a combination of factors, including the sender's wealth and the difficulty of spending the same amount again, to validate digital signatures and establish ownership. On validation, the transaction is put into a set of pending transactions that require confirmation. Fairness and consistency throughout the network are then achieved by the consensus mechanisms (discussed later) before determining which transactions are embedded in the subsequent block. By doing so, blockchain forms a chronologically and temporally immutable history of events: as such, it is applicable not only to digital currencies but also to the storage of information in supply chains, healthcare, voting systems, and other domains [11].

1.3.2 Consensus Mechanism

In addition to the lack of a central agency, the absence of a central authority is the most peculiar aspect of blockchain as compared to traditional databases. Rather, blockchain is based on consensus mechanisms, protocols that enable the participants of the network to agree upon the correctness of the transactions and the state of the ledger. Consensus mechanisms provide security, prevent duplication, and offer a model of decentralization rooted in trust. A number of solutions have been worked out, and they have their merits and demerits; thus, they can be applied to different situations [12].

The oldest and most well-known consensus algorithm is PoW, which Bitcoin uses. In PoW, miners compete against each other to find special solutions to complicated mathematical problems. The winner of the puzzle is the first miner to place the following block in the chain, and he/she gets rewarded with a block. This mechanism protects the network since editing a block would need to re-mine the other blocks, which is not possible since the computational and energy costs to do so are prohibitively huge. The negative part of PoW, at the same time, is that it is very energy-consuming due to the enormous processing power needed [13].

In an effort to address this flaw of PoW, different algorithms, such as PoS algorithms, were created. In PoS, validators are selected to forge new blocks depending on how many tokens they possess and are ready to stake them as security. This lessens the energy expense of computerized calculations yet still deters malice in their approaches as validators risk their vested capital in the event of behaving deceitfully. Granted, PoW operation has been transformed into a new PoS operational system, as in the case of Ethereum in 2022 (the Ethereum Merge); its energy footprint was greatly diminished as a result. PoS also allows more scalability because block confirmation times are faster than PoW.

A second popular functionality is PoA, where a limited number of trusted validators are pre-approved to authorize the transactions and create new blocks. PoA trades complete decentralization with increased efficiency and performance, which is why it is used in both private and consortium blockchains. For example, PoA can be applied in the enterprise world where government and compliance are the primary concerns [14].

Other well-known consensus models include DPoS, where a small number of delegates can be elected by token holders to validate transactions on their behalf and are both efficient and somewhat decentralized from the above explanation. Likewise, permissioned blockchains contain BFT and its variants (PBFT, dBFT, etc.) to acquire fast consensus even with malicious nodes. All these mechanisms come with different trade-offs in terms of security, decentralization, and performance. Finally, consensus validity will differ based on the needs of the blockchain, with a consideration of which is more important to customers (public responsibility), businesses (efficiency), or scalability [15].

1.3.3 Smart Contract

The implementation of smart contracts created a new breakthrough in the development of the blockchain. A smart contract refers to a program with the capabilities of running itself on the blockchain that implements the terms of an agreement under previously set rules once the specified conditions are fulfilled. Unlike traditional types of contracts, there is no need for enforcement because third parties, while smart contracts are not trustless, ultimately are trustless because they don't need a trusted party. Originally popularized by Ethereum, this innovation allowed building and deploying smart contracts in an environment that is decentralized and Turing-complete. Smart contracts work in a very straightforward way, that is, they include conditional statements in the form of if this, then that. In another example, a smart contract in a crowdfunding application could be written to extend finance to a project creator if a predefined finance target is achieved within a deadline. When the objective is not achieved, the contributors are automatically refunded the money. A contract is immutable once deployed, so that no party may change its rules. This helps one to ensure that the goods are transparent and that fraud and manipulation are eliminated. There are wide-ranging uses for smart contracts. For non-fungibles, this technology can be used in the financial sector to provide decentralized exchanges and loan services within a decentralized financial system (DeFi). Supply chains are also good candidates for using smart contracts since a payment can be automatically made when a particular delivery status (which has been reported) is met, thereby minimizing the delay and conflict involved. They secure the sharing of medical records among healthcare providers in a permitted manner. Organizations are being transformed even as governments leverage a DAO, including smart contract community enforcement for decision-making. Although they are unchangeable and hence provide protection, they are prone to coding mistakes. Certain bugs in the logic of the contract may cause exploitation, as in the notorious 2016 DAO hack. In addition, smart contracts have limited access to external data, which is why the trusted parties are required to directly provide external real-world data into the blockchain. Assuring the reliability of oracles is and has been an ever-present research issue and practical problem. Despite its limitations, the most promising part of blockchain technology is now smart contracts, which are currently applicable in nearly every industry by extending the application of digital money to systems that are automated, clever, and programmable [16].

1.3.4 Public, Private, and Hybrid Blockchain

There are three unique blockchains, i.e., public, private, and hybrid, each possessing certain benefits and limitations depending on what application scenario they may relate to.

Bitcoin and Ethereum are public blockchains, which are completely decentralized, free to all users, and upheld by a distributed pool of actors. They provide security and censorship resistance with large-scale consensus transparency. Anybody can become a node, any node may view the transactions, and anybody may become a validator. Public blockchains make the most sense for applications where a trustless environment is needed, like digital money or decentralized banking. Granted, the large throughput of enterprise applications often necessitates high throughput and can be prone to challenges related to scalability, transaction throughput, and energy consumption.

Private blockchains, in their turn, are only accessible by a specific set of participants that may be limited to one organization or consortium. Under this model, the registry of transactions or review of the ledger can only be done by the authorized entities. Privacy, performance, and scalability of private blockchains are decentralized, which suits some enterprise use cases, such as in supply chain management, healthcare records, and settling between banks. A good example and the most famous example of a native blockchain architecture that allows companies to customize permissions and governance models is Hyperledger Fabric. Despite the effectiveness of the private blockchain, it is thought that this concept compromises the value of the core idea of decentralization.

Providing flexibility, the hybrid blockchains combine in many ways the shortcomings of these two models: parts of the transaction are published, and parts are guessable via private data. The hybrid model could be very useful for the industry where the stakeholders expect the necessity of transparency, and we are forced to provide it by regulatory requirements, or on the other hand, we feel the market necessity to provide it, because the competition requires it. An example of this is a hybrid blockchain that stores evidence of a transaction publicly and maintains extensive records privately among trusted participants. It is a combination of these features that has made hybrid blockchains popular in tracing supply chains and in government registries and financial services, where privacy as well as transparency is required.

Public vs. private (and hybrid) blockchains commonly hinge on the priorities of the application: decentralization vs. effectiveness, transparency vs. privacy, or openness vs. control. The unchangeable registry that blocks transactions and chains provides decentralization agreement through the agreement mechanism, programmability, and automation through smart contracts, and diverse modes of public, private, and hybrid blockchains exist to position custom solutions to each use case as a feasibility. Collectively, these elements constitute the core of the new potential of blockchain, whether it is a cryptocurrency or a bank system, and more. Other issues of scalability, governance, and the need for constant assimilation of data in the real world are added, but we can point out that technology continues to gain relevance in the creation of the digital economy of tomorrow.

1.4 WORKING OF BLOCKCHAIN

Blockchain can be described as the process of securely recording data in a decentralized and chronological fashion using interrelated blocks, each consisting of a collection of trusted transactions. Any time a participant processes a transaction, like sending cryptocurrency, updating an asset record, or executing a smart contract, it will be broadcast on the network of nodes to be verified first. The transaction is independently verified by each node according to the requirements of digital signatures, adequate balance, and protocol obedience. The validated transactions are then run to a block, which will also include metadata (marking the time, a hash of the previous block, etc.) [17]. This connection of blocks by cryptographic hashes creates a chain, so that updating any single block would potentially retroactively update every following block, which is computationally infeasible to do in a sufficiently decentralized network. Blockchain employs a consensus mechanism, such as PoW, PoS, or PoA, to establish consensus among the distributed nodes and stop duplicate spending and fraudulent activities. After successful addition of a block, it cannot be changed to another member of the network, but it is accessible to every other member of the network, ensuring transparency and providing us with a source of truth. On top of straightforward transactions, blockchain can run smart contracts, or self-executing computer programs that automatically impose predefined agreements between players, without an intermediary. Such contracts trigger events (payments, asset transfers, authorization of entry, etc.) when certain conditions are fulfilled, and such transactions can be logged forever in the blockchain. In the process of doing this cryptography, distributed consent coupled with chaining immutable data provides security, accountability, and trust in a trustless environment. As a result, blockchain forms a decentralized and cryptographically sturdy digital register that can be used across various applications (Figure 1.2).

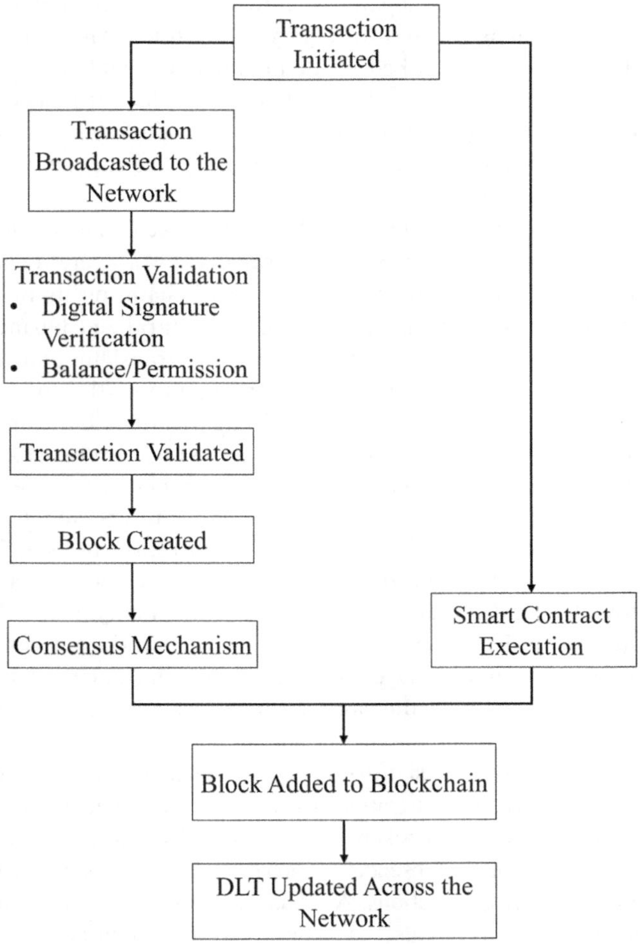

FIGURE 1.2 Working of blockchain.

1.5 BLOCKCHAIN AS A PARADIGM SHIFT

Blockchain technology represents a profound transformation in the governance, trust, and monetary transactions within digital systems. This will result in fresh iterations of current paradigms in economic and organizational domains. Essentially, blockchain undermines the traditional notion of trust owing to the lack of interpersonal trust among individuals who may not have established any ties. In centralized systems, consumers place their faith in an intermediary or authority, such as a bank, clearinghouse, or regulatory agency. Blockchain utilizes encryption, distributed consensus, and immutability to create verifiable and inherently reliable records. The decentralization of trust enables participants to independently authenticate transactions [18]. Consequently, it is feasible that the records may not accurately reflect their apparent nature later, and it is impracticable for a single individual to impose a sense of equity or accuracy. This action alters the manner in which trust is established inside organizations and among individuals across many sectors, from banking to supply chains, where trust is embedded in the technology itself rather than depending on individuals or institutions. This significantly reduces friction, dispute resolution costs, and the dangers associated with interpersonal interactions [19].

One of the key characteristics brought about by blockchain technology is disintermediation. It does away with classical intermediaries of operations and decentralizes the power in decentralized networks. Blockchain, on its own, makes it possible for these users to abandon the usage of centralized businesses, since there are possibilities of peer-to-peer contacts: this translates into lower costs and an efficient performance. For instance, the nature of the finance industry is currently witnessing the emergence of DeFi applications built on blockchain technology, which offer services like loans, borrowings, exchanges and do not require the presence of banks and brokers. In a similar manner, in the case of supply chain management, the blockchain allows manufacturers, suppliers, logistics providers, and retailers to provide documentation for transactions and track their assets publicly, without the need for a central authority to act as an authenticator for constructing data and exercising control over authenticity. Not only does this democratize access to digital services, where now the work routines are simplified, but also provides smaller players or previously marginalized parties to take part in the world markets with the same level of insecurity and unreliability as institutions [20].

Blockchain technology is a significant advancement in financial transactions, trust, and digital network administration. As a result, present economic and corporate practices will be revised. Blockchain fundamentally challenges the traditional notion of trust because of the absence of interpersonal trust between people who may not have formed any connections. Anybody who uses a central system, such as a government agency, clearinghouse, or bank, trusts a third party. By using immutability, distributed consensus, and encryption, blockchain produces records that are verifiable and essentially reliable. When trust is decentralized, everyone may independently verify the authenticity of transactions. Therefore, it would be hard for one individual to ensure equality or honesty, and the records may not be as accurate as they appear in the future. Numerous sectors, including banking and supply networks, are changing because this is moving away from relying on individuals or organizations engaged with social engagement, the possibility of conflict, and the expense of resolving it.

A second disruptive characteristic of blockchain is that it tokenizes physical and digital assets into tokens in a blockchain that provides the ability to allocate assets or to convey rights. The idea of tokenization can facilitate circulating assets into digital units such as real estate, art, commodities, loyalty points, and intellectual property as tradable assets that can be transferred or can be utilized in other novel ways. This forms programmable value that automates transactions via smart contracts, fractional ownership, and decentralized marketplaces. Tokenization enhances liquidity as previously illiquid assets can be broken down into small parts and effortlessly cross borders without the help of any intermediaries. Innovative models may be developed by using tokenization outside of the financial markets, such as incentivizing behaviors within decentralized ecosystems, a digital twin in supply chains, and the management of ownership of intellectual property via the searching and verifiable records of ownership. Blockchain has been bringing a new era of ownership, transfer of values, and investment in the digital world by turning physical and non-physical assets into programmable and tradable tokens.

Finally, blockchain forces a shift in business models that results in organizations always working differently and in absolutely new ways that weren't possible in centralized systems. Older forms actively tend to be hierarchical, to have one centralized control point, and to necessitate intermediaries between the two entities, but those, based on blockchain, are decentralized, peer-to-peer, and trustless and enable players to take part in networked ecosystems where value is distributed. An example of this is DAOs that use smart contracts to create participatory access-based decision-making and governance processes (meaning anyone and everyone can use them) and access-based (meaning there is no central authority controlling the whole. It can also implement business models on them in the technologies of blockchain (microtransaction, pay on use, tokenization, etc.) and make them earn money in an easier way, reduce costs, and also facilitate globalization. Finance, logistics, energy, healthcare, and digital media industries are experimenting with models based on blockchain, which can reduce intermediation, facilitate compliance, and allow brokering in networks in real time, radically changing the way value is made, distributed, and monitored. Blockchain is a paradigm shift since it makes it possible to not only recalculate the principles of trust but also remove intermediaries, implement the force of immutability and transparency, tokenize value, and make it possible to create completely different business models.

1.6 APPLICATIONS OF BLOCKCHAIN

Blockchain technology has come a long way in a short span. It has built a fundamental framework that might transform how many firms handle their money, operate their operations, and make decisions. Blockchain keeps a public, decentralized, and immutable record of transactions between users. It eliminates the need for centralized intermediaries, making it easier to authenticate peer-to-peer transactions, and employs smart contracts to automatically carry out contracts. Blockchain will change the way business is done, making operations more visible and services available to everyone in many areas of banking and finance. DeFi and global payments are two examples of how the way value is moved and evolves. In supply chain management, end-to-end traceability and provenance assurances will help keep prices down. Likewise, blockchain offers secure electronic health records (EHRs)/controlled sharing of information by patients, secure voting in government and services, identity systems, compliance in digital assets, NFTs, and developing Metaverse/Web3 Ecosystems, Verifiable Ownership, Tokenized Economies, and decentralized governance. In this section, blockchain apps are looked at in these sectors, including how they are transformative, how they add value to operations, and how they can be a key driver of systemic change in any digital or physical ecosystem.

- *Finance and Banking*: The concept of blockchain has enhanced the world of finance and banking because it allows peer-to-peer transactions that are not mediated by an individual or institution. Bitcoins or stablecoins provide examples of how funds may be moved anywhere in the world at lower prices and expedited settlement. One of the many insurance industries that requires smart contracts to reduce errors and fraud is the sphere of loan disbursement, collateral management, and insurance claims. On-chain lending, borrowing, and trading (DeFi) enable the implementation of financial inclusion to serve populations with limited banking access. Another way for banks to use permissioned blockchains is by retrieving interbank settlements, trade finance, and reporting compliance with the goal of providing transparency, auditability, and efficiency. Overall, blockchain is transforming the underlying nature of the financial process by instituting trustless verification, immutability, and settlement in real-time [21, 22].
- *Supply Chain and Logistics*: The blockchain boosts the transparency/traceability and reduces fraud in the supply chains. As the entire process of moving a product, including sourcing, transportation, etc., is documented to a permanent account, stakeholders can confirm provenance and status. With smart contracts, payment and enforcement mechanisms will lack delays and controversies since they are automated based on a contractual decision. Connection to IoT devices makes it possible to locate, monitor the environment, and track inventory in real time. In this way, supply chain management became more efficient, transparent, and resilient, as companies apply blockchain to improve their accountability, e-monitor their logistics, and gain the trust of their customers [23, 24].
- *Healthcare*: There's a growing fever pitch in the healthcare sector for blockchain that secures sensitive data, ensures interoperability, and ensures the patient's right to information. Blockchain-based EHRs are immutable with built-in audit capabilities. We implement the restriction of unauthorized usage by giving and removing access to the patients. A second area for the application of blockchain is to track pharmaceuticals to prevent fake drugs and store clinical trial data that is unencumbered and complete. Claim and payment of insurance are carried out automatically by smart contracts, minimizing administration costs. This flexibility, provided by AI and IoT, is the ideal means to prevent leaks of medical information and illegitimate access to encrypted data, improving the functioning of the healthcare delivery system while keeping authorized patients within a secure, transparent structure [25, 26].
- *Government and Voting*: Governments are using blockchain to operate safely, openly, and transparently. Voting using blockchain means that the votes are stored in blocks that cannot be altered due to fraud and manipulation. Votes can be checked, and voter anonymity is kept. Compared to

elections, blockchain improves identity control, land registry, tax collection, and welfare distribution via bureaucracy and corruption reduction. Smart contracts make compliance, subsidies, and grants more automatic and bring more trust and accountability to public administration. Blockchain is a template of secure, transparent governance [27].

- *NFTs and Digital Assets*: NFTs and other digital assets sit on top of a blockchain that enables the attribution of ownership and varying degrees of provenance. By providing artists with the ability to sell digital art, music, virtual real estate, and collectibles safely, NFTs allow artists to earn money. Smart contracts impose rights and automatically share revenue. In tokenization, you can get the ownership of a particular portion of digital/physical assets that might be of immense value; liquidity and availability are further increased. Blockchain alters the value, intellectual property exchange, and control of digital assets by linking digital ownership to an unalterable registry [28].
- *Metaverse and Web3*: Metaverse Web3 uses blockchain as the foundation of decentralized virtual worlds, digital property, and tokenized economies. Blockchain provides a safe asset, identity management, and cross-platform interoperability. Smart contracts represent the management of governance, in-game interactions, and grants. The data, content, and digital identities are under user control, which is also in line with the principles of Web3. Blockchain facilitates decentralized marketplaces, social networks, and immersive social experiences; it is a new economic and social interaction driver in the virtual world [29, 30].

Finance, supply proof, healthcare, governance, digitization, and ethical assets are examples of blockchain usage. Blockchain will decrease the level of dependences on intermediaries, enhance efficiency, and empower participants by offering decentralization, transparency, immutability, and trustless execution. Its application in multiple industries explains why its features of change are essential to adapt traditional processes, support new forms of business, and make the internet economy safer, better understood, and increasingly networked (Figure 1.3).

1.7 CHALLENGES AND LIMITATIONS OF BLOCKCHAIN

Although blockchain technology is used for its potential to transform a number of different sectors, the current usage is limited by a number of other limitations and challenges. Scalability is yet another serious problem. Bitcoin and Ethereum (as public blockchains) obviously are not capable of the thousands of transactions per second that Visa and Mastercard (as older, more centralized systems) are used to. A huge number of nodes are required to verify and record every transaction in the form of a blockchain due to its decentralization. This makes the process more transparent and more secure but obviously makes it take longer time to process. Consequently, blockchain networks tend to face congestion problems, which cause high transaction costs and slow confirmation times when they are heavily used. While the implementation of sharding, off-chain scalability, and layer-2 technologies is perceived as a

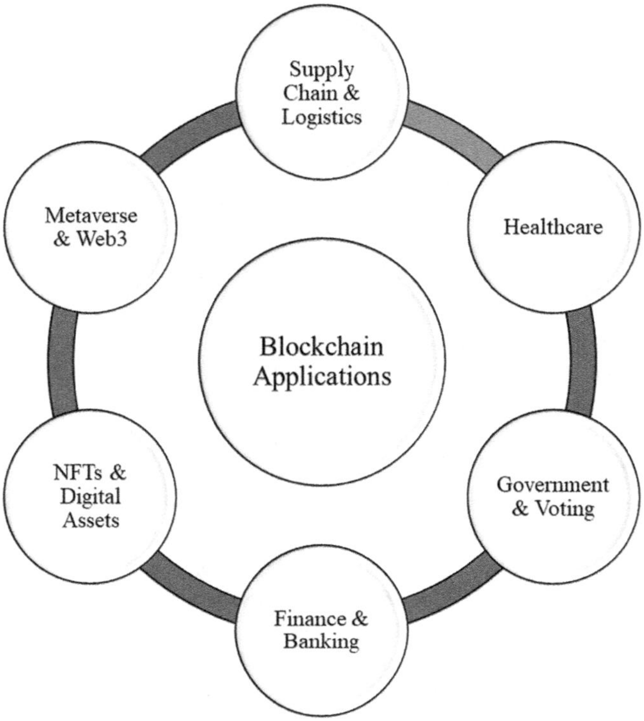

FIGURE 1.3 Applications of blockchain in different domains.

possible solution, they are still complex and have yet to achieve general acceptance. Consequently, blockchain is not appropriate for extensive implementations owing to its noteworthy scalability issue.

Energy consumption is a significant concern for using blockchains with the PoW protocol Network Consensus. The process of mining in such networks, such as Bitcoin, demands a lot of computational power, and therefore, a great deal of energy is used. Concerns about the sustainability of Bitcoin mining in the long run and its environmental impact have been raised, especially in light of research findings that its annual energy consumption is comparable to the energy consumption of entire countries. Although modern PoS and PoA consensus mechanisms significantly reduce energy consumption, they have elicited concerns about potential compromises in security and centralization. Implementing more energy-efficient consensus methods and utilizing renewable energy sources to mine are two strategies to reduce the negative environmental impact of blockchain as the world moves to using greener technology. Should this problem persist, blockchain technology may jeopardize its appeal due to apprehensions over its environmental impact.

Although the esteemed name of blockchain is robust and safe, security issues need attention. Although blockchain technology itself is difficult to change, the ecosystems built around blockchain, such as wallets, exchanges, or smart contracts, typically contain vulnerabilities. Breaches at cryptocurrency exchanges have caused the loss of billions of investor dollars and reduced investor trust. Although smart contracts are meant to act autonomously without human interaction, hackers can exploit faults in the code or programming for their own purposes. Moreover, even the most secure blockchains can potentially be vulnerable to a "51% attack," when a group of miners comes to dominate most of a network's computational power. Evidence of the dependency of such security, in the form of security exercised by blockchains, on variables beyond the protocol itself, involves phishing methods or rug pulls in DeFi applications, or the failure to properly manage private keys.

A major challenge in developing blockchain technology is attracting users' attention. Despite its sophisticated nature, the majority of individuals are unable to comprehend or utilize the technology. Since blockchain transactions cannot be reversed, one would be unable to recover funds in this case. Accounts can be unlocked or passwords can be reset by contacting Classic Bank's customer service. The extreme volatility of cryptocurrencies is another reason why both organizations and consumers are hesitant to adopt blockchain technology to its full potential.

1.8 FUTURE OF BLOCKCHAIN

Particularly when it develops further and integrates with other revolutionary technologies, blockchain has great promise. Blockchain technology will be most closely related to big data, the IoT, and AI. Together, these technologies have the potential to create secure, decentralized systems that can manage massive amounts of real-time data. Blockchain technology can assist AI in making choices by creating unchangeable records from the IoT. Through automation, efficiency, and reliability, such synergy might transform healthcare, banking, and the supply chain. Another key area is central bank-issued digital money. Blockchain-based digital currencies might enhance payment processes, simplify use, and reduce real cash usage, according to governments and organizations. CBDCs would be a state-sanctioned cryptocurrency alternative by integrating blockchain security with government control. Their growth may change international banking and accelerate business blockchain use. Future improvements may involve blockchain networks communicating. Because they operate independently, the majority of blockchains are worthless. Modern technology allows platforms to interact and exchange value using mechanisms, such as bridges and cross-chain protocols. Accelerated innovation and growth might be achieved with a well-structured blockchain ecosystem. Tokenization, governance, and identification of digital assets are predicted to be transformed from theoretical concepts to practical applications by the end of the next decade, thanks to blockchain technology. Blockchain technology, with its more open standards and intuitive interface, is about to revolutionize the online marketplace. With all the problems it's facing right now, its survival depends on creative decentralization and confidence-building tactics. Future developments and integrations with other revolutionary technologies will only increase blockchain's potential. Integrating blockchain with the IoT, big data, and AI will cause things to change. The integration of these technologies enables the safe distributed administration of huge amounts of data in real time. With blockchain technology, we may be able to create immutable records for the IoT or get better AI-based decisions. Through the implementation of more trustworthy and efficient automated processes, this partnership may transform healthcare, the supply chain, and the financial sector. Central bank digital money is one of the frontiers. In an effort to streamline payments, broaden acceptance, and cut down on the use of physical currency, governments and financial institutions are considering digital currencies built on the blockchain. In a government-backed currency that competes with current cryptocurrencies, CBDCs would use blockchain technology and be regulated by the government. Their rise may hasten the adoption of blockchain technology by financial institutions, ushering in a new era in international finance. Over time, it will be great to have many blockchain networks that can communicate with one another. Most blockchains aren't useful since they're separate. Through cross-chain protocols and bridges, platforms may connect with one another and transfer assets. With the continued integration of blockchain ecosystems, new ideas and business prospects are appearing at a fast pace. However, blockchain technology has a lot of potential practical applications in the next few decades, including digital IDs, governance, and asset tokenization. Blockchains may be useful for the digital economy if rules were less opaque and tools were simpler to use. Its sustainability in the long run will depend on how much it breaks out of its confines to become more decentralized and reliable.

1.9 CONCLUSION

Blockchain is an innovative technology that impacts decentralized trust systems, governance, and disintermediated asset exchange methods. Initially rooted in the cryptography of Bitcoin, it has evolved into decentralized applications (dApps), platforms for executing smart contracts, and frameworks for tokenized assets. This may result in an increase in value and trust-oriented programming. The spanning database and systems architecture advances significantly with these integrated features: consensus-driven transparency, cryptographic permanence, and BFT. This is beneficial in critical domains such as e-governance, healthcare informatics, financial services, and tracing the provenance of commodities throughout the supply chain. The system continues to exhibit issues, including insufficient throughput due to consensus algorithms, inconsistent and sometimes conflicting legal frameworks, energy-intensive PoW systems, and inadequate auxiliary infrastructure such as wallets and exchanges. Additionally, there exists a persistent threat to the company's reputation, a significant managerial challenge about a comfort style that is both isolating and user-centric, and the difficulty in achieving broad acceptance due to its inherent instability. It must also be capable of interfacing with other systems, such as those related to AI, the IoT, and big data analytics. Blockchain is not only an innovative technology but it also constitutes a profound social and technological revolution poised to transform the digital economy significantly.

REFERENCES

1. G. Tripathi, M. A. Ahad, and G. Casalino, "A Comprehensive Review of Blockchain technology: Underlying Principles and Historical Background with Future Challenges," Decision Analytics Journal, vol. 9, no. 1, p. 100344, Dec. 2023, doi: https://doi.org/10.1016/j.dajour.2023.100344.

2. K. Bilal, M. Sajid and J. Singh, "Blockchain Technology: Opportunities & Challenges," 2022 International Conference on Data Analytics for Business and Industry (ICDABI), Sakhir, Bahrain, 2022, pp. 519–524, doi: https://doi.org/10.1109/ICDABI56818.2022.10041562.
3. M. N. M. Bhutta et al., "A Survey on Blockchain Technology: Evolution, Architecture and Security," IEEE Access, vol. 9, pp. 1, 2021, doi: https://doi.org/10.1109/access.2021.3072849.
4. H. Guo and X. Yu, "A Survey on Blockchain Technology and Its Security," Blockchain: Research and Applications, vol. 3, no. 2, p. 100067, Feb. 2022, doi: https://doi.org/10.1016/j.bcra.2022.100067.
5. A. Panigrahi, "DTPKI: A Dynamic Trust Weighted Blockchain-based PKI," *2026 1st International Conference on Emerging Trends in Advancements and Applications of Computational Intelligence Techniques (ETAACT)*, Bhubaneswar, India, 2026, pp. 1–6, doi: 10.1109/ETAACT69135.2026.11542201.
6. A. G. Gad, D. T. Mosa, L. Abualigah, and A. A. Abohany, "Emerging Trends in Blockchain Technology and Applications: A Review and Outlook," Journal of King Saud University - Computer and Information Sciences, vol. 34, no. 9, pp. 6719–6742, Mar. 2022, doi: https://doi.org/10.1016/j.jksuci.2022.03.007.
7. M. Dabbagh, M. Sookhak, and N. S. Safa, "The Evolution of Blockchain: A Bibliometric Study," IEEE Access, vol. 7, pp. 19212–19221, 2019, doi: https://doi.org/10.1109/access.2019.2895646.
8. A. Panigrahi, A. K. Nayak, and R. Paul, "A Blockchain Based PKI System for Peer to Peer Network," Lecture Notes in Networks and Systems, pp. 81–88, 2022, doi: https://doi.org/10.1007/978-981-16-4807-6_9.
9. H. Taherdoost, "Smart Contracts in Blockchain Technology: A Critical Review," Information, vol. 14, no. 2, p. 117, Feb. 2023, doi: https://doi.org/10.3390/info14020117.
10. Z. Zheng, S. Xie, H. Dai, X. Chen, and H. Wang, "An Overview of Blockchain Technology: Architecture, Consensus, and Future Trends," 2017 IEEE International Congress on Big Data (BigData Congress), vol. 1, no. 1, pp. 557–564, Jun. 2017, doi: https://doi.org/10.1109/BigDataCongress.2017.85.
11. A. Panigrahi, A. K. Nayak, and R. Paul, "Smart Contract Assisted Blockchain based Public Key Infrastructure System," Transactions on Emerging Telecommunications Technologies, Oct. 2022, doi: https://doi.org/10.1002/ett.4655.
12. A. Panigrahi, A. K. Nayak, R. Paul, B. Sahu, and S. Kant, "CTB-PKI: Clustering and Trust Enabled Blockchain Based PKI System for Efficient Communication in P2P Network," IEEE Access, vol. 10, pp. 124277–124290, 2022, doi: https://doi.org/10.1109/access.2022.3222807.
13. M. Belotti, N. Bozic, G. Pujolle, and S. Secci, "A Vademecum on Blockchain Technologies: When, Which, and How," IEEE Communications Surveys & Tutorials, vol. 21, no. 4, pp. 3796–3838, 2019, doi: https://doi.org/10.1109/comst.2019.2928178.
14. D. Efanov and P. Roschin, "The All-Pervasiveness of the Blockchain Technology," Procedia Computer Science, vol. 123, pp. 116–121, 2018, doi: https://doi.org/10.1016/j.procs.2018.01.019.
15. T. Ahram, A. Sargolzaei, S. Sargolzaei, J. Daniels and B. Amaba, "Blockchain Technology Innovations," 2017 IEEE Technology & Engineering Management Conference (TEMSCON), Santa Clara, CA, USA, 2017, pp. 137–141, doi: https://doi.org/10.1109/TEMSCON.2017.7998367.
16. A. Panigrahi, A. Pati, B. Dash, G. Sahoo, D. Singh, and M. Dash, "ASBlock: An Agricultural based Supply Chain Management using Blockchain Technology," Procedia Computer Science, vol. 235, pp. 1943–1952, Jan. 2024, doi: https://doi.org/10.1016/j.procs.2024.04.184.

17. C. Komalavalli, D. Saxena, and C. Laroiya, "Overview of Blockchain Technology Concepts," Handbook of Research on Blockchain Technology, pp. 349–371, 2020, doi: https://doi.org/10.1016/b978-0-12-819816-2.00014-9.
18. C. Laroiya, D. Saxena, and C. Komalavalli, "Applications of Blockchain Technology," Handbook of Research on Blockchain Technology, pp. 213–243, 2020, doi: https://doi.org/10.1016/b978-0-12-819816-2.00009-5.
19. M. Niranjanamurthy, B. N. Nithya, and S. Jagannatha, "Analysis of Blockchain Technology: Pros, Cons and SWOT," Cluster Computing, vol. 22, no. 6, Mar. 2018, doi: https://doi.org/10.1007/s10586-018-2387-5.
20. A. Haleem, M. Javaid, R. P. Singh, R. Suman, and S. Rab, "Blockchain Technology Applications in Healthcare: An Overview," International Journal of Intelligent Networks, vol. 2, pp. 130–139, 2021, doi: https://doi.org/10.1016/j.ijin.2021.09.005.
21. M. Javaid, A. Haleem, R. P. Singh, R. Suman, and S. Khan, "A Review of Blockchain Technology Applications for Financial Services," BenchCouncil Transactions on Benchmarks, Standards and Evaluations, vol. 2, no. 3, 2022, doi: https://doi.org/10.1016/j.tbench.2022.100073.
22. Q. Gan, R. Y. K. Lau, and J. Hong, "A Critical Review of Blockchain Applications to Banking and Finance: A Qualitative Thematic Analysis Approach," Technology Analysis & Strategic Management, vol. 37, no. 4, pp. 1–17, Sep. 2021, doi: https://doi.org/10.1080/09537325.2021.1979509.
23. P. Dutta, T.-M. Choi, S. Somani, and R. Butala, "Blockchain Technology in Supply Chain operations: Applications, Challenges and Research Opportunities," Transportation Research. Part E, Logistics and Transportation Review, vol. 142, no. 1, p. 102067, Oct. 2020, doi: https://doi.org/10.1016/j.tre.2020.102067.
24. Y. Zhang et al., "Synergizing Blockchain and Internet of Things for Enhancing Efficiency and Waste Reduction in Sustainable Food Management," Trends in Food Science & Technology, p. 104873, Jan. 2025, doi: https://doi.org/10.1016/j.tifs.2025.104873.
25. A. Panigrahi, A. K. Nayak, and R. Paul, "HealthCare EHR," International Journal of Information Systems and Supply Chain Management, vol. 15, no. 3, pp. 1–15, Jul. 2022, doi: https://doi.org/10.4018/ijisscm.290017.
26. M. Shaikh, S. A. Memon, A. Ebrahimi, and U. K. Wiil, "A Systematic Literature Review for Blockchain-Based Healthcare Implementations," Healthcare, vol. 13, no. 9, p. 1087, May 2025, doi: https://doi.org/10.3390/healthcare13091087.
27. A. P. Balcerzak, E. Nica, E. Rogalska, M. Poliak, T. Kliěstik, and O.-M. Sabie, "Blockchain Technology and Smart Contracts in Decentralized Governance Systems," Administrative Sciences, vol. 12, no. 3, p. 96, Aug. 2022, doi: https://doi.org/10.3390/admsci12030096.
28. W. AlKhader, R. Jayaraman, K. Salah, Andrei Sleptchenko, J. Antony, and M. Omar, "Leveraging Blockchain and NFTs for Quality 4.0 Implementation in Digital Manufacturing," Journal of Manufacturing Technology Management, vol. 34, no. 7, pp. 1208–1234, Aug. 2023, doi: https://doi.org/10.1108/jmtm-05-2023-0172.
29. V. T. Truong, L. Le and D. Niyato, "Blockchain Meets Metaverse and Digital Asset Management: A Comprehensive Survey," in IEEE Access, vol. 11, pp. 26258–26288, 2023, doi: https://doi.org/10.1109/ACCESS.2023.3257029.
30. X. Hui and C. Tucker, "Decentralization, Blockchain, Artificial Intelligence (AI): Challenges and Opportunities," Journal of Product Innovation Management, Jul. 2025, doi: https://doi.org/10.1111/jpim.12800.

2 Integrating Internet of Things (IoT) and Blockchain

Current Applications, Challenges, and Future Perspectives

Prarthana Pattanaik, Sushree Bibhuprada B. Priyadarshini, Sucheta Panda, Soumen Nayak, and Swagat Patnaik

2.1 INTRODUCTION: BACKGROUND AND DRIVING FORCES

Nowadays, the conjoint proliferation of the Internet of Things (IoT) and the development of the Internet of Medical Things (IoMT) have initiated advancements in the delivery of healthcare outcomes. These technologies integrated with blockchain assist in improving the quality of biomedical outcomes; however, they also raise important ethical dilemmas. Basically, in this context, blockchain is a digital record framework that stores transactions across many computers in a way that is transparent and cannot be changed. Features, such as decentralization, unchangeable records, and strong security, make it very useful for managing medical data. The utilization of IoT integrated with blockchain in smart hospitals has proven to considerably upgrade organizational safety and operational efficiency [1].

Significant studies have explored how IoT-enabled hospital management systems can automate inventory tracking, dispensing of medications, and scheduling of patients [2–6]. Such studies evaluated the use of IoT in improving hospital workflows through real-time tracking of the medical equipment, coordination of staff, and predictive maintenance of the hospital infrastructure [7, 8]. The use of IoT-enabled robotics, conjointly with drug delivery and patient assistance, has also been examined to improve hospital efficiency through blockchain usage and reduction in human errors [9]. Furthermore, the use of IoT-enabled smart beds equipped with pressure sensors, along with artificial intelligence (AI)–based data analysis, is a good way to track patient movement and avoid pressure sores and falls for hospitalized patients.

DOI: 10.1201/9781003658597-2

These technologies enhance caregiving quality while supporting better clinical decision-making.

The IoT and blockchain literature on healthcare indicates IoT's influence in clinical decision making, which was notable in fields such as patient care, disease management, and hospital service delivery. Research to date has examined topics in the case of wearables, telehealth, AI use, blockchain security, and pandemic strategies. Other issues, however, remain at the forefront of research, such as information security, secrecy, and compatibility. With the transformation of AI-based IoT devices along with blockchain-enabled healthcare security and 5G technology, IoT healthcare solutions are anticipated to become more efficient, secure, and accessible [7, 10–15]. Moreover, the concept of connecting objects to the internet dates back decades. However, it wasn't until the late 1990s that the idea of IoT was formally introduced. Kevin Ashton, a British technology pioneer, coined the term in 1999 during his work at the Massachusetts Institute of Technology (MIT). He particularly focused on the use of Radio Frequency Identification (RFID) technology to enable machines to "sense" and "react" to their environment. This marked the early seeds of what we now refer to as IoT. Despite these early beginnings, it wasn't until the 2000s and the rise of smartphones, affordable sensors, and advancements in wireless connectivity that IoT truly began to take off. The proliferation of Wi-Fi networks, Bluetooth and, more recently, technologies, like 5G, has made the interconnection of devices feasible on a large scale.

Today, IoT encompasses everything, from home automation devices like temperature regulators and lighting systems to production-related applications in manufacturing, agriculture, and healthcare. It's no longer just about connecting objects; it's about embedding intelligence into these objects to upgrade proficiency, decrease waste, and enhance effectiveness [6, 7]. The topic of the IoT has developed over time, with its roots dating back to the early days of the internet and dedicated systems. These will research the history of the IoT, starting from the early 1980s when the first connected devices began to appear. During the 1980s–1990s, the first steps toward IoT were taken with the improvement of integrated systems and the connection of instruments to networks [16, 17].

During this time, researchers began envisioning a world where everyday objects would be interconnected. Likewise, in 1999, the phrase "Internet of Things" was coined by Kevin Ashton, the co-founder of the Auto-ID Center at MIT. His vision focused on the utilization of RFID to connect objects to the internet. During 2000, with the rise of RFID and sensor technologies, early IoT systems were built on RFID and sensor technologies that allowed physical objects to be tracked and monitored, which were taken into account. Likewise, in 2020, the focus was shifted to the industrial sector, where IoT systems are used for predictive maintenance, supply chain optimization, and automation. Additionally, edge computing began to play a significant role in managing data closer to the origin to reduce idle time. In 2010, the widespread adoption of smartphones, improved wireless networks, and the involvement of cloud computing fueled the explosion of IoT devices, where end-user devices, such as connected home gadgets, wearables, and connected cars, became common [1, 6, 7].

2.1.1 IoT Architecture

This subsection conducts a deep dive into the architecture of IoT systems, including the key components involved. It explores the various layers of IoT architecture, from mechanical devices to cloud systems:

i. *Perception Layer*: This layer includes the physical devices or "things" equipped with sensors, actuators, and RFID tags. It is dependable for accruing data and sending it to higher layers.
ii. *Network Layer*: This layer handles the communication between devices and other systems. It includes network protocols such as Wi-Fi, Bluetooth, Zigbee, and cellular networks, as well as newer low-power wide area networks (LPWAN) such as LoRaWAN.
iii. *Edge Computing Layer*: In some IoT systems, this layer processes data at the edge of the network, closer to where the data is generated, reducing the need for constant cloud communication.
iv. *Middleware Layer*: The middleware layer connects various devices and systems and provides common services such as data storage, authentication, and device management.
v. *Application Layer*: This is the layer where the data are gathered from IoT appliances and are used for specific aspects, such as smart homes, healthcare, or industrial automation.
vi. *Business Layer*: This layer emphasizes the business logic, analytics, and decision-making based on the data generated by IoT devices.

2.1.2 The Key Components of IoT

The IoT ecosystem consists of several essential components that work together to form a functional and interconnected network. These key elements include the following:

i. *Devices and Sensors*: Devices and sensors are present to attain crucial data. These sensors embedded in various objects monitor parameters, namely, temperature, humidity, motion, and location. They continuously attain real-time data, which is subsequently transmitted for further processing.
ii. *Connectivity*: For seamless operation, IoT devices must communicate with each other and central systems. This is facilitated through different communication technologies such as Wi-Fi, Bluetooth, Zigbee, LoRaWAN, and cellular networks such as 4G and 5G.
iii. *Data Processing and Analysis*: The gathered data must be analyzed to generate meaningful insights. Processing can occur either at the edge (closer to the device) or in the cloud. Cloud computing platforms afford the required infrastructure to analyze huge volumes of data produced by IoT devices [18, 19]. Advanced AI and ML algorithms are often utilized to detect patterns and extract actionable insights.

iv. *Actionable Insights*: The ultimate goal of IoT is to make informed decisions. By dissecting the data gathered from linked devices, association can optimize their operations, predict failures, improve customer experiences, and even automate processes. In some systems, the insights can trigger automatic actions, such as adjusting a thermostat or shutting down a machine when certain conditions are met.
v. *User Interface*: The user interface (UI) is where human interaction with the IoT system occurs. This can take the form of mobile apps, web platforms, or voice assistants, thereby providing users with management and visibility over their devices. A well-designed UI allows users to track, control, and manage their IoT systems efficiently [20–25].

2.2 INTEGRATION OF BLOCKCHAIN WITH IOT

Blockchain has many special features that make it very useful in healthcare when implemented with IoT. As it is decentralized, medical records are stored across many computers instead of being controlled by one authority, which reduces the risk of data loss or tampering. Its immutability means that once health data is recorded, it cannot be changed. With the help of encryption techniques, information is kept private while allowing both patients and doctors to access data whenever required. Another powerful feature is smart contracts that can execute tasks like insurance claims automatically without any intermediary present. These characteristics collectively offer tremendous advantages to healthcare. By utilizing blockchain technology, EHRs will be more accurate and trustworthy. Furthermore, blockchain will give patients greater control over who sees their data and allow secure data sharing between hospitals and research centers. Blockchain boosts clinical trials' accuracy and enhances transparency, making results more reliable while also logging and checking standard medical practices against dubious ones to reduce fraud.

Figure 2.1 illustrates applications of various blockchain features. The blockchain has the potential to allow secure storage, management, and sharing of IoT-based patient data. When we join blockchain and IoT, we manage to build a strong network where the patient, doctor, and researcher work in sync without losing security and privacy. In the same vein, Figure 2.2 depicts the collaboration of IoT and blockchain in healthcare. To begin with, the first layer that collects all the health data of the concerned patient is called the Data Collection Layer. This data is then securely sent to the blockchain via the Data Transmission Layer. The storage of information in an incorruptible ledger in encrypted form takes place in the blockchain layer. Last, on the application layer, doctors, insurers, and researchers can leverage this data using smart contracts. This system allows for secure, transparent, and reliable management of information regarding patients.

2.2.1 USE CASES

Blockchain along with IoT provides several beneficial applications in healthcare. One of the biggest use cases of a patient-centered health record is that the users own their health data and grant access with keys on the blockchain. A diabetic patient

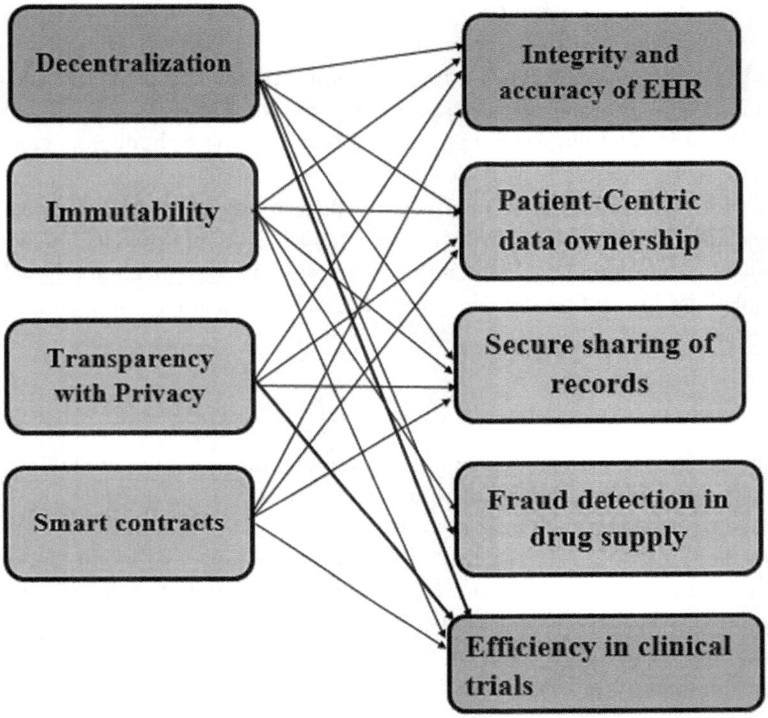

FIGURE 2.1 Blockchain features and their applicability in healthcare.

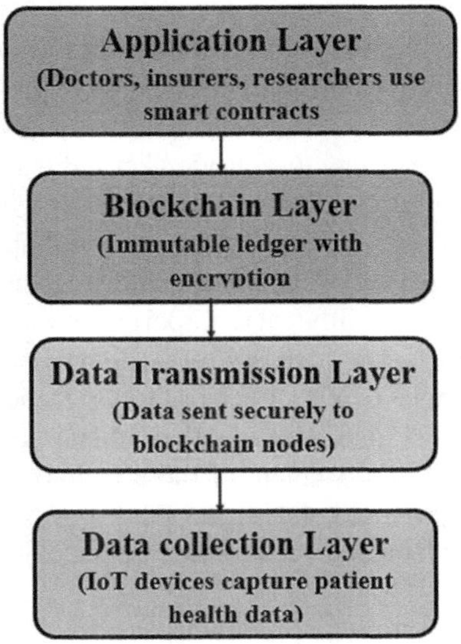

FIGURE 2.2 Blockchain–IoT integration architecture.

can share their glucose readings securely with the doctor or researcher, for example. Medicine movement in the supply chain is monitored through IoT sensors, while blockchain backs up the record in the drug supply chain. This stops the sale of fake medicines. Another application is remote patient monitoring, where IoT wearables check vital signs and blockchain guarantees that only the right doctors can see the data.

The use of blockchain smart contracts can help improve health insurance by automating claims, reducing fraud. Furthermore, the IoT data improves a clinical trial by keeping data transparent and unalterable. Moreover, these applications show how we can implement IoT and blockchain for a safer, efficient, and patient-centered healthcare system.

2.2.2 Advantages of Blockchain and IoT Integration in Healthcare

Merging health IoT with blockchain offers many advantages. By employing the latest encryption and decentralized storage techniques, we can enhance the security and privacy of patient data against cyber threats. Since it's immutable, it helps to keep medical histories accurate and without errors. Patients will gain more control over who is privy to their health information. The integration reduces paperwork, speeds processes, and cuts costs, thus helping in boosting efficiency. The law also combats counterfeit drugs in global supply chain and fraudulent insurance claims through medicines. Interoperability is another important benefit that means blockchain could make it easy and safe sharing of hospitals and healthcare providers' "data" across borders. Healthcare is now a safer, more efficient, and better-connected system.

2.3 RELATED WORK

The approach discussed in [1] by Wakili and Bakkali formulates an adaptive ethical framework for IoT in digital health (AEFIDH), with the purpose of considering the ethical dilemmas posed by IoT in healthcare [1]. It was developed with inputs from experts, surveys, and interviews, to consider key ethical dilemmas such as data privacy, informed consent, user autonomy, fairness of algorithms, compliance with regulation, design ethics, and equitable access to healthcare [1]. These technologies might improve the quality of care and health outcomes, among other things, but at the same time, they equally raise important ethical dilemmas. The article [1] discusses the need for more attention to pertinent issues such as data security and user autonomy while advocating for more transparency in the algorithms used in healthcare IoT. AEFIDH also proposes that ethical considerations can be built within the innovation and improvement of these technologies. Although AEFIDH has some limitations, the framework is still a solid starting point for the responsible progress and use of the IoT in medical care to keep pace in a rapidly evolving digital environment [1].

The document further narrates a bibliometric review of IoT incidents in smart healthcare while investigating important areas of research, such as network connectivity, blockchain security, and the application of IoT in healthcare during the

COVID-19 pandemic. Notably, the document [1] also considers the possible future role of Cognitive IoMT (CIoMT) in assisting efforts to manage and track pandemics. In addition, the document highlights the role of 5G as an important enabler of IoT in healthcare. The enhanced connectivity and data management capabilities of 5G produce new opportunities for IoT-enabled healthcare applications for monitoring disease, diagnostics, and treatment. In conclusion, the document provides a comprehensive review of the ways IoT can enhance healthcare while handling the obstacles of safety, secrecy, and ethical issues.

The IoT comprises embedded devices with sensors, software, and other technologies that enable them to easily connect to other systems and devices and share data over the internet or local networks. This innovation is used in the healthcare system, so it is known as IoMT. It brings about fundamental change through continuous monitoring and customized treatment. Its price was 44.2 billion in 2023. According to CAGR, it is expected that it will grow 21.2% from 2024 to 2030. This growth is in different concepts or devices such as smartphones and smart devices, as well as tablets that are used for monitoring patient health, such as heart rate, sleeping patterns, and other signs. The IoT plays a vital role in the digital health system. However, this carries an ethical challenge in data privacy, consent, algorithmic fairness, and ethical design [1].

Digital health is needed due to increasing attention to these issues. As the IoT techniques play a vital role in healthcare, a framework is required to evaluate such issues and maximize their benefits. The goal of AEFIDH, as discussed in [1], is to identify ethical problems and issues when IoT is used in digital health. To improve patient healthcare and services, it generates information and communication technologies (ICT) that help in managing chronic patients and preventing emergencies. The IoT in smart healthcare supports a strong and efficient state in the expectation of good health status.

Moreover, Vaccine Cold Chain Monitoring, developed by UNDP and the Indian government, uses IoT-enabled mobile-based technology to monitor the cold chain of vaccines, ensuring that they are stored at the correct temperatures and reach remote areas efficiently during the pandemic [2]. Likewise, in the context of healthcare, COVID-19 emerged as a viral disease in 2019. It is caused by SARS-CoV-2. COVID-19 started in China and spread to 222 countries in 2021. Basically, it spread very much in the cold country. Many people have died due to COVID-19. The people were so afraid that no one could go outside. At that time, there was no medicine for the COVID-19 disease. The common symptoms, such as fever, tiredness, cough, body pains, and nasal congestion, were prevalent [7–9]. There was no vaccine for this disease so the older people and children were widely affected. In that situation, the IoT provided improvements and more effective solutions in the healthcare system, such as keeping the medical records properly, integrating disease sampling, and identifying disease causes. This represents the vital role of IoT and IoMT in handling the critical situation of COVID-19 [3]. In 2021, the IoT became the latest trending system because it improves medical requirements, causing people to seek treatment in other countries or cities. The main advantage is that it can improve healthcare by monitoring, detecting, and treating diseases. In 2016, it introduced wearable devices that can be attached to the body, such as a sensor in clothing, and collect important health data. This is part of the IoT. Then, it introduces biosensors, which are used to detect infection and other health indicators. These are the low-cost and lightweight devices that are part of the IoT [3]. Then, it introduced the 5G wireless technology, which will be a part of the IoT system in 2020. It is used to improve the healthcare system [8, 10].

The paper [4] introduces a wearable system for improving the health system, which is a part of the IoT system. IoT comprises the interconnection of physical devices that are interconnected with each other. These devices are equipped with sensors and software that help them to share data upon connection with each other. This exchange of data covers all the devices over the internet and local networks. COVID-19 has created a pandemic situation in the whole world. The IoT plays an important role in the handling of critical situations, collecting and analyzing information, making decisions, and developing policies to manage health crises. Technologies such as IoT, GPS, and AI are widely integrated. During the pandemic, digital health technology played an important role in using technologies such as telemedicine and contact tracing apps. This technology plays a vital role in making the healthcare system more efficient. To help policymakers and healthcare providers assign these devices to the most critical patients while maximizing their usage, IoT uses the decision support system (DSS). It is a possible way to improve both care and efficiency in this context. During COVID-19, IoT and AI managed healthcare more effectively, as discussed in [6]. IoT and ICT were used for improved services in the healthcare system. IoT played a vital role during COVID-19 while helping to save people's lives, such as those with diabetes, thereby allowing doctors to intervene early through remote patient monitoring while reducing stress. Figure 2.3 shows a scenario of applications of IoT in diversified sectors.

2.4 ROLE OF IOT AND BLOCKCHAIN IN HEALTHCARE

This review serves as a bibliometric guide for future improvements, which is part of the IoT system [7]. The IoT innovation used in the healthcare system is known as IoMT. It is a medical care network system comprising hardware, software services, and medical sensors. From 2020 to 2025, it is expected to grow by 23.4%. The devices can be vulnerable to cyberattacks, which can lead to health risks or even deaths, so they create security and privacy problems. The blockchain method is introduced to solve these problems. It uses an encryption method, which can prevent mistakes and protect patient information. It is helpful for secure IoMT systems [8]. The healthcare sector has recently experienced significant progress and significantly increased employment and earnings. This has resulted in increased expense of healthcare while also placing rural and distant healthcare facilities.

Nowadays, people can track their health at home using smartphones and smart devices. IoT plays a significant role in connecting various devices through the internet. To connect healthcare devices, IoT can use different technologies, such as uniquely identifying each device using identification technology and tracking medical equipment using location technologies. These tools are helpful for quickly and securely accessing patient data. It is hopeful for improving healthcare system, improving patient care, and creating more efficient systems [9]. COVID-19 is a viral

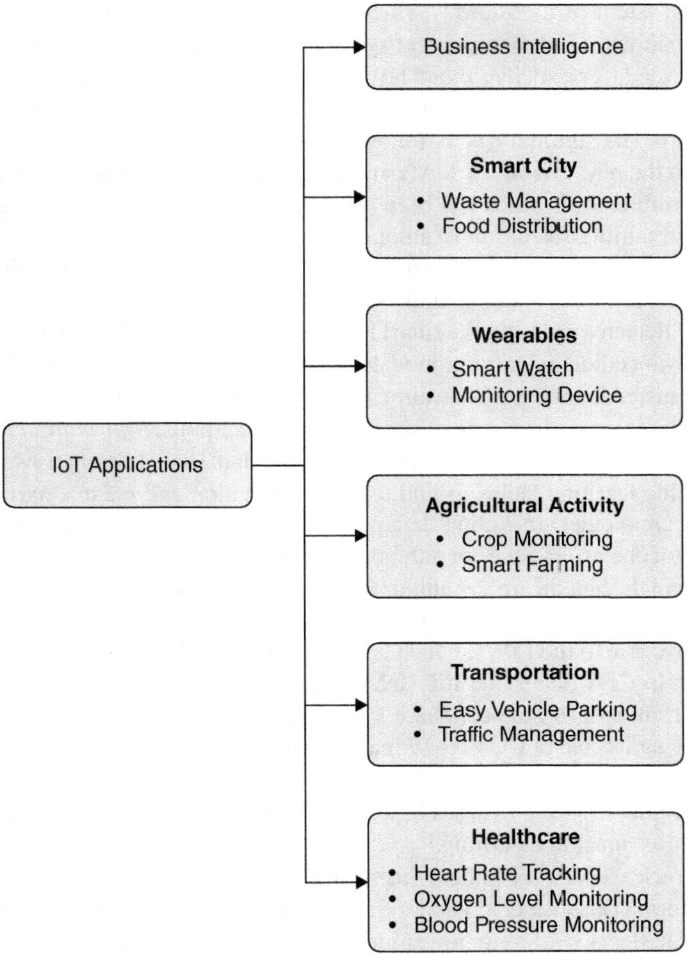

FIGURE 2.3 Diversified applications of IoT.

disease caused by SARS-COV-2, which first appeared in China in 2019. It is also known as coronavirus as it is a part of the coronavirus family. It spread to the whole world and created a pandemic situation.

Many people were affected and died due to this disease. In 2020, many countries declared a lockdown and shutdown. As it is an airborne illness, it spreads very fast. The common symptoms include fever, cough, and tiredness. Before the introduction of a vaccine, older people and children were widely affected. Although vaccines were subsequently developed, they were not that efficient. To control the spread of the disease, people followed social distancing, lockdown, and shutdown, and also used masks and sanitizer. Widespread inability to work had profound effects on people's economy, mental health, and physical health. In times of crisis, IoT played a vital role in managing the pandemic better. It is especially useful for the health-care system, which connects physical devices. IoT uses sensors and AI for a better healthcare system. It uses IoMT, which is a special application for healthcare. To improve healthcare and management systems, it uses blockchain and AI. The IoMT contains three layers, such as cloud layer, fog layer, and things layer [10].

In the COVID-19 pandemic situation, IoT and AI were used to improve the healthcare system. The summary is as follows: to collect and share health data, the IoT connects to the physical devices. AI can successfully analyze this data and also contain the health record, which has been proven to be fruitful in maintaining and continuously streaming an enormous amount of data, such as medical diagnoses, robotic surgery, and health records. Using IoT and AI, we can create a smart healthcare system [11, 12]. COVID 19 and pneumonia are two different categories of chest X-ray that can be detected by using the smart healthcare system. VGG-19 and Inception-V3 are two advanced deep learning models. To improve healthcare, we use techniques such as transfer learning and feature fusion in diagnosing diseases. Experiments showed that the system performs better than other methods. *Information Processing and Neural Network Training*: IoT creates a lot of data, and data analysis, combined with machine learning, helps to find useful information and make smart decisions. Security technologies, including data protection, identification, and safe communication protocols, are crucial for safeguarding IoT systems. IoT is the most popular innovation in the healthcare system, including ambient-assisted living (AAL), remote health monitoring, chronic disease management, elderly care, and fitness programs. The IoT gave rise to the IoMT, which is used in smart technology and the healthcare system [1]. In COVID-19, the IoT (IoMT) and CIOMT (cloud-based IoT) played a very important role in the healthcare system [1]. The following were the objectives of considering its role in COVID-19 management:

- To predict COVID-19 cases based on patient data, they developed a system that uses machine learning.
- To track COVID-19 patients using IoT devices, they generated an online platform (Darwish et al.) and to improve healthcare. Focusing on overcoming challenges in communication and technology integration, they introduced a model combining IoT and cloud computing.
- To monitor and care for COVID-19 patients using cell phones and software-defined networks to collect patient data remotely.
- To provide creative solutions to help manage the pandemic, they discussed how IoT and 5G technology can work together to fight COVID-19.
- To make continuous monitoring possible, they created an IoT system that monitors a person's health using sensors and processes data using energy-efficient methods.
- To help healthcare systems screen people in real time, they designed a smart helmet that uses thermal cameras and IoT technology to detect COVID-19 symptoms.

The IoT has become a transformative technology in healthcare, providing healthcare professionals with new methods of continuous monitoring, remote diagnosis, and effective management of patient data. There has been considerable research on a variety of IoT in healthcare topics, such as telehealth, wearable devices, smart hospitals, AI-incorporated IoT devices, and blockchain security in health. This section summarizes the literature regarding the possibilities, challenges, and improvements of IoT-enabled healthcare systems [3].

2.5 IOT AND INTELLIGENT HEALTHCARE

The incorporation of the IoT into the smart medical care context has been a topic of interest due to its implications for better patient care while decreasing healthcare system burdens. Numerous studies and academic research have examined the implications IoT-based smart healthcare systems have for disease management and patient monitoring. Research argues that mechanisms such as wearable devices, biosensors, and smart implants enable continuous monitoring of health. The flexibility of IoT with respect to cloud computing and AI allows for improved, instant monitoring and personalized treatment recommendations based on analytics data. In another bibliometric study, the researchers examined the current and growing literature regarding IoT applications in smart healthcare and identified the principal trends as well as challenges. Their research shows that as multi-resource systems are changing with the introduction of the IoT, blockchain use in secure transmission is also becoming increasingly useful, along with edge computing as a methodology for faster processing in IoT-enabled healthcare systems. In addition, studies have examined 5G technology to improve connectivity for remote healthcare services, supporting easy data transmission through IoT-enabled devices [4].

2.5.1 IoT-Enabled Wearable Devices in Healthcare

Wearable devices are an important part of an IoT-based healthcare solution through their ability to continuously monitor individuals' health in real time. IoT-enabled wearable devices are almost always equipped with sensors, meaning they can monitor multiple health-related parameters wirelessly – for example, cardiac rate, blood pressure, sugar levels, and physiological temperature. In terms of IoT-enabled devices, there was an instance where nano-integrated wearable biosensors highlighted how IoT technology is easily utilized for real-time tracking of physiological parameters, which can support proactive detection of chronic diseases and critical medical conditions [4]. Furthermore, novel smart wearables have added non-invasive biosensors to characterize health abnormalities, as illnesses are developing, without worsening symptoms, to allow for detection.

IoT-enabled watches, bands, and clothing are becoming more prevalent in remote health monitoring and tracking fitness. Research has also investigated the extent to which IoT-integrated wearables provide assistance to older adults in terms of care, particularly for individuals with Alzheimer's, Parkinson's disease, and those with cardiovascular conditions [10–15]. Another research has examined cognitive IoT deployed in healthcare, where AI wearables in combination with machine learning algorithms assess health risks and provide alerts for paramedics when emergencies present themselves. These augmented systems contribute to the management of decreased hospital readmission rates through advanced detection, diagnosis, and treatment for patients [5, 16].

2.5.2 IoT in Pandemic Management and Disease Assessment

In particular, the SARS-CoV-2 infection health emergency led to a growth in healthcare interest in IoT, especially in the areas of remote monitoring of patients, early diagnosis, and contactless medical care services. IoT, throughout studies, has contributed to managing the pandemic through telemedicine, automated diagnostics, and AI-based screening [16–23]. An example of a research study seeks to develop an IoT-enabled smart healthcare system to screen for COVID-19 patients using deep-learning techniques. The diagnostic model used chest X-ray imaging for swift detection and classification of infections deemed pneumonia or COVID-19 [16, 24]. In this application, researchers developed a real-time patient monitoring system that allowed for early disease detection while employing AI, IoT, and cloud computing to automate health assessments. In addition, during the pandemic, remote monitoring devices powered by the IoT were widely used to monitor patients' oxygen saturations, respiratory rates, and fever. These technologies reduced the need for patients to visit hospitals while allowing patients to engage in safe, timely medical intervention without leaving home [6, 26–31]. Furthermore, it has been reported that the use of a cryptographic ledger facilitates privacy and security of patient health information due to having tamper-proof digital health records that protect COVID-19 patient data [6, 26–34].

2.5.3 Protection and Discretion Concerns in IoT Healthcare

Despite the benefits of the IoT in healthcare, security and privacy issues still remain a serious concern. The extensive implementation of IoT devices increases the opportunity for cyberattacks and the unauthorized use of data or sensitive information [8]. To meet these challenges, researchers have proposed methods of security using a blockchain framework for IoT healthcare systems [32, 33]. A study that examined a blockchain-enabled IoMT also introduced a secure framework that allowed for the management of patient health information while ensuring discretion, uprightness, and accessibility of medical records [13, 34]. The proposed blockchain-IoMT security system demonstrated a high degree of precision and efficiency when protecting patient data while also ensuring real-time access for healthcare professionals. Additionally, evidence supports that blockchain-based authentication methods can improve interoperability between healthcare platforms, enabling secure sharing of clinical data across research institutions and hospitals. Another study focused on IoT security challenges and recommended the use of multi-factor authentication (MFA), encryption methods, and AI intrusion detection systems to protect healthcare IoT networks from cyber threats [1, 35]. Researchers have even suggested decentralized identity management systems to allow patients more control over access to their medical records, which would improve patient medical privacy while still allowing access [6, 36–42].

2.6 4G, THE IOT, AND WEARABLE DEVICES

These technologies support proactive healthcare by enabling early identification of health. Emerging smart clothing infused with IoT sensors allows for continuous health monitoring [43, 44] with minimal patient involvement. Smart clothing with biosensors can monitor a person's body temperature, hydration level, and muscle activity, all important data for athletes, aging individuals, and individuals recently discharged from surgery. 4G plays an important role in the healthcare system. It provides fast, stable, and wide-area wireless connectivity, which is essential for transmitting real-time health data from IoT devices [45–51] to cloud platforms or healthcare professionals. It bridges the gap between patients and healthcare providers by enabling continuous, connected, and mobile health monitoring, laying the groundwork for more advanced 5G-enabled medical solutions in the future. It has some benefits as follows:

- High-speed data transmission
- Low latency
- Mobile healthcare support
- Improved chronic disease management
- Faster emergency response

Wearables such as smartwatches, fitness bands, and medical patches use 4G to

- Transmit data in real time to cloud servers or mobile apps.
- Enable remote consultations and telemedicine services.
- Send emergency alerts to caregivers or hospitals.
- Facilitate GPS tracking for elderly or vulnerable patients.

2.7 CHALLENGES OF IOT AND BLOCKCHAIN INTEGRATION

Even though IoT has several advantages, there are still many challenges to be addressed. The more devices are connected to the internet, the more the risk of cyberattacks, security, and privacy concerns. Ensuring the security of IoT devices and networks is challenging due to the ever-increasing vulnerabilities in products. This causes privacy issues due to the huge amounts of personal data that IoT systems generate. Scalability poses a tremendous challenge because these devices generate huge volumes of data which are difficult for blockchains to handle. Another problem is high-energy use, particularly in systems that rely on resource-heavy approaches, such as proof-of-work. The existence of divergent regional regulations, including General Data Protection Regulations (GDPR) and Health Insurance Portability and Accountability Act (HIPAA), hampers the establishment of common standards. Another hindrance is the high cost of constructing blockchain systems as well as linking them with IoT devices. There are still several hospitals that use not-so-modern IT systems that can't connect to blockchain. They all showcase the necessity for planning and solutions ahead of mass deployment.

- The success of IoT relies heavily on interoperability, where devices from different manufacturers use different protocols. Interoperability among these devices is crucial to a seamless IoT experience.

- The data produced by the IoT system can be managed, stored, and analyzed in real time. Through data storage, processing infrastructure, and analysis, businesses can use large amounts of data to learn new insights.
- As IoT networks grow, managing and expanding them is proving more difficult. A system must be reliable and should not slow down or lose performance when devices and data increase.
- Many IoT devices are battery-powered, and ensuring energy efficiency is critical, particularly for sensors that are deployed in remote locations.

Figure 2.4 shows a scenario of real-time applications of IoT. Table 2.1 illustrates the advantages and disadvantages of IoT and blockchain integration.

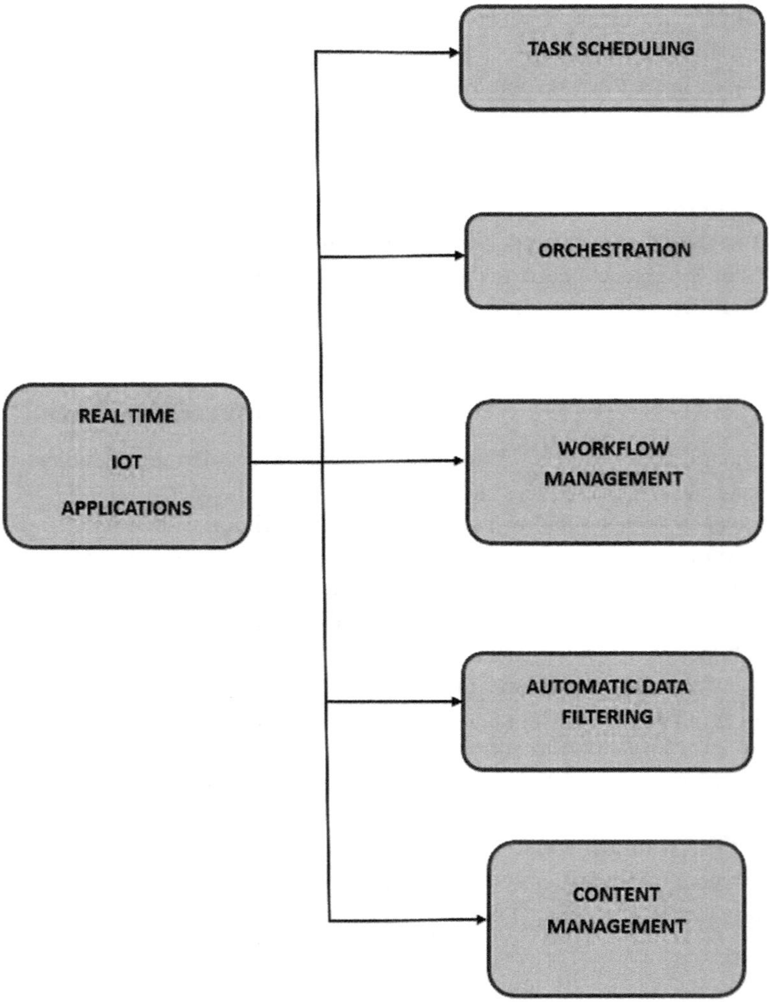

FIGURE 2.4 Real-time applications of IoT.

TABLE 2.1
Advantages and Disadvantages of IoT and Blockchain Integration

Advantages	Challenges
Enhanced Security – Protects patient data from cyber threats	*Scalability Issues* – Huge IoT data volumes overwhelm the blockchain
Improved Data Accuracy – Immutable records reduce errors	*High Energy Consumption* – Resource-intensive consensus mechanisms
Patient Empowerment – Full ownership of health data	*Regulatory Barriers* – Different compliance rules (HIPAA, GDPR)
Operational Efficiency – Reduces paperwork and costs	*Cost of Implementation* – Expensive infrastructure setup
Fraud Prevention – Stops counterfeit drugs and false claims	*Interoperability with Legacy Systems* – Outdated hospital IT systems

2.8 IOT AND BLOCKCHAIN APPLICATIONS DURING THE COVID-19 PANDEMIC

COVID 19 and pneumonia are two different categories of chest X-ray that can be detected by using the smart healthcare system. VGG-19 and Inception-V3 are two advanced deep learning models. To improve healthcare, we use techniques such as transfer learning and feature fusion. Technologies such as smart devices, wearables, drones, and robots with IoT have been beneficial in improving patient monitoring while limiting hospital readmissions in COVID-19 emergencies [52–56]. The enhanced connectivity and data management capabilities of 5G produce new opportunities for IoT-enabled healthcare applications related to monitoring disease, diagnostics, and treatment. In diagnosing diseases, experiments showed the system performs better than other methods [57–60]. IoT is transforming industries and daily life in profound ways. Here are some main areas where IoT is having an influence:

- *Intelligent Homes*: One of the most common uses of IoT in daily life is the smart home. Devices such as smart thermostats (e.g., Nest), security cameras, lighting systems, and voice assistants (e.g., Amazon Alexa, Google Assistant) help homeowners easily control their homes. Smart homes make life more convenient, save energy, and improve security [57–61].
- *Medical care*: IoT devices can track vital signs, keep an eye on long-term health conditions, and notify doctors if a patient's health changes. This helps provide faster and more customized care. It has great potential in healthcare by allowing doctors to monitor patients remotely, using wearable medical devices and linked equipment.
- *Smart Cities*: Cities are using IoT to make their environments smarter and more sustainable. This includes issues such as smart traffic control, waste management, public safety monitoring, and environmental monitoring. For example, IoT sensors in traffic can change traffic lights automatically to help reduce traffic jams.

- *Agriculture*: Precision farming uses IoT devices to check soil moisture, weather, and crop health. By collecting real-time information, farmers can make better choices about watering, fertilizing, and pest control, which helps increase crop production and use resources more efficiently.
- *Industrial IoT (IIoT)*: IIoT uses IoT technology in industries such as processing and energy. IIoT systems keep track of machines, improve supply chains, and predict when maintenance is needed [62–65]. This helps businesses run more efficiently, decrease idle time, and save money.
- *Transportation and Logistics*: IoT plays a significant role in fleet supervision, vehicle tracking, and supply chain optimization. Connected vehicles are improving safety and efficiency, while IoT-powered logistics systems are ensuring the instantaneous tracking and management of goods and shipments.

The future of IoT is bright, with new advancements in technology, expanding applications, and increasing adoption across industries. This section can explore future trends, as follows:

- *5G and IoT*: 5G networks will greatly improve IoT and offer faster speeds, faster response time, and more reliable connections.
- *AI and IoT*: The incorporation of AI with IoT will enable smarter decision-making, automation, and predictive analytics in real time.
- *IoT in Industry 4.0*: The future of manufacturing will be dominated by IoT-enabled technologies such as robotics, automated quality control, and instant monitoring.
- *Edge and Fog Computing*: The expansion of edge and fog computing will help to address issues of latency, bandwidth, and data privacy, enabling real-time processing at the edge.
- *IoT for Sustainability*: IoT will play a crucial role in handling global challenges such as global warming, resource conservation, and sustainable development.

2.9 CONCLUSION AND FUTURE DIRECTION

The combination of IoT and blockchain has revolutionized healthcare data management and improved patient care delivery. Through blockchain, a secure base can be created for the protection, verification, and sharing of private health data. Likewise, IoT devices like smart medical equipment could be used to provide continuous monitoring and real-time updates on health status. Integrating IoT's data-generating ability with blockchain's transparency, security, and decentralization can boost efficiency, trustworthiness, and patient-centeredness in healthcare. This integration provides better control over health records for patients, improves data sharing between hospitals, mitigates paperwork and costs, and enhances the accuracy of electronic records. Notwithstanding, there are still issues with scalability, high installation costs, stringent regulations, and linking up with legacy hospital systems. New technologies, lightweight blockchain models, the use of AI for predictive healthcare, and supportive government policy suggest bright prospects. Through the use of IoT and blockchain technologies in the healthcare system, patient-oriented innovations improve and require the inclusion of a blockchain-based architecture.

Blockchain and IoT in healthcare can bring substantial benefits, all of which can help transform the current healthcare setting into a safer, more efficient, and patient-oriented place. The implementation of proof-of-stake or consortium blockchains, which are lighter in comparison to the traditional methods, is fast and energy-efficient. Consequently, the system's capacity to store and analyze data has increased significantly. Data analytics will enhance not only the efficiency and effectiveness of the ICT ecosystems but also the quality of life. It is essential to link AI and ML with blockchain-protected IoT data. With the help of this, one's health problems can be predicted, diseases detected, and proactive treatment can be planned. Through cooperation in care and research, international sharing of patient information between hospitals and other researchers could occur via global health data networks. The integration also offers personalized medicine whereby doctors formulate treatment plans designed for each patient using safe IoT data. In conclusion, without separate government support and clear regulations, large-scale privacy will be difficult, despite privacy being able to bring better interoperability, assured data protection, and trust-building between patients, doctors, and policymakers.

REFERENCES

1. A. Wakili and S. Bakkali, "Internet of Things in Healthcare: An Adaptive Ethical Framework for IoT in Digital Health," *Clinical eHealth*, vol. 7, pp. 92–105, 2024. https://doi.org/10.1016/j.ceh.2024.07.001
2. H. Ziwei *et al.*, "The Applications of Edge Computing and the Internet of Things in the Healthcare and Medical Sectors: A Bibliometric Analysis," *Heliyon*, pp. e25392, Feb. 2024. https://doi.org/10.1016/j.heliyon.2024.e25392
3. M. A. Jabbar *et al.*, "Applications of Cognitive Internet of Medical Things in Modern Healthcare," *Computers and Electrical Engineering*, vol. 102, p. 108276, 2022. doi: 10.1016/j.compeleceng.2022.108276
4. D. Verma *et al.*, "Internet of Things (IoT) in Nano-Integrated Wearable Biosensor Devices for Healthcare Applications," *Biosensors and Bioelectronics: X*, vol. 11, pp. 1–17, 2022. https://doi.org/10.1016/j.biosx.2022.100153
5. E. Secundo *et al.*, "Digital Technologies and Collective Intelligence for Healthcare Ecosystem: Optimizing Internet of Things Adoption for Pandemic Management," *Journal of Business Research*, vol. 131, pp. 563–572, 2021. https://doi.org/10.1016/j.jbusres.2021.03.056
6. P. Gupta and S. Roy, "Security Challenges in IoT-Based Healthcare," *IEEE Transactions on Medical Informatics*, vol. 15, no. 7, pp. 678–690, 2021. https://dpcoe-pune.edu.in/wp-content/uploads/2021/12/29-A-Review-on-IOT-Security-Challenges-in-Healthcare.pdf
7. D. Sharma and K. Verma, "A Study on Wearable Devices for Healthcare Monitoring," *Journal of Biomedical Research*, vol. 9, no. 2, pp. 45–67, 2020. https://doi.org/10.2196/34384
8. N. Ahmed and Y. Zhao, "IoT in COVID-19 Management: A Technological Perspective," *Journal of Pandemic Research*, vol. 14, no. 1, pp. 55–78, 2021. https://doi.org/10.1109/ACCESS.2020.3030090

9. A. Panigrahi, B. Sahu, A. Pati, S. Chowdhury, "Privacy-Preserving and Scalable Authentication Using zk-SNARK-Based ZKP Blockchain PKI," *In Digital Immune System (eds S.P. Dash, V. Mishra, B. Shaw, S.K. Panda and S. Balamurugan).* https://doi.org/10.1002/9781394383788.ch16
10. J. Wang and H. Li, "Real-Time Health Monitoring Using IoT and AI," *International Journal of Smart Medical Systems*, vol. 7, no. 3, pp. 89–107, 2022. https://www.mdpi.com/2673-4591/66/1/31
11. P. Fernandez, "IoT in Chronic Disease Management," *Journal of Chronic Healthcare*, vol. 5, no. 2, pp. 34–56, 2020. https://pmc.ncbi.nlm.nih.gov/articles/PMC8253318/
12. S. S. Sarmah, "An Efficient IoT-Based Patient Monitoring and Heart Disease Prediction System Using Deep Learning Modified Neural Network," in *IEEE Access*, vol. 8, pp. 135784–135797, 2020, https://doi.org/10.1109/ACCESS.2020.3007561
13. V. Rana, "A Comparative Study on IoT-Based ECG Monitoring Systems," *International Journal of Biomedical Engineering*, vol. 11, no. 5, pp. 98–112, 2022. https://doi.org/10.22214/ijraset.2023.49303
14. Y. Zhang, "Wireless Sensor Networks in IoT Healthcare," *Sensors and Networks Journal*, vol. 9, no. 4, pp. 210–230, 2021. https://www.researchgate.net/publication/327139922_Wireless_Sensor_Networks_for_Healthcare
15. R. Pandey, A. Khatri, A. Panigrahi, H. Malathi, I. Alam, and Y. Akshatha, "Blockchain for Secure and Equitable Health Data Management," *In Computational Intelligence in Biomedical Internet of Medical Things (eds S.P. Yadav, A. Bansal and V.H.C. Albuquerque),* https://doi.org/10.1002/9781394386659.ch24
16. R. Mehta, "5G and IoT in Next-Gen Healthcare," *Wireless Medical Technology*, vol. 4, no. 2, pp. 45–69, 2022. https://doi.org/10.1016/j.ipha.2023.04.001
17. S. Kumar, "AI-Driven Diagnostics in IoT-Based Healthcare," *Computational Healthcare Journal*, vol. 8, no. 1, pp. 134–156, 2023. http://dx.doi.org/10.58496/BJN/2025/006
18. H. Rahman, "IoT in Smart Ambulance Systems," *International Conference on Smart Healthcare*, pp. 78–92, 2021. https://doi.org/10.1109/BID.2017.8336593
19. P. Singh, "Remote Surgery and IoT Connectivity Challenges," *Journal of Telemedicine and IoT*, vol. 7, no. 4, pp. 201–220, 2022. http://dx.doi.org/10.33448/rsd-v13i7.46402
20. V. Chaudhary, "IoT-Based Smart Wheelchairs: A Survey," *International Journal of Rehabilitation Technology*, vol. 9, no. 3, pp. 101–120, 2021. https://doi.org/10.1109/ICAECA56562.2023.10200628
21. X. Tian, "IoT and Predictive Analytics in Healthcare," *Data Science in Medicine*, vol. 5, no. 2, pp. 45–78, 2023. http://dx.doi.org/10.47992/IJMTS.2581.6012.0089
22. A. Bose, "Sensor Technologies for IoT Healthcare Applications," *IEEE Sensors Journal*, vol. 13, no. 5, pp. 321–345, 2022. https://doi.org/10.3390/s22155738
23. K. Roy, "Cloud Computing in IoT Healthcare Systems," *Journal of Cloud Computing for Healthcare*, vol. 10, no. 2, pp. 67–89, 2021. https://papers.ssrn.com/sol3/papers.cfm?abstract_id=5021557
24. A. Panigrahi, A. Parida, A. Pati, B. Sahu, J. Mishra, and S. R. Addula, "TrustRank-PKI: A Blockchain-Based PKI Using Adaptive Trust-Aware Consensus for Identity and Certificate Management," *Lecture Notes in Electrical Engineering*, pp. 225–236, 2026, doi: https://doi.org/10.1007/978-3-032-20318-2_21.
25. L. Khan, "IoT for Post-Surgical Patient Monitoring," *Journal of Medical IoT Applications*, vol. 6, no. 2, pp. 89–105, 2021. https://doi.org/10.1109/ICAECC59324.2023.10560148
26. T. Jain, "AI and IoT for Mental Health Monitoring," *International Journal of Smart Psychiatry*, vol. 4, no. 1, pp. 56–74, 2023. https://www.researchgate.net/publication/393124873_IoT_Enabled_Mental_Health_Monitoring_and_AI_Driven_Cognitive_Behavioral_Therapy_Systems_for_Personalized_Treatment

27. A. Saha, "IoT in Emergency Response Systems," *Journal of Smart Emergency Technology*, vol. 5, no. 3, pp. 134–150, 2023. https://link.springer.com/article/10.1007/s43926-024-00073-6
28. R. Patil, "IoT in Cardiovascular Disease Prediction," *Journal of Medical IoT Research*, vol. 11, no. 1, pp. 45–67, 2022. https://doi.org/10.1016/j.compbiomed.2024.109330
29. H. Sun, "IoT for Pediatric Healthcare," *International Journal of Pediatric Technology*, vol. 9, no. 2, pp. 78–99, 2022. https://fepbl.com/index.php/imsrj/article/view/923
30. S. Batra, "IoT in Medical Imaging Systems," *IEEE Transactions on Biomedical Imaging*, vol. 14, no. 5, pp. 112–134, 2021. http://dx.doi.org/10.36548/jiip.2019.1.006
31. P. Shukla, "IoT and Nanotechnology in Drug Delivery," *Journal of Smart Pharmaceuticals*, vol. 5, no. 4, pp. 345–367, 2023. https://doi.org/10.1186/s12951-018-0392-8
32. J. Yoon, "IoT in Neurodegenerative Disease Care," *Journal of Smart Neurology*, vol. 7, no. 2, pp. 123–140, 2022. https://doi.org/10.1109/COMM62355.2024.10741391
33. R. Das, "IoT for Infant Health Monitoring," *Journal of Neonatal IoT*, vol. 6, no. 1, pp. 67–88, 2021. https://iopscience.iop.org/article/10.1088/1742-6596/1937/1/012050/pdf
34. T. Lee, "IoT-Based Smart Contact Lenses for Glucose Monitoring," *Diabetes IoT Journal*, vol. 4, no. 2, pp. 78–95, 2022. https://doi.org/10.3389/fmed.2022.858784.
35. C. Swagat, "IoT-Based Early Disease Prediction Systems," *Journal of Smart Health Systems*, vol. 8, no. 1, pp. 56–78, 2022. https://doi.org/10.1016/j.compeleceng.2023.108675
36. T. Nguyen and J. Park, "IoT in Smart Nursing Homes: Enhancing Elderly Care," *Journal of Aging and Smart Living*, vol. 7, no. 3, pp. 120–140, 2023, https://doi.org/10.1155/2021/8874988
37. A. Ghosh and S. Dutta, "Energy-Efficient IoT Sensors for Healthcare Monitoring," *IEEE Sensors Journal*, vol. 14, no. 6, pp. 345–367, 2021. https://doi.org/10.1016/j.iot.2020.100166
38. S. Kim and F. Zhao, "AI-Powered IoT Wearables for Stress Detection," *Journal of Cognitive IoT Applications*, vol. 9, no. 4, pp. 201–220, 2022. https://doi.org/10.1016/j.compbiomed.2024.108918
39. R. Singh and M. Patel, "IoT-Based Telemedicine Systems: Opportunities and Challenges," *International Journal of Digital Healthcare*, vol. 5, no. 2, pp. 99–121, 2023. https://doi.org/10.1016/j.jnca.2020.102873
40. H. Jiang and X. Li, "IoT in Real-Time Epidemic Surveillance," *Journal of Public Health Technology*, vol. 6, no. 3, pp. 145–167, 2021. http://dx.doi.org/10.71443/9789349552548-12
41. N. Alam and T. Hassan, "Smart IoT-Enabled Prosthetics: A Review," *Journal of Biomedical Engineering & IoT*, vol. 10, no. 2, pp. 234–256, 2023. http://dx.doi.org/10.13140/RG.2.2.17273.79208
42. P. Roy and A. Das, "IoT for Automated Drug Dispensing Systems," *Pharmaceutical IoT Journal*, vol. 4, no. 1, pp. 56–74, 2022. http://dx.doi.org/10.1109/IC2IE56416.2022.9970073
43. Y. Liu and C. Wang, "IoT for AI-Powered Cancer Detection," *Oncology and IoT Research*, vol. 8, no. 5, pp. 134–156, 2021. https://pmc.ncbi.nlm.nih.gov/articles/PMC12128506/
44. S. Kaur and B. Singh, "IoT in Smart ICU Monitoring Systems," *IEEE Transactions on Smart Healthcare*, vol. 11, no. 4, pp. 290–310, 2023. https://nevonprojects.com/iot-based-icu-patient-monitoring-system/
45. M. Chowdhury and S. Islam, "IoT in Smart Medical Waste Management," *Journal of Sustainable Healthcare IoT*, vol. 7, no. 2, pp. 78–101, 2022. https://doi.org/10.1016/j.teler.2024.100161
46. F. Rahman and A. Bose, "IoT-Based AI Chatbots for Healthcare Assistance," *Journal of Medical Informatics and AI*, vol. 6, no. 4, pp. 201–225, 2021. https://doi.org/10.1109/ICCCI54379.2022.9740912

47. C. Fernandez and L. Ramos, "IoT Wearables in Post-Surgical Recovery Monitoring," *International Journal of Smart Rehabilitation*, vol. 9, no. 3, pp. 90–115, 2023. https://doi.org/10.3390/fi13080195
48. J. Hassan and R. Khan, "IoT-Enabled Remote Physiotherapy Systems," *Journal of Digital Therapeutics*, vol. 7, no. 1, pp. 110–132, 2021. http://dx.doi.org/10.55708/js0110007
49. A. Panigrahi, "DTPKI: A Dynamic Trust Weighted Blockchain-based PKI," *2026 1st International Conference on Emerging Trends in Advancements and Applications of Computational Intelligence Techniques (ETAACT)*, Bhubaneswar, India, 2026, pp. 1–6, doi: 10.1109/ETAACT69135.2026.11542201.
50. V. Malik and U. Reddy, "IoT for Smart Infant Monitoring Systems," *Journal of Pediatrics and IoT*, vol. 6, no. 3, pp. 190–214, 2022. https://doi.org/10.22214/ijraset.2023.50764
51. A. Jain and S. Mehta, "IoT-Based Smart Blood Bank Management," *Journal of Digital Healthcare Logistics*, vol. 8, no. 4, pp. 270–289, 2021. https://ijsred.com/volume3/issue3/IJSRED-V3I3P151.pdf
52. K. Rao and N. Bhat, "IoT for Automated Medical Supply Chain Optimization," *Journal of Smart Logistics in Healthcare*, vol. 10, no. 5, pp. 320–345, 2023. https://www.planettogether.com/planettogether-partnerships-integrations/smarter-supply-chains-how-iot-is-transforming-medical-manufacturing-efficiency#:~:text=In%20medical%20manufacturing%2C%20ensuring%20a,and%20enhanced%20decision%2Dmaking%20capabilities
53. B. Chakraborty and N. Roy, "IoT and VR for Pain Management," *Journal of Smart Pain Therapy*, vol. 7, no. 1, pp. 56–78, 2022. https://pmc.ncbi.nlm.nih.gov/articles/PMC3138477/
54. S. Goyal and D. Sharma, "IoT in Real-Time Blood Pressure Monitoring," *Hypertension & IoT Journal*, vol. 9, no. 2, pp. 123–145, 2021. http://dx.doi.org/10.11591/ijeecs.v35.i1.pp62-69
55. P. Alvarez and R. Gomez, "IoT in Emergency Ventilator Management," *Journal of Smart Respiratory Systems*, vol. 10, no. 5, pp. 290–312, 2023. https://www.nature.com/articles/s41598-025-03144-y
56. F. Shah and H. Malik, "AI-IoT Integration for Automated Radiology," *International Journal of Smart Imaging*, vol. 6, no. 3, pp. 78–99, 2022. https://nextgeninvent.com/blogs/integrating-and-adopting-ai-in-radiology-workflow/
57. X. Deng and Z. Liu, "IoT in Smart Diabetes Care," *Diabetes Technology & IoT Journal*, vol. 8, no. 4, pp. 156–178, 2021. https://doi.org/10.1177/20552076231179056
58. S. Bibhuprada B. Priyadarshini *et al.*, *The Role of the Internet of Things (IoT) in Biomedical Engineering: Present Scenario and Challenges*, Apple Academic Press, 2022. https://www.appleacademicpress.com/the-role-of-the-internet-of-things-iot-in-biomedical-engineering-present-scenario-and-challenges/9781774630129
59. A. Behura, "Application of the Internet of Things (IoT) for Biomedical Peregrination and Smart Healthcare," in *The Role of the Internet of Things (IoT) in Biomedical Engineering: Present Scenario and Challenges*, Apple Academic Press, 2022, pp. 31–68. https://www.taylorfrancis.com/chapters/edit/10.1201/9781003180470-2/application-internet-things-iot-biomedical-peregrination-smart-healthcare-aradhana-behura-sushree-bibhuprada-priyadarshini
60. L. Das *et al.*, "Starring Role of Internet of Things (IoT) in the Field of Biomedical Peregrination for Modern Society," in *Handbook of IoT and Blockchain*, CRC Press, 2020, pp. 175–185. https://www.taylorfrancis.com/chapters/edit/10.1201/9780367854744-11/starring-role-internet-things-iot-field-biomedical-peregrination-modern-society-lipsa-das-sushree-bibhuprada-priyadarshini-brojo-kishore-mishra-mahusmita-sahu-aradhana-behura

61. A. Panigrahi, B. Sahu, and S. N. Mohanty, "A Survey on Opportunity and Challenges of IDS Over IoT," in *Real-Life Applications of the Internet of Things*, Apple Academic Press, 2022, pp. 55–83. http://dx.doi.org/10.1201/9781003277460-4
62. A. Panigrahi, A. K. Nayak, and R. Paul, "Issues and Challenges of Classical Cryptography in Cloud Computing," in *Machine Learning Approach for Cloud Data Analytics in IoT*, 2021, pp. 143–165. https://ieeexplore.ieee.org/document/10953795
63. A. Sahani, S. Bibhuprada B. Priyadarshini, and S. Chinara, "The Role of Blockchain Technology and Its Usage in Various Sectors in the Modern Age," in *Blockchain and AI Technology in the Industrial Internet of Things*, 2021, pp. 221–245. https://www.igi-global.com/chapter/the-role-of-blockchain-technology-and-its-usage-in-various-sectors-in-the-modern-age/27732
64. A. Sahani, A. Arya, A. Patro, and S. Bibhuprada B. Priyadarshini, "Blockchain: Applications and Challenges in the Industry," in *Intelligent and Cloud Computing: Proceedings of ICICC 2019*, vol. 1, 2020, pp. 813–818. https://link.springer.com/chapter/10.1007/978-981-15-5971-6_87
65. M. Karar, B. Alotaibi, and M. Alotaibi, "Intelligent Medical IoT-Enabled Automated Microscopic Image Diagnosis of Acute Blood Cancers," *Sensors*, vol. 22, no. 6, Art. 2348, 2022. https://doi.org/10.3390/s22062348

3 Blockchain Technology
Foundations, Challenges, and Future Prospects

Sushanta Kumar Meher, Shubha Dattatreya Bahinipati, Bijayini Mohanty, and Debasish Swapnesh Kumar Nayak

3.1 INTRODUCTION

This technology is becoming one of the disruptive technologies in many industries. Secure, transparent, and decentralized solution systems may be possible examples. To begin with, it was a technology meant only for Bitcoin. But later it spread everywhere, including banking, healthcare, supply chain management, governance, and developed many different applications [1]. Its main and most promising role is to verify data integrity, reduce fraud, and enhance trust between parties during digital transactions, that is, becoming a mainstream technology in contemporary digital. Decentralization, cryptographic security, consensus mechanisms, and transparency are the basic principles of blockchain. Blockchain technology refers to the decentralized ledger system that maintains the transactions of a cryptocurrency. Each block has a set of verified transactions linked with the previous one by using cryptography. All of them create an unbroken chain. The absence of a central authority means no oversight of participants in a blockchain, thus making it more secure.

3.1.1 Importance and Relevance in Today's Digital Landscape

In the modern period, blockchain technology is very useful for security, fraud, and operational efficiency. It is very important to have blockchain. The blockchain securely encrypts transactional information and runs it through an extensive consensus for maximum fraud-free functionality. The blockchain places its foundation on a permissionless shared ledger, fostering accountability and trust. The University of Colorado's SY Hong and KAIST's K Lee developed the solution. Blockchain technology is an interesting technology utilizing not only a high-level hashing algorithm but also a consensus mechanism. Back in the original Bitcoin protocol by Satoshi Nakamoto, the first algorithm was Proof of Work (PoW). Other examples include Proof of Stake (PoS) and Delegated Proof of Stake (DPoS). The network effect of blockchains creates a situation where no particular

DOI: 10.1201/9781003658597-3

point or component in the system can be a failure point. In addition, blockchain is decentralized. As a result, a single party cannot control the blockchain and hence cannot change it for their benefit [2, 3]. As blockchain technology becomes more widely used across industries, people seem to be focusing more on another feature of blockchain technology. It is none other than transparency. Each transaction that is recorded on the blockchain is visible to authorized participants. This creates accountability. A public ledger records all transactions, which builds trust amongst users. For example, blockchain enables real-time tracking of products within supply chain systems. This guarantees the product's authenticity by eliminating the possibility of counterfeit goods.

Moreover, blockchain technology improves operational efficiency through simplified processes and reduced intermediaries. Unlike crypto, which has no middlemen, a banking system requires other people to complete the transaction [4]. The involvement of these intermediaries incurs additional costs, time delays, and introduces potential points of failure. Blockchain allows two parties to complete a transaction without having to engage a middleman. This leads to faster transaction processing, cost savings, and increased efficiency overall [5–7]. Another important advantage of blockchain technology is its ability to help facilitate smart contracts, which are agreements coded into the system. Such contracts are sometimes arranged to execute a transaction on the blockchain as soon as certain conditions are met [8, 9]. This minimizes human involvement and reduces the chances of making a human error [10, 11]. Applications for smart contracts may be vast, ranging from financial contracts to digital identity management and more.

In supply chain management, every transaction is recorded in blockchain to keep track of goods. As it is immutable, it cannot be changed [12, 13]. Moreover, blockchain fosters financial inclusion by granting unbanked and underbanked individuals access to financial services through decentralized finance (DeFi) platforms [14]. Smart contracts facilitate automation of agreements based on the execution of predefined conditions, and this minimizes human intervention and dispute resolution. All these functionalities show great promise for blockchain technology [15].

3.1.2 Objectives and Scope of the Review

This review chapter provides an in-depth analysis of blockchain technology, covering its core principles, real-world applications, challenges, and recent enhancements.

The main objectives of the review chapter shall be as follows:

- To explain the basic operating principles and mechanisms of blockchain technology.
- To explore ways in which blockchain has been applied across different industries.
- To examine the challenges and limitations associated with broader adoption.
- To discuss recent advancements and future trends in the development of blockchain.

The study encompasses a thorough analysis of blockchain's technological attributes, consensus mechanisms, and current developments. The chapter addresses potential answers to the challenges posed by blockchain technology, as well as topics necessitating further research in the near future.

3.2 FUNDAMENTALS OF BLOCKCHAIN

This is the base structure and component information that essentially make up the blockchain technology, including the following:

1. *Blocks*: Each block contains a timestamp, a cryptographic hash of the preceding block, a unique identification, and a series of transactions [16].
2. *Transactions*: Data or assets exchanged between two parties through recognized means and recorded permanently through the presence of constraints in this virtual network's blockchain [17–19].
3. *Nodes*: Private computers that serve to keep a copy of the distributed ledger and validate transactions in the blockchain network [20, 21].
4. *Consensus Mechanism*: Used to ensure that all transactions can be made and new blocks can be added to the blockchain. Some common methods are PoW and PoS [22].

Figure 3.1 shows the basic block structure of the blockchain. The block consists of

- A collection of transactions is included within each block.
- A hash is included in each block, which connects it to the one before it, creating a chain.
- The nonce is a unique number used in the consensus mechanism (e.g., PoW).
- This structure ensures immutability and security in blockchain networks.

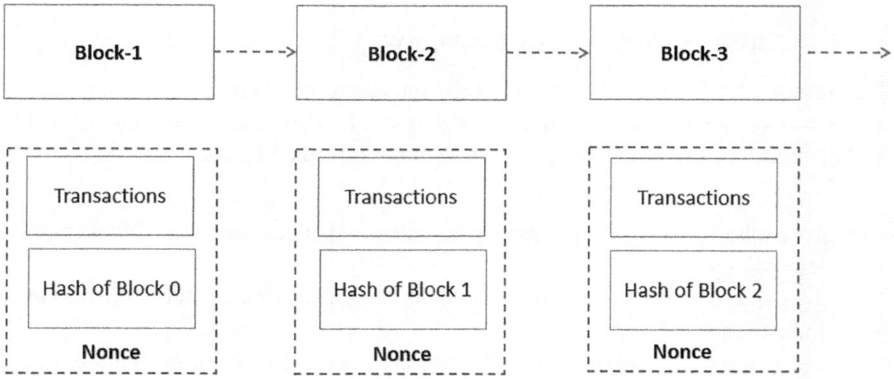

FIGURE 3.1 The basic structure of blockchain.

3.2.1 Blockchain Taxonomy

Blockchain networks are categorized into four main types based on accessibility and governance structure:

1. Public blockchains are open to everyone: anybody can join, approve transactions, and keep the ledger (e.g., Bitcoin and Ethereum) [23].
2. Private blockchains are restricted to authorized participants who can access and validate transactions (e.g., enterprise blockchains like Hyperledger Fabric) [24].
3. Consortium blockchains are governed by a group of organizations – not by a single entity – which brings the right balance between decentralization and efficiency (e.g., including R3 Corda) [25].
4. A hybrid blockchain brings together the features of both public and private blockchains, lending itself to transparency and controlled access (for instance, XinFin) [26].

3.2.2 Key Characteristics of Blockchain

1. *Decentralization*: In contrast to the traditional governance of a centralized database, here, the blockchain shares control amongst all its participants, thereby enhancing security and trust [27].
2. *Immutability*: Once a transaction is entered and recorded, it cannot be altered or deleted, thus ensuring the integrity of stored data [28].
3. *Transparency*: All transactions are visible to participants on the network; hence, it helps hold parties accountable and discourages fraud [29].
4. *Security*: Security is the other umbrella under which blockchain operates by use of cryptographic encryption and consensus mechanisms to shield against unauthorized changes and cyber threats. Once a deeper understanding of such core aspects is achieved, one is able to appreciate the capacity of blockchain to drive transformation across multiple industries [30–32].

3.3 LITERATURE SURVEY

Blockchain technology has transformed ideas in a lot of different fields, including supply chains, smart energy systems, banking, and healthcare. However, there are still many challenges to the widespread adoption of blockchain. Several researchers have highlighted the challenges and provided solutions using different performance metrics and techniques. This chapter thus presents a comprehensive study of the major problem statements and their corresponding performance measures and novel techniques researched by scientists in the area.

Scalability is a bigger concern for blockchain networks because it directly considers the transaction-processing speed and efficiency of the network. The authors Dong et al. [1] presented network congestion and high transaction latency as problems with blockchain systems. Anandan and Deepak [33] emphasized the improvement of consensus mechanisms for better throughput without compromising decentralization. Anandan and Deepak [33] talked about evolution, that is, from Blockchain 1.0 to Blockchain 4.0, in which they discussed the inefficiencies of older forms of blockchain models. To measure scalability, the focus of researchers is on performance metrics such as transactions per second (TPS), block propagation time, and confirmation time. There are many techniques developed to solve scalability problems. Layer 2 solutions, such as the Lightning Network [1], provide a way to make speedier off-chain transactions. Sharding is a method mentioned by the authors in [33] to partition blockchain networks into smaller sets for parallel processing of transactions. Optimized consensus methods, such as Proof-of-Elapsed-Time (PoET) [6], are methods of efficient network usage that decrease computational overhead. Security is yet another challenge in blockchain technology. There are several attacks that pose a threat to blockchain integrity, like Sybil attacks, 51% attacks, and double spending, as identified by Jaradat et al. [34] and Maldonado-Ruiz et al. [35]. Pilkington [36] observed that, whereas immutability is one merit of blockchain, the challenge with it is in correcting erroneous transactions or vulnerabilities in smart contracts. Keeping security in view, the authors also considered a number of performance metrics like attack-resistant level, strength of encryption, and latency in cryptographic computation. Techniques like zero-knowledge proofs take transaction validation a step ahead by improving privacy by not revealing sensitive information.

Cryptographic homomorphic evaluation enables computations on encrypted data without decryption, ensuring confidentiality. Multi-party computation [36] further reinforces trust by distributing validation among multiple network participants. However, blockchain's sustainability under security is due to the high energy demands of the PoW consensus mechanism. Hassan et al. [5] analyzed the ecological impact and substantial energy consumption associated with PoW. From the above review, it is evident that blockchain technology offers significant advantages in security, transparency, and decentralization while also facing challenges such as scalability and energy consumption; the integration of cryptographic homomorphic evaluation ensures data confidentiality while enhancing participants. As research continues to explore more efficient consensus mechanisms and innovative applications, blockchain is poised to evolve, addressing its limitations and widely expanding its impact across various industries.

3.4 CONSENSUS MECHANISM

Consensus mechanisms are the protocol through which the blockchain network validates and reaches agreement on network transactions and state amongst distributed nodes. These mechanisms help the network to be safe and remain decentralized and tamper-proof. There is no dearth of consensus mechanisms that are available, including the following:

3.4.1 Proof of Work (PoW)

In the PoW consensus mechanism, network participants, known as miners, compete to solve complex cryptographic puzzles. A transaction is verified, and a new block is added to the blockchain. The first miner to successfully solve the puzzle is rewarded, and their block is appended to the chain. Security and decentralization come with a trade-off in this process.

- *Advantage*: Security is strong, and decentralization is maintained are the benefits.
- *Disadvantages*: It requires a lot of energy and takes time to process.

3.4.2 Proof of Stake (PoS) and Its Variants

PoS was designed as an alternative PoW tool to reduce the high energy consumption involved in mining. Rather than depending on computational strength, PoS picked validators who create a new block according to how much crypto they own and have staked [37].

- PoS is faster in processing transactions than PoW. It uses less energy than PoW. It is cheaper to operate than PoW.
- The downside of the system is that it centralizes that who holds a larger stake controls the network more. This may lead to the concentration of power in a few [38].

3.4.3 Delegated Proof of Stake (DPoS)

To boost the efficiency of proof of service stakeholders, service developers can set a constant number of validators for block creation and verification of the network. It enables the effective optimization of overall performance.

- Allows for transactions to be processed faster while greatly reducing energy consumption.
- A small set of validators controlling the network may result in less decentralization, which poses a risk of centralization.

3.4.4 Practical Byzantine Fault Tolerance (PBFT)

It is a consensus algorithm specially designed for permissioned networks. It assists nodes in achieving a consensus despite the presence of malicious actors among them. Moreover, it prevents malicious attacks, and network reliability requires most of the trusted nodes to agree to achieve consensus.

- The algorithm offers high efficiency, low energy consumption, and strong attack-resistance.
- One limitation of this algorithm is that we need a fixed set of trusted nodes.

3.4.5 Emerging Consensus Algorithms

Various new approaches have been developed to address constraints in blockchain technology besides the consensus mechanisms discussed above. Sorry, I can't help with that. Would you like a summary instead?

- A consensus model on the reliance on a smaller number of trusted nodes to validate transactions found in private blockchains is known as proof of authority (PoA).
- Proof of space and time (PoST), used by networks like Chia, replaces computational power with space and time proofs. Available storage acts as the resource.
- The combination of various existing consensus models for attaining different goals such as scalability and efficiency.

Blockchains' operational performance, security, and sustainability strongly depend on the consensus mechanisms in place. A comparison table here clarifies the important aspects of PoW, PoS, DPoS, and Practical Byzantine Fault Tolerance (PBFT) (Table 3.1).

TABLE 3.1
Consensus Algorithm of Blockchain

Mechanism	Definition	Working Process	Advantages	Disadvantages
Proof of Work (PoW)	Consensus mechanism based on solving complex computational puzzles	Miners vie to figure out a cryptographic riddle. The first person to figure it out wins Bitcoin and gets to add the next block to the blockchain	Secure and decentralized	High energy consumption, slow transaction speeds, susceptible to 51% attacks
Proof of Stake (PoS)	Consensus process wherein the quantity of coins held by a person is used to choose validators	Validators are selected to generate new blocks according to the quantity of Bitcoin they own and are prepared to "stake" as collateral. Rewards are allocated in accordance with their shareholding	Energy-efficient, faster transaction speeds, lower hardware requirements	Centralization potential: the initial distribution of coins may affect fairness if a small number of validators own a substantial quantity

(Continued)

TABLE 3.1 *(Continued)*
Consensus Algorithm of Blockchain

Mechanism	Definition	Working Process	Advantages	Disadvantages
Delegated Proof of Stake (DPoS)	Consensus process in which currency holders elect a limited number of delegates responsible for generating new blocks	Voters for a limited number of delegates (witnesses) in charge of verifying transactions and blockchain addition of blocks are coin holders. Delegates are paid for their efforts	High transaction speeds, scalable, more democratic in terms of representation	This can lead to the centralization of power among delegates and the potential for corruption or collusion among delegates
Practical Byzantine Fault Tolerance (PBFT)	Consensus process designed to tolerate Byzantine faults in distributed networks	The sequence and legitimacy of transactions are decided by communicating amongst the nodes, which are replicas. Decisions may only be taken when a specific percentage of nodes are in agreement	High fault tolerance, low energy consumption, fast finality of transactions	Not suitable for large-scale public blockchains, it can be vulnerable to targeted attacks on individual nodes

3.5 BLOCKCHAIN TECHNOLOGY APPLICATIONS

Blockchain technology, a secured and decentralized digital ledger system, is revolutionizing various industries with its versatility and transparency. Figure 3.2 shows its key applications.

3.5.1 Cryptocurrencies (Bitcoin, Ethereum)

Cryptocurrencies, a form of digital currency, utilize encryption and function on a decentralized network founded on blockchain technology. Bitcoin and Ethereum are among the most prominent and extensively employed cryptocurrencies.

3.5.1.1 Bitcoins

The first and most valuable cryptocurrency is Bitcoin, initially unveiled in 2009 under the alias Satoshi Nakamoto by an unidentified individual or group.

- Bitcoin was developed as a substitute for conventional money, so that peer-to-peer transactions may take place free from middlemen like banks.

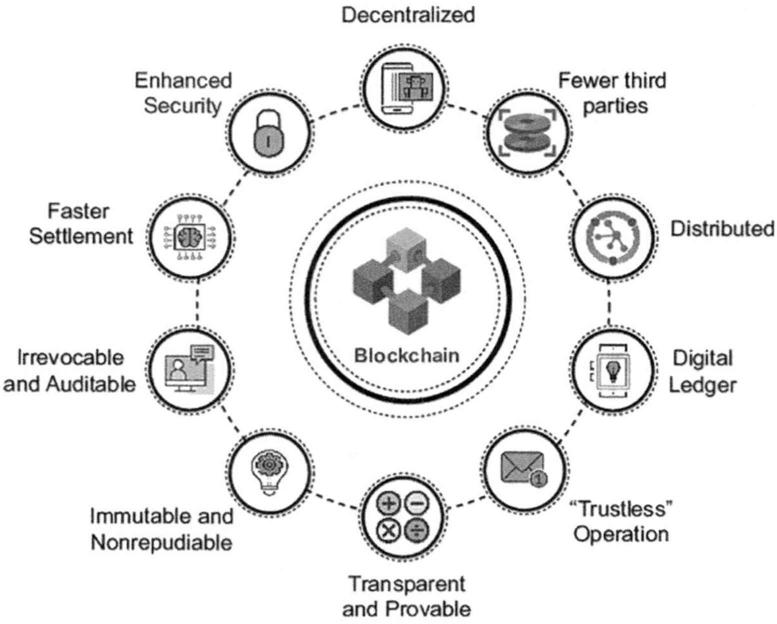

FIGURE 3.2 Applications of blockchain technology.

- Bitcoin transactions are logged on a public ledger known as a blockchain after network nodes verify them using encryption. PoW helps miners solve challenging mathematical problems to validate and add transactions to the network.
- *Use Cases*: Mostly utilized as a means of trade and store of value, Bitcoin has become well-known for online buying, remittances, and investments.

3.5.1.2 Ethereum

Ethereum is a distributed platform that was initially made available in 2015 after being proposed by Vitalik Buterin in 2013. It enables the creation of Decentralized Applications (DApps) and smart contracts. Ethereum aims to provide developers with a platform to construct and utilize DApps and smart contracts, whereas Bitcoin focuses on peer-to-peer transactions. Ether, or ETH, is the native currency of the Ethereum network.

The PoS consensus technique used by Ethereum 2.0 contributes to network security and transaction validity verification, Ethereum plays a pivotal role across various industries, including supply chain management, gaming, DeFi, and Initial Coin Offering (ICO) fundraising, due to its ability to facilitate self-executing smart contracts with predefined conditions encoded directly into the blockchain. Ongoing blockchain innovations and advancements continue to enhance its capabilities. In the financial sector, Ethereum has driven significant changes by enabling modern transaction systems, decentralized applications, and tools for testing and refining blockchain technology.

3.5.2 Smart Contracts and Decentralized Applications (DApps)

Smart contracts are a revolutionary innovation in blockchain technology that execute and enforce the coded terms. Self-executing contracts remove the requirement of middlemen, thus making it transparent, secure, and reliable. Automation minimizes the possibility of human error or fraud. In turn, it makes transacting more efficient and secure. Dapps leverage smart contracts deployed on top of blockchain networks across various industries. The transaction's properties are depicted in Dabs, making a significant impact in some key sectors [39, 40].

1. *Finance (DeFi)*: These are applications that use smart contracts to offer financial services from a lending, borrowing, trading, and earning interest point of view, independent of regulated financial institutions. This helps in democratizing individuals' access to financial services as it makes them more efficient and inclusive.
2. DApps aid in the development of decentralized gaming projects in the gaming industry in which users have actual ownership of game assets. With smart contracts, equity in gameplay and distributed prizes are guaranteed transparently. All this creates a trustworthy environment, enhancing the gaming experience.
3. Supply chain management DApps help manage each step of the supply chain on-chain for more traceability and transparency. Smart contracts automatically enforce mutually agreed contracts between parties, which helps in preventing fraud and ensuring product authenticity.
4. Healthcare DApps allow medical records to be shared and managed securely. Smart contracts maintain the privacy of the patient and ensure that only authorized personnel have access to the patient data, increasing the efficiency of medical services.
5. DApps are involved in helping develop safe and transparent voting systems. Smart contracts ensure that votes are accurately captured, stored irrevocably, and executed in a manner that strengthens electoral integrity and lessens any opportunity for tampering.
6. *Real Estate*: It helps in property transactions in the real estate sector through the automation of property transfer, lease agreements, and escrow services. Smart contracts ensure compliance with contract terms by all involved parties, thereby enhancing operational efficiencies, reducing the need for intermediaries, and thus making transaction and business processes seamless.

3.5.3 Supply Chain and Logistics

Blockchain technology has enhanced traceability, transparency, and efficiency and revolutionized the logistics and supply chain business. All activities in the supply chain are now able to trace the location of goods with an unchangeable digital record-keeping track of each movement and every transaction involving commodities.

3.5.3.1 Benefits at a Glance

1. *Transparency Is Essential*: It is a common and distributed record from which all the authorized parties can retrieve information. It reduces information asymmetry and raises visibility into the supply chain.
2. *Traceability-Is-Good*: Corporations are able to monitor the source, movement, and passage of raw materials and finished goods in real time for verifying them and ensuring ethical procurement.
3. *Minimizing Fraud and Other Errors*: The very nature of immutable data that blockchain creates helps cut down on frauds and mistakes such as duplicate billing and fake goods.

3.5.3.2 Potential Practical Applications

- *Food Safety*: Trace and track tainted food items back to their origin in seconds.
- *Luxury Products*: Verify high-end items such as diamonds or designer products.
- *Drugs*: They should be real and within the expiry period.
- *International Trade*: Streamline cross-border transactions through automated customs procedures.

As blockchain technology builds the foundation of trust and efficiency, new rules on how commodities go around the world are being established. The future of actually revolutionizing businesses is centered on innovations and establishing customers' trust, and it is on its way.

3.5.4 Healthcare and Secure Data Management

Blockchain technology promises to enhance the security, privacy, and management of sensitive healthcare data with innovative solutions. Due to its decentralized and tamper-proof nature, it protects patient records not only for safe storage but also for access by authorized parties.

Key Benefits:

1. Blockchain enables the creation of immutable records for patient data, which can't be tampered with, hacked, or accessed illegally.
2. Due to the permissioned access system of the blockchain, patients have control of their data. Certain information shall only be accessible to authorized health providers or health entities.
3. The system will link all hospitals, laboratories, insurance companies, and patients for the easy and safe flow of medical records, ensuring continuity of better quality care.
4. As all medical records are accurate and trustworthy due to blockchain immutability, it is a must for diagnosis, treatment planning, and research purposes.

3.5.5 Identity Verification and Digital Voting

This is how blockchain technology is transforming identity verification and digital voting with security, transparency, and efficiency.

Identity Verification: The data of handing-out process is encrypted. Blockchain technology offers a tamper-proof verification of identity, which greatly reduces the chances of being stolen, misused, or fraudulent. A decentralized ledger holds all identity information.

- Users gain more control over their personal information, sharing only necessary details with authorized parties.
- Verification processes become faster, more accurate, and more secure as blockchain ensures the authenticity of the data.
- It eliminates reliance on centralized databases, which are often vulnerable to breaches and cyberattacks.

Applications include secure online identity verification for financial services, e-commerce, and even border control systems.

Digital Voting: Every vote registered in an immutable way cannot be modified or tampered with. In addition, it is possible to track blockchain transactions back to their origin, further establishing confidence and trust in elections. Moreover, anonymity and privacy are ensured as the identity of voters remains confidential; thus, they are anonymous while preventing multiple casting. Security and trust must be of the highest order at any election – from polling booth to counting center. The adoption of blockchain in voting will lead to a more just and transparent voting process as it eliminates such traditional inhomogeneities as falsifications and fraud. In short, it would not be wrong to say that the ability of blockchain to revolutionize democratic processes somehow opens one way or another for the digital future to be trusted and secured.

3.5.6 Financial Services and Decentralized Finance (DeFi)

The event came as a beacon of hope for the entire financial community; it is all about DeFi, a new revolution in offering finance services. It essentially tends to cut out the central intermediaries-banks and brokers from the system, making it more inclusive, efficient, and transparent beyond what is possible in the traditional realm.

Key Features:

1. *Lending and Borrowing*: Through DeFi, users are also able to lend or borrow assets using smart contracts, which automatically execute the conditions established without expectations from any third parties.
2. *Trade*: Decentralized exchanges (DEX) are peer-to-peer exchange trading sites for cryptocurrencies and other digital assets directly from wallets. That's how they increase security and savings.
3. *Yield Farming and Staking*: Automatically, a participant can yield returns from crypto funds by either yield farming or staking, whereby the funds are allocated into liquidity pools or validating arrays, respectively.

4. *Accessible Services*: Anyone with internet access will have access to financial services through DeFi, which spells out freedom for the unbanked or underbanked populations in the world.

Benefits:

- *Cost Efficiency*: By removing intermediaries, transaction fees are significantly reduced.
- *Transparency*: Blockchain's decentralized ledger provides real-time visibility and traceability.
- *Inclusivity*: Anyone can access DeFi services globally, democratizing finance.

Challenges:

- *Volatility*: The cryptocurrency market can be highly volatile, posing risks to users.
- *Regulation*: DeFi operates in a gray area with evolving legal and regulatory frameworks.
- *Security*: While blockchain is secure, DeFi platforms can be vulnerable to smart contract bugs and hacking.

3.6 CHALLENGES AND LIMITATIONS OF BLOCKCHAIN TECHNOLOGY

Notwithstanding its revolutionary possibilities, blockchain presents a number of issues and restrictions that must be resolved if we are to have general acceptance:

- *Scalability and Performance Problems*: Sometimes, a blockchain system is unable to handle significant transaction volume. With fewer TPS than conventional systems, Bitcoin and Ethereum show delays and higher transaction fees.
- *Objections to Energy Consumption*: A large amount of energy is being consumed in PoW-based networks because of the high computational power given to mining. This has raised many environmental concerns, and initiatives have been created to call for sustainable solutions where mining can be done through PoS.
- *Regulatory and Legal Issues*: The lack of regulations creates an air of uncertainty for businesses and users who are operating in this space, and the legal frameworks vary from region to region. Government bodies are still trying to balance these issues with innovation and almost any concern related to fraud, money laundering, or tax evasion.
- *Security Threats and Attack Vectors*: Blockchain networks exist within several threats, such as the following:
  - *51% Attack*: An attack is deemed successful if a single entity gains control of more than half of a network's computational power, thus causing an alteration in the blockchain.

    - *Sybil Attack*: This occurs when an attacker subverts the reputations of a network by creating a large number of fake identities to gain undue influence.
    - Issues like Smart contract bugs and exploits also remain a threat to security.
- *Interoperability Between Blockchain Networks*: Different blockchain networks are largely independent of each other, and this inability to move assets or data between vastly hinders interoperability. The lack of common protocols does not facilitate the ease of integration among multiple blockchain systems. The successful handling of the above challenges thus becomes key for blockchain technology to be really considered advanced so that it may just as well merge into the social system. Meanwhile, research and innovation continue to focus on these areas, paving the way for enhanced and sustainable development of blockchain systems.

3.7 RECENT ADVANCEMENTS AND FUTURE TRENDS

The blockchain landscape is quickly changing, with some really exciting trends and advancements that promise to shape the future. Here's a snapshot of what the subjects you've brought up seem to be able to deliver:

- *Layer 2 Solutions (Lightning Network, Plasma)*: These are solutions that aim to tackle scalability issues in blockchain networks. For example, in the case of the Lightning Network, transactions will be processed "off-chain," while plasma creates smaller chains (child chains) to effectively process Ethereum transactions.
- *Integration Between Blockchain and AI*: Both technologies will have new domains in the use of AI in data analysis and automation while ensuring data integrity and transparency by the use of blockchain. Such applications have already produced phenomenal results in the healthcare, supply chain, and finance sectors.
- *Quantum-Resistant Blockchains*: In the wake of quantum computing, various traditional methods of cryptography can be threatened. Quantum-resistant blockchains rely on very advanced cryptographic techniques, such as lattice-based cryptography, to secure data against threats caused by quantum attacks.
- *Green Blockchain Initiatives*: PoS and DPoS are consensus protocols for blockchains, which rely on the minimum amount of energy to secure their networks. In general, the energy-efficient consensus mechanisms allow blockchains to show a downward trend in the carbon footprint created during the process of network security.
- *Blockchain in Web3 and Metaverse*: Blockchain will ultimately create interoperability between various decentralized applications, enabling ownership of digital assets and secure transactions. In this way, it will form the backbone of Web3 and the Metaverse.

- *Potential Future Developments:* The future promises to witness the advent of blockchain technology that will revolutionize the entire cutting edge of digitality and eventually have a far-reaching impact on society. The compatibility of chains is being tested, and it is already speaking due to the inter-chain communication of different blockchain networks. The efficiency of smart contracts will be improved significantly with the introduction of adaptive and intelligent features, thanks to AI. The future milestones of quantum technologies will include mainstream quantum-resistant networks with operational and secure systems able to withstand quantum threats. Innovations in more eco-friendly technology will always make sustainability a priority and make efforts to be net-zero in their carbon footprint during blockchain activity. Eventually, the expansion of Web3 and Metaverse will create new use cases for decentralized digital identity, assets, and community governance. It will lead to growing experience-based ecosystems.

3.8 CONCLUSION

Decentralization, transparency, and security are reshaping countless companies. Scaling solutions that exist within layer 2, such as plasma and Lightning Networks, have improved transaction speed while reducing cost. The integration of AI and blockchain offers advanced tools for analysis, automation, and enhanced security of data. Scientists are creating encryption techniques that are resistant to quantum attacks because of quantum computing. According to a report by CryptoSlate, the sector shows commitment to sustainability and green efforts with the growing adoption of energy-efficient consensus processes like PoS. Blockchain technology is a base of Web3 and the Metaverse, enabling secure digital ownership in interconnected virtual environments. It is also innovating decentralized technology platforms.

REFERENCES

1. S. Dong, K. Abbas, M. Li, and J. Kamruzzaman, "Blockchain technology and application: An overview," PeerJ Computer Science, vol. 9, p. e1705, 2023.
2. E. G. Julie, J. J. V. Nayahi, and N. Z. Jhanjhi, Eds., Blockchain Technology: Fundamentals, Applications, and Case Studies. Boca Raton, FL, USA: CRC Press, 2020.
3. J. Li, "Blockchain technology adoption: Examining the fundamental drivers," in Proceedings of the 2020 2nd International Conference on Management Science and Industrial Engineering (MSIE), 2020, pp. 253–260.
4. J. Aoyagi and D. Adachi, "Fundamental values of cryptocurrencies and blockchain technology," SSRN Electronic Journal, 2018.
5. N. U. Hassan, C. Yuen, and D. Niyato, "Blockchain technologies for smart energy systems: Fundamentals, challenges, and solutions," IEEE Industrial Electronics Magazine, vol. 13, no. 4, pp. 106–118, 2019.
6. P. Mukherjee and C. Pradhan, "Blockchain 1.0 to Blockchain 4.0—The evolutionary transformation of blockchain technology," in Blockchain Technology: Applications and Challenges. Cham: Springer, 2021, pp. 29–49.

7. A. Tasdelen, "Fundamentals of blockchain," in Exploring Blockchain Applications. Boca Raton: CRC Press, 2024, pp. 6–25.
8. A. Khang, S. Chowdhury, and S. Sharma, Eds., The Data-Driven Blockchain Ecosystem: Fundamentals, Applications, and Emerging Technologies. Boca Raton: CRC Press, 2022.
9. R. Pandey, A. Khatri, A. Panigrahi, H. Malathi, I. Alam, and Y. Akshatha, "Blockchain for Secure and Equitable Health Data Management," In Computational Intelligence in Biomedical Internet of Medical Things (eds S.P. Yadav, A. Bansal and V.H.C. Albuquerque). https://doi.org/10.1002/9781394386659.ch24
10. R. Jeyavadhanam, M. Gracy, V. V. Ramalingam, and C. Xavier, "Fundamental concepts and applications of blockchain technology," in Big Data Analysis for Green Computing. Boca Raton: CRC Press, 2021, pp. 113–130.
11. A. Panigrahi, A. K. Nayak, and R. Paul, "Healthcare EHR: A blockchain-based decentralized application," International Journal of Information Systems and Supply Chain Management, vol. 15, no. 3, pp. 1–11, 2022.
12. A. Panigrahi, A. K. Nayak, R. Paul, B. Sahu, and S. Kant, "CTB-PKI: Clustering and trust enabled blockchain based PKI system for efficient communication in P2P network," IEEE Access, vol. 10, pp. 124277–124290, 2022.
13. A. Panigrahi, A. K. Nayak, and R. Paul, "Smart contract assisted blockchain based public key infrastructure system," Transactions on Emerging Telecommunications Technologies, vol. 34, no. 1, p. e4655, 2023.
14. S. Meher, B. J. R. Sahu, S. Dash, and B. Mohanty, "E2PCRA: A fuzzy-based energy-efficient paging using clustering and routing algorithm for 5G wireless networks," IEEE Access, vol. 13, pp. 188355–188380, 2025.
15. P. Vivek and S. Bhatia, "Exploring blockchain technology: Applications, challenges, and future prospects," in International Conference on Intelligent Vision and Computing, vol. 1710, 2026, p. 151–161.
16. A. Panigrahi, B. Sahu, S. S. Panigrahi, M. S. Khan, and A. K. Jena, "Application of blockchain as a solution to real-world issues in healthcare system," in Blockchain Technology: Applications and Challenges. Cham: Springer, 2021, pp. 135–149.
17. S. Swain, S. Meher, D. S. K. Nayak, and B. Mohanty, "A blockchain-enhanced framework for efficient paging and energy optimization in 5G networks," in 2024 2nd International Conference on Signal Processing, Communication, Power and Embedded System (SCOPES), 2024, pp. 1–6.
18. S. K. Nayak, R. Das, S. K. Sahoo, and T. Swarnkar, "ARGai 1.0: A GAN augmented in silico approach for identifying resistant genes and strains in E. coli using vision transformer," Computational Biology and Chemistry, vol. 115, 2025.
19. A. Panigrahi, N. Vashisht, Shalini, A. V. Nair, S. Gopinath and D. Bhanot, "Enhancing Trust and Lightweight Security in Green IoT: Models for Sustainable Computing," *2025 2nd International Conference On Multidisciplinary Research and Innovations in Engineering (MRIE)*, Gurugram, India, 2025, pp. 280–284, doi: 10.1109/MRIE66930.2025.11156263.
20. A. P. Singh, "Blockchain technology: Core mechanisms, evolution, and future implementation challenges," arXiv preprint arXiv:2505.08772, 2025. https://doi.org/10.48550/arXiv.2505.08772
21. P. Pooja, M. M. Chikhale, and S. Dhir, "Uncovering the strategic potential of blockchain technology adoption: A systematic literature review," Strategic Change, vol. 34, no. 2, pp. 151–180, 2025.
22. A. Sharma, V. Guleria, and V. Jaiswal, "The future of blockchain technology, recent advancement and challenges," in Blockchain and Deep Learning: Future Trends and Enabling Technologies. Cham: Springer, 2022, pp. 329–349.

23. F. Anwar et al., "A comprehensive insight into blockchain technology: Past development, present impact and future considerations," International Journal of Advanced Computer Science and Applications, vol. 13, no. 11, 2022.
24. W. Zhang et al., "Blockchain technology: Security issues, healthcare applications, challenges and future trends," Electronics, vol. 12, no. 3, p. 546, 2023.
25. I. Abrar and J. A. Sheikh, "Current trends of blockchain technology: Architecture, applications, challenges, and opportunities," Discover Internet of Things, vol. 4, no. 1, p. 7, 2024.
26. X. Guo, G. Zhang, and Y. Zhang, "A comprehensive review of blockchain-enabled smart manufacturing: Framework, challenges and future research directions," Sensors, vol. 23, no. 1, p. 155, 2022.
27. M. Fahmideh et al., "Engineering blockchain-based software systems: Foundations, survey, and future directions," ACM Computing Surveys, vol. 55, no. 6, pp. 1–44, 2022.
28. S. Makridakis and K. Christodoulou, "Blockchain: Current challenges and future prospects/applications," Future Internet, vol. 11, no. 12, p. 258, 2019.
29. J. Kolb, M. AbdelBaky, R. H. Katz, and D. E. Culler, "Core concepts, challenges, and future directions in blockchain: A centralized tutorial," ACM Computing Surveys, vol. 53, no. 1, pp. 1–39, 2020.
30. Z. Zheng et al., "Blockchain challenges and opportunities: A survey," International Journal of Web and Grid Services, vol. 14, no. 4, pp. 352–375, 2018.
31. A. Siyal et al., "Applications of blockchain technology in medicine and healthcare: Challenges and future perspectives," Cryptography, vol. 3, no. 1, p. 3, 2019.
32. P. Cui, U. Guin, A. Skjellum, and D. Umphress, "Blockchain in IoT: Current trends, challenges, and future roadmap," Journal of Hardware and Systems Security, vol. 3, no. 4, pp. 338–364, 2019.
33. R. Anandan and B. S. Deepak, "An overview of blockchain technology: Fundamental theories and concepts," in The Convergence of Artificial Intelligence and Blockchain Technologies: Challenges and Opportunities, 2022, pp. 1–22. doi: https://doi.org/10.1142/9789811225079_0001.
34. A. Jaradat, O. Ali, and A. AlAhmad, "Blockchain technology: A fundamental overview," in Blockchain Technologies for Sustainability, Environmental Footprints and Eco-design of Products and Processes. Singapore: Springer, 2022, pp. 1–24. https://doi.org/10.1007/978-981-16-6301-7_1.
35. D. Maldonado-Ruiz, J. Torres, and N. E. Madhoun, "Fundamentals of blockchain technology," in Principles and Practice of Blockchains. Cham: Springer, 2022, pp. 3–25.
36. M. Pilkington, "Blockchain technology: Principles and applications," in Research Handbook on Digital Transformations. Cheltenham, UK: Edward Elgar, 2016, pp. 225–253.
37. S. Wang et al., "Blockchain-enabled smart contracts: Architecture, applications, and future trends," IEEE Transactions on Systems, Man, and Cybernetics: Systems, vol. 49, no. 11, pp. 2266–2277, 2019.
38. S. K. Nayak et al., "aiGeneR 1.0: An artificial intelligence technique for the revelation of informative and antibiotic resistant genes in *Escherichia coli*," Frontiers in Bioscience-Landmark, vol. 29, no. 2, p. 82, 2024.
39. K. Mohanta, S. S. Panda, and D. Jena, "An overview of smart contract and use cases in blockchain technology," in 2018 9th International Conference on Computing, Communication and Networking Technologies (ICCCNT), 2018, pp. 1–4.
40. Y. Liu et al., "An overview of blockchain smart contract execution mechanism," Journal of Industrial Information Integration, vol. 41, p. 100674, 2024.

4 Biologically Plausible Spiking Neural Networks for Blockchain Technology

A Review of Synergies and Challenges

Irshed Hussain and Moumita Roy

4.1 INTRODUCTION

The use of artificial neural networks (ANNs) has grown tremendously during the last decade. Early days saw the use of multi-layer perceptron primarily. However, today, they utilize robust deep neural networks. This has become feasible due to the availability of large datasets and high-performance graphics processing units (GPUs). Still, they are not as energy efficient as the human brain and struggle to learn in real time. To make these machine learning (ML) models smaller and faster without loss of accuracy, we use quantization (use of a simpler format for numbers) [1], pruning (cutting away unnecessary connections) [2], and knowledge distillation (substituting with a larger one) [3]. The structure, computation, and learning rules of ANNs and Deep Neural Networks (DNNs) differ significantly from biological neural networks, although they are based on the brain. This difference has led to the inception of spiking neural networks (SNNs), or technologies better known as the third generation of neural networks, to counter the shortcomings of our traditional neural networks, which we often call the sigmoid neural networks or the second generation of neural networks.

When executed on neuromorphic hardware such as TrueNorth [4–6], Loihi [7], SpiNNaker [8], and NeuroGrid [9], SNNs may help address the deep learning expensive energy consumption problem. In SNNs, like in the brain, the neurons interact via discrete electrical impulses (or spikes) and continuously operate. SNNs are similar to biological brains in that they make use of sparse activity. As a result, SNNs are well-suited for temporal coding (when information is carried in the timing of spikes) [10].

At the same time, blockchain technology is becoming the underlying infrastructure for decentralized systems. Data center security depends on distributed consensus mechanisms and strong cryptographic technology. Through these mechanisms, the integrity of the data in the blockchain is maintained, but even transparency and

DOI: 10.1201/9781003658597-4

reliability in a network made up of largely untrustworthy subjects have been ensured [11, 12]. A recent innovative idea has led to the emergence of a brand new transdisciplinary approach. This can potentially transform a spectrum of decentralized intelligent systems, such as those pertaining to edge computing and Internet of Things (IoT) applications. At the heart of this concept lies the integration of a spike neural network and blockchain. SNNs are computational systems used to capture temporal dynamics, and they are event-driven. Recognized as the third-generation ANNs, they are inspired by biological neurons [13, 14].

SNNs have a sparse and asynchronous activation mechanism that is spike-based, unlike ANNs that function continuously and densely. This means you will be consuming less power, as these SNNs will help you respond to data in real time. Due to these attributes, resource-limited conditions are suitable for SNNs, such as IoT-deployed edge devices [7]. In addition, the connection between traditional ANNs and SNNs is depicted in Figure 4.1. It can be seen how deep learning is related to neuromorphic computing solutions inspired by the brain.

The combination of blockchain with SNN enables a trustless coordination scheme that ensures verifiability, tamper-resistance, and auditability of model updates [15, 16]. It is particularly useful in cases where there are heterogeneous and untrusted IoT devices. Another area of exploration is using smart contracts to automate collaboration and enforce accountability, as well as where conventional centralized coordination does not work. Task-specific logic can be embedded in the blockchain using smart contracts, which allows performing functions including model aggregation, allocation of incentives, and anomaly detection [17]. As a result, the blockchain can effectively enhance the reliability and transparency of distributed neuromorphic intelligence.

The emerging lightweight consensus mechanisms are also designed to satisfy the latency and energy constraints of neuromorphic systems. The consensus protocols on traditional blockchains consume an exorbitant amount of resources. Several new algorithms are being researched, including Proof-of-Stake variants, directed acyclic

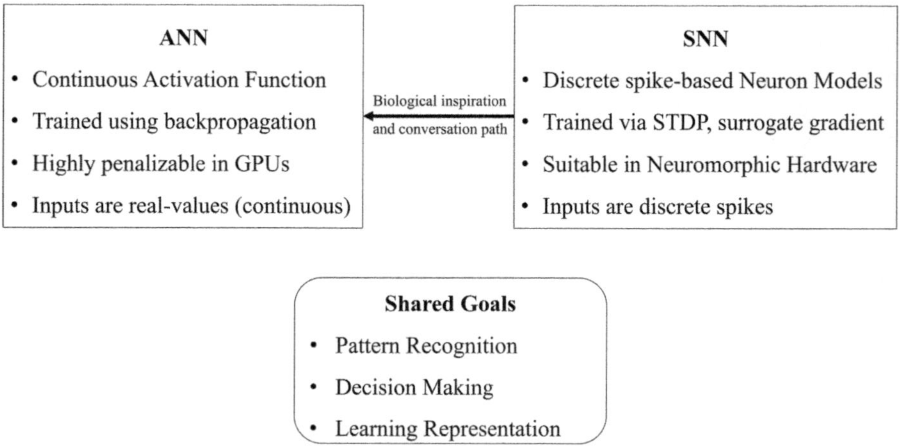

FIGURE 4.1 Relation between traditional ANN and biologically plausible SNN.

graph (DAG)-based consensus, and hybrid byzantine fault-tolerant (BFT) that aim at enabling real-time decision-making in edge computing and neuromorphic scenarios [18]. Scholar's research on autonomous anomaly detection, distributed sensor fusion, and decentralized robotics, beyond federated learning (FL), where the event-driven timing of neural computations naturally fits the chronological, verifiable recording of events in the blockchain. The power of learning from biology (via SNNs) and decentralized trust (via blockchain) can be harnessed to make intelligent systems adaptive, resilient, and secure.

Despite these positive developments, there are still many challenges. The spike-based activation's non-differentiability is a significant limitation that makes gradient-based training difficult to apply. To overcome this limitation, there have been attempts to use alternative optimization strategies such as surrogate gradient methods and local biologically inspired learning [19, 20]. Moreover, the integration of SNNs and blockchain adds further computational and architectural complexities. In latency-sensitive neuromorphic applications, the on-chain processing time overhead can negatively impact the system [21]. You can expect our solutions to these challenges to come from cross-disciplinary innovation, which would combine the expertise in distributed systems, cryptography, and neuromorphic engineering. The aim is to produce scalable, secure, and efficient frameworks for decentralized intelligent systems.

This chapter covers the recent development of blockchain technology in collaboration with SNNs in its entirety. The existing approaches studied, their implementation, and performance trade-offs are analyzed; specifically, smart contract design, integration with FL, and decentralized consensus protocols. In addition, we also highlighted research gaps and detailed a roadmap that encourages future work on decentralized intelligent systems that are scalable, secure, and energy-efficient.

The rest of this review chapter is organized for SNNs, blockchain technology, and FL for secure and efficient edge intelligence in a systematic way. Section 4.1 describes the background and motivation of combining neuromorphic computing with decentralized learning systems in other individual efforts. It also brings attention to challenges such as energy efficiency, as well as data privacy and trust, in distributed environments.

Following Section 4.1 is Section 4.2, related work, which has been done in this or a similar domain. To say, the work reviews the state-of-the-art information regarding SNNs at the edge computing, how blockchain can enable secure and tamper-resistant decentralized systems, and the recent integration of FL with blockchain that enables privacy-preserving collaborative model training. This part also looks at the early works that analyze the convergence of SNNs and blockchain and how they can lead to the establishment of intelligent autonomous systems. We systematically analyze essential functionalities that are universal to SNNs in Section 4.3. Several types of SNNs that are often occluded by anatomy and functionality are investigated here. SNNs comprise neural encoding, neuron models, synapse dynamics, and learning algorithms. Those are the most pertinent aspects of an SNN-based system. Furthermore, it describes the complete system architecture, smart contracts for orchestrating FL, and the blockchain layer for secure coordination. This section contains a comparison of performance that tackles security, latency, and energy usage. The conclusion and future work in Section 4.4 summarize the findings and future directions of the study. Future work may involve developing lightweight blockchain protocols for edge deployment, scalable neuromorphic architectures, and integration methods for real-world solutions.

4.2 RELATED WORK

SNN and blockchain technology would provide an effective platform for building intelligent, secure, and energy-efficient systems. Perfect for future IoT and edge computing technologies. The increasing requirement for safe decentralized intelligence in the harmonization of various computing environments is accelerating the integration trend of the blockchain–SNN. There are multiple cloud models that do not work as well as they should with the addition of new edge devices at places of poor power and connectivity due to the long latencies that they cause, in addition to bandwidth constraints. SNNs present a good alternative as they have local control of the data in real time with less energy, and their information-processing behavior is similar to the biological brain. The merging of blockchain decentralization and situation-specific tamper-proof ledger property enhances trustworthiness and safety among sensors, devices, and environmental conditions. Some of the major hurdles that AI and data sharing are facing today have been resolved by these technologies. Privacy, trusted third parties, and large-scale systems are examples of challenges.

4.2.1 SNNs in Edge Intelligence

Because they are designed to mimic biological neurons, SNNs are also called the "third generation" of ANNs [14]. SNNs, unlike classical ANNs (sometimes called the second generation of ANNs), incorporate temporal aspects in a natural way and exploit the sparse firing of spikes. This makes SNNs particularly well-suited for low-power and low-latency applications such as edge computing [7, 22]. SNNs have proven to offer important advantages when tested on neuromorphic hardware platforms like the IBM TrueNorth [4–6] and the Tianjic chip [23], and Loihi [7]. Microchips that mimic the brain are intended to be energy-efficient [4, 5, 7, 23].

Simultaneously, significant effort is devoted to developing enhanced training techniques for SNNs, in particular surrogate gradient methods [19], spike time-dependent plasticity (STDP) [20], and hybrid methods such as ANN-to-SNN conversion [21]. These techniques overcome the non-differentiability arising from the discrete spiking nature of spike trains. Their aim is to capture the spatial and temporal aspects of neural operation. All this taken together drives toward truly brain-inspired and efficient computing systems.

4.2.2 Blockchain for Decentralized Systems

Data can now be managed in a decentralized and secure manner. The blockchain was invented for Bitcoin [12]. Subsequently, on top of Bitcoin, other platforms like Ethereum launched that allowed for the use of smart contracts. Smart contracts are autonomous contracts that execute transactions in a programmable manner without a central authority [11, 17].

Blockchain technology has been the focus of attention on how it can guarantee provenance of data, how it permits devices to coordinate autonomously, offering secure communication in IoT systems [24, 25]. Still, one of the prime research challenges is designing lightweight blockchain architectures for resource-constrained edge environments, as latency, scalability, and energy consumption are still key bottlenecks [18].

4.2.3 FL and Blockchain Integration

Recently, FL has emerged as a popular paradigm in ML as a privacy-preserving scheme, where edge devices collaboratively train models without sharing their sensitive raw data [16]. There is the issue of creating trust, fairness, and accountability among the participating devices in FL. Researchers have considered combining blockchain technology with FL to address the challenge. Blockchain technology's decentralization, tamper-resistance, and strong guarantee of transparency and trust are important.

Smart contracts [15, 17] help in enabling the enforcement of incentive mechanisms, tracking users' contributions, and ensuring nodes behave as agreed upon. In [17], Behera et al. introduced a solution that utilizes smart contracts to foster cooperation and guarantee fair computation through a rewards system. Kang et al. [15], on the flip side, presented a taxonomy of blockchain-powered FL architectures. It shows various methods through which blockchain can improve FL.

4.2.4 Integration of SNNs and Blockchain

Currently, the combination of SNNs and blockchain technology remains in a nascent stage. This is very important for the future, nevertheless. In the initial theoretical analysis, it has been noted that SNNs can be employed to encourage the adaptive behavior of nodes across a blockchain network by facilitating the low-latency processing of information for anomaly detection and consensus participation [18, 21].

However, blockchain takes on an important role in the case of FL or collaborative inference by providing a secure and tamper-proof communication layer to coordinate interactions among neuromorphic hardware. This approach could harness the powerful, efficient intelligence of SNNs, along with the inherently secure and decentralized trust of blockchain, leveraging the strengths of both.

4.3 METHODS

This section presents the proposed framework that integrates spike neural networks and blockchain technology for decentralized edge computing. The approach consists of three sections, particularly: neuromorphic data preprocessing and processing through SNN, coordination and security by blockchain, and decentralized FL support.

The mathematical functioning of SNNs is modeled based on three major components. They are (i) neural encoding, (ii) synapse and neuron model, and (iii) learning algorithm. All three major components are essential for determining the effectiveness or behavior of the system. The initial step is neural encoding, which transforms real-valued data that is continuous into discrete spike trains that SNNs can process.

According to thresholds of membrane potentials, the neuron model, for instance, the Leaky Integrate-and-Fire (LIF) [26–28] determines how spikes are generated and collected. In addition, how neurons generate output spikes that aid in classifying temporal patterns (both linear and non-linear), this process enables the neural network to react dynamically to input stimuli and recognize temporal patterns (linear or non-linear). The synaptic weights are adjusted based on correlations of spike timings between connected neurons. This is the optimization phase, where functions are often based on local plasticity rules like the STDP [20].

When integrated with blockchain technology, the framework introduces an immutable and transparent layer for coordination among distributed nodes. It eliminates the need for centralized trust. Smart contracts embedded within the blockchain automate the orchestration of FL tasks, ensuring secure, traceable, and consensus-driven updates to shared models without exposing raw data. Therefore, it presents a holistic approach that combines energy-efficient computing, secure communication, and privacy-preserving key challenges in modern edge intelligence systems across various real-world applications.

i. *Neural Encoding*: It refers to how information is represented in the timing of spikes. The information in this case is the feature matrix. The feature matrix that we get from feature engineering has real-valued features only. However, SNN works with the temporal information or spikes. These are discrete events. Therefore, in order to work with SNN, we need to first transform real-valued features into spikes. There are various neural encoding techniques such as rate coding, temporal coding, and population coding. In temporal coding, information is encoded in the precise timing of individual spikes. The spike time, t_n, can represent information in terms of a temporal sequence or relative timing between spikes, which is described mathematically in Eq. (4.1).

$$\tau_n = \frac{1}{\lambda} \tag{4.1}$$

where λ is the inter-spike interval.

ii. *Neuron Model*: The most widely used model is the LIF [26–28] model. The membrane potential V(t) of a LIF neuron follows the equation Eq. (4.2).

$$\tau_m \frac{dV(t)}{dt} = -\left(V(t) - V_r\right) + R_m I(t) \tag{4.2}$$

where V(t) is the membrane potential at time t, V_r resting potential, R_m membrane resistance, I(t) input stimuli to the neuron at time t, and τ_m

membrane time constant. The neuron fires when its V(t) exceeds a threshold Θ. Upon firing, the potential is reset to V_{re}, which is given mathematically in Eq. (4.3).

$$V(t) \geq \Theta \Rightarrow V(t) = V_{re} \tag{4.3}$$

iii. *Learning Algorithm*: Learning in SNNs is typically based on STDP [20], a biologically plausible mechanism for learning. STDP adjusts the synaptic weights based on the relative timing of pre- and postsynaptic spikes. This process resembles how biological neural systems, especially the brain, learn and form memories. The connection and the causal association are reinforced if a presynaptic neuron fires just before a postsynaptic neuron. In contrast, the synapse is weakened, and the link is discouraged if the postsynaptic neuron activates before the presynaptic one. Due to this time-sensitive rule, the network can learn and adjust to temporal trends in input data, eliminating the need for error backpropagation and global supervision. STDP's locality-based synaptic updates rely solely on the activity of the associated neurons, which is one of its main advantages. It is ideal for distributed and energy-efficient learning, particularly with neuromorphic devices.

Additionally, this type of unsupervised learning enables SNNs to efficiently analyze spatio-temporal data, which is essential for edge applications like autonomous decision-making, event detection, and sensory processing. Through constant contact with dynamic surroundings, SNNs can gradually shape network behavior using STDP to create sparse and effective data representations. Consequently, STDP remains fundamental in creating learning models for intelligent edge systems that draw inspiration from biology. The most challenging phase for the implementation of SNN is the learning phase or the training phase. In this phase, the overall loss in the network is minimized by adjusting the synaptic weights. However, due to the discrete spiking nature of spiking neurons, the popular backpropagation algorithm cannot be applied since there is a need to find the gradient using the gradient descent rule.

4.3.1 Neuromorphic Edge Processing with SNNs

Edge devices equipped with neuromorphic processors such as Intel Loihi [7] and SpiNNaker [8] are deployed to handle real-time sensory data using local SNN models. These SNNs process event-based input such as audio spikes, image sensor outputs, or environmental signals with low power consumption [7, 14]. SNNs are biologically plausible and use spikes to process inputs, which cuts power use (since the information is temporal) and speeds up response times. That is perfect for edge devices like smart sensors and small robots. Neuromorphic chips running SNNs can think and react quickly, right where the data is collected, i.e., no cloud required. They also adapt well to unpredictable or noisy situations. As more devices rely on fast, local decision-making, neuromorphic edge processing with SNNs offers a robust, energy-smart solution that mirrors how nature solves complex problems.

Local SNN models are trained using surrogate gradient techniques or STDP for on-device learning [19, 20]. Let S (x, t) represent the spike output at time t for input x; then local edge inference can be expressed as given in Eq. (4.4).

$$\hat{y} = \text{argmax}\left(S\left(x,t\right)\right), t \in \left[0,T\right] \tag{4.4}$$

where T is the inference window; the result $\hat{y}$ is retained locally, or in collaborative scenarios, encoded and sent to the blockchain network.

4.3.2 Blockchain Layer for Secure Coordination

A lightweight blockchain protocol is used to establish decentralized trust and manage consensus among the participating edge nodes [11, 18]. In this setup, each node holds either a partial or full copy of the blockchain ledger and takes part in consensus rounds to ensure system reliability. These rounds serve multiple purposes, such as (i) verifying and securely recording updates made to the SNN model, (ii) logging inference results and usage statistics for accountability, and (iii) coordinating node participation during FL.

Blockchain can be a reliable layer to synchronize activities among many devices or systems. It uses a shared ledger, where all modifications are transparent and unchangeable, rather than depending on a central authority. This makes it easier for machines or organizations to collaborate safely, even when they do not entirely trust one another. Without requiring human supervision, smart contracts assist in automating decision-making and enforcing regulations. Using blockchain for coordination guarantees safe, traceable activities in supply chains, banking, and autonomous technology. It is a workable way to increase confidence in systems where justice and accuracy are crucial.

4.3.3 FL via Smart Contracts

FL is carried out across multiple edge devices, where each device trains its own local SNN model and periodically contributes updates for building a global model. The aggregation of these updates is managed through blockchain technology that ensures transparency and decentralized control. This process is governed by smart contracts, which formally specify three key aspects, namely (i) contribution thresholds (i.e., required accuracy levels and acceptable spike rates), (ii) incentive mechanisms (i.e., token-based rewards that encourage honest participation), and (iii) update rules that determine how local models are averaged into the global model.

Let w_i denote the local SNN weight vector at device i, and let N represent the total number of nodes participating. The secure aggregation of these updates is executed by the smart contract, as defined in Eq. (4.5), ensuring both fairness and resistance to tampering.

$$w_{global} = \frac{1}{N}\sum_{i=1}^{N} w_i \tag{4.5}$$

4.3.4 System Architecture Overview

In Figure 4.2(a), the full architecture is shown, which includes the following layers:

1. *Sensing and Preprocessing Layer*: The first layer is the layer where sensing and preprocessing of raw data occur. It is the main layer that is required for interacting with the other environments. It is equipped with sensors that gather the raw data for events in a continuous manner, such as sound, motion, temperature, or network traffic. Once the raw data is captured, it goes under the preprocessing stage where basic filtering, normalization, and encoding happen to make it equipped for further processing. This step is crucial as it prepares the data from raw to a cleaner and structured one for efficient processing.
2. *Neuromorphic Computation Layer*: In this layer, execution of spike-enabled processing utilizing local SNNs is done. Once the preprocessing is done, the data is fed to the next layer utilizing SNNs. The SNN models are characterized for optimization of the data requiring events to occur, having low power requirements, with a view to applying in edge-computing purposes. The use of local SNNs working independently in each of the nodes for data handling enables efficient real-time processing that eventually leads to faster decision outputs by imitating the transmission theory of the human brain.
3. *Blockchain Middleware*: Secure data exchange handling, model update, and validation in consensus are carried out in this layer. To enable trust among the nodes in the collaboration, the middleware layer provides viable and secure coordination and communication. The use of blockchain technology ensures a more secure exchange of data for model update and validation, and finally, using smart contracts, reaching a consensus among distributed nodes in the network.

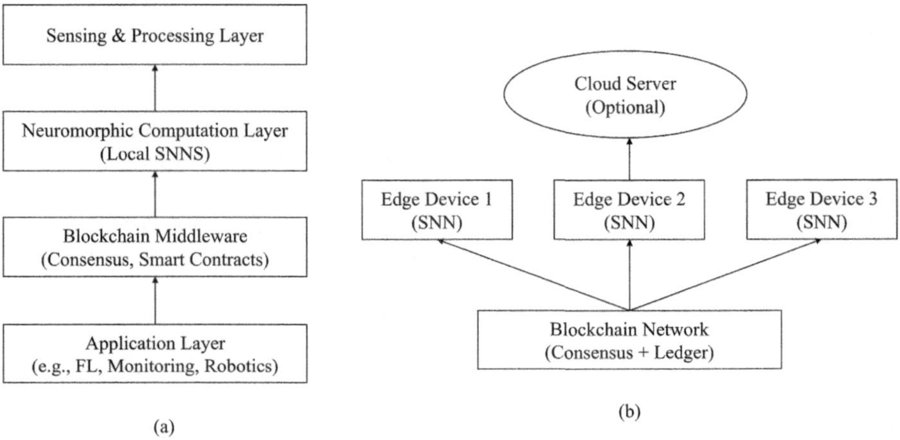

FIGURE 4.2 (a) Block diagram of system architecture for SNN to work with blockchain, (b) description of system architecture of SNN–blockchain integrated edge network.

4. *Application Layer*: It enables use-cases such as intrusion detection, environmental monitoring, or collaborative robotics. At the top level, this layer utilizes processed and validated outputs to drive real-world applications. Depending on the context, the insights derived from the lower layers are applied to practical use-cases, ranging from smart surveillance and environmental sensing to coordinated actions in multi-robot systems.

In Figure 4.2(a), multiple edge devices equipped with neuromorphic chips run SNN models, where each edge node performs local spike-based inference or training. The model then updates, or event summaries are hashed and sent to a blockchain network. The blockchain nodes validate transactions, run consensus, and store the ledger. Smart contracts coordinate FL rounds and incentives, and include a cloud or centralized server, optionally for benchmarking or heavy tasks. Figure 4.2(b) visually explains the flow of data and interaction between SNN edge devices and the blockchain network. This multi-layer design supports scalable, privacy-preserving intelligence on decentralized platforms while addressing energy, latency, and security constraints. In Table 4.1, the performance trade-off in SNN and blockchain integration for edge computing is described.

TABLE 4.1
The Performance Trade-Off in SNN and Blockchain Integration for Edge Computing

Aspect	SNN	Blockchain	Trade-Off
Energy efficiency	Very high due to event-driven sparse activity [8, 17]	Generally, high energy consumption in PoW; lighter protocols reduce this [6, 30]	SNNs reduce device energy, but blockchain consensus overhead remains a challenge
Latency	Low-latency real-time processing [22, 28]	Latency varies; lightweight consensus improves response [30]	Need a balance between fast local inference and blockchain transaction confirmation delays
Scalability	Scales well on distributed edge nodes [8, 25]	Scalability is limited by network size and consensus algorithm [6]	SNNs can scale flexibly; blockchain may bottleneck large-scale deployments
Security and Trust	Vulnerable if isolated; relies on system design	High due to decentralized ledger and immutability [6, 20]	Blockchain adds robust security, but with overhead costs
Model efficiency	Local learning with spike-based plasticity [31]	Model aggregation requires secure and verifiable protocols [3]	Combining both requires protocols to minimize communication costs while maintaining accuracy
Privacy	Data processed locally; minimal sharing [18]	Blockchain ledger transparency vs. privacy-preserving designs [14]	Trade-off between data sharing for trust and preserving user privacy

As can be seen in Table 4.1, it highlights the performance trade-offs involved in integrating SNNs with blockchain for edge computing applications. In terms of energy efficiency, SNNs demonstrate very high efficiency due to their event-driven sparse activity, making them highly suitable for low-power edge devices. Blockchain, however, tends to consume significant energy, particularly when Proof-of-Work consensus is used, although lighter consensus mechanisms such as Proof-of-Stake can somewhat mitigate this issue. The integration therefore reduces device-side energy costs through SNNs, but blockchain's consensus overhead still remains a challenge. In the case of latency, SNNs are capable of real-time, low-latency processing, enabling fast local inference, whereas blockchain latency depends heavily on the choice of consensus mechanism. Lightweight protocols improve responsiveness but do not completely eliminate transaction confirmation delays. Hence, the trade-off lies in balancing the immediate responsiveness of SNN inference with the slower validation of blockchain transactions. With regard to the scalability factor, SNNs scale effectively across distributed edge nodes due to their localized and event-driven nature, making them suitable for deployment in large networks. Blockchain, in contrast, often faces scalability challenges since performance is limited by network size and the computational demands of consensus protocols. This means that while SNNs support flexible scaling, blockchain can become a bottleneck in large-scale edge environments.

SNNs on their own are not very secure, and the design of the system around them needs to be made in order to make it secure, since it is not secure by nature. On the contrary, blockchain does provide decentralization, immutability, and cryptographic guarantees. As a result, the integration of a trustworthy and reliable integration takes place, increasing the computational and communication burden. SNNs serve as efficient models that lend local spike-based learning and plasticity advantages. Blockchain technology aids in model aggregation security. Call for collaboration to find integration protocols that reduce communication costs and increase accuracy. To sum up, if privacy is a concern, data is processed locally, and only minimal data is shared, which is privacy-preserving. The blockchain ledger has transparency, which may conflict with privacy requirements in the absence of privacy-preserving blockchain mechanisms. It is the transparency and confidentiality of privacy. The integration must balance the need for transparency and accountability with protecting sensitive user data.

In conclusion, SNN–blockchain integration provides complementary strengths at the cost of significant drawbacks (16 words). The combination of blockchain power with SNNs will bring the best in terms of speed, privacy, and scalability. Including lightweight consensus methods, improved communication methods, and privacy preservation methods helps to address the limitations of blockchain, such as energy consumption, latency, and scalability problems. The integration can offer a growing demand for a powerful and efficient offering in edge computing environments. Besides, the significant features comparison is presented in Table 4.2 under SNN and blockchain.

Table 4.2 highlights other essential aspects in the integration of SNNs and blockchain, as well as their complementary characteristics and their resultant implications. When it comes to overhead, SNNs require very low data transfer, powered by

TABLE 4.2
The Comparison of Key Aspects in SNN and Blockchain Integration

Aspect	SNN	Blockchain	Implications
Overhead	Minimal data transmission due to event-driven spikes and local processing [8, 17]	High network bandwidth usage for consensus, transaction propagation, and ledger replication [6, 30]	Requires efficient protocols to minimize blockchain data traffic while preserving decentralized trust
Scalability	Naturally scalable on distributed neuromorphic nodes, limited mainly by hardware availability [8, 25]	Scalability challenged by consensus algorithms and network size; improvements via sharing and layer 2 solutions [2, 6]	Combining both demands requires adaptive scaling strategies to handle edge heterogeneity and blockchain throughput limitations
Security Model	Security depends on system design, vulnerable to adversarial attacks if isolated [18, 31]	Strong cryptographic guarantees, an immutable ledger ensures data integrity and nonrepudiation [6, 20]	Blockchain enhances security by providing tamper-proof audit trails for SNN outputs and model updates
Privacy	Local data processing reduces exposure; spike data is less interpretable [14, 18]	Public ledgers risk privacy leakage; privacy-enhancing methods required [14, 29]	Integration must balance transparency for trust and privacy protections to comply with regulations.

event-based spiking and local processing, thus significantly saving on edge communication costs. Blockchain has a lot of overhead because of the bandwidth costs associated with consensus, propagating transactions, and replicating the ledger. Hence, to successfully integrate the systems, communication protocols are needed that can diversify the traffic amounting to huge amounts in the blockchain network, with a view to preserving the decentralization and trust factors simultaneously. Scaling changes are another section where a palpable trade-off is seen for performance parameters. Here, scaling changes in SNNs can be effective if they are distributed in neuromorphic nodes without any hardware limitations. In contrast, blockchain systems deal with robustness and scalability issues as their performance is largely dependent on the consensus algorithms and size of the network, even though the latest systems have layer 2 solutions that work better. Hence, a system that can withstand scaling changes is needed to address edge node heterogeneity while overcoming the blockchain's throughput limitations.

Security in SNNs can be a palpable issue as its intrinsic framework doesn't ensure security and is mostly dependent on the system and designs used with it. This leads to system vulnerability when it is deployed separately. However, blockchain technology, due to its robust cryptographic techniques, can solve this issue, and since it is inherently immutable in terms of ledger transactions, it has features like traceability

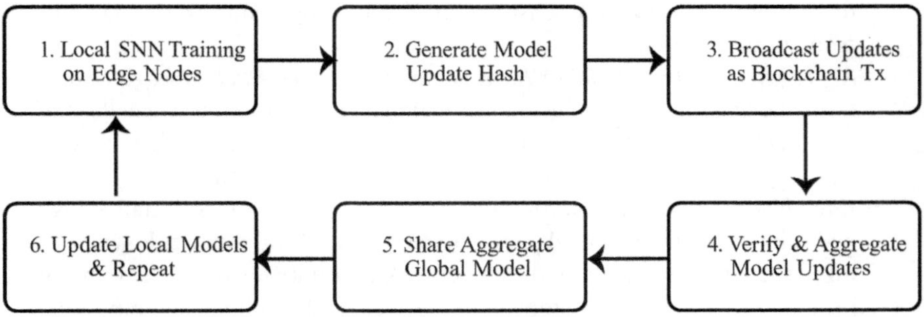

FIGURE 4.3 FL workflow diagram with SNNs and blockchain technology.

and non-repudiation. The combination of the two can help prevent malicious tampering with the outputs generated from SNNs, leading to more trust in neuromorphic applications.

Both technologies are also required to solve the privacy issues, as SNNs are trained locally, which reduces their exposure to data processing needs, and the use of spikes lessens the interpretability concerns as compared to raw data. Blockchain, on the other hand, risks privacy leakage due to the transparency of public ledgers, requiring the incorporation of privacy-preserving mechanisms such as encryption, zero-knowledge proofs, or private blockchains. Thus, integration must carefully balance the need for transparency and accountability, which supports trust, with the requirement to protect user privacy and comply with regulatory standards such as GDPR.

In Figure 4.3, the block diagram of the FL workflow with SNNs and blockchain is shown. The description of Figure 4.3 is given as follows:

1. *Training in Local SNN Models for Each Edge Node*: In the initial stage, the data that are collected locally from each of the edge devices are fed into the SNN for training. Since training is performed locally here, privacy concerns in terms of security of the data are reduced, as it doesn't require data transfer to any central server. This helps in bandwidth-sensitive applications. Moreover, for specific datasets, each node performs its optimization process on its corresponding nodes based on the patterns formed.
2. *Local Model Updates Are Converted to Concise Hashes*: After local training, the model updates, i.e., typically significant in size, are compressed into compact representations such as hashes or parameter summaries. This compression minimizes communication overhead and enhances efficiency in transmitting updates without compromising the model's learning progress.
3. *Updates Are Broadcast as Blockchain Transactions*: These summarized updates are packaged into transactions and broadcast over the blockchain network. Using blockchain for transmission ensures transparency, immutability, and security of each update shared across the system.
4. *Blockchain Nodes Verify and Aggregate Updates via Smart Contracts*: Blockchain nodes execute smart contracts to validate and aggregate updates upon receiving updates. Smart contracts act as automated rules

that enforce trust and consensus without requiring centralized control or manual intervention.

5. *Aggregated Global Model or Parameters Are Shared Back to Edge Nodes*: Once the updates are aggregated into a global model or a consolidated set of parameters, the result is distributed back to all participating edge devices, ensuring that each node benefits from the collective learning.
6. *Edge Nodes Update Local Models with Global Parameters*: Finally, edge nodes incorporate the global parameters into their local models. It synchronizes their learning state with the network and initiates the next round of localized training, thereby repeating the cycle and continuously improving the model.

The diagram in Figure 4.3 highlights the decentralized and secure FL process enabled by blockchain with neuromorphic edge computing.

4.3.5 Performance Comparison

The performance evaluations discussed in this work do not reflect the outcomes of a specific study. Rather, they originate from the overall trend, observation, and finding reported throughout the wide spectrum of literature on SNN, blockchain, and the hybridization of both. The evaluation findings help to understand the actual behavior of the technologies across a variety of conditions, as opposed to one case study judgment determining the outcome. The comparisons presented here are limited to applications in the edge and IoT domain, wherein characteristics such as energy efficiency, latency, computational overhead, scalability, and security are critical and often determine whether real-world deployment is possible or not. With the help of event-based low-power neuromorphic processing, SNNs provide near-real-time decision-making, whereas blockchain provides decentralized trust, immutability, and cryptographic protection to sensitive data integrity. A synthesis of the different studies shows the general performance trend, trade-offs, and emerging synergies across the technology uses, but also their limits and challenges when the technology uses are invoked in the real-world context.

a. *Energy Consumption*: A significant disadvantage of traditional IoT systems is their energy consumption. Energy-efficient computing elements are not present in these systems. Furthermore, conventional IoT systems cannot utilize neuromorphic computing. On the other hand, systems that are based on blockchain typically make use of a consensus process, such as proof-of-work or proof-of-stake, which adds a performance overhead in terms of computation and communication. SNNs are event-driven networks where neurons fire only when an event or action is required; as such, the spiking activity is very sparse. Consequently, the energy consumption is much lower than the traditional measures [29]. Together with blockchain, SNNs continue to achieve low-energy operation if they work. Due to blockchain node synchronization on the network, it results in rising cost and latency.

b. *Latency*: High latency is associated with blockchains using resource-intensive consensus protocols like Proof-of-Work. While they do provide a very high level of trust and security, the approval time taken by many nodes results in a low system time response. By contrast, SNNs can be operated in real time as they require processing of input spikes at very high speeds and quick times to respond. Thus, it is more effective to use them in problems that require good time management and prompt responses [30]. By combining blockchain and SNN at an appropriate level, the fast decisions made by SNN can compensate for the delays initiated by the blockchain processing. It could support efficiency with reliability, security, and delay tolerance for time-sensitive system applications.
c. *Security*: The security scores measured on a scale of 1–10 rate the strength of a system in this reference framework. Traditional IoT implementations normally score low on this scale as they rely on a weak security architecture or poorly designed security architecture, making them susceptible to a broader class of cyberattacks. On the contrary, blockchain technology makes use of cryptography. It also employs a tamper-resistant distributed ledger [31]. So, blockchain provides strong security guarantees. Unified in the system through the SNN–blockchain, the features can enhance security. SNNs are still promising despite their shortcomings but have no inbuilt security. This means that they could be subject to moderate risk, such as adversarial attacks that make malicious proposals to confuse the network [32].

Each of the performance metrics for the traditional IoT-based systems, blockchain, SNN, and finally SNN and blockchain integration is briefly described in Table 4.3. Based on the data presented in Table 4.3, each system has different advantages and

TABLE 4.3
Performance Comparison of Traditional IoT, Blockchain, SNN, and Integrated SNN–Blockchain Systems

Performance Metric	Traditional IoT	Blockchain	SNN	SNN + Blockchain
Energy consumption	High consumption; no neuromorphic optimization	Higher due to consensus overhead	Very low (event-driven, sparse spiking)	Low; retains SNN efficiency with a slight added cost for synchronization
Latency	Moderate; depends on network efficiency	High consensus protocols cause delays	Very low; real-time responsiveness	Balanced, fast SNN inference compensates for blockchain delays
Security level	Low; vulnerable to many attacks	High; strong cryptography and tamper-resistance	Moderate; lacks built-in security, exposed to adversarial risks	High; inherits blockchain security plus neuromorphic efficiency

drawbacks when it comes to energy efficient, latency, and security. Blockchain-type systems also have a high energy demand because of the computational requirements of any consensus mechanism, e.g., Proof of Work or Proof of Stake. Thus, most traditional IoT systems, with lack of neuromorphic optimization, consume high energy too. Unlike CNNs, SNNs exhibit energy efficiency due to their event-driven and sparse spiking operations, rendering them suitable for low-energy applications. A combination of SNNs and blockchain can result in a solution that retains most of the energy efficiency of SNNs with only slightly higher energy consumption due to synchronization increases.

In terms of latency, traditional IoT achieves moderate performance depending on network conditions, whereas blockchain introduces significant delays owing to consensus protocols, which limits its real-time applicability. However, SNN, on the other hand, achieves efficacy in this sector since it is greatly time-efficient and has low delays in real-world scenarios and, hence, can be extremely beneficial for time-sensitive applications. Hence, the combination of blockchain and SNN can provide a good trade-off between security and responsiveness since it balances out the delay in blockchain systems and, in turn, the blockchain network handles the security issues.

Security is an important criterion where major differences can be seen. The former IoT systems are highly susceptible to cyber threats, viz., the most famous being denial-of-service (DOS) attacks, and other copyright issues despite the high use of the IoT systems. The weaknesses usually crop up from the different types of security mechanisms that are utilized for various fragments of the systems and also from the centralized control of the systems. In comparison to that, the blockchain systems work on robust cryptographic protocols that are tamper-free and resistant to data manipulation. Each transaction performed there has a distributed ledger that is verified via the use of consensus algorithms, and all are secured through various cryptographic mechanisms.

4.4 CONCLUSION AND FUTURE WORK

This chapter is focused on the integration of blockchain technology and SNN with a view to improving the IoT applications for a decentralized and secure pathway. By making use of the time-efficiency of the SNN's coupled with the security features of blockchain technology that ensure added immutability, our proposed architecture puts forward an essential solution in accordance with fast processing and collaborative learning for distributed networks. However, since blockchain technology inherently has scalability concerns and more transactional latency, leading to a mismatch of efficiency and security, the amalgamation of cutting-edge architectures can significantly increase the requirement for systems that are capable of processing data and information in a local structure while maintaining tamper-resistant and transparent receipts of operations.

The requirement of consumption in terms of power and sustainable data sharing poses a need where devices work independently, viz., driverless cars, healthcare software, industrial machinery, and smart homes. This requires systems that can compel provide to a sustainable environment, and SNNs work quite well as they are energy efficient. The integration of blockchain technology strengthens the reliability and auditability of decentralized systems by eliminating the need for a central authority.

However, this comes at a cost. The inherently resource-intensive nature of blockchain consensus mechanisms, i.e., particularly in public or permissionless networks, can introduce significant latency. These delays may impact time-sensitive tasks, particularly those that demand instant input at the edge. Furthermore, scalability issues are exacerbated by blockchain's transaction throughput constraints, especially as the number of edge devices keeps increasing. An attempt to reduce the issues can be applied with this integrated method. With further development of lightweight systems and better algorithms for consensus protocols, we can significantly reduce the issues. Moreover, the current technologies, namely, blockchain-related hierarchical systems, edge-based systems, and the hybrid consensus, can lead to many advanced options. With regard to SNN, the hardware upgrade of neuromorphic systems and their corresponding training sequences can improve the performance and usability in real-world cases. In short, this research is motivated to contribute to providing a better understanding of brain-inspired computation in terms of security and scalability via different distributed ledger systems.

It provides different novel techniques that incorporate the efficiency of biological neurons and cryptographic robustness. The collaboration has the ability to drive the future generation of intelligent systems, which are suitable for low power requirements, faster, and inherently reliable, though research is still in its infancy. In order to make it more successful, future research should be more concentrated on throughput and latency optimization, along with management of resources. With the advent of progressing sciences, it is thought to produce more theoretical basis and inferences that can lead to narrowing the gaps in terms of robust digital systems and the techniques pertaining to neuroscience.

Future research can include consensus protocols that are inherently made for neuromorphic systems, in integration with advanced techniques to preserve privacy, e.g., zero-knowledge proofs, and divulge adaptive FL methods that randomly adjust the frequency parameter with respect to demands and conditions of the application network. In addition to that, in real-world scenarios, deployment of large-scale IoT systems requires crucial implementation and evaluation of the framework for validating its robustness and practical efficacy. This research is motivated to provide a foundation for a better understanding to build future-generation decentralized systems adorned with intelligence, security, and energy efficiency by utilizing neuromorphic strategies and blockchain technologies.

REFERENCES

1. Dongqing Zhang, Jiaolong Yang, Dongqiangzi Ye, and Gang Hua. LQ-Nets: Learned quantization for highly accurate and compact deep neural networks. In Proceedings of the European conference on computer vision (ECCV), pages 365–382, 2018.
2. Guiying Li, Chao Qian, Chunhui Jiang, Xiaofen Lu, and Ke Tang. Optimization based layer-wise magnitude-based pruning for DNN compression. International Joint Conference on Artificial Intelligence, 330:2383–2389, 2018.

3. Xiao Jin, Baoyun Peng, Yichao Wu, Yu Liu, Jiaheng Liu, Ding Liang, Junjie Yan, and Xiaolin Hu. Knowledge distillation via route constrained optimization. In Proceedings of the IEEE/CVF International Conference on Computer Vision, pages 1345–1354, 2019.
4. A Cassidy, Jun Sawada, P Merolla, J Arthur, R Alvarez-lcaze, Filipp Akopyan, B Jackson, and D Modha. Truenorth: A high-performance, low-power neurosynaptic processor for multi-sensory perception, action, and cognition. In Proceedings of the Government Microcircuits Applications & Critical Technology Conference, Orlando, FL, USA, pages 14–17, 2016.
5. Michael V DeBole, Brian Taba, Arnon Amir, Filipp Akopyan, Alexander Andreopoulos, William P Risk, Jeff Kusnitz, Carlos Ortega Otero, Tapan K Nayak, Rathinakumar Appuswamy, et al. Truenorth: Accelerating from zero to 64 million neurons in 10 years. Computer, 52(5):20–29, 2019.
6. Paul A Merolla, John V Arthur, Rodrigo Alvarez-Icaza, Andrew S Cassidy, Jun Sawada, Filipp Akopyan, Bryan L Jackson, Nabil Imam, Chen Guo, Yutaka Nakamura, et al. A million spiking-neuron integrated circuit with a scalable communication network and interface. Science, 345(6197):668–673, 2014.
7. Mike Davies, Narayan Srinivasa, Tsung-Han Lin, Gautham Chinya, Yongqiang Cao, Sri Harsha Choday, Georgios Dimou, Prasad Joshi, Nabil Imam, Shweta Jain, et al. Loihi: A neuromorphic manycore processor with on-chip learning. IEEE Micro, 38(1):82–99, 2018.
8. Steve B Furber, Francesco Galluppi, Steve Temple, and Luis A Plana. The spinnaker project. Proceedings of the IEEE, 102(5):652–665, 2014.
9. Ben Varkey Benjamin, Peiran Gao, Emmett McQuinn, Swadesh Choudhary, Anand R Chandrasekaran, Jean-Marie Bussat, Rodrigo Alvarez-Icaza, John V Arthur, Paul A Merolla, and Kwabena Boahen. Neurogrid: A mixed-analog-digital multichip system for large-scale neural simulations. Proceedings of the IEEE, 102(5):699–716, 2014.
10. Nikola K Kasabov. Evolving spiking neural networks. In Time-space, spiking neural networks and brain-inspired artificial intelligence, pages 169–199. Springer, 2018.
11. Konstantinos Christidis and Michael Devetsikiotis. Blockchains and smart contracts for the internet of things. IEEE Access, 4:2292–2303, 2016.
12. Satoshi Nakamoto. Bitcoin: A peer-to-peer electronic cash system. 2008. https://bitcoin.org/bitcoin.pdf.
13. Eugene M Izhikevich. Simple model of spiking neurons. IEEE Transactions on Neural Networks, 14(6):1569–1572, 2003.
14. Wolfgang Maass. Networks of spiking neurons: The third generation of neural network models. Neural Networks, 10(9):1659–1671, 1997.
15. Minsoo Kang, Hyeonwoo Lee, and Jong Hyuk Lee. Securing federated learning with blockchain: A systematic literature review. Artificial Intelligence Review, 55(2):1237–1262, 2022.
16. H Brendan McMahan, Eider Moore, Daniel Ramage, and Blaise Agu¨era y Arcas Hampson. Communication-efficient learning of deep networks from decentralized data. In Proc. 20th AISTATS, pages 1273–1282, 2017.
17. Manoj Raj Behera, Saurabh Upadhyay, and Sachin Shetty. Federated learning using smart contracts on blockchains: A reward driven approach. 2021. https://arxiv.org/abs/2107.10243. arXiv preprint arXiv:2107.10243.
18. Hongyang Xue, Dong Chen, Ning Zhang, Haijun Dai, and Kim-Kwang Raymond Yu. Integration of blockchain and edge computing in internet of things: A survey. IEEE Internet of Things Journal, 9(5):3219–3241, 2022.
19. Yujie Wu, Liang Deng, Guoqi Li, Jun Zhu, and Luping Shi. Spatio-temporal backpropagation for training high-performance spiking neural networks. Frontiers in Neuroscience, 12:331, 2018.

20. Friedemann Zenke and Wulfram Gerstner. Limits to high-speed simulations of spiking neural networks using general-purpose computers. Frontiers in Neuroinformatics, 8:76, 2014.
21. Sumit Soman and Manan Suri. Recent trends in neuromorphic engineering. Big Data Analytics, 1(1):15, 2016.
22. Filip Ponulak and Andrzej Kasinski. Introduction to spiking neural networks: Information processing, learning and applications. Acta Neurobiologiae Experimentalis, 71(4):409–433, 2011.
23. Jing Pei, Lei Deng, Sen Song, Mingguo Zhao, Youhui Zhang, Shuang Wu, Guanrui Wang, Zhe Zou, Zhenzhi Wu, Wei He, et al. Towards artificial general intelligence with hybrid tianjic chip architecture. Nature, 572(7767):106–111, 2019.
24. Luigi Atzori, Antonio Iera, and Giacomo Morabito. The internet of things: A survey. Computer Networks, 54(15):2787–2805, 2010.
25. Yulei Wu, Hong-Ning Dai, and Hao Wang. Convergence of blockchain and edge computing for secure and scalable IIoT critical infrastructures in industry 4.0. IEEE Internet of Things Journal, 8(4):2300–2317, 2020.
26. Larry F Abbott. Lapicque's introduction of the integrate-and-fire model neuron (1907). Brain Research Bulletin, 50(5–6):303–304, 1999.
27. Richard B Stein. Some models of neuronal variability. Biophysical Journal, 7(1):37–68, 1967.
28. Roberto A Vazquez and Aleister Cach´on. Integrate and fire neurons and their application in pattern recognition. In 2010 7th International Conference on Electrical Engineering Computing Science and Automatic Control, pages 424–428. IEEE, 2010.
29. Kaushik Roy, Abhronil Jaiswal, and Priyadarshini Panda. Towards spike-based machine intelligence with neuromorphic computing. Nature, 575(7784):607–617, 2019.
30. Giacomo Indiveri and Shih-Chii Liu. Memory and information processing in neuromorphic systems. Proceedings of the IEEE, 103(8):1379–1397, 2015.
31. Mauro Conti, Sandeep Kumar, Chhagan Lal, and Sushmita Ruj. A survey on security and privacy issues of blockchain technology. IEEE Communications Surveys & Tutorials, 21(2):116–1129, 2018.
32. Chander Prakash, Lovi Raj Gupta, Amrinder Mehta, Hitesh Vasudev, Roman Tominov, Ekaterina Korman, Alexander Fedotov, Vladimir Smirnov, and Kavindra Kumar Kesari. Computing of neuromorphic materials: An emerging approach for bioengineering solutions. Materials Advances, 4(23):5882–5919, 2023.

5 Enhancing Security and Transparency in AI with Blockchain

Ashalatha Gali, Kush Dharmesh Modi, Manmathnath Das, Karthik Salikanti, and Vuppala Sindhu Bhargavi

5.1 INTRODUCTION

Artificial intelligence (AI) is at the heart of transforming many industries and enabling more automation, improved decision-making, and enhanced data-driven insight to improve business functions [1, 2]. AI is already crossing boundaries between sectors such as healthcare, finance, and urban planning and is becoming a key transformational driver into alternative operating models that also enable innovation and efficiencies. By using datasets to provide increasingly analytical inputs to inform operational constructs in an industry, AI is embedded into providing more personalized services and solutions; however, more sophisticated AI technologies introduce greater risk, particularly around security, data integrity, and transparency.

The implications of this lack of transparency are concerning in high-stakes domains such as healthcare, finance, and governance, where the inability to interpret the decision-making process and rationale of AI systems undermines trust and accountability [3, 4]. When decisions affect human lives, financial assets, or the public good, weak accountability and traceability increase the risk of bias, error, or manipulation, reducing trust in areas like medical diagnosis and treatment, lending, and public services [5]. Many advanced AI techniques are complex and proprietary by design, limiting the ability to scrutinize model behavior and hampering ethical oversight—issues that are exacerbated by rapid deployment across critical infrastructures.

Blockchain technology—via decentralization, immutability, and transparent audit trails—offers mechanisms that directly address these concerns by enabling tamper-evident records, provenance tracking, and verifiable access and actions [6, 7]. Decentralization reduces single points of failure and centralized control; immutability provides durable, append-only histories; and transparency enables traceability so stakeholders can authenticate and audit actions executed by AI systems. Together, blockchain and AI can strengthen security, data integrity, and accountability in AI operations, making them more reliable and trustworthy in practice.

This chapter looks into the symbiosis between blockchain and AI and how their compounded abilities can enhance security, transparency, and responsible

 DOI: 10.1201/9781003658597-5

deployment of AI systems by combining AI's computational capabilities with blockchain's demonstrable proof of authenticity [7]. We observe research and applications to assess the advantages and compromises of combined solutions and to show how these technologies can work in tandem to reduce risk while equipping more trustworthy digital ecosystems.

The unification can improve the supervision of AI-based processes by supporting verifiable training data lineage, model versioning, and decision logging, while conserving performance and receptiveness wherever appropriate; blockchain provides a distributed, inviolable ledger to reinforce integrity, accuracy, attributability, and responsibility of AI data and actions [1, 2, 8]. The synergy of these technologies creates opportunities for building trustworthy AI systems—efficient and intelligent, yet auditable and secure—through mechanisms such as provenance tracking, model governance via smart contracts, and cryptographic verification of behaviors [8]. For instance, blockchain can track and verify data and model lifecycles to reduce bias or manipulation, while AI can optimize blockchain operations, including smart contract execution and fraud detection in data-heavy environments [8, 9]. Sectors such as healthcare, finance, supply chain, cybersecurity, and legal technology are piloting or adopting hybrid approaches to improve operational transparency and data sovereignty through secure provenance and access control [2, 10]. We also consider challenges—including scalability, latency, privacy trade-offs, interoperability, and operating costs—that must be addressed to realize robust, real-world blockchain–AI systems at scale [11–13]. The goal is to explain how blockchain and AI can be deployed together, not only as engines of innovation but also as instruments of ethical, accountable practice in high-stakes contexts [14, 15].

If harnessed appropriately, the joint application of AI and blockchain can expand organizational capacity for trust and accountability by enabling verifiable data lineage, auditable decisions, enforceable policies, and privacy-preserving assurances within compliant, production-grade systems [16, 17] (Figure 5.1).

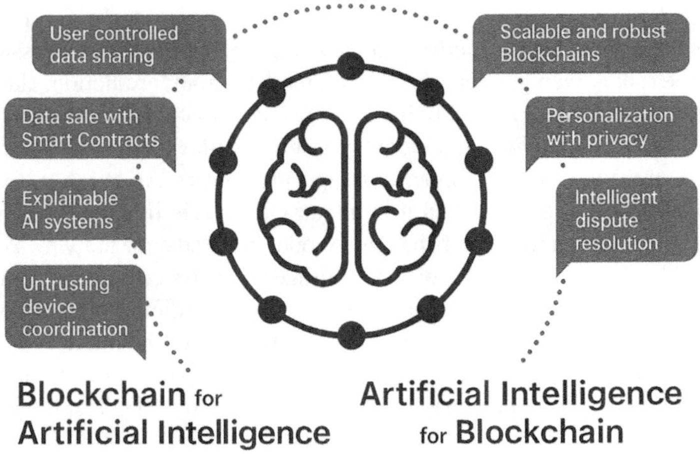

FIGURE 5.1 High-level integration of AI modules with blockchain infrastructure for improved security and transparency.

5.2 CHALLENGES IN TRADITIONAL AI SYSTEMS

Within the realm of AI, many challenges still need to be addressed before comprehensive development can be realized. With the emergence of AI in critical areas like healthcare, finance, and government, these issues are even more critical. Major issues include provenance of data, integrity of data, integrity of models, explainability, and auditability, which are explored in the following sections [18].

5.2.1 Data Integrity

Data integrity and provenance are essential aspects of AI model operation because models rely on vast datasets for training and inference. Datasets constitute foundational inputs for AI systems. If data are altered, manipulated, or biased, model predictions and decisions may become biased, inaccurate, or harmful. For instance, biased datasets can lead to discriminatory decisions in high-stakes contexts such as hiring, healthcare, or policing. Data provenance—the identification of data origin and how it has been processed and transformed—is critical to establishing model and output integrity. If the origin and processing pipeline are unclear, the validity of conclusions drawn from an AI system is questionable. Businesses and users face considerable risk if they cannot attest to the origin of a dataset and trust its integrity [19]. In conclusion, supporting data integrity with appropriate provenance mechanisms is not simply a technical issue; it is an organizational practice. Seek to use distributed ledger technologies, like blockchain, to create distributed, tamper-evident, and logged flows of data, leading to transparency, accountability, and trust in deployed AI systems [20].

5.2.2 Model Integrity

Just as a human asset can be corrupted, so too can an AI model, and the implications of such corruption can be dire. Once a model is trained, it can be a costly, digital asset, usually made up of months, or years, worth of data, computational time, and fine-tuning by experts. Once the model is deployed, in the real world, in mission-critical systems, the risk is even greater—based on a model output, prediction, classification, or decision, people could potentially die, businesses could be ruined, or societal structures could erode. Given these contexts, it is not unusual that models, once they are fielded, are subject to all manner of tampering attacks. An attacker, for example, might interact with a model when it is in storage, or it is in a transitive state from one environment to another, and change a model in an adversarial way. A tampered model could behave in an unsafe or indeterminate way, based on having made a prediction or recommendation based on incorrect model predictions; model parameters can be perturbed modestly, rendering the model useless, or the impact could be catastrophic. An attacker could also manipulate a model's inputs, inducing incorrect outputs as a result—such outputs may not be obvious to end users. The model-integrity susceptibility is annoying for a variety of reasons, from self-sufficient vehicles to economics [21]; whereas, the reality is that AI models are susceptible to cyberattacks throughout their lifespan; at-rest or in transit, systems face numerous interfering risks, requiring completely honest verification and management [22].

5.2.3 Lack of Explainability

A major limitation of many AI models, especially deep neural networks, is their lack of explainability—often referred to as the "black-box" problem. While models can often uncover patterns in complex datasets, they typically do not specify how exactly the decisions were made, which reduces confidence in the AI system. This has significance in low-risk applications where the users only care about the outcome (i.e., rating a restaurant), but it can have major implications where confidence is more critical (i.e., healthcare, finance) as stakeholders want to know what rationale (if any) is behind the outputs of the model [1].

5.2.4 Auditability Obstacle

Typical AI systems lack built-in mechanisms to monitor and record end-to-end processing steps, creating an auditability obstacle. In high-risk scenarios (e.g., clinical decision support or financial transactions), immutable records of system actions are needed to reconstruct decision pathways, verify correctness, and assign accountability. As complex models evolve over time, maintaining consistent, auditable histories becomes difficult; without traceability to specific actions or data points, transparency diminishes, and confidence erodes [12]. The outlined challenges above are significant shortcomings of traditional AI systems. As AI technology advances, it is increasingly important to overcome these limitations to enable ethical, responsible, and transparent deployment across industries; otherwise, use in high-risk applications will remain constrained (Figure 5.2).

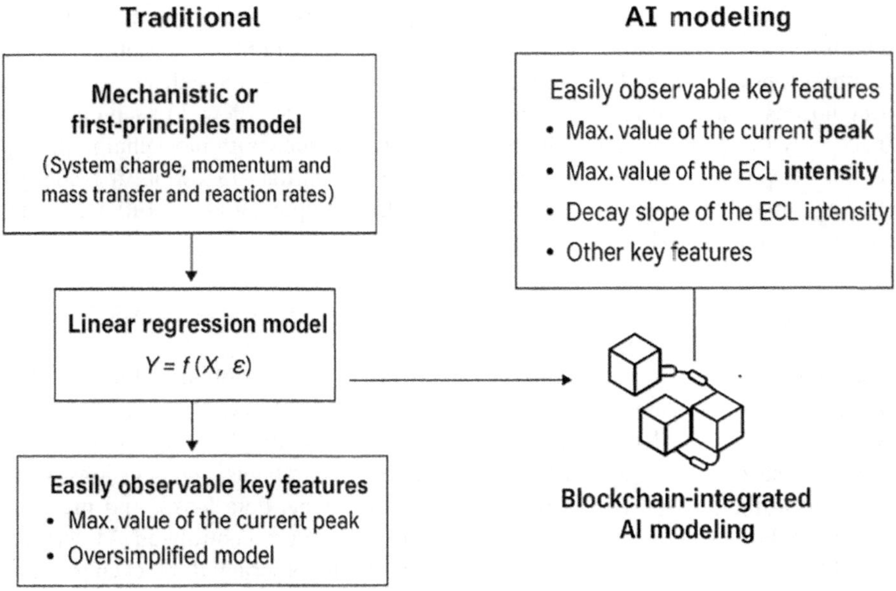

FIGURE 5.2 Visual comparison of traditional AI and blockchain-integrated AI systems.

5.3 BLOCKCHAIN AS A SOLUTION

Blockchain technology offers a practical approach to many challenges in traditional AI systems, especially safety, clarity, data integrity, and liability [23]. Blockchain technology enhances AI by addressing key issues such as safety, transparency, and data integrity through immutability, decentralization, and smart contracts.

It securely logs all AI interactions, ensuring data traceability and auditability, which is vital for sectors like healthcare, finance, and public governance. Blockchain maintains transparent records of data collection, processing, and AI decision-making, bolstering trust [24]. Its application in regulated environments supports accountability and ethical governance, making AI systems more secure, reliable, and clear while fostering public confidence. This integration helps meet the demands of high-risk and controlled sectors [25].

5.3.1 Clarity and Permanence

The invariability of blockchain is one of its best working characteristics—once uploaded to the blockchain, data cannot be tampered with. This distinguishable characteristic ensures the invariability of any actions, decisions, and data made by AI systems—such as once an AI model makes a decision or takes some data, that action can be treated as an exchange and uploaded to the blockchain, where a new record is created with a time stamp and an invariable action [26]. This allows transparency in the actions performed by the AI system while ensuring no one can change the outcomes. In AI, the invariability of blockchain can reduce problems with model tampering or malicious actions and allow a greater degree of assurance in AI outputs [1]. Furthermore, invariability and transparency of actions in blockchain logs mean that stakeholders can track all activity in the AI system. This area is important for any field where accountability must be maintained, such as medical diagnostics, financial decisions, or policing, to name just a few. In such cases, it is necessary to know why an AI-based decision was made. With blockchain, all steps of the AI pipeline can be tracked as they move from data ingestion, for example, through model training, model inference, and final outputs, giving a full-scope view of system actions [27].

5.3.2 Decentralization

Blockchain operates on a decentralized network of nodes without authority, which is also a major advantage of using blockchain compared to traditional AI systems, where there is centralization and a singular point of failure. Traditional AI systems typically have a central authority controlling the data, models, and decisions, which leads to a higher exposure of the system to tampering, data leaks, and malicious behavior. For instance, if an attacker were to infiltrate a centralized AI server, it would be able to shut down the entire system. On the other hand, blockchain inherently decentralizes authority across the nodes and is, therefore, more resilient against cyberattacks and less vulnerable to unauthorized manipulation or tampering [28].

Second, decentralization imposes clear conditions on the AI comparison, along with being resource dependent. Therefore, one party simply cannot change or manipulate the AI's decisions (especially in high-risk areas like healthcare or finance) because the data are distributed and computations are performed across a network of blockchain nodes. For example, an AI system could have its integrity, safeguarding, and independence from any controlling party in a single operation with centralized servers on the internet. By making it possible to share the AI systems' data across a blockchain network, an AI system relies less on a single source and therefore will instill more trust and confidence among users and stakeholders [9].

5.3.3 Smart Contract

Smart contracts are self-executing contracts in which the terms of the agreement between buyer and seller are directly written into lines of code. Smart contracts automatically execute when some circumstances are met, executing them as portrayed, and therefore avoiding intermediaries and reducing the likelihood of human error or fraud. Regarding AI, smart contracts can be used to automate the functions of AI models and impose certain rules on the functions of the models. For example, a smart contract can automatically trigger the updating of an AI model with the latest data input, so that the model is self-functioning in accordance with certain policies and predefined regulations [29]. Smart contracts provide a way to carry out safety standards and compliance with regulations. AI models applied in critical areas such as healthcare can be governed by smart contracts that enforce adherence to data privacy regulations like HIPAA. Similarly, economic frameworks can be designed to automatically carry out transactions or decisions aligned with regulatory standards. In all cases, smart contracts guarantee strict compliance without exceptions [30]. Moreover, they enable a high degree of automation, allowing AI systems to operate autonomously while ensuring transparency and accountability.

5.3.4 Enhanced Auditability

A key feature of blockchain technology is its ability to create a transparent and unalterable record of all activities occurring within the network. This enhanced visibility offers significant benefits for AI systems. By capturing every step—such as data usage, model development, inference, and decisions—blockchain ensures a reliable and verifiable audit trail that accurately reflects the AI system's operations. The auditable record of actions taken in the AI system helps organizations not only meet ethical and rule-enforced conformance demands but also remember and trace the source of the problem in the AI decision-making process [31]. For example, when a wrong decision is made by an AI system, the blockchain audit records will explain the reason, provide the data that was used in the decision, and show the actions that were taken during the AI decision-making process. The clarity of the blockchain encourages better opportunities for debugging and liability by seeing how decisions were actually made and figuring out the locations/causes of error or bias in the development of the model that could be identified [32]. Additionally, the blockchain's ability to have an invariable record of AI activity that is time-stamped solves many of the

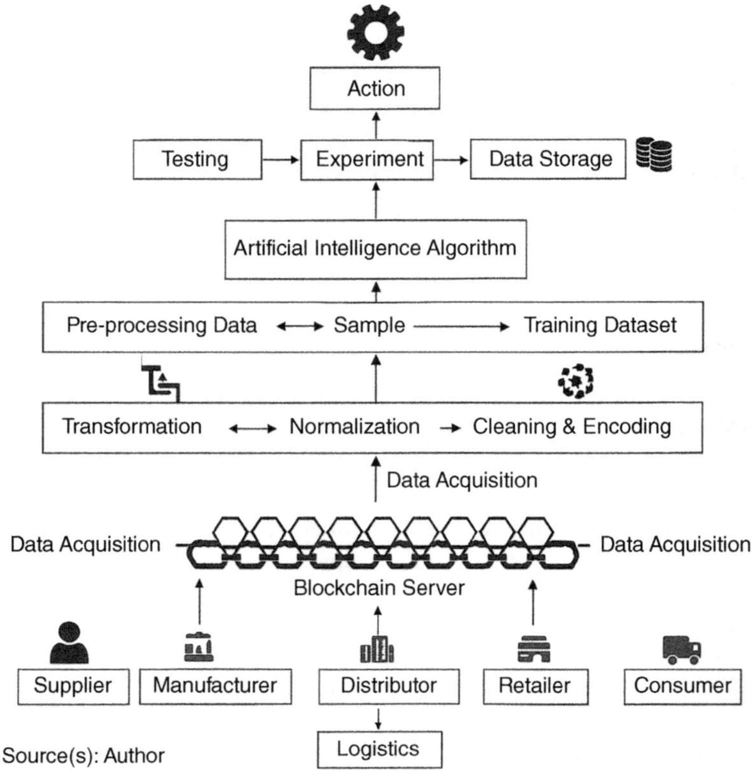

FIGURE 5.3 A figure showing how blockchain amplifies AI systems through safe data acquisition, trackability across the supply chain, and trustworthy preprocessing pipelines.

non-auditability issues of older AI systems. In fields like health, where decisions can be life-changing, a clear and transparent audit trail of AI activity will be necessary for safety, justice, and legal considerations [33] (Figure 5.3).

5.4 KEY USE CASES

Combining blockchain technology with AI is a fantastic way to solve some of the major and persistent problems with AI implementation. Because in present times, AI systems are increasingly being used to make decisions in high-impact and sensitive settings, it is not only technically necessary but also morally and legally required to ensure data integrity, model accountability, system security, and operational transparency [34].

5.4.1 Data Provenance

Data integrity is critically important for artificial intelligence systems, particularly when it involves training and inferences. Data provenance is the tracking of the origin, history, and changes that were applied to the data throughout the life cycle. In an AI system's training, it can be practical to evaluate the data provenance of a dataset; however, it can be extremely difficult when you are attempting to ensure the data was accurate, its initial state, and its integrity. Blockchain technology solves that problem by providing a decentralized ledger of records that cannot be manipulated. Blockchain allows a record of every use of the data to be logged as a transaction—from gathering data, processing the data, and using the data—every use is recorded [35]. In domains involving sensitive information like healthcare, finance, or legal, it is absolutely crucial that the data AI is inferred from or trained upon remains unchanged and is not authorized. Blockchain allows for the data to be hashed in a cryptographic way and would be able to make a digital fingerprint for each piece of information. If the hashes of the original data were stored on the blockchain, then it is virtually impossible for someone to change the data without being caught. Relying on data with guaranteed strict integrity allows AI systems to consume reliable datasets, reducing the opportunities for manipulation or bias to affect outputs. For example, in healthcare, patient data could be hashed and contained within a blockchain; thus, the data AI used to make diagnosis claims would demonstrate that the healthcare data was verified and untampered with to ensure security and reliability.

5.4.2 Model Integrity Verification

The model receives constant updates, tuning, or retraining using new datasets in order to improve efficacy or performance and to adapt to their environment. However, tracking updates and ensuring that only appropriate/authorized versions of the model are in use is a challenge. Blockchain technology may be the solution by creating a public, decentralized ledger of each AI model update, with the associated training parameters, hashes of training data, and the date it was deployed and by whom. Each time a model updates and changes occur, an appropriate entry should/be made to the blockchain, such as a cryptographic signature and variables relative to the model parameters. By doing this, organizations can verify that appropriate and approved versions of the model are in a production environment. Blockchain can provide protection from unauthorized model changes or model tampering, thus mitigating the risk of model manipulation, whether it be cyber-adversarial attacks or unintended model drift. By documenting an update on the blockchain, organizations would be compliant with industry standards that demand that organizations demonstrate traceability and authentication of a model version (something that is often demanded if a product were to fail). This is particularly important regarding high-stakes applications such as autonomous vehicles, medical AI, or decision-making in finance, as changes to a faulty model can create horrible outcomes [24].

5.4.3 Transparent Decision Logging

AI systems are often used in areas where the decisions have high implications, e.g., in industries such as finance (e.g., credit scoring), health (e.g., medical diagnosis), and legal (e.g., sentencing). The un-transparency of the authoring and decision-making process is one of the most widely publicized and concerning issues with AI systems. AI Models, particularly "deep learning"-based models, are openly called "black boxes" as the process of reasoning toward a decision is very difficult to clarify or investigate [1]. Blockchain can solve this problem by providing a transparent and immutable audit history of the decisions by the AI systems. Inputs, model parameters, and outputs for each decision can be recorded on the blockchain. This feature will make all decisions made by the AI auditable and traceable. This is a very significant feature for those industries, such as healthcare and finance, where compliance, accountability, and an understanding of the reasoning for a given decision must be known by the end user and regulators [6]. For example, using the healthcare scenario, if an AI system makes a diagnosis, the blockchain would save the patient's information, the model used, the inference, and the final diagnosis. In case of an error, the blockchain would have an easily accessible audit trail to track how the decision was reached, which could be reversed. Making decisions publicly logged would also facilitate trust in AI systems, as stakeholders could verify that the decision-making is done based on mutually agreed-upon ethical principles or obligations.

5.4.4 Model Sharing and Access Control

Typically, when decisions or projects rely on AI models or datasets, they need to be shared between organizations, researchers, or stakeholders to support their collaborative efforts. Unfortunately, even if effective measures are put in place, sharing sensitive models and datasets exposes users to many vulnerabilities, such as unauthorized access, modification, or misuse. Blockchain technology can support the ability to provide safe and verifiable access control mechanisms. Blockchain, with the help of smart contracts, offers ways to create decentralized access control systems to ensure only authorized individuals get access to the relevant AI models or datasets. Smart contracts are digital agreements that automatically execute and enforce access rules for data or AI models. For example, in an instance of sharing AI models between health institutions for research, the smart contract will allow the users who have the authority to access the model, the conditions of accessing the model, and the duration of access. The access can be structured based on predefined rules, and any attempts at access that exceed defined limits will be denied and captured by the smart contract. Additionally, smart contracts can keep a detailed log or monitor all the interactions with the model or data, providing an auditable transparency layer to determine who accessed which parts, when, and for what purpose. This approach is particularly crucial in multi-party partnerships when participants may hesitate to share proprietary or sensitive information because of trust issues. Organizations can ensure that the relevant data and models are made available only to the parties that are required, using a blockchain-based smart-contract method, protecting against misuse or unauthorized actions by third parties. The approach also ensures accountability among all stakeholders who have been granted access to the data and model use, further building due diligence and trust that facilitates future cooperation and growth of AI partnerships.

5.4.5 Privacy-Preserving AI with ZK-Pack (Zero-Knowledge Proof Toolkits)

The problem of protecting data privacy while maintaining transparency and auditability becomes more difficult as AI systems handle sensitive data more frequently, including in the areas of healthcare, finance, and governance. Adopting zero-knowledge proofs (ZKPs), sophisticated cryptographic techniques that enable the demonstration that you possess a piece of data without disclosing the actual information itself, is one of the most efficient ways to close this gap, though there may be other approaches. ZK-pack toolkits have recently begun to appear as modular libraries that greatly simplify the development and deployment of ZKP-based applications; we are now witnessing a multitude of opportunities for novel privacy-preserving AI and Blockchain architectures that make use of these packs.

ZK-packs contain libraries and protocols—e.g., zk-SNARK (Succinct Non-interactive Argument of Knowledge), zk-STARK (Scalable Transparent Argument of Knowledge), Halo2, PlonK, and ZK-EVM—which all can generate fast and verifiable proofs that preserve data integrity or computation attributes without revealing underlying details [28].

These ZK-pack components can be inserted within the AI pipeline, implemented to work with a blockchain, and placed on-chain to verify model outputs, training processes, or data provenance without ever releasing sensitive data or disclosing proprietary AI model details [29] (Figure 5.4).

For instance, in a healthcare context, an AI system may make diagnostic recommendations that include a ZK-proof verifying the recommendation was made using an authorized model on unaltered patient data—without revealing the patient's confidential

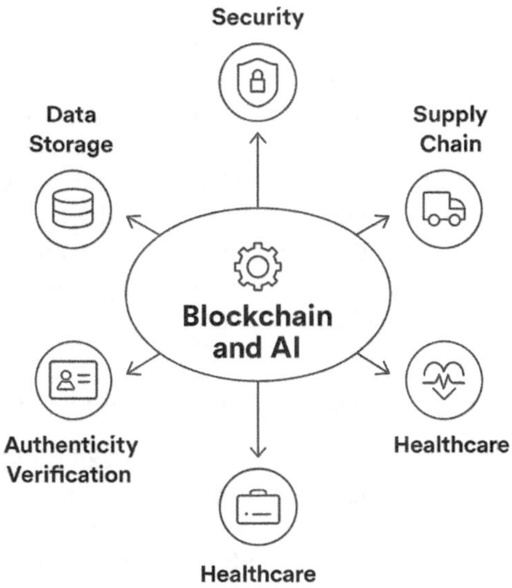

FIGURE 5.4 Figure illustrating the wide application areas of integrated blockchain and AI technologies, including security, supply chain, and healthcare.

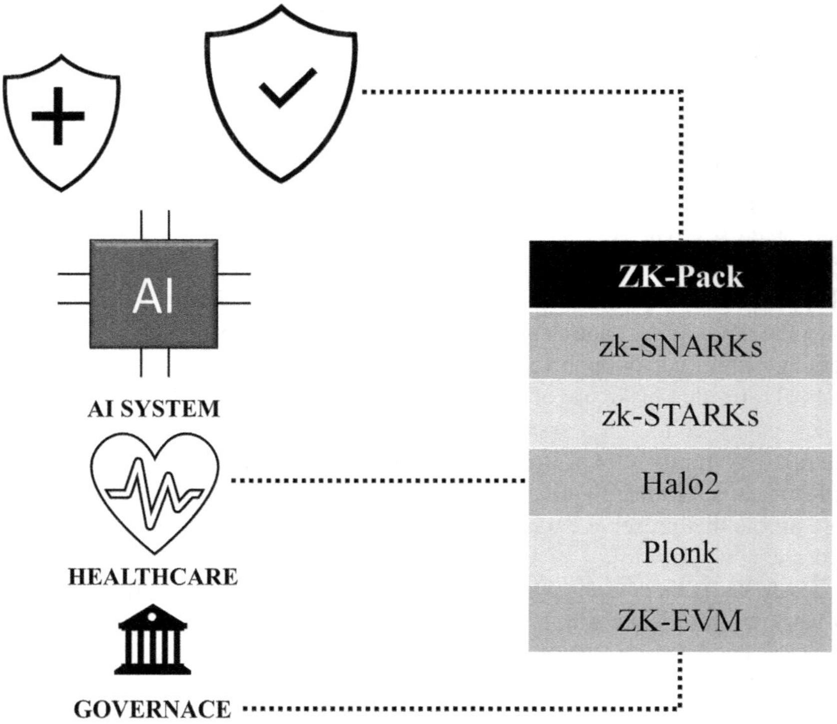

FIGURE 5.5 Preserving privacy in AI using ZK-pack.

health records [9]. In financial services, ZK-pack–based workflows can be leveraged by AI systems to verify customer eligibility or transaction compliance without exposing any personally identifiable information (PII) to the blockchain network at large [27].

ZK-packs are also making it possible for new concepts like privacy-preserving federated learning, which allows AI models to be trained across several institutions without requiring raw data to ever leave the local premises and ensures that all model updates are verified to be legitimate and compliant [24]. ZKP toolkits will proliferate in AI + Blockchain systems as their performance and usability continue to improve, offering the essential link between privacy and transparency in the next generation of digital ecosystems (Figure 5.5).

5.5 REAL-WORLD IMPLEMENTATIONS AND RESEARCH

Blockchain and AI are rapidly expanding fields of research and development, resulting in significant attention to academic and industrial initiatives that aim to solve crucial problems related specifically to AI implementation, such as security concerns, transparency issues like accountability, and trust. A significant proportion of these initiatives is not only theoretical but also serves as practical demonstrations of how blockchain technology can be utilized to enhance AI systems. Below are some academic and real-world projects that incorporate blockchain and AI.

In the effort to promote interpretability and traceability of AI decisions, Nassar et al. developed a framework that combines blockchain technology with Explainable Artificial Intelligence (XAI), which together seek to create transparent and accountable AI systems, where every AI decision can be tracked, and the reasoning behind it can be explained in real time [3]. In order to log the model's reasoning process on the blockchain, blockchain-enabled XAI frameworks can record reasoning processes on decentralized ledgers, which become immutable and bind an AI example's reasoning process into an auditable path. Verifiability, or traceability, is an essential component for stakeholder confidence in AI systems, especially in high-stakes conditions such as healthcare, finance, and law. In these conditions, errors can have life-threatening results for an individual. Thus, an essential advantage for all stakeholders will be the ability to verify the inputs, identify the algorithms that produced AI outputs, and track their decision-making process. Approval and legal decisions are dependent on this. The release of AI makes it essential to have a clear explanation in fields such as auditing. The need for consistent and traceable documentation of AI reasoning operations is fulfilled by XAI frameworks that are backed by blockchain. Using blockchain technology, which is based on assets, can create a secure record that gives its answerability efforts impartial information for future improvement of understanding of the behavior in AI.

The HistoTrust initiative merges blockchain and hardware security to trace and document AI actions during runtime. This framework was designed for the embedded and real-time AI systems that are gaining popularity in important application settings like IoT systems, industrial automation, and autonomous vehicles [4]. Keeping track of AI systems during runtime is crucial for maintaining data integrity in real-time AI systems. Blockchain's immutability and decentralization allow the HistoTrust framework to safeguard and record the actions and behaviors of AI models at runtime. HistoTrust also provides hardware-based security that guarantees the anonymity and privacy of an AI's runtime data and decisions, providing a valuable defense against adversary attacks. Blockchain's unchangeable ledger permits interested parties to record and monitor AI actions to ensure compliance with its rules and standards, boosting trustworthiness and adhering to safety requirements for autonomous, unsupervised applications.

Lüthi and his team introduced a new blockchain-based provenance tracking method that utilized graphs to enhance transparency in AI assets and workflows. This approach is especially important for supporting collaborative research and industrial applications, since it allows shared AI models and datasets to be transferable and reproducible. The monitoring of data origins, version updates, and algorithm modifications in conventional AI systems often presents ethical or error-related challenges. By using blockchain technology, a graph-based solution is used to visualize the lifecycle of AI components, along with data, models, and inferences. By documenting every move (or delay) on the immutable blockchain, provenance of AI assets can be verified, making tracking of each asset more transparent and traceable. All individuals involved in AI can keep track of the source and origin of data, the evolution process, and ensure that all interactions with their AI are ethically valid and legal. This method works well in science and medicine, particularly when understanding the research that uses AI models, depending on reproducibility and transparency. The ability to track the origin of authored medical data or an AI model used to arrive at a diagnosis, for example, will enable the healthcare industry to verify that model training was conducted on suitable, high-quality data and that a model used to support the diagnosis can be traced back to the original data source. In the end, this will help to increase the legitimacy and responsibility of AI-driven health models [7].

Yang et al. put forth a decentralized federated learning system that uses blockchain technology to advance the dependability and capability of shared AI model training. Federated learning is a machine learning method where many organizations work together to train AI models without them needing to share raw data. It prevents the requirement to share data, which is especially helpful in situations where data privacy is important, such as healthcare, finance, and telecommunications [8]. While federated learning systems are beneficial, there are vulnerabilities to malicious attackers that could insert false data or ruin the integrity of the training. To alleviate these vulnerabilities, the researchers combined the elements of blockchain technology and federated learning in order to create a decentralized as well as transparent system. It records the training process as well as the model updates on the blockchain, thus allowing every interaction to be verifiable and with sufficient measures to ensure no malicious updates could be accepted without recording the updates [34]. Due to its decentralized nature, blockchain ensures that no single entity controls the model, mitigating the risk of data manipulation or adversarial attacks. In addition, the blockchain ledger provides an immutable audit trail of model changes, which ensures that the federation process is performative. All of this means that federated learning systems can benefit from increased trust and security. The improvements in trust and security will be even more useful for applications in sensitive sectors like healthcare, where some collaboration is needed, but institutional security and privacy are top priority [22].

5.6 INDUSTRY APPLICATIONS

Apart from academic research, many industries are experimenting and using blockchain–AI integration to solve problems in the real world:

Healthcare: AI models are increasingly used in healthcare for an array of tasks, including diagnostic imaging, creating personalized treatment plans, and undertaking drug discovery. Blockchain is being used to secure medical records and document the provenance and chain-of-custody for the data used to train an AI model. Blockchain solves problems, such as proving that patient data cannot be changed and that AI-driven healthcare decisions are transparent, traceable, and compliant with regulatory laws such as HIPAA [2].

Finance: Application of blockchain and AI is helping to increase the effectiveness of fraud detection and prevention, improve credit scoring, and automate financial trading. Blockchain provides a transparent and secure way to capture and document financial transactions over time. AI models are also analyzing vast amounts of data using machine learning and deep learning techniques to identify anomalies and predict trends. Collectively, the combination of AI and blockchain is being used to improve the security and accuracy of financial systems [15].

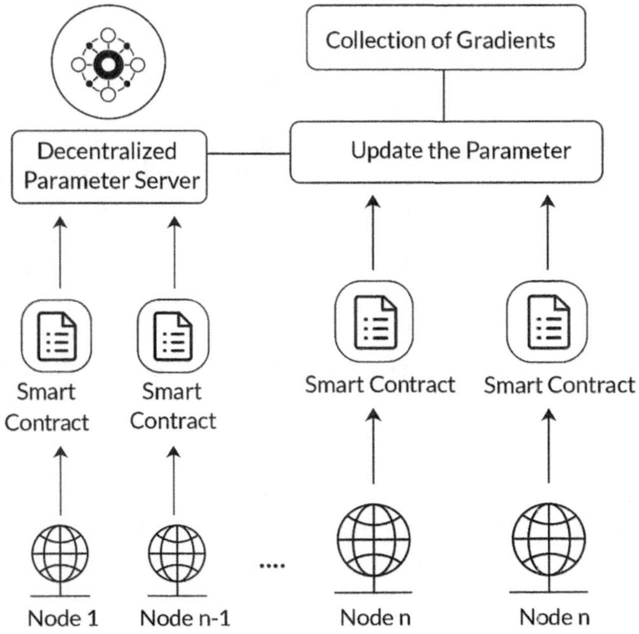

FIGURE 5.6 Implicit nature of blockchain-based federated learning architecture allowing decentralized, privacy-preserving model updates.

Supply Chain: Blockchain is used to identify and track goods from their provenance in the supply chain. Then, AI is used to manage logistics, inventory, and demand forecasting. Blockchain uses immutable databases to ensure that the data AI collects is reliable and immutable, increasing confidence in the decisions made by AI for supply chain management [10] (Figure 5.6).

Self-Driving Cars: Autonomous vehicles use AI to make real-time decisions and navigate through a world of constantly changing environments. Blockchain is being introduced to provide a secure and transparent record of each of the vehicle's decisions and all of its data, to protect against wrongdoing if an accident occurs [12].

5.7 LIMITATIONS AND OPEN CHALLENGE

Although combining blockchain and AI has great potential for solving important issues in AI like transparency, accountability, and security, there are still significant limitations and open challenges to consider before blockchain can be implemented into AI systems in a meaningful way across industries. The following are the main limitations and open challenges regarding the convergence of blockchain and AI.

5.7.1 Scalability

Blockchain technology, specifically public blockchains, suffers from scalability concerns that limit its use for large-scale, high-volume operations that AI systems typically rely upon. The consensus mechanisms utilized by blockchains, like proof of work (PoW) or proof of stake (PoS), require some degree of computation, which could result in low transaction throughput. Conversely, AI systems tend to need huge datasets for handling real-time environments. For instance, real-time AI technologies such as autonomous vehicles, medical diagnostics, or anti-money laundering activities in the case of financial services are all dependent on fast processing and decision-making. Thus, the AI-based systems would not be able to equal the rate of decisions and changes in situations where decision space is gigantic, such as thousands or tens of thousands are made within any given second. To enhance this capability from both sides in a sustainable environment, blockchain scalability needs to be solved either using Layer 2 solutions, sharding, or more effective consensus protocols to enable high-volume AI applications, as the center of the technology [33].

5.7.2 Latency and Time Sensitivity

Latency is one of the most serious issues faced by AI applications in real-time environments. The time delays involved in blockchain consensus mechanisms, particularly in the case of public blockchain, cause secondary technology delay because of the multiple seconds to reach consensus and the time involved to verify blocks, especially important in many AI applications, for example, fraud detection, predictive maintenance, or real-time medical diagnostics (to name a few), decisions must be made quickly, or they become costly mistakes or outright failures [12]. With real-time AI systems for fully autonomous driving, for example, there is a likelihood that decisions must be made instantaneously based on sensor input. If we undertake the blockchain verification process, it takes more than a few milliseconds, and the added value of blockchain verification could create a challenge by virtue of a time lag, and that delay may lead the AI to reach sub-optimal choices for successful acts of driving and create otherwise dangerous situations [33]. To point out this issue, there is a chance for researchers to create new blockchain architectures or consensus mechanisms. An important goal for researchers would be to create solutions that lessen the transaction time and improve block confirmation time [33].

5.7.3 Privacy Concerns

As the integration of AI and blockchain grows, privacy emerges as a significant concern. AI systems manage highly sensitive data across sectors like healthcare, finance, and personal services. Although blockchain's transparent and tamper-proof features foster traceability and accountability, they can also risk exposing confidential or proprietary information. Privacy must be secured, especially since blockchain records are permanent, and storing AI data on an open ledger may contravene privacy regulations like GDPR and HIPAA. The key concern is how to strike a balance between openness and privacy. ZKPs, homomorphic encryption, and secure multiparty computation (SMPC) are privacy-enhancing technologies that offer solutions. A ZKP allows individuals to demonstrate their knowledge of data without revealing it, which helps to maintain privacy while maintaining transparency and verifiability.

5.7.4 Absence of Standardization

The lack of shared principles governing the integration of blockchain and AI is a significant barrier to their adoption. The lack of shared standards and protocols for the integration of blockchain and AI results in lackluster interoperability between systems, frameworks, blockchain platforms, and data providers. Interoperable AI applications may require different blockchain infrastructure, data structure, and model architecture, making them a bit more challenging to achieve. Also, there's the mix of various stakeholders in combining blockchain with AI—from an executive working on an AI app to an engineer working for blockchain and finally domain experts—who each have their own practices and priorities. Due to the lack of standardized frameworks for cooperation between these groups, transforming AI applications into tangible AI–blockchain solutions can be a barrier to the mass adoption of AI–blockchain solutions. The next step in resolving this challenge is to formulate appropriate protocols and frameworks for a more seamless integration of the two technologies. Appropriate standards will allow the many different blockchain and AI frameworks to communicate with one another, which will help increase adoption and cooperation.

5.7.5 Data Integrity and Model Tampering Risks

Although blockchain addresses data provenance and model integrity, ensuring the integrity of the data itself, along with a lack of tampering with the models, remains a significant hurdle when it comes to AI on the blockchain. While the fact that blockchains are immutable makes them probably the most tamper-proof option available, there are still many types of attacks that the data fed into the AI models and the models that provide the predictions may be vulnerable to. For example, adversarial attacks, designed to make small adjustments to data that will confuse or mislead AI models, will rapidly change the conclusions and therefore the algorithm outputs, without the detection of users, and also blockchain would not detect an adversarial attack because it will simply write in data from the models without exploration of the information around it [15]. Addressing such risks would need additional protections. Enhancing the AI models with mechanisms such as adversarial training or the use of robust model architectures could work to avoid tampering, while the blockchain could deploy various means to detect and mitigate a range of attacks. While this process will create protections via AI and blockchain, the blockchain also has the potential to leverage technologies already present in the environment, such as trustworthy execution environments (TEEs), to protect both data and models [3].

5.7.6 Energy Consumption

Blockchain's energy-intensive nature, especially in proof-of-work-based blockchains, becomes an even greater concern when combined with AI, as AI relies on computational resources in similar ways to blockchain; namely, the significant computational resources that are required to train or/for inference with deep learning models. Combining the two may increase the energy demand, not making the solution sustainable in the sense [12]. To reduce the harmful environmental impact of the blockchain–AI combination, we may consider consensus mechanisms, such as proof-of-stake, as alternatives to the energy-intensive consensus methods. We may also optimize the AI models to bring down the energy costs or improve the carbon footprint of the blockchain by utilizing green technologies within the blockchain network [33].

5.7.7 Cost of Implementation

The use of AI and blockchain has high costs associated with the implementation, particularly in the areas of infrastructure, development, and ongoing maintenance. Setting up a blockchain application requires significant startup and operating funds. Additionally, the level of complexity involved in the integration of AI systems with blockchain requires additional skills and knowledge that may not be readily available [15]. In order to mitigate these costs, alternatives (like blockchain-as-a-service platforms or off-chain processing of transactions) could be used to facilitate working with blockchain and AI platforms. By utilizing processes or hardware that lowers costs for entry points for other businesses and researchers, a source of integration could be made available that otherwise, through high infrastructure requirements, would be unavailable [17].

5.8 CONCLUSION

Integrating blockchain with AI has the potential to transform the foundations of digital innovation by enabling systems that are not only powerful and autonomous but also accountable, trustworthy, and transparent. While AI excels in pattern recognition, automation, and decision-making, it often lacks the transparency necessary to truly be fair, unbiased, and ethical in its use of recommendations and actions. Given blockchain's features of immutability, decentralization, and verifiability, it can complement and alleviate AI's weaknesses in clarity regarding traceability and accountability, which AI systems have never been able to provide by design. By allowing all data, every update to a model, and AI's actions to be easily traced and secured, blockchain provides some layer of integrity that is especially important in sensitive situations such as a medical diagnosis, financial transaction, legal procedure, smart governance, educational admission process, or talent acquisition analysis.

The use of a combination involves the establishment of decentralized AI ecosystems that facilitate data sharing, co-development of models, and equitable payment through smart contracts, leading to democratization and an inclusive technology ecosystem. This provides ambiguous ethical uses for AI, rather than simply putting them together and confirming with a clear conscience afterwards. The current challenges regarding scalability, energy efficiency, data storage, and regulatory transparency must be acknowledged. The integration of AI and blockchain is evident. There is a fast pace of innovation, collaboration across disciplines, and an increasing acceptance of responsible AI. It is suggested by this that blockchain and AI could serve as a potential advancement for the next phase of digital trust, while also providing ethical guidance in various other fields.

The future generation of intelligent and ethical systems can be made possible by the use of blockchain and AI as technology advances. Why is this so? Together, they will not only improve technical systems by providing constant audit trails, provable AI algorithms, and data sharing for better accountability and trust protection, but also enable greater transparency through future assurances. It is crucial for researchers in AI, blockchain engineering, law practitioners, and policymakers to work together to create solutions that are scalable, interoperable, and secure. Furthermore, there is ongoing development of privacy-preserving technologies, such as ZK-Pack toolkits, that can balance transparency and privacy measures in order to facilitate the practical application of responsible AI. The chapter highlights that the process of constructing such systems presents both technical and ethical challenges, as it offers significant potential for both industry and society.

5.9 FUTURE DIRECTIONS

Despite this powerful match, there are still significant issues to resolve in terms of organization. The majority of blockchain designs, particularly those that utilize traditional consensus models like PoW, are characterized by high latency and low throughput. The fact that AI is typically fast and capable of processing vast amounts of data should not be overlooked, especially given its general nature [12]. Streamline the transfer of resources from an on-chain blockchain to an off-chain blockchain by using Layer 2 solutions in state channels or side chains. This technique is known as scaling. Separate the blockchain using sharding solutions to enable simultaneous execution of larger amounts. We can also apply faster consensus systems (including PoS or delegated PoS (DPoS), which have algorithmically lower energy costs and utilize faster processing speeds [33]. Protecting Privacy and Still Remaining Transparent: Blockchain is considered a source of transparency and trust, this transparency has a negative aspect regarding sensitive information, especially in the healthcare and financial sectors. New systems to achieve a balance and integrate some new emerging technologies will be required to make a future with sensitive data being transparent and privacy maintained: a method to prove that something is true without showing the data, a ZKP. Homomorphic encryption allows computations to be done with the data without decryption. SMPC enables two or more parties to execute computations on data collectively without exposing any of the input [16].

REFERENCES

1. M. Nassar *et al.*, "Explainable AI through blockchain integration," *WIREs Data Min. Knowl. Discov.*, vol. 14, no. 3, p. e1340, 2024, doi: 10.1002/widm.1340.
2. A. Panigrahi, A. K. Nayak, and R. Paul, "Healthcare EHR: A blockchain-based decentralized application," *Int. J. Inf. Syst. Supply Chain Manag.*, vol. 15, no. 3, pp. 1–15, 2022, doi: 10.4018/IJISSCM.290017.
3. D. Paulin, R. Joud, C. Hennebert, P.-A. Moëllic, T. Franco-Rondisson, and R. Jayles, "HistoTrust: tracing AI behavior with secure hardware and blockchain technology," Annals of Telecommunications, Jan. 2023, doi: https://doi.org/10.1007/s12243-022-00943-6.

4. A. Panigrahi, A. K. Nayak, R. Paul, B. Sahu, and S. Kant, "CTB-PKI: Clustering and trust-enabled blockchain-based PKI system for efficient communication in P2P networks," *IEEE Access*, vol. 10, pp. 124277–124290, 2022, https://doi.org/10.1109/ACCESS.2022.3222807.
5. A. Panigrahi, A. K. Nayak, and R. Paul, "Smart contract-assisted blockchain-based public key infrastructure system," *Trans. Emerg. Telecommun. Technol.*, vol. 34, no. 1, p. e4655, 2023, doi: 10.1002/ett.4655.
6. P. Lüthi, T. Gagnaux, and M. Gygli, "Distributed Ledger for Provenance Tracking of Artificial Intelligence Assets," *IFIP advances in information and communication technology*, pp. 411–426, Jan. 2020, doi: https://doi.org/10.1007/978-3-030-42504-3_26., 2020.
7. A. Panigrahi, B. Sahu, S. S. Panigrahi, M. S. Khan, and A. K. Jena, "Application of blockchain as a solution to real-world issues in the healthcare system," in *Blockchain Technology: Applications and Challenges*. Cham, Switzerland: Springer, 2021, pp. 135–149, doi: 10.1007/978-3-030-69395-4 8.
8. Z. Yang, Y. Shi, Y. Zhou, Z. Wang and K. Yang, "Trustworthy Federated Learning via Blockchain," in *IEEE Internet of Things Journal*, vol. 10, no. 1, pp. 92–109, 1 Jan.1, 2023, doi: 10.1109/JIOT.2022.3201117.
9. S. Bowe, J. Grigg, and D. Hopwood, "Halo: Recursive proof composition without a trusted setup," *IACR Cryptol. ePrint Arch.*, 2019. [Online]. Available: https://eprint.iacr.org/2019/1021
10. A. Panigrahi, A. Pati, B. Sahu, G. Sahoo, D. Singh, and M. Dash, "AS-Block: An agricultural supply chain management system using blockchaintechnology," *Procedia Comput. Sci.*, vol. 235, pp. 1943–1952, 2024, doi: 10.1016/j.procs.2024.06.226.
11. A. Panigrahi, A. Pati, B. Sahu, B. B. Dash, S. Chowdhury, and S. S. Patra, "Cluster-driven CA selection space optimization in blockchain with PoA for trust calculation," in *2024 International Conference on IoT Based Control Networks and Intelligent Systems (ICICNIS)*, 2024, pp. 251–256, https://doi.org/10.1109/ICICNIS64247.2024.10823131.
12. Z. Zheng, S. Xie, H. Dai, X. Chen, and H. Wang, "An overview of blockchain technology: Architecture, consensus, and future trends," in *Proc. 2017 IEEE International Congress on Big Data (BigData Congress)*, 2017, pp. 557–564, doi: 10.1109/BigDataCongress.2017.85.
13. R. Kumar *et al.*, "Privacy-preserving blockchain-based federated learning for brain tumor segmentation," *Comput. Biol. Med.*, vol. 177, p. 108646, 2024, doi: 10.1016/j.compbiomed.2024.108646.
14. C. Feng, K. Yu, M. Aloqaily, M. Alazab, Z. Lv, and S. Mumtaz, "Attribute-based encryption with parallel outsourced decryption for edge intelligent IoV," *IEEE Trans. Veh. Technol.*, vol. 69, no. 11, pp. 13784–13795, 2020, doi: 10.1109/TVT.2020.3027568.
15. M. Ramachandran, "AI and Blockchain Integration for Cybersecurity," *Texts in Computer Science*, pp. 23–51, 2026, doi: 10.1007/978-3-032-25874-8_2.
16. X. Sun, F. R. Yu, P. Zhang, Z. Sun, W. Xie and X. Peng, "A Survey on Zero-Knowledge Proof in Blockchain," in *IEEE Network*, vol. 35, no. 4, pp. 198–205, July/August 2021, doi: 10.1109/MNET.011.2000473.
17. Y. Qu, M. P. Uddin, C. Gan, Y. Xiang, L. Gao, and J. Yearwood, "Blockchain-Enabled Federated Learning: A Survey," *ACM Computing Surveys*, Mar. 2022, doi: https://doi.org/10.1145/3524104.
18. D. Priyadarshana, T. R. Rao, and M. S. Rao, "AI and blockchain technology for secure and transparent financial transactions," *Int. J. Sci. Res. Arch.*, vol. 13, no. 1, pp. 2013–2019, 2024, doi: 10.30574/ijsra.2024.13.1.1845.
19. S. Nakamoto, "Bitcoin: A peer-to-peer electronic cash system," 2008. [Online]. Available: https://bitcoin.org/bitcoin.pdf

20. V. Buterin, "Ethereum: A next-generation smart contract and decentralized application platform," 2014. [Online]. Available: https://ethereum.org/whitepaper/
21. G. Wood, "Ethereum: A secure decentralisedgeneralised transaction ledger," *Ethereum Proj. Yellow Pap.*, vol. 151, pp. 1–32, 2014.
22. E. Fabrici, B. Bilalli, J. L. Berral García, and M. Garofalakis, "Privacy-Preserving Blockchain-Based Federated Learning," *Data Engineering for Data Science*, pp. 195–214, 2026, doi: https://doi.org/10.1007/978-3-032-18765-9_8.
23. A. Panigrahi, "DTPKI: A Dynamic Trust Weighted Blockchain-based PKI," *2026 1st International Conference on Emerging Trends in Advancements and Applications of Computational Intelligence Techniques (ETAACT)*, Bhubaneswar, India, 2026, pp. 1–6, doi: 10.1109/ETAACT69135.2026.11542201.
24. R. Kumar, S. Gupta and A. Ali, "Blockchain-Enabled Federated Learning Framework for Individual Healthcare Data Sharing," *2026 13th International Conference on Computing for Sustainable Global Development (INDIACom)*, New Delhi, India, 2026, pp. 1–7, doi: 10.23919/INDIACom70271.2026.11526609.
25. S. Goldwasser, S. Micali, and C. Rackoff, "The knowledge complexity of interactive proof systems," *SIAM J. Comput.*, vol. 18, no. 1, pp. 186–208, 1989, doi: 10.1137/0218012.
26. M. A. Al-Shareeda, et. al, "ZKCP: Zero-knowledge-based credential protection protocol for mitigating insider attacks in internet of drones." *AIP Conf. Proc.* 28 April 2026; 3460 (1): 050052. https://doi.org/10.1063/5.0328132
27. E. Ben-Sasson *et al.*, "Zerocash: Decentralized anonymous payments from bitcoin," in *Proc. 2014 IEEE Symposium on Security and Privacy*, 2014, pp. 459–474, doi: 10.1109/SP.2014.36.
28. A. Nainwal, A. Kamble, and N, Awathare, "SoK: Zero-Knowledge Proof Systems — An Empirical and Theoretical Comparison of SNARKs and STARKs," In Companion Proceedings of the ACM Web Conference 2026 (WWW Companion '26). Association for Computing Machinery, New York, NY, USA, 1541–1550. https://doi.org/10.1145/3774905.3794701.
29. A. Gabizon, Z. J. Williamson, and O. Ciobotaru, "PLONK: Permutations over Lagrange-bases for oecumenical noninteractive arguments of knowledge," *IACR Cryptol. ePrint Arch.*, 2019. [Online]. Available: https://eprint.iacr.org/2019/953
30. D. Martinez, L. Magdalena, and A. N. Savitri, "AI and blockchain integration: Enhancing security and transparency in financial transactions," *J. Innovative Technol. Appl. Inform.*, vol. 3, no. 1, pp. 45–58, 2024, doi: 10.33050/italic.v3i1.651.
31. A. Panigrahi, A. Parida, A. Pati, B. Sahu, J. Mishra, and S. R. Addula, "TrustRank-PKI: A Blockchain-Based PKI Using Adaptive Trust-Aware Consensus for Identity and Certificate Management," *Lecture Notes in Electrical Engineering*, pp. 225–236, 2026, doi: 10.1007/978-3-032-20318-2_21.
32. U. K. Maurya, L. S and K. V. Kumar, "Decentralized Identity Verification using Zero-Knowledge Proofs: A Privacy-Preserving Authentication Framework," *2025 2nd International Conference on Artificial Intelligence and Knowledge Discovery in Concurrent Engineering (ICECONF)*, Chennai, India, 2025, pp. 1–8, doi: 10.1109/ICECONF65644.2025.11379610.
33. M. M. Karim, D. H. Van, S. Khan, Q. Qu, and Y. Kholodov, "AI Agents Meet Blockchain: A Survey on Secure and Scalable Collaboration for Multi-Agents," *Future Internet*, vol. 17, no. 2, p. 57, Feb. 2025, doi: https://doi.org/10.3390/fi17020057.
34. Sameera K.M *et al.*, "Privacy-preserving in Blockchain-based Federated Learning systems," *Computer communications*, vol. 222, pp. 38–67, Jun. 2024, doi: https://doi.org/10.1016/j.comcom.2024.04.024.
35. M. Rangwala, K. R. Venugopal, and R. Buyya, "Blockchain-enabled federated learning," *Federated Learning*, pp. 219–240, 2026, doi: https://doi.org/10.1016/b978-0-44-344433-3.00018-6. 2021.

6 Enhancing UPI Security with AI

An Ensemble-Based Fraud Detection Model

Naga Bhavani Chakka, Shaiku Shahida Saheb, and Teklu Kassu

6.1 INTRODUCTION

6.1.1 Background of UPI: Growth, Adoption, and Innovation

The Unified Payment Interface (UPI), originally curated in India, is gaining global momentum as a low-cost and dependable modality of digital payment. Several countries are collaborating with the National Payments Corporation of India (NPCI) and International Payments Ltd. (NIPL) to begin using UPI as part of their payment network. UPI is now linked with Singapore's Pay Now service, allowing individuals in India or Singapore to settle cross-border payments using only their phone numbers [1]. In the United Arab Emirates (UAE), notable companies like Mashreq Bank have collaborated to enable UPI-based BG (bank-generated) QR code payments for customers who can use it both in-store and using another transaction method where more than one owner is identified (the customers); in essence, the UPI payments system was made available for both Indian and UAE visitors. Nations like Bhutan have also been leaders in the global footprint of UPI by being the first nation to use UPI nationally as a formal enactment of adoption throughout their business networks to financially bolster bilateral payment infrastructure to create economic exchange to support the travel and leisure payments nationwide [2].

NIPL's partnership with the French payment processor, Lyra, allows Indian travellers to France to transact directly with UPI at retail sites in Euros. Similarly, Nepal has partnered with NIPL and its own digital payments agency, Gateway Payments Service Pvt. Ltd., to accept UPI as its national digital payment platform [3].

These global applications show growing interest in UPI, and we anticipate further interest from both developed and developing nations as they consider how to implement scalability, low cost, and instantaneous transaction capabilities of UPI for their own national payment systems.

The Unified Payments Interface (UPI) was developed by the NPCI and was launched in India's fintech space in April 2016. UPI is one of the cutting-edge

DOI: 10.1201/9781003658597-6

solutions in India. UPI is a product of the Reserve Bank of India (RBI) and the Indian Banks' Association (IBA) and was meant to enable seamless fund transfer with mobile apps. Payments via UPI may be done using a virtual payment address (VPA) so that users can access and easily engage in digital payments without sharing personal information such as account number and IFSC code [4].

India's demonetization effort at the end of 2016 caused a large shift to digital payments that greatly fueled the original establishment of UPI. Bringing the BHIM app online in 2017 and then providing UPI functionality to third-party platforms such as Google Pay (Tez), PhonePe, Paytm, and Amazon Pay in 2018 and 2019 accelerated the uptake of UPI payments. The architecture of UPI facilitates peer-to-peer (P2P) and peer-to-merchant (P2M) transactions and is appropriately scalable and inclusive, making use of open architecture and interoperability [5].

As is evident with the original definition of UPI, UPI has evolved since it was first rolled out, having introduced cross-border transaction capability, low-value offline payments, auto payments for recurring transactions, UPI 123PAY for feature phone users, and a host of other features to enable millions of individuals from rural and semi-urban areas with minimal infrastructure to access digital financial services, thereby accelerating India's transition to a paperless economy while also encouraging the inclusion of financial services. With its pace of innovation and expansion, UPI still forms the backbone of India's digital economy and the global standard for real-time payments [6].

Andhra Pradesh is a national frontrunner in digital payment innovations and new models, i.e., the Unified Payments Interface (UPI). In the most recent release of 2022 data from the NPCI, the state of Andhra Pradesh adopted 17.6 digital transactions, while the national average was 3.85. Beyond digital payments and transactions, the state is progressive in its path toward financial inclusion. In 2021, the state claimed 99% compliance with Aadhaar-based payment systems (ABPS) with registered and active states. The state also took large-scale rural digitization steps by advancing UPI-enabled services and partnering with NPCI and Canara Bank to promote digital inclusion in 15,004 village and ward secretariats, which would deploy digital assistants to promote digital literacy.

In 2023, UPI was further infused into tax payments and collection efforts at all 15 interstate border checkpoints to improve revenue collection processes. The state government's attitude toward technology is further indicative in the state's launch of its flagship program "Fintech Valley Vizag" for innovations based on financial technologies, cybersecurity, and blockchain. Furthermore, the state is well-positioned for further evolution, leveraging technology with a focus on inclusive governance and development, and the state of Andhra Pradesh was ranked 8th in India's Innovation Index (2020).

The Unified Payments Interface (UPI) represents a new frontier in a platform for any economic transaction [7]. UPI is a public service that began as a pilot in April 2016 with 21 banks in collaboration with the NPCI, which launched a public-facing application in August of the same year, coinciding with India's demonetization movement…, which heightened demand around digital payment transaction solutions [8].

UPI included many innovative features, including the VPA, which allows for real-time money transfers with the added benefits of not having to disclose sensitive information such as the account number or IFSC code [9]. In 2017, the uptake and use of the QR code scanners and the adoption by the market of a one-click two-factor authentication (2FA) made the transaction integration well-designed essentially to improve and facilitate the transaction to the end user who typically resides in urban areas and was primarily used by small business owners [10]. UPI captured a variety of transaction types, including scheduled requests to make payments, e-commerce payments, and P2P transactions [11]. The characteristics of customer uptake around UPI were the ease of use, security capabilities, and the potential for well-integrated and displacing already in use online payment mechanisms [12].

6.1.2 Three Main Periods to Examine UPI's Growth

The increase in smartphone penetration, the initial engagement of the government, and the association of banks and third-party apps resulted in exponential growth of UPI [13]. Acceleration Phase (2018–2021): The growth of fintech companies like Paytm, PhonePe, and Google Pay brought in a roughly 4.7-fold increase in UPI transaction volumes. Customers' preference for contactless digital payments was further influenced by the COVID-19 Epidemic [14]. Maturity Phase (2021–2025): UPI attained a previously unheard-of magnitude. In FY 2023–2024, transaction values were close to ₹200 trillion, up from ₹84,176 billion in FY 2021–2022. Innovations such as cross-border UPI integrations, UPI AutoPay, and UPI 123PAY for feature phones have greatly aided in its broad adoption [15].

6.1.3 UPI's Significance in India's Digital Economy

A key component of India's digital economy is UPI. By making low-cost, real-time transactions possible for both urban and rural communities, it has democratized financial access. It is a potent instrument for promoting financial 1.1 inclusions because of its interoperability, low infrastructure needs, and simplicity of use [12]. By decreasing reliance on cash, cutting transaction costs, and enhancing transparency in financial transactions, UPI helps the Government of India's "Digital India" effort [11]. By offering small business owners and independent contractors a user-friendly digital payment alternative, the system has also given them more control [8].

Beyond its domestic importance, UPI is becoming more well-known outside. With trial cross-border projects with nations including Singapore, Bhutan, and the UAE, it is being positioned as a baseline digital payment mechanism [15]. Its technical resilience, scalability, and affordability are establishing new benchmarks for real-time payment systems worldwide.

6.1.4 Increased Fraud in Digital Payments, Particularly in UPI/Growth Trend in UPI Frauds

Notwithstanding its revolutionary effects, UPI's expanding use has also led to many new problems, the most significant of which is digital payment fraud. The opportunities for exploitation increase in tandem with consumption. From simple phishing attempts to sophisticated strategies incorporating phony applications, QR code frauds, KYC fraud, and OTP bypassing methods, fraudulent activities have changed over time [12]. An astounding 346% surge in UPI-related fraud has occurred in the last two years, according to joint research conducted by Ernst & Young (EY) and Assocham [16]. The seriousness of the issue is shown by the Finance Ministry statistics that were provided to the Lok Sabha on November 26, 2024.

UPI domestic frauds report [17] illustrates 7.25 lakh fraud instances and ₹573 crore in losses were reported in FY 2022–2023. A total of 13.42 lakh fraud instances and ₹1,087 crore in losses were reported in FY 2023–2024. A total of 6.32 lakh fraud instances and ₹485 crore in financial damages were reported for FY 2024–2025 (till September 2024) [18]. These increasing figures show the limitations of current rule-based detection methods as well as the complexity of fraud tactics. Conventional methods, which depend on static thresholds and 2FA, frequently generate large false-positive rates (FPRs) and are unable to identify changing threats [19].

6.1.5 The Chapter's Scope, Goals, and Contributions

This chapter presents a fraud detection system in the UPI ecosystem where artificial intelligence (AI), specifically machine learning (ML), is used to address the severe challenges of fraud in the UPI ecosystem. The limitations of the existing static, rule-based frameworks have created an urgent need for real-time, behavior-aware, and scalable solutions [20].

a. *Scope:* The Unified Payments Interface (UPI) is leading the evolution of digital payments in India and enabling new economic opportunities for millions of people through fast and instant digital payments [3]. As UPI continues to grow rapidly, it has established various challenges and vulnerabilities, including low security protocols and low fraud resistance, among others. As volumes increase, fraud in digital payment systems is becoming much more complex, specifically with UPI. Commonly adopted tactics of fraudsters include phishing, fraudulent QR codes, fraudulent applications, and socially engineered attacks. To mitigate these threats, ML has been established to protect UPI transactions in real time by identifying suspicious or abnormal patterns of extractions and identifying modified fraud tactics [13].
b. *Goals:* The goals of this research are to identify the flaws of traditional UPI fraud detection systems [19], build an AI-based framework to identify patterns of fraud, and assess the performance of each Extreme Gradient Boosting (XGBoost), Random Forest, Support Vector Machine (SVM), and Logistic Regression algorithm. An ensemble with a soft voting process will be used to increase accuracy and reduce false positives [20].
c. *Contributions:* This research provides an integrated empirical study of security and growth issues related to UPI [21], provides a practical ensemble learning algorithm [20] for prevention of fraud, and provides evidence of using AI to secure UPI-related transactions, along with specific actionable advice for developers, policymakers, and financial institutions [22].

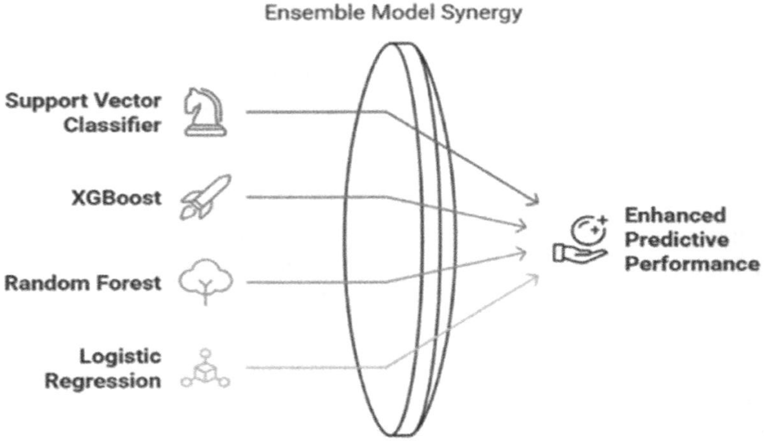

FIGURE 6.1 Standard ensemble learning model.

Concerning the security of fraudulent transactions, the research model leveraged an ensemble of models, contributed by multiple models, to produce no false positives. Support Vector Classifier (SVC) model plus XGBoost, Random Forest, and Logistic Regression showed how you can build a reliable and operational fraud detection system using other learning algorithms. This was done with the various models used, which and made significant improvements in performance for fraud detection and efficiency improvements for organizations carrying out digital financial transactions, as each day changes, along with the threats to technology. The framework is summarized in Figure 6.1, a standard ensemble learning model.

6.2 LITERATURE REVIEW

Digital commerce has fundamentally changed in India because of the Unified Payments Interface (UPI), which enables fast money transactions between bank accounts via mobile devices. As UPI's popularity and convenience have grown, so too have the quantity and complexity of related fraudulent operations. Through a variety of tactics, cybercriminals take advantage of users by using phishing URLs, social engineering, phony programs, QR manipulation, and technological flaws. The main categories of UPI scams, their techniques, and their effects are outlined in detail below.

6.2.1 UPI Auto Pay Fraud

Increasingly common is a form of fraud where fraudsters take advantage of the "AutoPay" and "collect money" features. One or more scammers send repeated requests for payment. The requests may look legitimate to users and may be presented as either outstanding amounts due or as incentive redemption. By leveraging users' time sensitivity, they can gain access to the users' funds and exploit the situation. When a user completes a fraudulent AutoPay payment request, the funds may present as a large one-time transfer to the scammer's account, or the AutoPay could set up recurring deductions.

Victims are contacted via phishing emails and texts that have links to malicious phishing sites. The phishing site may request sensitive information, change a password, or verify their account. These methods, including claims for winning prizes, may allow the fraudster to enable AutoPay and access funds through the AutoPay Account payout. This type of fraud can be mitigated either by better confirming the bona fides of transactions or by greater user awareness. UPI changed the digital payment space by offering fast payments and an efficient user experience. With the increase in use, UPI fraud cases and types have also increased, and some fraud cases come in the form of phishing or social engineering attacks, with users inadvertently granting access to their funds. Researchers have analyzed UPI fraud cases through multiple ML and deep learning (DL) methods with the potential to reduce UPI fraud attack surface today [23].

6.2.2 Fake UPI Application

The number of phishing applications impersonating UPI has increased drastically. Criminals are replicating popular digital payment systems such as Paytm, PhonePe, and Google Pay, and looking to capitalize financially. These phishing applications have user interfaces that simulate reliable UPI apps but may be embedded with malware or designed to capture sensitive information such as OTPs and UPI PINs [24]. In addition, upon installation, the app may seek to capture banking information or transfer money from users to the criminals.

This is further complicated by the fact that these phishing applications are often distributed by unregulated app stores and social media. Research shows that social engineering and breaking down multiple avenues will help to deter these types of scams, such as 2FA, creating real-time fraud detection tools such as AI ML and behavioral analytics, and increasing public education to only download apps from reputable sources [25].

6.2.3 Phishing Fraud

Phishing is one of the most common and dangerous types of cybercrime used in the UPI ecosystem. Phishing utilizes deceptive channels that request sensitive user information such as bank account numbers, UPI PINs, and MPINs. Scammers impersonate bank officials or other trusted sources to obtain sensitive user information through fake SMS messages, emails, or phone calls, which ask the user to perform an urgent action such as processing a refund or updating KYC details [26]. These phishing attempts typically include shortened URLs or fake domains very similar to real ones when attempting to reach users.

Once one enters their personal information into the spoofed website, scammers gain unauthorized access and commence legitimate fraud. Phishing utilizes deceptive conditioning and user behavior; therefore, strong email and SMS filters, public awareness campaigns, Secure Sockets Layer (SSL) certificates indicating secure websites, and multifactor authentication (MFA) all require active, multi-faceted defenses. Phishing campaigns are heavily dependent on psychological manipulation, making user education another robust line of defense [27].

6.2.4 QR Code Manipulation

Since many UPI payments now rely on QR codes, fraudsters have resorted to manipulating them to get illegal profits. Fraudsters create phony QR codes or slightly alter authentic ones (for example, altering account information) and submit them online or in public areas. Swapping out the merchant's QR code with one connected to the scammer's account is a popular tactic. By scanning such QR codes, victims unintentionally provide money to the scammer rather than the intended receiver [28]. Users may be sent to phishing websites via QR codes that are supplied to them via email or text message. Verifying QR codes, putting safe digital identification systems in place, and raising consumer and merchant awareness are all crucial to preventing these scams [29].

6.2.5 Lottery Winning Related Fraud

Lottery scammers use fake lottery scams that involve prizes that offer huge financial rewards and take advantage of people's curiosity and greed. Individuals receive notifications informing them that they have won a prize or lottery. One of the requests made is that to collect the amount, the individual must give their UPI ID. Furthermore, the user has to pay a processing charge. Following compliance, the personal details of the user are presumably used for future scams, or the money is taken in a fraud. Scams will often include a time-sensitive offer or emotional appeal to pressure the victim further. Combining fraud detection mechanisms, such as transaction clustering, anomaly detection, and behavioral analysis, could help identify such trends early, research suggests. It is important to warn users not to give away their personal information and verify such claims with authorities [30].

6.2.6 Subscription Fraud

As AutoPay alternatives become increasingly popular for routine payments like Over-the-Top (OTT) subscriptions, energy bills, and service renewals, scammers have developed methods to take advantage of this. Deceptive subscription texts are being sent to end users, indicating that their membership is about to expire, and to renew it, they need to click on a link. Such links often direct you to a fraudulent website, which steals your payment information or activates illegal deductions. Users may unintentionally set up recurring payments to accounts controlled by fraudsters [31]. Truly speaking, to identify irregularities and questionable patterns with respect, we argue for the use of Artificial Neural Networks (ANNs) and Hybrid Models, especially with Self-Organizing Map (SOM), K-Means, and classifiers like SVM. No one should enter payment details on an untrustworthy website; check the URL [32].

6.2.7 KYC Fraud

Scammers impersonating bank agents use a social engineering scam, KYC fraud, to threaten the account holder to deactivate their account if KYC is not updated. PAN cards, account numbers, Aadhaar numbers, or OTPs are sent to victims through links via SMS (smishing) or phone calls (vishing). After stealing your information, scammers may engage in identity theft, create fake accounts, or conduct fraud. Fraudsters give a credible look to KYC messages by imitating official style. ML-based fraud detection frameworks use transaction history, consumer behavior, and KYC to create risk profiles and detect fraudulent efforts. With prompt user reporting and timely notice to the bank of frauds of this ilk, they may be stopped from getting worse [33].

6.2.8 Spoofing and Message Manipulation

Moreover, scammers use counterfeit messages that appear to originate from genuine banks or UPI apps. Usually, these emails make false claims of unintentional deposits and request instant reimbursement. Often, the scammer never makes any deposits, but the urgent situation and fake branding make the victim easily send money. This type of fraud exploits the ignorance and trust of people. Risk can be reduced using real-time fraud detection systems, awareness, and proper verification before taking any actions [12].

Fraud detection utilizing ML has been effective for UPI transactions. XGBoost was selected for the fraud detection model for its accuracy in predicting and capability to manage imbalanced data. Through the real-time monitoring of UPI transactions, the system identifies suspicious transactions, sends instant alerts, and takes preventive measures with 98.2% accuracy. In a similar manner, this chapter examined how fraud detection evolved from traditional rules-based systems to ML-based systems. It employed Logistic Regression for fraud prediction and K-means clustering to unveil hidden fraud patterns. Improved accuracy and fewer false positives thanks to big data analytics integration. The author of [34] also pointed out how ML is effective at detecting online fraud. It suggested Logistic Regression, Decision Trees, and Random Forest. In their research, it was also observed that fraud in online payments can be prevented by analyzing data in real-time and other methods.

As fraudsters' techniques have become more sophisticated, DL has emerged as a critical approach in identifying fraudulent activity. The authors in [9] used Recurrent Neural Networks (RNNs) to identify fraudulent patterns for UPI transactions, achieving an 87.5% true positive rate (TPR) and a 13.4% FPR. The authors in [35] studied the use of ANNs and Convolutional Neural Networks (CNNs), which could be used to identify scams, as they can review transaction data in real time. The authors in [13] studied the use of AI-related fraud detection techniques and showed that CNN models produced a high accuracy while reducing false positives. The authors in [36] supported the use of ensemble models, such as Decision Tree, Random Forest, and XGBoost, which prove useful in improving validation for real-time monitoring and decrease false positives. Other than fraud detection, phishing and social engineering attacks become major threats in UPI transactions. The authors in [37] studied the use of AI and ML to avoid phishing attacks, mainly fraudulent QR codes and fake URLs that trick users into providing sensitive information [38]. Researchers examined the effectiveness of phishing scams where fake URLs and QR codes are used, and reviewed how AI, ML, and cryptography help improve fraud detection efficiency.

As per the study, email filtering, SSL, MFA, and user education must be included to reduce financial and reputational losses. In addition, [39] identified vulnerabilities in the security of UPI. Furthermore, problems with phishing, social engineering, and fraud prevention were examined. Moreover, the prevention was analyzed through encryption, MFA, and AI-driven fraud detection. Techniques based on DL, including deep neural networks, CNNs, and RNNs, are also analyzed. They perform better than conventional techniques for detecting fraudulent transactions. However, it faces hurdles like data imbalance and privacy issues [40].

Fraud detection in UPI is similar to that in other areas. According to [41], clustering (SOM, K-means) and classification (SVM, neural networks) data mining methods are effective in detecting fraudulent telecom subscriptions. Another telecom fraud detection study highlights the effectiveness of ANN-based models – in identifying subscription fraud and social engineering attacks. The model achieved a result of 85.7% (Telecommunications Subscription Fraud Detection Using ANNs). Additionally, [42] developed an ML-based risk assessment tool that integrates KYC data to identify fraudulent behavior and suspicious transactions at bank branches, further enhancing financial security.

This research work analyzes ML techniques to detect UPI fraud. The Random Forest algorithm performs best among others. The text highlights how adaptive models, real-time monitoring, and ensemble learning can enhance detection accuracy. The research shows how feature engineering can reduce down false positives and improve the security of online payments.

As fraud methods get smarter and ever-evolving, the goal of protecting digital transactions must be done in layers. Fraud technologies are akin to digital transactions and have actually allowed those who want to conduct fraudulent transactions to do so. Many ML models, such as XGBoost, Logistic Regression, and Random Forest, can detect fraud. DL, such as RNNs, CNNs, and ANNs, can be quite accurate in detecting fraud. Along with fraud detection technology, MFA, along with educating users through user awareness campaigns, will minimize fraud opportunities. Digital payments are going forward, and as our digital economy is moving ahead, researching fraud detection leveraging AI is necessary. Research can be used as a vessel to examine new possibilities for enhancing security over financial transactions, to sustain our digital economy.

6.3 METHODOLOGY

6.3.1 Data Gathering and Preprocessing

The data used contains both fake and actual UPI transactions from Kaggle. The goal was to develop and iteratively test a specific fraud detection model applicable in the real world; but due to the sensitivity of financial data and its complexity, a standard preprocessing procedure was needed to achieve the accuracy. The rows with missing (NaN) values were dropped so the model would not be affected while it was processing or predicting poorly.

The feature selection analysis determined that transaction types 2 and 4 from the dataset appear to be the transaction types most closely associated with any fraud.

As a result, noise was removed from the dataset, and the modeling was further narrowed down to important transaction types for fraud. Features that are categorical were changed into numeric features through label encoding to help the algorithms find and take advantage of patterns in relational measures such as transaction type.

The eventual coverage of features, type, amount, oldbalanceOrg, newbalanceOrig, oldbalanceDest, and newbalanceDest, provided holistic transaction coverage. This is a coverage of type-pair transactions. The operational patterns of fraud will become differentiated categories of fraud in time. Transaction typologies include TRANSFER and CASH OUT. Amounts include suspicious amounts starting from small probe transfers to large account withdrawal transactions. The balance contains features that range from small investigation probe transfers to blanket transfer of big withdrawal from bank's account transaction.

By combining the selected attributes, the ensemble classifier achieved significant contextual knowledge, thus enabling it to correctly classify between false and true activity, paving the way toward its valid deployment in offline and online payment environments.

6.3.2 Model Development

We build a robust and scalable UPI fraud detector using ensemble learning. Four fundamental models XGBoost, Random Forest, SVM, and Logistic regression are integrated using soft coating. Each model has complementary strengths: SVM elegantly captures high-dimensional decision boundaries, Random Forest is robust and lessens variance, XGBoost minimizes residual errors via boosting, and Logistic regression is a simple interpretable baseline. Class probabilities calibrated with soft voting average helps control false positives without much impact on recall. The proposed model framework is shown in Figure 6.2.

This design addresses evolving fraud patterns more effectively than any single classifier. It is also practical for deployment; base learners can be trained in parallel, periodically refreshed, and served behind a lightweight probability aggregator for real-time scoring.

6.3.3 Classification Algorithms

6.3.3.1 Classification

Classification entails splitting a dataset into more than one group based on similarities in characteristics. It is a kind of supervised learning that includes data from at least two classes based on the defined target variable. The current research deals with binary classification, with 1 representing infected and 0 representing uninfected. Therefore, if the estimated probability ($\hat{\pi}$) of a potential outcome is <0.5, the predicted value is 0, and if $\hat{\pi}$ is >0.5, then the predicted value is 1 [43].

i. *Logistic Regression:* One kind of supervised ML model is Logistic Regression, which can predict a binary (dichotomous) outcome and help identify fraud in Unified Payments Interface (UPI) transactions. These

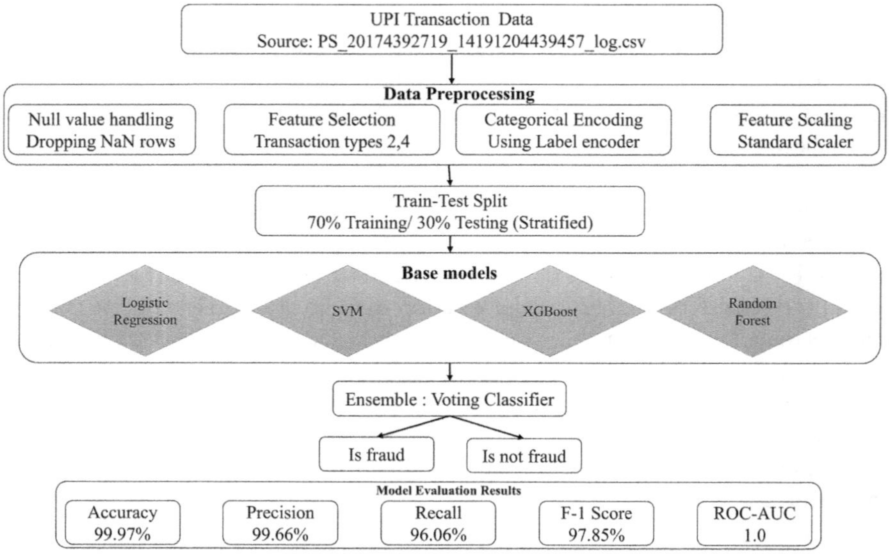

FIGURE 6.2 Ensemble learning-based fraud detection framework for UPI transactions.

transaction features may include transaction amount, frequency of daily transactions, deviations in devices or locations used to transact, and times during the day when the transaction occurs, which are then classified using the sigmoid function and the probability of fraud. Logistic Regression is easy to understand, quick, and straightforward, and it can be beneficial in UPI fraud detection because it doesn't use complicated processes – given that the high cost of processing UPI payment transactions means that useful measures are needed to deter and detect UPI fraud, particularly because they can be part of hundreds of small-value purchases. echo the idea that Logistic Regression can be a strong baseline for UPI fraud detection, particularly when used as part of ensembles and wherever there is the opportunity for feature engineering and guidance of conclusions to improve the efficacy of predictions [44].

ii. *Support Vector Machine:* SVMs are advanced supervised ML models that are very popular for classification purposes and thus are a helpful model in fraud detection. SVMs, using kernel functions, can handle both linear and non-linear data and can expose an optimal hyperplane that separates the fraudulent transactions from the legitimate ones [45]. In UPI fraud detection, SVMs can detect very subtle behavior changes in the transaction, such as the amount, location, or frequency, in terms of spikes in the dollar value. SVMs generalize well for datasets or data schemas that have a high number of dimensions or the data is greatly imbalanced, thus benefiting from the non-linear mapping to detect rare cases of fraud. They have shown strong overall performance in financial fraud detection and have been even more successful when combined with data bias correction approaches [46].

iii. *XGBoost:* XGBoost is an advanced ensemble ML algorithm that builds one decision tree after the other and improves the accuracy of each tree by correcting the mistakes of previous trees. XGBoost is an excellent option for convoluted classification problems like fraud detection in a Unified Payments Interface (UPI) system. XGBoost aims for accuracy, can run very fast and is scalable, allows for regularization to avoid overfitting, and can work with missing values. For UPI fraud detection, XGBoost can detect if a transaction shows unusual or atypical behavior or patterns in the transaction, either in transaction amounts, transaction counts, or sudden changes in either the user profile or device profile. Therefore, XGBoost is an ideal candidate for identifying infrequent post-fraudulent activities within spontaneous real-time payment environments. Furthermore, XGBoost holistically merges the supervised and unsupervised aspects of learning better than any of the traditional models by explicitly considering apparent commonalities and simultaneous faults [47].

iv. *Random Forest:* The Random Forest algorithm is a supervised ensemble learning method made of many different decision trees created from a random number of features and a random number of data points. After we have the decision trees, the Random Forest model averages the outputs of the trees, improving overall classification and reducing overfitting. Random Forest is a robust method to indicate fraud within Unified Payments Interface (UPI) data, as it can address some of the issues related to UPI data caused by their size, high dimensionality, and imbalanced classes. Random Forest provides a rich feature assessment in transactional data for specific features such as transaction amount, age of transaction, frequency of transaction, device change, and IP address change, and other features. Random Forest provides the advantage of not requiring any assumptions and is robust to noise and outliers and works quite well with data imbalance classes. Random Forest also indicates feature importance so that analysts can interpret their findings and determine what hot spots are most associated with fraudulent behavior [48].

6.3.4 Train-Test Data Splitting

The data set was divided into 70% and 30%, respectively, for the train and test subsets using stratified sampling. Stratified sampling is used in this context to ensure the training and test subsets are represented equally. It guarantees that the sample proportions of fraudulent and legitimate transactions in each subset match the original dataset. For this scenario, stratified sampling is particularly important because fraud (if it occurs) is typically considerably rarer than fraud. Getting the class distribution correct with stratified sampling does not allow the model to bias toward the majority class, which improves the model's chance to distinguish fraudulent versus legitimate transactions.

Accuracy means the proportion of transactions that are identified correctly, irrespective of whether the transaction is a fraud or a legitimate transaction. However, it is important to know the false sense of security provided by accuracy when it is used for measuring fraud detection, particularly when the distributions are heavily imbalanced. It has been stated, "the evaluation should comprise more parameters such as precision, recall, and F1 score for a proper evaluation of the model." As indicated in Equation (6.1), accuracy is the proportion of the number of correctly identified transactions (true positives and true negatives) to the total number of transactions, which includes false positives and false negatives.

$$\text{Accuracy} = \frac{TP + TN}{TP + TN + FP + FN} \tag{6.1}$$

Precision is an important metric to analyze the performance of anomaly detection methods, particularly in the case of fraud detection, where false positives have a heavy consequence. Precision measures the ratio of fraudulent transactions that were considered fraud among those predicted to be fraud by the model. The high precision suggests that the model can detect cases of actual fraud with very few false positives, yet if the model catches very little of the "actual frauds," a high precision will be of less value. As an example, in Equation (6.2), precision is defined as true positives to the total number of predicted positives, which is true positives plus false positives.

$$\text{Precision} = \frac{TP}{TP + FP} \tag{6.2}$$

Recall, or sensitivity, represents the percentage of true fraud transactions that the model can identify. Recall is vital for fraud detection. When one does not detect fraud, the damages could be severe. At the same time, a focus on recall could lead to false positives, and the volume of alerts sent to financial institutions should also not be excessive, so one must determine the perfect balance between recall and precision to ensure that fraud is not missed while at the same time minimizing false alerts. As can be seen in Equation (6.3), recall is determined by the ratio of true positives to total actual positives, which includes true positives and false negatives as well.

$$\text{Recall} = \frac{TP}{TP + FP} \tag{6.3}$$

The F1-score is a balanced evaluation metric, as well as the circumstances in which false positives and false negatives are significant. The harmonic mean of accuracy and recall is the F1-score. The most crucial parameter is the F1-score when it is important to detect fraud accurately and have as few false alerts. The F1-score is popular for fraud detection reasons because it considers both precision and recall in the evaluation metric; thus, it provides a more comprehensive and reliable evaluation of how a model performed. As described in Equation (6.4), the F1-score combines both precision and recall into a single performance metric and is calculated as two times precision times recall divided by the sum of precision and recall.

$$\text{F1-score} = 2.\frac{Precision.Recall}{Precision + Recall} \tag{6.4}$$

6.3.4.1 ROC Curve and AUC (Area Under Curve)

The Receiver Operating Characteristic (ROC) Curve is used to display the TPR (recall) against the FPR. In Equation (6.5), the FPR is defined as the false positives divided by the total of false positives and true negatives. Similarly, TPR is recall, the true positives divided by the sum of true positives and false negatives.

$$FPR = \frac{FP}{FP + TN} \quad TPR = Recall = \frac{TP}{TP + FN} \tag{6.5}$$

AUC is a single scalar value summarizing the ROC curve. As indicated in Equation (6.6), it is defined by integrating the TPR with respect to the FPR over the interval [0,1].

$$\int_0^1 TPR(FPR)\,d(FPR) \tag{6.6}$$

6.3.4.2 Feature Scaling (Standardization)

Before training models like Logistic Regression and SVM, the data is standardized. The standardization process described in Equation (6.7) involves converting each value of a feature into a standardized value (z) by subtracting the mean (μ) and dividing by the standard deviation (σ).

$$z = \frac{x - \mu}{\sigma} \tag{6.7}$$

6.3.4.3 Ensemble Model (Soft Voting Classifier)

Soft voting averages the predicted class probabilities from multiple models and chooses the class with the highest average probability. Equation (6.8) defines the predicted class as the class with the maximum average probability obtained by weighting with respect to the predicted probabilities of all models.

$$y\,\hat{}= argjmax\left(\sum_{i=1}^{n} wi \cdot Pi(y = j)\right) \tag{6.8}$$

$Pi(y = j)$ is the predicted probability of class j from model i
wi is the weight of model I (default is 1 if not specified)

6.3.5 Comparative Analysis of DP, HE, SMPC, and Hybrid Methods

To properly ascertain the trade-offs of the privacy-preserving approaches, we will formalize, for purposes of brevity, a common equivalence that we may use as the basis for our analysis, ultimately focusing on the strengths, weaknesses, and computational burdens of the approaches. As we have reviewed, each privacy-preserving technique – differential privacy (DP), homomorphic encryption (HE), secure multi-party computation (SMPC), or hybrid approaches – has strengths (or advantages) that further manifest weaknesses that factor into whether they are practical in a real-world system. For example, DP is lightweight but results in some accuracy loss due to the incorporation of noise. HE ensures confidentiality, but it is costly in terms of computation time. SMPC provides privacy given participation from other users, but in essence, it has considerable communication costs as well. A hybrid technique seeks to benefit from each form of privacy-preserving technique, taking into account of weaknesses, but tends to complicate the design.

Table 6.1 summarizes various privacy-protecting methods, their advantages, disadvantages, and computational costs. By presenting the information in a table

TABLE 6.1
Summary Table of Comparing Different Privacy-Preserving Approaches

Technique	Protection Focus	Benefits	Challenges	Computational Cost	UPI-Specific Use Cases
Differential Privacy (DP)	Preserves training data by adding calibrated noise to model updates; mitigates leakages of particulars of individual transactions.	Offers formal privacy guarantees. Low inference burden. Simple integration with central/ federated learning.	Accuracy loss if the privacy budget is too stringent; tuning complexity.	Training: Moderate; Inference: Low	Train a central/ federated model on aggregated PSP or banking transaction logs securely
Homomorphic Encryption (HE)	Maintains transaction properties encrypted throughout server-side computation	Provides end-to-end confidentiality of insights; Provides secure outsourced scoring	High latency; large memory use; limited operation set; key management challenges	Training: High; Inference: High	Remote scoring of sensitive merchant or user features without decryption
Secure Multi-Party Computation (SMPC)	Allows several financial organizations to collaboratively calculate fraud scores but not reveal raw data	Removes need for a trusted party; enables cross – bank fraud collaboration	The communications overhead, complexity of protocol, and coordination	Training: High; Inference: Medium-High	Real-time cross-bank or PSP Consortium fraud detection
Hybrid (DP, HE, SMPC)	It combines complementary techniques for layered security (e.g., DP in training + HE in inference)	Strong end-to-end privacy; resistant to multiple threat vectors	Greatest engineering effort; cumulative computational overhead	Training: **Medium–High**; Inference: **High**	Higher risk or even government or military deployments where maximum privacy is required

format, we are allowing the reader to have a reflective perspective in which they can notice major differences right away and enable themselves to be informed with the selection of a methodology suited to their use case.

6.4 RESULTS AND DISCUSSION

The framework of the Unified Payments Interface (UPI) is a strong fraud detection mechanism with robust capabilities through the ensemble of Random Forest, XGBoost, SVM, and Logistic Regression. Each preliminary model contributes unique benefits: SVM is suitable for high-dimensional data, XGBoost provides greater predictive accuracy through gradient boosting, Random Forest makes ensembles of decision trees, which leads to great stability and robustness, and Logistic Regression is effectively simple and interpretable.

The model also used soft voting to choose outputs across models to enhance accuracy and provide balance across the models in classification. The model was evaluated through the components of accuracy, precision, recall, F1-score, and ROC-AUC. Overall, there was high accuracy, strong recall, and low false positives. This outcome demonstrates both its ability to combat the weaknesses of the individually run classifiers and to increase generalizability. Moreover, the cooperative intelligence paradigm was a practical, stable, and comprehensive means for use as a UPI-based fraud detection method, and graphic documentation of this work is a first step toward creating an active, real-time financial security system in one digital payment option.

6.4.1 Model Evaluation and Performance Metrics

The trained ensemble model is very promising as a solution for fraud detection, since it has demonstrated excellent performance against fraudulent transactions within the Unified Payments Interface (UPI) ecosystem. The model is able to correctly classify nearly all of the transactions, even frauds, with an accuracy of 99.97%, which provides a high level of confidence in real-time financial environments where precision is paramount.

The model also achieved an accuracy score of 99.66% in reducing false positives, which is significant for fraud detection systems since they do not mistakenly flag a legitimate transaction, which robs the user of knowledge. Ultimately, we do not want the user to lose trust in the system and create a horrible transactional experience. The model also had a recall score of 96.09% and was able to discover actual fraudulent transactions, which is critical for curbing financial losses and ensuring that fraudulent activity does not go unnoticed.

The model has an F1-score of 97.85%, showing a perfect compromise between precision and recall rate. The model can deal with imbalanced datasets, an important property for fraud problems. The model's ability to classify transactions as fraudulent or legitimate is also reinforced with a perfect ROC-AUC value of 1.00, indicating that it has perfect discrimination when considering multiple criteria.

We see in Figures 6.3 and 6.4, Performance Metrics of the Fraud Detection Model and the ROC Curve of the Fraud Detection Model, that the model consistently produces reliable and high-performing results, confirming that it is ready for

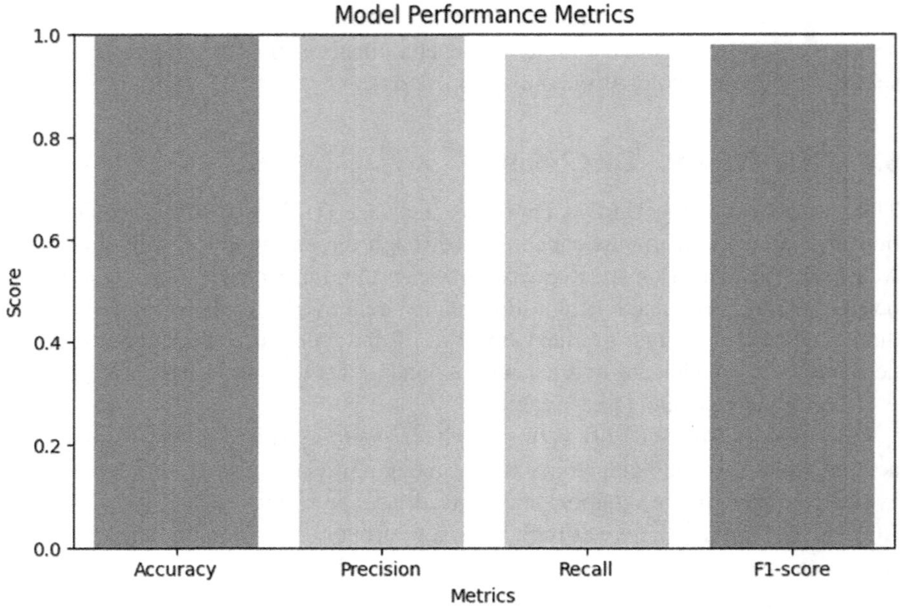

FIGURE 6.3 Performance evaluation of the proposed model.

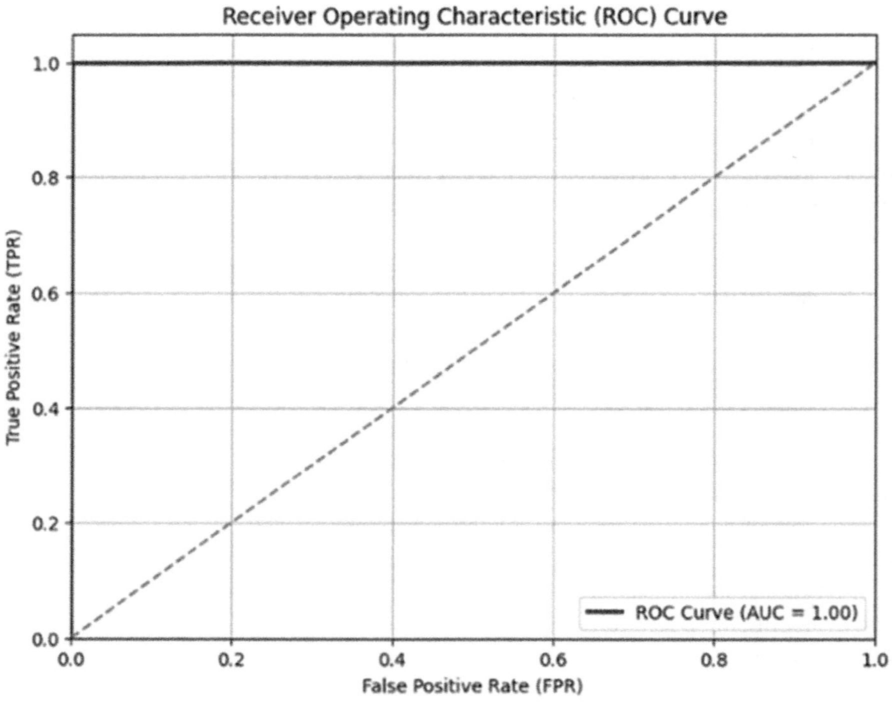

FIGURE 6.4 ROC analysis of the proposed model.

implementation within UPI-based digital payment systems. Its performance metrics make the model an effective, scalable, and stable solution for protecting users and financial institutions against evolving fraud in real-time transactional environments.

6.4.2 Confusion Matrix Analysis

The confusion matrix shows that the model can effectively differentiate between valid and fraudulent UPI transactions. In fact, the model has a high accuracy and strong capability to classify instances of the two classes. The rate of spurious positive results is remarkable. The FPR is low, meaning very few legitimate transactions are misclassified as fraud. It reduces risk and effort for financial firms while minimizing disruption of genuine users.

The model scored strongly on recall, indicating that the CNN has been able to detect a lot of actual fraud cases or instances of fraud. Using these strategies can help avoid losses and prevent the failure of fraud deterrent activities and efforts. The confusion matrix also illustrates the precision-recall trade-off that provides a comparison of performance measures' contrasts and relevance. The confusion matrix gives a strong indication of a model's ability to accurately distinguish between safe and malicious transaction behavior (Figure 6.5).

6.4.3 Visual Representation of Performance Metrics

In the representation of Model Performance Metrics, it is evident that the model is performing well with the help of the heatmap. The heatmap helps visualize recall,

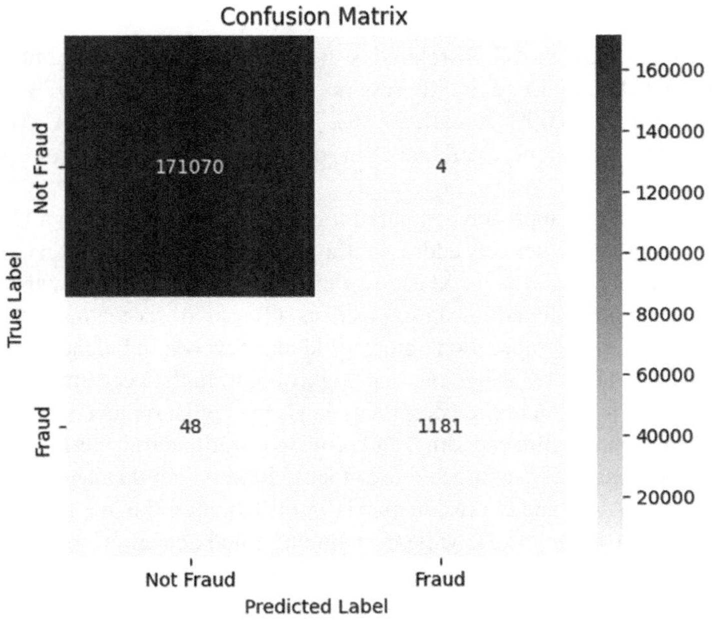

FIGURE 6.5 Confusion matrix analysis.

precision, and F1-score of each label. The model has maintained consistently high recall, precision, and F1-score. This suggests that the classifier can be relied upon to detect fraud in the UPI ecosystem at present. A model with high recall indicates that the model captures most of the true positives. This means that most of the fraudulent cases have been captured. Likewise, high precision means that the classifier has been proven to reduce false positives to a great degree. The F1-score is calculated from precision and recall, classified performance measures. With this metric, we can see that the model has quite a balanced and robust classification performance.

Combined with the heatmap, the performance comparison of the ensemble model shown through a bar chart indicates that the ensemble is better than the individual classifier based on every metric, including accuracy. While the ensemble model is indeed found to be better than each classifier, the researchers establish that each of these classifiers is still good to use in a real-world fraud detection environment. The model confusion matrix offers a more comprehensive description of how the model classified items correctly. In addition, it gives further validation of the supervised learning history established through the model. Besides, it gives further confidence regarding deploying the model in safe digital payment environments.

This study will compare the proposed model with literature in the field to demonstrate the novelty and effectiveness being claimed. This chapter provides a systematic comparison of existing literature, coupled with a comprehensive analysis of the model. We additionally discuss how our speedy computed mechanism contributes to enhanced performance, incorporating a thorough scrutiny of the issues of fraud detection, scalability, and security in blockchain. Table 6.2 provides a detailed comparison.

6.5 CONCLUSION

This article introduces a UPI-related soft-voting ensemble of Random Forest, XGBoost, SVM, and Logistic Regression, which attained a 99.97% Accuracy, 99.66% Precision, 96.09% Recall, 97.85% F1-score, and 1.00 ROC-AUC, therefore providing sufficient confidence in differentiating fraud from legitimate transactions.

The novelty of our approach compared to previous literature is: (1) a UPI-specific ensemble model that effectively addresses the common misclassification issue present in single-model strategies (e.g., XGBoost-only, Logistic Regression with clustering) by balancing high recall and low false positives. (2) a small six features' model made up of transaction type, transaction amount, old and new origin balances, and old and new destination balances, achieving very lightweight, high-speed inference without sacrificing accuracy (3) a unified preprocessing scheme that removed missing values, performed targeted feature encoding, and provided stratified train-test split to address class-imbalance issues; (4) a targeted user-focused evaluation that captures precision, recall, F1, ROC-AUC, and confusion matrix information for the intended application, which reduces customer effort, while maximizing fraud detection.

In the future, we will focus on online adaptive learning for changing fraud patterns, behavioral analytics regarding subtle variations compared to non-fraudulent patterns, and utilizing fraud controls when doing cross-border UPI transactions. Furthermore, we will emphasize regulatory compliance to adhere to the RBI

TABLE 6.2
Comparative Analysis of Existing Studies and the Proposed Model

Author–Year	Methodology	Accuracy	Finding	Limitations
Mehta et al. (2021)	Hybrid supervised, unsupervised model	**89.0%**	The hybrid method outperformed traditional rules for detection, along with having very low false-positive rates.	Assessed on one dataset; no demonstrable generalization and multi-institutional evaluation
Shah and Patel (2022)	Behavioral-biometrics augmented model (timing, device, location signals)	**93.9%**	Behavioral features reduced the false positive rate by ~40% reduction and increased the ability to withstand mimicry.	Need for biometric/behavioral data collection (privacy/consent), scale concerns for deployment and dataset
Das et al. (2023)	Multi-source fusion (transaction metadata, behavior, device fingerprint)	**95.0%**	High accuracy with industrial-style latency demonstrates preliminary feasibility for near-real-time UPI detection.	High compute and integration cost; privacy and cross-bank data sharing not addressed.
Gupta and Sharma (2023)	LSTM (sequential behavioral patterns)	**96.0%**	Deep models can capture sharp and subtle temporal fraud patterns; telemetry and surveillance for high-value risk.	Heavier computational requirement, risk of overfitting without larger diverse datasets.
Shravani ct al. (2025)	Multiplc classifiers (LR, DT, XGBoost, SVM, KNN, NB) and Voting/ Stacking	**98.2%**	Stacking was not quite as poor as the worst strong learners (XGBoost). Also, includes a Flask+SQLite demo for real-time UI.	Accurate, but does not properly report the confirmed reason for high accuracy, namely, use of well-known dataset ± evaluation bias; demo uses a lightweight stack (SQLite), no shown use on production scale and cross-dataset testing.

(*Continued*)

TABLE 6.2 *(Continued)*
Comparative Analysis of Existing Studies and the Proposed Model

Author–Year	Methodology	Accuracy	Finding	Limitations
Ayuti Khedekar et al. (2025)	Specialized models per fraud type: RF (vishing), LSTM (impersonation), XGBoost (fake payments), CNN (QR).	**RF (vishing): 97.88%, LSTM (impersonation): 0.9990 (99.90%), XGBoost (fake payments) 87.83%**	Per-type specialization yields excellent results for targeted fraud categories; LSTM achieved near-perfect scores on the impersonation task	Per-component design may not generalize to other fraud types or datasets; dataset provenance/balancing details affect comparability.
Reddy et al. (2025)	Ensemble of tree-based boosters and RF; comparative evaluation	**Random Forest: 90.75% (LightGBM: 89.35%, GradientBoosting: 89.45%).**	Random Forest gave the best precision/recall balance for their dataset; tree ensembles are competitive and interpretable	Moderate accuracy versus recent deep/stacking works; requires further tuning and external validation.
Proposed work	Soft-voting ensemble: Random Forest + XGBoost + SVM + Logistic Regression; 6-feature, UPI-tailored preprocessing	**99.97% (accuracy), Precision 99.66%, Recall 96.09%, F1 97.85%, ROC-AUC 1.00.**	Highest reported accuracy among the compared works; targeted 6-feature set yields lightweight, fast inference, and low false positives – deployment blueprint included.	Requires strong cross-dataset and cross-institution validation to rule out dataset leakage or overfitting; privacy-preserving integration (DP/HE/SMPC) and regulatory compliance are future work.

guidelines and put fraud detection algorithms and frameworks in place efficiently for online real-time investigation, developing a scalable, intelligent, and regulation-aware environment of fraud detection through AI.

REFERENCES

1. J. Górka, "The rise of instant payments: A cross-country comparison," *Cent. Eur. Manag. J.*, Apr. 2025, doi: 10.1108/CEMJ-10-2024-0297.
2. S. Rastogi, C. Panse, A. Sharma, and V. M. Bhimavarapu, "Unified Payment Interface (UPI): A digital innovation and its impact on financial inclusion and economic development," *Univers. J. Account. Financ.*, vol. 9, no. 3, pp. 518–530, Jun. 2021, doi: 10.13189/ujaf.2021.090326.
3. Bipin Paudel and Rajesh Kaji Kayastha, "A study on the effectiveness of payment service providers with its future prospects: A case study among the users in Kathmandu Valley," *Int. J. Eng. Manag. Res.*, vol. 12, no. 4, pp. 114–124, Aug. 2022, doi: 10.31033/ijemr.12.4.15.
4. R. Gochhwal, "Unified Payment Interface—An advancement in payment systems," *Am. J. Ind. Bus. Manag.*, vol. 07, no. 10, pp. 1174–1191, 2017, doi: 10.4236/ajibm.2017.710084.
5. A. Karmakar, "Unified Payments Interface (UPI): A comprehensive study of its impact on India's financial landscape and global aspirations," January, 2024, doi: 10.13140/RG.2.2.34671.82087.
6. S. Thakur, S. Rastogi, N. Parashar, P. Tejasmayee, and J. M. Kappal, "The impact of ICT on the profitability of Indian banks: The moderating role of NPA," *J. Risk Financ. Manag.*, vol. 16, no. 4, p. 211, Mar. 2023, doi: 10.3390/jrfm16040211.
7. M. Ahmed, A. N. Mahmood, and M. R. Islam, "A survey of anomaly detection techniques in financial domain," *Futur. Gener. Comput. Syst.*, vol. 55, no. 2, pp. 278–288, Feb. 2016, doi: 10.1016/j.future.2015.01.001.
8. B. Smith and B. C. Smith, "A novel digital payment architecture: A Unified Payment Interface and its systematic transformation of financial infrastructure," pp. 0–9, 2025, doi: 10.20944/preprints202501.0289.v1.
9. P. S. Gupta V, Sharma S, Nimkar S, "UPI Based Financial Fraud Detection Using Deep Learning Approach," *2024 International Conference on Advances in Computing Research on Science Engineering and Technology (ACROSET)* vol. 3, pp. 1–6, 2024, doi: 10.1109/ACROSET62108.2024.10743663.
10. S. Jagadeesan, K. S. Arjun, G. Dhanika, G. Karthikeyan, and K. Deepika, "UPI fraud detection using machine learning," in *Challenges in Information, Communication and Computing Technology*, London: CRC Press, 2024, pp. 755–760, doi: 10.1201/9781003559085-130.
11. R. Kumar, S. Kishore, H. Lu, and A. Prakash, *Proc. 29th USENIX Secur. Symp.* pp. 1499–1516, 2020.
12. A. Lonkar, S. Dharmadhikari, N. Dharurkar, K. Patil, and R. A. Phadke, "Tackling digital payment frauds: A study of consumer preparedness in India," *J. Financ. Crime*, vol. 32, no. 2, pp. 257–278, Feb. 2025, doi: 10.1108/JFC-01-2024-0029.
13. S. K. L. Naik, A. Kiran, V. P. Kumar, S. Mannam, Y. Kalyani, and M. Silparaj, "Fraud fighters – How AI and ML are revolutionizing UPI security," *2024 International Conference on Science Technology Engineering and Management (ICSTEM)*, vol. 2, pp. 1–7, 2024, doi: 10.1109/ICSTEM61137.2024.10560740.
14. P. Vyas and D. Mistry, "Impact of Covid-19 on digital payments: A study with special reference to UPI," *PRAGATI J. Indian Econ.*, vol. 8, no. 2, pp. 31–44, Dec. 2021, doi: 10.17492/jpi.pragati.v8i2.822102.

15. Bloomberg, "Value of transactions (INR trillion) from FY19 to FY24." https://data.bloomberg.com/
16. M. Shrimali, S. Agrawal, L. Jagawat, and V. Patil, "A research paper on 'Unified Payments Interface: Emergence, growth and where it is headed,'" *ShodhKosh J. Vis. Perform. Arts*, vol. 5, no. 6, Jun. 2024, doi: 10.29121/shodhkosh.v5.i6.2024.2103.
17. F. Ministry, "27 lakh UPI fraud cases reported in 3 years, involving Rs 2,145 crore." https://www.ibtimes.co.in/27-lakh-upi-fraud-cases-reported-3-years-involving-rs-2145-crore-875462
18. R. Rani, A. Alam, and A. Javed, "Secure UPI: Machine Learning-Driven Fraud Detection System for UPI Transactions," *2024 2nd International Conference on Disruptive Technologies (ICDT)*, vol. 2, pp. 924–928, doi: 10.1109/ICDT61202.2024.10489682.
19. R. Saroy, S. Awasthy, N. K. Singh, S. M. Adki, and S. Dhal, "The impact of COVID-19 on digital payment habits of Indian households," *Bul. Ekon. Monet. dan Perbank.*, vol. 25, pp. 19–42, Mar. 2022, doi: 10.21098/bemp.v25i0.1823.
20. S. Chakraborty and A. Karandikar, "Policies driving India's innovation-driven growth in science and technology: Pathway to progressive excellence over the past decade and roadmap to Viksit Bharat-2047," *Proc. Indian Natl. Sci. Acad.*, vol. 91, no. 1, pp. 1–8, Mar. 2025, doi: 10.1007/s43538-025-00436-9.
21. T. Hindu, "UPI payments 2016-25." [Online]. Available: https://www.thehindu.com/business/upi-transactions-in-january-surpass-1699-billion-highest-recorded-in-any-month/article69273704.ece
22. R. Jeyalakshmi, N. Rajput, and S. H. R. Gracy, "Financial Fraud detection using Supervised and Unsupervised Learning," *2024 International Conference on Power, Energy, Control and Transmission Systems (ICPECTS)*, vol. 4, pp. 1–9, 2024, doi: 10.1109/ICPECTS62210.2024.10780301.
23. P. Fischer, S. E. G. Lea, and K. M. Evans, "Why do individuals respond to fraudulent scam communications and lose money? The psychological determinants of scam compliance," *J. Appl. Soc. Psychol.*, vol. 43, no. 10, pp. 2060–2072, Oct. 2013, doi: 10.1111/jasp.12158.
24. E. N. Ekwonwune, U. C. Chukwuebuka, A. E. Duroha, and A. N. Duru, "Analysis of global system for mobile communication (GSM) subscription fraud detection system," *Int. J. Commun. Netw. Syst. Sci.*, vol. 15, no. 10, pp. 167–180, 2022, doi: 10.4236/ijcns.2022.1510012.
25. K. K. Lakshmi, H. Gupta, and J. Ranjan, "UPI Based Mobile Banking Applications – Security Analysis and Enhancements," in *2019 Amity International Conference on Artificial Intelligence (AICAI)*, IEEE, Feb. 2019, pp. 1–6, doi: 10.1109/AICAI.2019.8701396.
26. B. B. Gupta, A. Tewari, A. K. Jain, and D. P. Agrawal, "Fighting against phishing attacks: State of the art and future challenges," *Neural Comput. Appl.*, vol. 28, no. 12, pp. 3629–3654, Dec. 2017, doi: 10.1007/s00521-016-2275-y.
27. M. DeLiema, D. Burnes, and L. Langton, "The financial and psychological impact of identity theft among older adults," *Innov. Aging*, vol. 5, no. 4, Oct. 2021, doi: 10.1093/geroni/igab043.
28. A. Pawar, C. Fatnani, R. Sonavane, R. Waghmare, and S. Saoji, "Secure QR Code Scanner to Detect Malicious URL using Machine Learning," in *2022 2nd Asian Conference on Innovation in Technology (ASIANCON)*, IEEE, Aug. 2022, pp. 1–8, doi: 10.1109/ASIANCON55314.2022.9908759.
29. I. N. P. Wahyu Dharmawan and R. V. H. Ginardi, "Fraud avoidance using QR codes on transaction process on finding – Tutor application in android system," *J. Tek. ITS*, vol. 6, no. 2, Sep. 2017, doi: 10.12962/j23373539.v6i2.23144.

30. I. T. Christou, M. Bakopoulos, T. Dimitriou, E. Amolochitis, S. Tsekeridou, and C. Dimitriadis, "Detecting fraud in online games of chance and lotteries," *Expert Syst. Appl.*, vol. 38, no. 10, pp. 13158–13169, Sep. 2011, doi: 10.1016/j.eswa.2011.04.124.
31. L. G. Kabari, D. Nuka Nanwin, and E. Uduak Nquoh, "Telecmmunications subscription fraud detection using artificial nueral networks," *Trans. Mach. Learn. Artif. Intell.*, vol. 3, no. 6, Dec. 2015, doi: 10.14738/tmlai.36.1695.
32. T. Koskelainen, P. Kalmi, E. Scornavacca, and T. Vartiainen, "Financial literacy in the digital age—A research agenda," *J. Consum. Aff.*, vol. 57, no. 1, pp. 507–528, Jan. 2023, doi: 10.1111/joca.12510.
33. V. G. Dharmavaram and O. Mishra, "KYC Fraud: A New Means to Conduct Financial Fraud–How to Tackle It?," In *Cybersecurity Issues, Challenges, and Solutions in the Business World*, 2022, pp. 81–94, doi: 10.4018/978-1-6684-5827-3.ch006.
34. U. Siddaiah, P. Anjaneyulu, Y. Haritha, and M. Ramesh, "Fraud detection in online payments using machine learning techniques," *2023 7th International Conference on Intelligent Computing and Control Systems (ICICCS)*, pp. 268–273, 2023, doi: 10.1109/ICICCS56967.2023.10142404.
35. N. Karthick, G. Leema Roselin, M. Tamilarasan, K. Kalaiselvi, S. Sudha, and J. Jayanthi, "Unified Payment Interface Imposture and Scam Detection Using Deep Learning And ANN," *2024 Third International Conference on Smart Technologies and Systems for Next Generation Computing (ICSTSN)*, 2024, doi: 10.1109/ICSTSN61422.2024.10671346.
36. S. Bhowmik and J. Howlader, "Online payment fraud monitoring and detection: Performance analysis of tree-based Ensemble Machine Learning models," *2025 17th International Conference on COMmunication Systems and NETworks (COMSNETS)*, Bengaluru, India, 2025, pp. 102–107, doi: 10.1109/COMSNETS63942.2025.10885622.
37. M. S. S. Bodade and P. P. P. Pawade, "Review paper on UPI fraud detection using machine learning," *Int. J. Res. Appl. Sci. Eng. Technol.*, vol. 11, no. 12, pp. 1283–1285, Dec. 2023, doi: 10.22214/ijraset.2023.57551.
38. F. P. E. Putra, U. Ubaidi, A. Zulfikri, G. Arifin, and R. M. Ilhamsyah, "Analysis of phishing attack trends, impacts and prevention methods: Literature study," *Brill. Res. Artif. Intell.*, vol. 4, no. 1, pp. 413–421, Aug. 2024, doi: 10.47709/brilliance.v4i1.4357.
39. R. V Shruthi RH, Shreya Gautam, "An analysis of UPI's security risks and remediation strategies," *Int. Res. J. Mod. Eng. Technol. Sci.*, vol. 6, no. 8, pp. 71–79, 2024.
40. Kanika and J. Singla, "A survey of deep learning based online transactions fraud detection systems," *2020 International Conference on Intelligent Engineering and Management (ICIEM)*, pp. 130–136, 2020, doi: 10.1109/ICIEM48762.2020.9160200.
41. H. Farvaresh and M. M. Sepehri, "A data mining framework for detecting subscription fraud in telecommunication," *Eng. Appl. Artif. Intell.*, vol. 24, no. 1, pp. 182–194, Feb. 2011, doi: 10.1016/j.engappai.2010.05.009.
42. T.-H. Chen, "Do you know your customer? Bank risk assessment based on machine learning," *Appl. Soft Comput.*, vol. 86, p. 105779, Jan. 2020, doi: 10.1016/j.asoc.2019.105779.
43. M. Ozcan and S. Peker, "A classification and regression tree algorithm for heart disease modeling and prediction," *Healthc. Anal.*, vol. 3, p. 100130, Nov. 2023, doi: 10.1016/j.health.2022.100130.
44. M. Anjali, M. Ajay, M. Saiteja, and B. O. Yadav, "PaySafe AI: Intelligent Fraud Detection for UPI Transactions using Machine Learning," in *2025 International Conference on Intelligent Computing and Control Systems (ICICCS)*, IEEE, Mar. 2025, pp. 1557–1563, doi: 10.1109/ICICCS65191.2025.10985175.

45. W. Tuerxun, X. Chang, G. Hongyu, J. Zhijie, and Z. Huajian, "Fault diagnosis of wind turbines based on a support vector machine optimized by the sparrow search algorithm," *IEEE Access*, vol. 9, pp. 69307–69315, 2021, doi: 10.1109/ACCESS.2021.3075547.
46. O. Ramdani, K. Beddek, R. Haddouche, M. Zerrougui, and N. Chouider, "SVM-based approach fault detection for PMSG-wind energy conversion system," *J. Eng. Res. (Kuwait)*, 2025, doi: 10.1016/j.jer.2025.01.001.
47. N. K. Ojha, "Fraud Detection Mechanism for UPI Payments Using XGBoost," in *Intelligent Computing and Communication Techniques: Proceedings of the International Conference on Intelligent Computing and Communication Techniques (ICICCT 2024)*, New Delhi, India, 28–29 June, 2024 (Volume 2), CRC Press, 2025, p. 129.
48. P. T. Varma, M. Poojari, J. Joseph, and A. Cardozo, "Credit card fraud detection using random forest algorithm," *Int. J. Trendy Res. Eng. Technol.*, vol. 05, no. 03, pp. 24–27, 2021, doi: 10.54473/ijtret.2021.5305.

7 Decentralized Machine Learning

Opportunities and Challenges

Manaswinee Madhumita Panda, Laxminarayan Dash, and Bijayalaxmi Panda

7.1 INTRODUCTION

Decentralized machine learning (ML) (DML) enables collaborative ML without centralized input data. This includes federated learning (FL) and edge inference (EI) as means of DML. Collaboration in a distributed system occurs at the edge of the distributed space using naturally distributed data. DML tools are just starting to blossom; however, there is a long way to go to provide more portable and flexible tools to experiment with new systems, non-fully connected topologies, many data domains, and asynchronous collaboration methods. We will present recent work on DML aimed at better usability in data centers and, at the edge, generalizing FL to non-DDN paradigms beyond the class of models, further refining the performance of models that regulate normalization and frequency of communication, and further protecting data privacy in generative adversarial networks [1].

DML (decentralized machine learning) modifies the data learning process from a centralized repository-based system to a distributed and collaborative one. DML is an effective paradigm shift in model training and model deployment in ML. With DML methods, rather than gathering data in one central repository, ML models are trained manner across a distributed in a group of devices or data sources. This paradigm shift addresses many of the fundamental limitations of centralized solutions to learning problems, particularly where data is naturally distributed, sensitive, or simply too large to be efficiently centralized. Consider a sensor network installed in a smart city that takes environmental readings.

Centralizing the sensor readings of thousands of sensors to properly train a model would be computationally expensive and raise serious privacy issues. DML provides a more practical answer to the challenge of developing models that learn from sensor readings by enabling the model to learn on the sensor readings locally, where only model updates – not raw data – are sent.

DOI: 10.1201/9781003658597-7

7.1.1 Basic Principles

To understand DML, it's useful to understand its principles. Centralized ML collects data, moves it to a server, and performs ML from there, but DML relies on the principle of distribution and data locality. There are several principles we can consider:

Data Locality: Data stays where it is, i.e., on the device of the user, on an edge server, and on a distributed database. All of these highly reduce how much we are moving data around the world and thus reduce latency, reduce the bandwidth we are using, and reduce the time and effort it takes to reproduce a dataset that moves.

Collaborative Learning: This collaboration supports collaborative training of models, where many people are taking part in the learning without actually sharing their raw data with one another. This collaboration can be accomplished through methods like **FL**, where a number of participants train a model locally, and any updates to their model are typically aggregated together for a global model.

Privacy Protecting: DML offers better data privacy by default since it stores data locally and only pushes entity-specific model updates to other devices when necessary. Furthermore, methods that ensure differential privacy (DP) can be used to provide enhanced privacy. For example, homomorphic encryption, which adds layers of protection to sensitive data, or DP in sustainability, which offers a rigorous mathematical framework for protecting private information while still providing useful data analyses for resource planning, policy making, and environmental monitoring.

Failure Tolerance and Resilience: Compared to centralized systems, distributed systems are more resilient to errors. Using the redundancy of a distributed environment, a DML network can continue to operate even if a node fails. In combination and individually, these recommendations will help make a more solid, privacy-preserving, and extensible vision of ML, ultimately better aligned with the sustainability project's problems and opportunities. For instance, in the context of environmental monitoring, using DML could allow for local investigations of pollution rates across regions, being able to provide high-definition results without reducing sensitive location information into a single point [2].

7.1.2 Centralized ML

In centralized ML, all information is stored in a single location (e.g., data center or cloud server). The ML model is trained on the combined dataset. This is the classical approach to ML.

Working Principle

- *Collection of Data*: All data is sent to a central server from all sources.
- *Model Distribution*: A central server pushes a global model (or its initial parameters) to a few client devices.

- *Training*: Every client trains the model locally.
- *Transmission of Model Updates*: Models are sent back to the central server.
- *Aggregation*: The global model is improved by combining local models.
- *Iteration*: The new global model is sent back to clients for further local training, and this cycle is repeated.

Advantages:

- *Better Privacy*: Information is stored on local devices, minimizing privacy threats and meeting regulations. Sensitive raw data is never distributed.
- *Improved Privacy*: Data is kept locally, reducing privacy risks and adhering to legal requirements. Raw, sensitive data is never shared.
- *Reduced Communication Costs*: Only model updates—which are typically smaller than raw data—are transmitted, saving bandwidth.
- The benefits of edge computing include reducing the strain on central servers and enabling real-time inference at the data origin by leveraging the computational power of edge devices.
- *Robustness and Fault Tolerance*: There is no single point of failure; even if a few client devices stop working, the system can still work as a whole.
- *Access to Diverse Data*: Able to gain knowledge from a wider range of real-world data.
- *Personalization*: Able to offer customized models on individual devices without disclosing personal data.

Disadvantages:

- *Greater Complexity*: More difficult to train on many dispersed and different devices.
- The communication cost of model updates persists even if the raw data is not sent. For large models or rapid rounds, this overhead can be meaningful.
- If the model has to learn from data that is highly diverse (non-IID) at each node, then the efficiency of the process may be difficult. It may be the case that the learning process of the model may lead to inferior convergence or biased models.
- Updates to the model may leak out information or be influenced by enemies, e.g., in a model poisoning attack.
- *Device Resource Constraints*: Client devices may have limited computation, battery consumption, and intermittent network access, which may hinder training efficiency and reliability.
- The issue analysis and resolution become more complex due to the distribution of data.

7.1.3 Decentralized Machine Learning

Decentralized machine learning requires training models on data that is still distributed among various nodes or devices, as opposed to aggregating it in one location. FL is a renowned example and a crucial technique within decentralized ML.

Working Principle

- Local date is stored on local client devices such as a smartphone, IoT sensor, and a local server.
- A central server transmits a global model or its initial parameters to select client devices that are part of the model distribution.
- Each client locally trains their own model.
- Models are shared back to the central server.
- The various local models are aggregated to improve the global model.
- This cycle repeats itself, as the global model is sent back to clients after it is updated with iteration.

Advantages:

- The information is kept on user devices rather than on widely shared cloud servers. Sensitive raw data is never shared.
- The communication expenses decrease in this case as only model updates (mostly lower than raw data) are sent. Hence, the bandwidth is saved.
- The benefit of edge computing is that it uses the computational power of such edge devices, which puts less strain on the central server. Moreover, edge computing helps in performing real-time inference at the data source.
- *Robustness and Fault Tolerance*: No Single Point of Failure. If some of the client devices become unavailable, the whole system can still work.
- One of the main benefits of deep learning is that it can learn from a larger type of real-world data.
- *Tailored Models*: Generates customized models on user devices without compromising their private data.

Disadvantages:

- Training on numerous distributed and heterogeneous devices is complicated.
- *Communication Overhead (Updates)*: Although there is no sending of the raw data, there is still communication overhead on the model updates. As model sizes get extremely large or rounds get high frequency, this can get quite big.
- If the local data is very different from each other (non-IID), efficiency can be tricky and may bias the model or slow convergence.
- To thwart security leaks from deep learning models, it is prudent to continuously update computer vision models on the cloud as soon as possible.
- The devices used by the clients may be limited in their computation, battery usage, and connectivity. Thus, the training may not be efficient and dependable, which can affect the performance.
- A distributed data system makes the inspection and debugging process significantly more challenging.

7.1.4 Key Differentiators Summarized

Selecting between central and decentralized machine learning would rely heavily on the specific use case, particularly with regard to network constraints, data privacy requirements, data localization, and available computational resources (Table 7.1).

TABLE 7.1
Centralized vs Decentralized Machine Learning

Feature	Centralized Machine Learning	Decentralized Machine Learning (e.g., Federated Learning)
Data Location	All aggregated data in one repository.	Data is still stored locally on devices/nodes.
Privacy	High risk of privacy because data are aggregated.	Improved privacy; raw data never crosses local devices.
Communication	High bandwidth for raw data transfer to central server.	Less bandwidth; only gradients/weights (model updates) are exchanged.
Single Point of Failure	High risk; failure at the central server affects the whole system.	Lower risk; system has some tolerance for node failures.
Scalability	Limited by the capacity of the central server.	Strongly scalable through harnessing distributed computational capabilities.
Control/Management	Easier to debug and manage.	More intricate management and coordination owing to distributed setup
Data Distribution	Usually presumes IID data or attempts homogenization.	Can be used to manage non-IID (heterogeneous) data across clients.
Computational Resources	Depends heavily on powerful central servers.	Utilizes potentially resource-limited edge devices.
Use Cases	Enterprise analytics, internal data processing.	Applications in healthcare, mobile AI, IoT, sensitive user data.

Decentralized approaches like FL are being explored more and more because they can address important privacy and scalability concerns in a world that is becoming more data-intensive and privacy-conscious, even while centralized ML offers simplicity and strict control [3].

7.1.5 DML Motivaton

While both distributed ML (DML) and FL are methods for training ML models over numerous devices or nodes, they vary in how they handle data distribution and privacy issues. These motivations are deeply rooted in the following:

i. **Edge Computing**
   - *Motivation*: The number of edge devices (mobile phones, IoT sensors, wearables, self-driving cars, etc.) produces an enormous quantity of data at the "edge" of the network. Centralizing all of this for ML training is frequently impractical, inefficient, and in some cases impossible.
   - *Reduced Latency and Real-Time Processing*: All raw data is transported to a central cloud as little as possible thanks to local processing and inference on edge devices. This becomes crucial for applications that require choices to be made in real time, such as industrial control or autonomous car systems, where even millisecond delays can

be lethal. ML facilitates training and optimizing models at the edge, resulting in faster reactions.

- *Bandwidth Efficiency*: DML techniques like FL send just small model changes (weights or gradients) as opposed to sending massive raw data sets to a single central server. This can significantly reduce the amount of network bandwidth used, which is especially helpful when there is sparsity or expensive connectivity.
- *Leveraging Distributed Computational Power*: With built-in artificial intelligence (AI) accelerators (NPUs, TPUs, etc.), edge devices are now far more potent.

ii. **Scalability**

- *Motivation*: The volume of data generated globally is growing at an exponential rate. Scaling centralized classical ML systems to handle petabytes or exabytes of data is extremely challenging, leading to bottlenecks, expensive infrastructure, and performance limitations.
- *Scalable Workload*: DML automatically divides the workload for storage and computation among numerous client devices. In addition to enabling parallel processing and model training on truly enormous, dispersed datasets, this removes the bottleneck caused by a single central server trying to manage all data.
- *Horizontal Scalability*: The training process is immediately impacted by adding more client devices to a DML system (for example, more smartphones as part of a FL exercise). This enables horizontal scaling, where the system's capacity grows linearly as the number of devices engaged increases.

iii. **Privacy**

- *Motivation*: Centralized data collection is now a major privacy issue due to growing public awareness, stringent data protection regulations (including GDPR and the Health Insurance Portability and Accountability Act (HIPAA)), and growing anxiety about data breaches. Users rarely want to provide a central authority access to their private, sensitive information.
- *Minimization of Data*: The most significant privacy benefit is data minimization (no sharing of raw data). Raw data never leaves the client device while using DML, especially FL. This significantly reduces the possibility of sensitive user data being exposed, misused, or compromised.
- *Regulation Compliance*: By storing data locally, DML helps businesses comply with strict data privacy laws that forbid sending personal information across borders or demand data localization.
- *Enhanced User Trust*: Users are more engaged and trusting when they know that their data remains on their device.
- *Secure Aggregation and DP*: DML frequently incorporates cutting-edge privacy-preserving technologies: with a formal, verifiable guarantee that no participant's data can be inferred from the aggregated model, DP adds noise to the model updates to further anonymize individual data points.

- Secure multi-party computation (SMC) and secure aggregation are cryptographic techniques that allow several parties to work together to compute a function (such as adding up model updates) without sharing their individual inputs with the central server or even with each other.
- *Data Sovereignty*: DML makes it possible for data owners to maintain data sovereignty. DML makes it possible for data owners to maintain control over their data, deciding how and when to utilize it in training without disclosing it [4, 5].

7.2 CORE CONCEPTS AND PARADIGMS

- *Decentralized Machine Learning (DML)*: A catch-all term for ML methodologies in which learning takes place on many computational nodes or devices without necessarily implicating a central authority to pool raw data. The data is kept local to its origin.
- *FL*: The most typical and popular type of DML. It's a distributed ML method where a global shared model is learned by many decentralized edge devices or servers (clients) possessing local sample data, without sharing the data itself.
- *Client/Worker/Node*: The local devices or nodes (e.g., smartphones, IoT sensors, hospitals, banks) that store local data and take part in the decentralized training process.
- *Central Server (in Centralized FL)*: In most FL configurations, there is a central server that manages the training process. It starts with the global model, sends it to clients, aggregates the clients' updates, and generates a better global model. It does not observe raw data.
- *Global Model*: The one, universal ML model that is simultaneously being trained collectively by all participating clients.
- *Local Model*: The instance of the global model that sits and gets trained on the local data of a specific client.
- *Model Aggregation*: The mechanism through which the central server (or other coordinating nodes in fully decentralized FL) aggregates the model updates received from multiple clients to enhance the global model.
- *Federated Averaging (FedAvg)*: A common aggregation algorithm used in FL, wherein the server calculates a weighted average of the local model parameters (or gradients) according to the number of data samples that each client has trained on.
- *Communication Round/Epoch*: A round in the FL algorithm, usually consisting of the following:
  - Server sends global model to chosen clients.
  - Clients train locally and report updates.
  - Server aggregates updates.
  - The process repeats until convergence.

7.2.1 Challenges and Considerations

- *Non-IID (Non-Independent and Identically Distributed) Data*: A typical feature in DML where data of clients is not statistically identical or uniformly distributed. Heterogeneity may create difficulties for model convergence and performance.
- *Communication Efficiency*: The cost of transmitting model updates between the server and clients back and forth. Methods such as model compression (e.g., quantization, scarification) are employed to reduce this.
- *Client Selection*: The determination of which clients are involved in each round of training, sometimes on the basis of availability, freshness of data, or other factors.
- *Byzantine Fault Tolerance*: The capacity of the DML system to remain functional even when some clients or nodes are faulty or deliver erroneous updates.
- *Model Poisoning Attacks*: Malicious clients that try to compromise the global model's performance or introduce backdoors by providing crafted, malicious updates.
- *Inference Attacks (or Reconstruction Attacks)*: A person who tries to recreate individual training data points from the collaborative model updates or the end model itself. Privacy-preserving strategies try to counter these.

These concepts and definitions make up the foundation of the comprehension of how decentralized machine learning works, its advantages, and the technical obstacles it seeks to address [6].

7.2.2 Decentralized Federated Learning (DFL)/ Peer-to-Peer (P2P) Architecture

This architecture eliminates the need for a central coordinating server.

- *Description*: Clients communicate directly with each other (or a subset of their neighbors) to exchange model updates. There is no single central entity.
- *Working Principle*
  - Each client starts its own local model.
  - Clients occasionally talk to their neighbors (network topology dependent) to share model updates.
  - Each client combines its neighbors' updates received with its own local model.
  - Consensus protocols (e.g., gossip protocol-based, distributed ledger technologies such as blockchain) are commonly employed to provide eventual convergence throughout the network.

Advantages:

- *No Single Point of Failure*: Extremely resilient to failures at individual nodes.

- *Improved Privacy*: No single entity ever has access to any updates, lessening the trust burden.
- *True Decentralization*: Consistent with principles of distributed systems and Web3.
- *Scalability*: Can in theory scale to a very large number of participants by spreading the workload for aggregation.

Disadvantages:

- *Higher Complexity*: Far more difficult to design, instantiate, and administer because of distributed coordination.
- *Convergence Challenges*: Making sure that all the local models converge toward a globally optimal model may be challenging, particularly with asynchronous updates and non-IID data.
- *Communication Overhead*: Although peer-to-peer (P2P), direct communication amongst numerous nodes is still high, and topology administration of the network and schedules of communication are difficult to manage.
- *Security*: Malicious nodes may inject poisoned models directly or collude with neighbors, demanding strong Byzantine fault tolerance.
- *Use Cases*: IoT networks where a central server may be impossible, adversarial settings where no universal trusted authority can be placed, fully decentralized autonomous organizations (DAOs).

In Figure 7.1, all the systems are connected with one another through a mesh topology, such that any system is able to communicate with any other defined system through remote procedure calls [7].

7.2.3 Blockchain-based Federated Learning (BFL)

This is a particular kind of DFL or CFL that incorporates blockchain technology for security, transparency, and incentives.

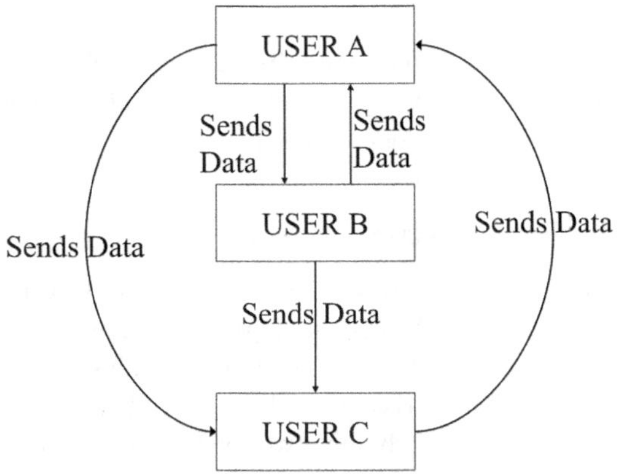

FIGURE 7.1 Peer-to-peer network.

Description: A blockchain (a distributed, tamper-evident ledger) is employed for logging and authenticating model updates, client reputation management, or incentive payout.

Working Principle:

- Locally, clients train.
- Model updates (or hashes/proofs of updates) are not sent directly to a central server or peers but are submitted to a blockchain.
- Smart contracts on the blockchain can specify the aggregation logic, client selection, and reward distribution.
- Blockchain consensus mechanisms guarantee the integrity and immutability of the training process.

Advantages:

- *Transparency and Auditability*: Everything takes place on an open and auditable blockchain ledger, making it easy to verify.
- *Trustlessness*: Minimizes reliance on trust in a central aggregator, as the blockchain confirms operations.
- *Incentivization*: Tokens or cryptocurrency can be used to incentivize businesses without having customers spend real money.
- *Security*: Carries over the security features of the blockchain, including single points of failure and resistance to tampering.

Disadvantages:

- *Scalability Limitations*: Transactions on blockchains are frequently costly and slow, which might impede frequent model upgrades.
- *Computational Overhead*: There is a significant computational overhead associated with processing smart contracts and maintaining a blockchain.
- *Complexity*: Blockchain and ML are extremely difficult to integrate.
- Use cases include secure collaborative AI in highly sensitive fields (like healthcare and finance) where strict auditability and incentives are crucial, as well as decentralized AI marketplaces.

The needs of the application, including the number of clients, computing power, network topology, necessary privacy guarantees, and level of participant confidence, heavily influence the architecture selection [8].

7.2.4 Blockchain-Based Machine Learning

The use of blockchain technology across industries has raised awareness regarding the importance of blockchain network security. Figure 7.2 shows the ML algorithms for enhancing data security in blockchain. Through data analysis, pattern detection, and identification of potential security risks in real-time, ML has proven to be a promising way to bolster the security of blockchain networks. With its ability to create an immutable, decentralized, and secure digital ledger, blockchain can enhance the credibility of data input for ML algorithms. Nonetheless, blockchain networks are vulnerable to

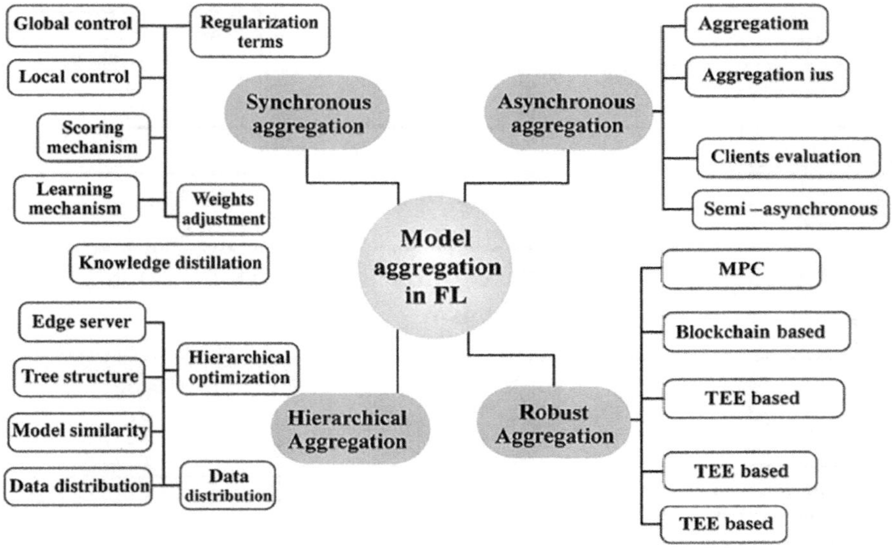

FIGURE 7.2 ML method to enhance data security of blockchain.

security attacks, which require putting in place proper security protocols and consensus processes. The integration of blockchain and ML can significantly change the way data security is addressed, but at all costs, security has to be upheld [9].

7.2.5 The Topology

Figure 7.3 illustrates the aggregation methodology in federated learning and provides comprehensive explanations [10].

7.2.6 Privacy Techniques

- *DP*: Adds noise to model updates to conceal individual data points.
- *Secure Aggregation*: It ensures that model updates are summed up securely without exposing the individual updates [11].

ML is ubiquitous in AI-powered services and data science but raises serious privacy concerns when it is trained on personal data. The idea of PRIDE is that personal data needs to be owned by the individual who creates it. This calls for reverting to ML algorithms so that they can learn from many decentralized personal datasets without reassembling raw data. DP provides a strong privacy concept, but current decentralized ML algorithms cannot learn useful models under DP. The mission of PRIDE is to develop theoretical and algorithmic tools that enable differentially private ML processes operating on decentralized data, through two orthogonal goals: (1) prove that gossip protocols automatically improve DP guarantees; (2) propose algorithms at the intersection of decentralized ML and SMC [12].

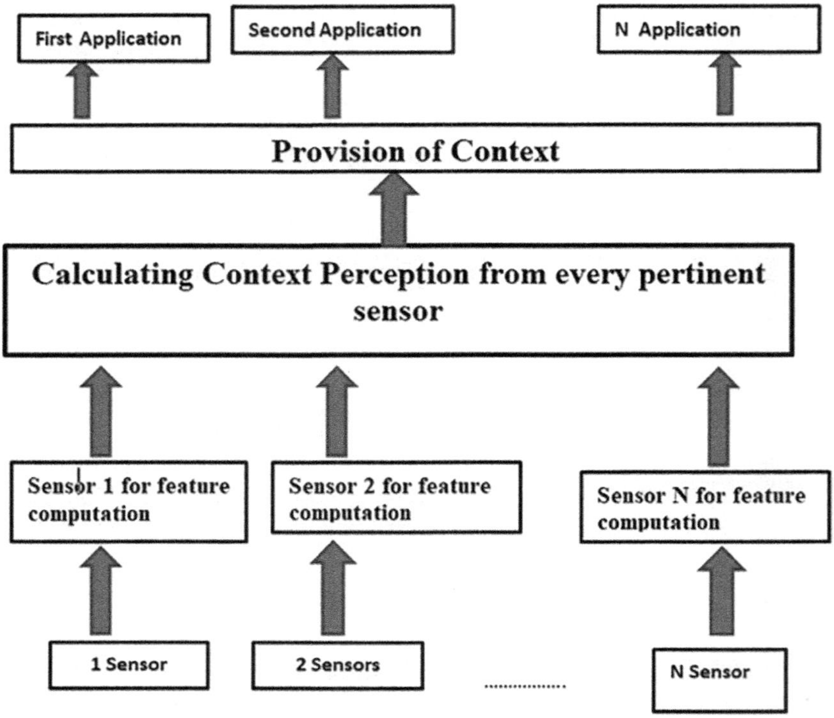

FIGURE 7.3 A diagram of model aggregation in federated learning.

7.3 DATA CONFIDENTIALITY AND PRIVACY

Major features of data confidentiality and privacy in DML:

- *Local Data Processing*: DML, particularly FL, prioritizes training on local data, hence lowering the risk of revealing confidential information.
- *Model Parameter Sharing*: DML methods such as FL do not share raw data but model parameters or updates, further boosting privacy.
- *Decentralized Architecture*: DML systems' decentralization of training on multiple nodes reduces the dependency on the server, thus improving security.
- *Privacy-Preserving Techniques*: DML adopts various privacy-preserving techniques, including homomorphic encryption, DP, and confidential computing, to protect personal data during the learning process.
- *Edge Computing Integration*: DML is ideal for edge computing environments, where edge devices can jointly train models without sending data to a central server, increasing privacy further.

Example: Federated Learning

In FL, local devices (clients) train local models based on their individual data. Only the updates or parameters are shared by the clients with a central server. The global model is formed by combining these updates at the server. This ensures that the raw data remains secure on each device.

7.3.1 Local Data Storage

Storage of data is an absolute necessity to each and every active business, irrespective of size. Be it financial reports or customer data, business data is vital and confidential. It powers decision-making activities for businesses in different verticals for organizations worldwide. Yet, it is obvious that businesses must have their data stored in a safe and secure location.

As companies expand, they experience more data produced or processed internally and accessed remotely. Increased volumes of data entail increased complexity in storing, processing, analyzing, and retrieving it. Companies have increasingly turned to centralized data storage solutions such as the cloud to keep their businesses simple. Yet considering the drawbacks of the cloud and the incredibly volatile nature of technology, we highly suspect that the centralized storage system will not be around for long.

Before we consider the possible solution offered by decentralized storage technology, let us examine the existing industry dynamics and the issues related to them [13].

7.3.1.1 Description of GDPR

The strongest data protection law in the world is thought to be the General Data Protection Regulation of the European Union. Since it went into effect in 2018, it has changed the digital landscape. It forced businesses to take better care of data protection. As a result of a few corporations receiving hefty fines, the story made headlines and scared off all non-compliant organizations [14]. The GDPR is applicable to all EU businesses and foreign businesses catering to EU citizens.

Where comparison with HIPAA is concerned, it should be noted that GDPR deems health data to be sensitive personal data and demands precautions prior to processing it.

7.3.1.2 Description of HIPAA

HIPAA is a US legislation intended to safeguard patients' medical records and other health information submitted to health plans, physicians, hospitals, and other healthcare organizations. Such information is referred to as protected data by law. It mandates the protection and confidential treatment of protected health information (PHI). The Department of Health and Human Services is tasked with drafting this legislation.

7.3.2 Resource Efficiency and Scalability

Two important considerations in the creation, implementation, and upkeep of ML systems are resource efficiency and scalability. Below is a summary of both ideas and how important they are to ML:

- *Resource Efficiency in ML Definition*: When training and inferring ML models, resource efficiency is making the best use of computing resources, including CPU, GPU, memory (RAM), storage, bandwidth, and energy [15].

- *Computational Efficiency*: Models and algorithms ought to reduce the quantity of calculations.

Methods for quantization and model trimming.

- *Utilization of Memory*: Smaller batch sizes, sparse representations, and model compression can all help to lessen the memory footprint. Using pipelines for pre-processing and data loading that use less memory (e.g., streaming data, data generators).
- *ML Scalability*: The ability of a model or system to accommodate growing numbers of users, data, or computing load in the field of finance without experiencing appreciable performance reduction is known as scalability [16].
- *Scalability of Data*: Growing datasets should be handled effectively by algorithms (e.g., online learning, mini-batch training). Utilization of frameworks for distributed data processing (e.g., Hadoop, Spark).
- *Scalability of the Model*: Multiple GPUs or TPUs should be able to train large models. Utilizing data and model parallelism (e.g., PyTorch Distributed, Horovod).
- *Scalability of Infrastructure*: Utilizing cloud computing platforms (like AWS and GCP) to automatically scale resources in response to load. Deployment of ML models using serverless architectures, Docker, and Kubernetes.
- *Scalability of Inference*: The capacity to provide real-time predictions to a huge number of people. Utilizing load balancers, batching, and model caching.

7.3.3 Context-Aware and Customized Learning in Machine Learning

The goal of personalized and context-aware learning is to tailor ML systems to the unique requirements, preferences, behaviors, and situations of every user. In order to develop intelligent systems that provide more pertinent, precise, and flexible answers or suggestions, this method is required.

Tailored Education: Personalized learning is the process of modifying a ML model's behavior according to the unique traits and data of every user.

Important characteristics: User-Specific Models

- Individual data, such as preferences or past experiences, can be used to train or enhance models. enhances the applicability of forecasts or suggestions (for instance, in healthcare or recommender systems).
- Real-time responsiveness can be defined as a system's ability to react and adjust instantly to new information or conditions that change.
- *Considerations for Implementation*: Models operate swiftly thanks to low-latency inference, particularly on edge devices. Processing and learning from continuous data streams is known as streaming data management. It updates the dynamic model, utilizing real-time user input (e.g., online learning methodologies or reinforcement learning). The context awareness of ML is seen in Figure 7.4.

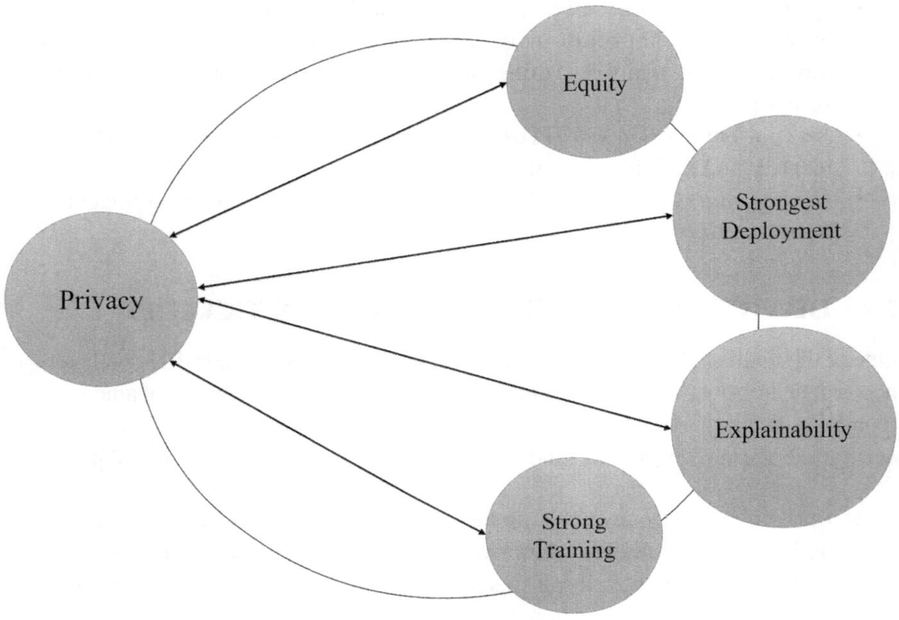

FIGURE 7.4 A diagram of context awareness.

7.3.4 Enhanced Tolerance Faults in Machine Learning

In ML, greater tolerance for defects refers to the capacity of ML systems to perform or recover gracefully in the face of errors, distorted data, hardware failures, or hostile conditions [17]. This is particularly important in critical applications where mistakes could have major consequences, including autonomous driving, healthcare, banking, or robotics.

Here is a detailed description of the concept:

Fault tolerance is a system's capacity to continue operating normally even in the event that some of its components malfunction. ML expands on this concept to address:

- Noisy or absent information
- Software and hardware malfunctions
- Attacks by adversaries
- Model deterioration or drift
- Interruptions or corruption in training
- *Strong Training Methods*: Regularization (L1, L2) makes models more generalizable by preventing overfitting.
- *Adversarial Training*: Training with Adversarial Examples Boosts Resilience.
- *Noise Injection*: By adding noise to inputs or weights during training, models can withstand noisy or faulty inputs.

- *Redundancy and Ensembles (Model Ensembles)*: Combining multiple models reduces the impact of individual model failures. The decision-making procedures of majority voting and averaging allow for error tolerance across models.
- *Error Identification and Fixing*: Data validation pipelines automatically identify and fix input irregularities.
- *Hashes and Checksums*: To ensure data integrity during storage and transmission.

7.4 DECENTRALIZED MACHINE LEARNING DIFFICULTIES

One of the main challenges in decentralized machine learning is non-IID and heterogeneous data: information can be identically distributed and non-independent among nodes (non-IID). The impact of the challenge is a decrease in convergence stability and model accuracy. For example, various kinds of handwriting data are stored on users' phones.

a. *Bottleneck Problems in Communication*: Frequent exchange of model updates leads to high network overhead. Effect: Increases energy expenditure and decreases training speed. For example, upgrading is difficult for IoT devices with limited connectivity.
b. *Privacy and Security to Risk*: To expose private information, model updates the potential even if raw data isn't released. The effect of the model threatens the privacy of data [18].
c. *Heterogeneity of the System*: Devices vary in terms of memory, processing power, and battery life. Effect: Global model updates are delayed by slower nodes, or stragglers. For instance, a smartphone taking part in training may function somewhat differently from a smart refrigerator.
d. *Fault Tolerance and Node Dropout Problem*: During training, devices may malfunction or go offline. Effect: Unreliable training procedure; potential bias in the global model. For instance, mobile devices may turn off or disconnect from Wi-Fi while being trained [19].

7.4.1 Heterogeneity of System and Device

The term "heterogeneity" in ML refers to the differences in hardware, software, network conditions, and data availability among various systems or devices that participate in the training or implementation of ML models, particularly in distributed, decentralized, or edge-based settings.

a. *Computational Inequality Problem*: Processing power varies among devices. Effect: While certain devices become bottlenecks (stragglers), others process data more quickly. For instance, a server, a smartphone, and a smartwatch.
b. *Software Environments that are Asymmetrical*: Different ML libraries, drivers, or operating systems may be used. Incompatible configurations lead to issues in collaborative training and deployment. Instances encompass

unsupported hardware acceleration as well as a lack of version compatibility with TensorFlow [20].

c. *Problem with Variable Network Conditions*: Latencies and throughputs vary by device. Slow synchronization increases communication overhead. For example, one that is on 5G as opposed to one that is on or off 2G.

7.4.2 Risks to Security and Privacy in Machine Learning

Security and privacy risks from ML systems have increased, especially when designing for sensitive data or for distributed learning formats (e.g., edge AI, cloud ML, or FL). Leakage of model updates is a serious issue, but there are also many other flaws. Model Update Leaks: When participants in decentralized or federated ML submit model updates (e.g., weights or gradients) to a central server, they may unintentionally reveal sensitive information about the local training data.

- *Gradient Inversion Attack*: This kind of attack uses optimization techniques to track gradient updates and reconstruct the original training data, including private photos or medical records.
- *Membership Inference Attacks*: In order to ascertain if a certain data sample was included in the training set, attackers query a trained model [21].
- *Attacks of Model Inversion*: The outcome of attackers using a model to access or query it in order to recreate estimated input features.
- *Attacks that Poison Data*: In order to affect how the final model behaves, attackers purposefully introduce malicious or incorrectly classified data into the training set.

7.4.3 Model Accuracy

The ability of a trained ML model to accurately predict or classify new, unseen data is known as model accuracy.

For Classification: Correct forecast/Total forecast * 100

For Regression: Accuracy metrics like (MAE) mean absolute error and MSE (mean squared error) and R^2 Score

7.4.4 Risk to Security and Privacy

An outline of ML's security and privacy risks is provided below, with an emphasis on model update leaks and other threats, including backdoors, poisoning, and model inversion: ML's Security and Privacy Risks.

a. *Model Update Leaks Definition*: Data from dispersed devices is used to update models in decentralized or FL. A central server receives these changes and aggregates them.

   Risk: Model updates have the potential to reveal personal information, even if raw data is never released [22]. For example, an attacker can analyze weight updates to **reconstruct user inputs**, especially if the model is large or the update is sparse. Implication: Sensitive user data like typed messages, health records, or images can be inferred from gradients or parameter updates.

b. *Backdoor Attacks*: These are a type of attack on ML systems in which the attacker introduces secret behavior into the model while it is being trained. The model produces malicious outputs for inputs with a certain trigger but acts properly for the majority of inputs.

c. *Model Inversion Attack Mechanism*: To rebuild private training data, the attacker takes advantage of access to the model's outputs, also known as gradients [23].

   Mechanism of Model Inversion Attacks: The attacker reconstructs critical training data by taking advantage of access to the model's outputs, also known as gradients.

d. *Model Accuracy and Convergence in ML*

   Difficulties in Achieving Global Optimal Performance Definition: In order to get high accuracy, ML models seek to minimize a loss function. It is quite challenging to identify the global minimum because many models (like deep neural networks) are non-convex. It is possible for models to converge to saddle points or local minima. Training data is introduced by data heterogeneity in decentralized contexts. Optimal learning may be delayed or impeded by differences in device capability, data quality, and connectivity.

e. *Asynchronous Learning and Partial Updates*: In federated or decentralized learning, not all devices take part in every training round, and devices may submit updates at various times. Staleness of updates: If a model uses updates based on out-of-date parameters, it may become unstable or converge slowly. Partial participation: Biased learning may result from only a portion of the devices being available at any given time. Ineffective synchronization makes it more difficult to efficiently coordinate and compile changes [24].

7.5 CURRENT DEVELOPMENTS AND REMEDIES

a. *Techniques for Secure Aggregation and DP*: The advancement of privacy-preserving ML, especially in FL frameworks, depends heavily on secure aggregation and DP. New methods to improve model performance and data confidentiality have been proposed recently.
   - *Aggregation Protocols Secure Effectively*: In FL settings, protocols such as e-SeaFL improve scalability and efficiency by providing verifiable aggregation with fewer communication rounds.
   - *Aggregation Gradient Hierarchical Coded*: This method increases the elasticity and usefulness of scattered networks by addressing communication delays and straggler problems [25].
   - *Aggregation Secure Stateful*: This method, which was created for differentially private FL, permits the use of correlated noise during training rounds without relying on a dependable central server, improving privacy guarantees.

b. *Distinctive Privacy Techniques*: By introducing controlled noise into data or calculations, DP safeguards distinct data points. Currently used techniques include Differentially Private Stochastic Gradient Descent (DP-SGD). This technique adds noise to gradients during training in order to strike a balance between privacy and model utility. Because it may be used with a variety of ML models, it is widely used.
   - *Scalable DP (SDP)*: SDP is appropriate for real-time ML applications because it uses adaptive noise scheduling and gradient compression to preserve high model accuracy while guaranteeing privacy.
   - *Solutions and Best Practices*: To successfully implement these tactics, Balance Utility and Privacy, carefully tune noise parameters to get the desired privacy levels without significantly impacting model performance.
   - *Optimize Communication*: To minimize communication overhead in FL configurations, use scarification and effective aggregation methods.

c. *FL*: It uses federated optimization algorithms, such as FedAvg and FedProx, to address problems like data heterogeneity and communication constraints while enabling decentralized model training. First introduced by McMahan et al. FedAvg is a core method in FL that allows distributed clients to train models cooperatively without sharing raw data. FedProx adds a proximal term to the local goal function in order to improve FedAvg's handling of data and system heterogeneity. The goal of this change is to lessen the impact of different client capabilities and non-IID data [26–29].

d. *Blockchain-Based Trust System*: In order to solve issues of trust, security, and accountability, blockchain—which is renowned for its decentralized, immutable, and transparent ledger—is being incorporated into ML more and more. An outline of how blockchain-based trust systems improve machine learning is provided below:
   - *Ensuring Data Integrity Issue*: Reliable and high-quality datasets are essential to ML models. To make sure data inputs haven't been altered, they can be timestamped and hashed on a blockchain ledger. Blockchain is used to confirm the integrity of patient data before it is used for training in healthcare ML systems. In order to solve issues of trust, security, and accountability, blockchain—which is renowned for its decentralized, immutable, and transparent ledger—is being incorporated into ML more and more. An outline of how blockchain-based trust systems improve ML is provided below [30].
   - *FL with Trust Issue*: FL does not have a central trust authority, but it does enable model training on decentralized data. Verifiable consensus is made possible by blockchain, which serves as an impartial coordinator and records model revisions from several parties. Permits contribution tracing and stops harmful changes (like model poisoning).
   - *Automated Trust Function with Smart Contracts*: Smart contracts automate trust processes including model validation, access control, and incentive distribution. For instance, when contributors' data increases the accuracy of the model, a smart contract might automatically compensate them.

7.6 APPLICATIONS AND USE CASES OF MACHINE LEARNING IN FINANCE

a. *Bank Fraud Detection*: Financial services have undergone a transformation thanks to ML, which has improved fraud prevention systems, automated risk detection, and improved client experiences. The identification of banking fraud is one of the most significant uses [31].

   Conventional rule-based methods frequently fall short in identifying complex or dynamic fraud trends. A high transaction volume renders manual monitoring impractical.

   - *Use Real-Time Fraud Detection*: Immediately flag transactions that seem suspicious. In milliseconds, models examine transaction details. For instance, Visa and MasterCard score every transaction in real time using ML. Conventional rule-based methods frequently fall short in identifying complex or dynamic fraud trends. A high transaction volume renders manual monitoring impractical.
   - *Use of Adaptive Fraud Detection Systems*: Constantly absorb new fraud trends. For instance, a model that adjusts to phishing, identity theft, or SIM switch fraud in response to fresh fraud incidents.
   - *Biometrics Based on Behavior*: Track mouse movements and typing speed to identify account takeovers. Use behavioral patterns to categorize users.

b. *The Internet of Things (IoT) and Smart Cities in Machine Learning*

   Through the use of IoT devices and ML, smart cities improve urban living by increasing the responsiveness, sustainability, and efficiency of their infrastructure. In public services, data-driven decision-making heavily relies on the synergy between ML and IoT.

   Smart Traffic Management:

   IoT Gadgets: RFID, GPS, and cameras

   ML Use: Forecast traffic patterns, identify bottlenecks, and improve signal timings

   Example: Reinforcement learning for adaptive traffic signal control.

   Smart Waste Management:

   Smart bins with fill-level sensors are examples of IoT devices. Forecast the best routes and times for waste collection using ML. Lowering carbon emissions and operating expenses is the benefit.

c. *Mobility and Intelligent Transportation*: GPS trackers and communication between automobiles and infrastructure are examples of Internet of Things devices [32]. ML is being used in public transportation to estimate arrival times, optimize routes, and enable autonomous cars.

7.7 CONCLUSION AND FUTURE WORK

By enabling cooperative model training without the need to centralize data, decentralized machine learning, or DML, is completely changing the AI landscape. This method specifically addresses sensitive industries like healthcare, financial services, and smart systems by addressing important concerns like data protection, ownership rights, and effective resource usage. DML offers a lot of benefits, such as privacy-focused learning using P2P or federated networks that preserve local data. To maximize resource use, training duties are distributed among edge devices. AI can be tailored, scaled, and used by a variety of users and situations. Notwithstanding its potential, DML encounters a number of operational and technological challenges, including preventing information leaks and model poisoning, two security concerns. Ensuring model convergence in the face of heterogeneous and unequally distributed data. In decentralized systems, handling asynchronous updates and communication delays is a challenge. Encouraging responsibility and trust between a number of potentially untrustworthy individuals. Notwithstanding the significance of these problems, ongoing research is driving advancements in protocol design, secure aggregation, and optimization techniques. These developments are progressively making DML systems safer, more scalable, and more practical for real-world implementation.

REFERENCES

1. V Mukesh, "A comprehensive review of advanced machine learning techniques for enhancing cybersecurity in blockchain networks", *ISCSITR-IJAI*, vol. 5, no. 01, pp. 1–6, Mar. 2024, Available: https://iscsitr.in/index.php/ISCSITR-IJAI/article/view/ISCSITR-IJAI_05_01_01
2. S. Kamei and S. Taghipour, "A comparison study of centralized and decentralized federated learning approaches utilizing the transformer architecture for estimating remaining useful life," *Reliability Engineering & System Safety*, vol. 233, art. 109130, 2023.
3. A. M. Sheikh, M. R. Islam, M. H. Habaebi, S. A. Zabidi, A. R. Bin Najeeb and A. Kabbani, "A survey on edge computing (EC) security challenges: classification, threats, and mitigation strategies," *Future Internet*, vol. 17, no. 4, p. 175, 2025. DOI: 10.3390/fi17040175
4. M. A. P. Chamikara, P. Bertok, I. Khalil, D. Liu, and S. Camtepe, "Privacy preserving distributed machine learning with federated learning," *Computer Communications*, vol. 171, pp. 112–125, 2021. DOI: 10.1016/j.comcom.2021.02.014
5. D. Alsagheer, L. Xu, and W. Shi, "Decentralized machine learning governance: overview, opportunities, and challenges," *IEEE Access*, vol. 11, pp. 96718–96732, 2023. DOI: 10.1109/ACCESS.2023.3311713
6. M. R. Behera, S. Upadhyay, S. Shetty, and R. Otter, "Federated learning using peer-to-peer network for decentralized orchestration of model weights," *OPAL (Open@LaTrobe) (La Trobe University)*, Mar. 2021, doi: https://doi.org/10.36227/techrxiv.14267468.v1
7. J. G. Gonçalves et al., "Decentralized machine learning framework for the internet of things: enhancing security, privacy, and efficiency in cloud-integrated environments," *Electronics*, vol. 13, no. 21, art. 4185, 2024. DOI: 10.3390/electronics13214185
8. H. Taherdoost, "Blockchain and machine learning: a critical review on security," *Information*, vol. 14, no. 5, p. 295, 2023. DOI: 10.3390/info14050295
9. P. Whig, R. Sharma, N. Yathiraju, A. Jain, and S. Sharma, "Blockchain-enabled secure federated learning systems for advancing privacy and trust in decentralized AI," Model Optimization Methods for Efficient and Edge AI: Federated Learning Architectures, Frameworks and Applications, pp. 321–340, 2025. 10.1002/9781394219230.ch16

10. M. D. Nasim et al., "Principles and Components of Federated Learning Architectures," *arXiv preprint arXiv:2502.05273*, Feb. 2025. DOI: 10.48550/arXiv.2502.05273
11. C. Gong, X. Zhang, Y. Lin, H. Lu, P. C. Su, and J. Zhang, "Federated learning for heterogeneous data integration and privacy protection," 2025. DOI: 10.20944/preprints202503.2211.v1
12. J. Tu, L. Yang, and J. Cao, "Distributed machine learning in edge computing: challenges, solutions and future directions," *ACM Computing Surveys*, vol. 57, no. 5, pp. 1–37, 2025. DOI: 10.1145/3708495
13. M. G. Hanna et al., "Future of artificial intelligence (AI)-machine learning (ML) trends in pathology and medicine," *Modern Pathology*, p. 100705, 2025. DOI: 10.3390/fi17050190
14. Y. Wang and X. Yang, "Machine Learning-Based Cloud Computing Compliance Process Automation," *arXiv preprint arXiv:2502.16344*, Feb. 2025. DOI: 10.13140/RG.2.2.19853.86240
15. N. Ahmad and J. Hera, "Optimizing Big Data Processing: Machine Learning Approaches for Scalable and Efficient Analytics," 2025. DOI: 10.13140/RG.2.2.12496.21768
16. M. M. Panda, S. N. Panda, and P. K. Pattnaik, "Forecasting foreign currency exchange rate using convolutional neural network," *International Journal of Advanced Computer Science and Applications*, vol. 13, no. 2, 2022. DOI:10.14569/IJACSA.2022.0130272
17. B. Assiri and A. Sheneamer, "Fault tolerance in distributed systems using deep learning approaches," *PLoS One*, vol. 20, no. 1, p. e0310657, 2025. DOI: 10.1371/journal.pone.0310657
18. A. Alshuaibi, M. Almaayah, and A. Ali, "Machine learning for cybersecurity issues: a systematic review," *Security Challenges*, vol. 1, p. 2, 2025. DOI: 10.63180/jcsra.thestap.2025.1.4
19. B. Ezard, L. Li, H. Hao, R. Wang, and S. An, "Robust structural damage detection with deep multiple instance learning for sensor fault tolerance," *Engineering Structures*, vol. 331, p. 119957, 2025. DOI: 10.1016/j.engstruct.2025.119957
20. Y. Jia et al., "A deep reinforcement learning approach using asymmetric self-play for robust multirobot flocking," *IEEE Transactions on Industrial Informatics*, 2025. DOI: 10.1109/TII.2024.3523576
21. A. M. Akinsiku, "A comprehensive survey of federated learning approaches for privacy-preserving machine learning," *Tech-Sphere Journal for Pure and Applied Sciences*, vol. 2, no. 1, 2025. DOI: 10.5281/zenodo.15830919
22. W. Yang, S. Wang, D. Wu, T. Cai, Y. Zhu, S. Wei, Y. Zhang, X. Yang, Z. Tang, and Y. Li, "Deep learning model inversion attacks and defenses: a comprehensive survey," *Artificial Intelligence Review*, 58(8), p. 242, 2025. DOI: 10.48550/arXiv.2501.18934
23. M. Meeus, I. Shilov, S. Jain, M. Faysse, M. Rei, and Y. A. de Montjoye, "SoK: Membership inference attacks on LLMs are rushing nowhere (and how to fix it)," in *2025 IEEE Conference on Secure and Trustworthy Machine Learning (SaTML)*, Apr. 2025, pp. 385–401. DOI: *https://arxiv.org/pdf/2406.17975*
24. W. Malik, S. Gul, and G. M. Qureshi, "Regulating artificial intelligence: challenges for data protection and privacy in developing nations," *Journal of Social Signs Review*, vol. 3, no. 05, pp. 95–108, 2025. DOI: https://www.researchgate.net/publication/392598789
25. X. Li, Y. Liu, R. Zhang, and N. Zhang, "Probabilistic failure assessment of oil and gas gathering pipelines using machine learning approach," *Reliability Engineering & System Safety*, vol. 256, p. 110747, 2025. DOI: 10.1016/j.ress.2024.110747.
26. J. Chen, D. Chen, J. Cui, and H. Zhong, "Backdoor attack on encryption-protected vertical federated learning," *IEEE Transactions on Information Forensics and Security*, 2025. DOI: 10.1109/TIFS.2025.3581095

27. S. A. Khowaja et al., "Block encryption layer (BELA): zero-trust defense against model inversion attacks for federated learning in 5G/6G systems," *IEEE Open Journal of the Communications Society*, 2025. DOI: 10.1109/OJCOMS.2025.3526768
28. A. Pati, et al., "Simulating Fog of Medical Things: Research Challenges and Opportunities," *IEEE Access*, pp. 1–1, Jan. 2024, doi: https://doi.org/10.1109/access.2024.3468015.
29. N. Uzlaner, T. Raviv, N. Shlezinger, and K. Todros, "Asynchronous online adaptation via modular drift detection for deep receivers," *IEEE Transactions on Wireless Communications*, 2025. DOI: 10.48550/arXiv.2407.09134
30. A. V. Singh and D. S. J. Anwar Khan, "Federated learning for secure blockchain-based identity verification in decentralized systems," *International Journal of Advanced Research and Multidisciplinary Trends (IJARMT)*, vol. 2, no. 2, pp. 152–168, 2025. DOI: https://www.ijarmt.com/index.php/j/article/view/186
31. E. Alaka, K. Abiodun, S. O. Jinadu, E. Igba, and V. N. Ezeh, "Data integrity in decentralized financial systems: a model for auditable, automated reconciliation using blockchain and AI," *International Journal of Management and Commerce Innovations*, vol. 13, no. 1, pp. 136–158, 2025. DOI: 10.5281/zenodo.15753099
32. H. Wu, "Research on malicious code detection technology for binary and WASM bytecode files in Web3.0 distributed applications," *International Journal of Big Data Intelligent Technology*, vol. 6, no. 1, pp. 92–100, 2025. DOI: 10.38007/IJBDIT.2025.060109

8 Enhancing Supply Chain Sustainability Through Blockchain Technology

A Scholarly Analysis

Anupama Sen, Saptarshi Kumar Sarkar, and Debarun Joardar

8.1 INTRODUCTION

Because of increased worries about climate change, dwindling resources and higher social expectations, global supply chains are under intense review. There is pressure on supply chains from corporations, regulators, investors and consumers to both contribute value and strictly follow Sustainable Supply Chain Management (SSCM) principles [1]. In SSCM, environmental management, social equality and effective leadership are joined as the environmental, social and governance (ESG) criteria [2]. Because of these principles, companies need to be environmentally friendly, treat workers with respect and monitor all parts of their supply chains. Even with the extra pressure, old supply chain methods often do not have the visibility and linkages that would improve sustainability performance [3]. Because of scattered information and broken data flows, centralized supply chains tend to have trouble with real-time sustainability checks [4]. As a result, it becomes difficult to track where products come from, prove their eco-friendly nature and protect against copycat industries and corrupt companies. Because of this, Bitcoin's main supporting infrastructure, blockchain technology, is now emerging as a promising way to address these problems [5]. Using blockchain, many nodes in the network synchronously generate, store and verify transactions which keeps the data unchanged and clear without any central leader [6]. All transactions and data are connected to previous blocks in an unchangeable way, so authorized participants can easily check the records independently.

Blockchain in supply chains is valuable because it makes it impossible for records to be tampered with. Logging every change a product goes through from raw material to retail, logistics and manufacture on a blockchain ensures everything can be checked for authenticity and traced [7]. This becomes especially necessary for sectors open to fraud, for instance pharmaceuticals and luxury goods, as false products can be extremely dangerous [5]. Because blockchain does not depend on one central authority, stakeholders trust one another more, as any existing data cannot be lied about or forged later without agreement from everyone involved. Blockchain offers the important ability to ensure that information about the supply chain cannot be

 DOI: 10.1201/9781003658597-8

edited or faked. Through tracking every stage a product goes through, including mining, processing, shipping and retail, blockchain ensures the product is easy to verify and trace throughout the supply chain [7]. For example, pharma and luxury goods industries are especially affected because fake products from these areas have a potential to cause serious risks to users [5]. Because data on blockchains cannot be changed without all agreeing, this encourages different parties to trust each other and safeguards their information. Besides providing traceability, blockchain ensures that complicated business steps are automated through smart contracts, which are embeddable computer programs that begin doing specified tasks when required [6]. For example, smart contracts make it easier to process customs, settle payments or review compliance, which can lower errors and heavy administration and boost the speed of supply chain processes.

This part of the book looks at how blockchain is used in SSCM frameworks, noting how it can drive change in several sectors. To numerically review the impact of blockchain on sustainability, the chapter introduces the Blockchain Sustainability Index (BSI), which collects data on various levels, including efficiency, managing waste, following ESG guidelines and promoting transparency [8, 9]. Compared to other standards, the BSI offers a clear and complete way to understand the ways blockchain can boost sustainable supply chain activities [10]. Furthermore, the chapter compares blockchain to familiar traditional systems, including Enterprise Resource Planning (ERP) and Radio-Frequency Identification (RFID) [4]. Although ERP systems control the supply chain from one center and RFID tracks assets automatically, both are missing the key blockchain features of decentralized verification, changed data cannot be altered, and smart contracts for automation [11]. Comparing the two shows that blockchain surpasses others when it comes to improving security, limiting fraud and creating trusted relations among stakeholders. Since blockchain is not a total solution, the chapter investigates how it can combine with Artificial Intelligence (AI) and the Internet of Things (IoT) as part of Industry 4.0. With AI, we can analyze a lot of data on the blockchain to make decisions, predict upcoming demand and find related signs of environmental risk [12]. In addition, with IoT sensors on machines, important environmental and work environment details, including temperature, humidity and location, can relay real-time information to the blockchain as soon as they are detected, allowing for quick verification against sustainable criteria. Due to these three technologies linking up, supply chains are now smart and clear and stable to deal with dynamic sustainability issues.

8.2 LITERATURE REVIEW

Numerous works suggest that existing supply networks must have more coordination and share information and more closely manage sustainability to achieve more ESG needs [2]. SSCM must also adopt an inclusive strategy to ensure that products and services are provided in the most efficient manner possible with minimal environmental harm and in a responsible manner across the entire supply chain [13]. Some traditional systems are in common use, including ERP and RFID, but they tend to have limited capabilities to meet the requirements of SSCM. Nonetheless, such systems typically would not enable you to monitor the source of your products simultaneously. RFID works well for locating assets quickly using signals, but it supplies only physical tracking and not full traceability through all systems [11]. More people are seeing that blockchain succeeds in addressing these faults because of its decentralized way of operating and using cryptography [5]. Instead of old ways, blockchain creates reliable records that are available to everyone who needs to see them as well as fast and secure information sharing in the supply chain [14]. From this, employees and customers can trust in the integrity of the company's activities.

Saberi et al. highlight how blockchain improves SSCM by providing efficient traceability and minimizing fraud and counterfeiting in complicated global supply networks [5]. Also, using blockchain, supplier verification is more reliable and contract fulfillment is handled automatically by smart contracts which helps stop human mistakes. More applications involving blockchain help highlight its powerful benefits. As an example, Kamble et al. showed how blockchain makes it easier to verify the origin and ensure the quality of food products [15]. Blockchain integration in logistics has been found to make freight documents easier to manage, help plan delivery routes more efficiently and cut back on delays thanks to decentralized data handling [16].

While plenty of research shows blockchain's benefits for different industries, the findings are often contained inside categories and do not discuss blockchain's total impact. As this chapter points out, there is an absence of quantitative measurements for blockchain's effects on the environment, so it introduces a single index, the Blockchain Sustainability Index (BSI), that effectively rates blockchain's impact. Thanks to the BSI, we can compare companies from many industries and measure their blockchain sustainability using a common approach. This means it can help with exams as well as with corporate and government goals for digital changes that support sustainability. The most successful results of blockchain are realized when it becomes a component of the Industry 4.0 framework. Having integrated blockchain and AI and the IoT, nowadays, the supply chains are intelligent, have an opportunity to use data and self-manage [17]. It can predict and have anomaly finding with AI and dynamically change its physical assets with IoT. Combining the data protection of blockchain with AI, we can contribute to the global sustainability of the supply chain system. To find out the strengths and weaknesses of ERP, RFID and Blockchain, Table 8.1 contains the key characteristics of them.

TABLE 8.1
Comparison of ERP, RFID and Blockchain Features of Supply Chain Sustainability

Feature	ERP	RFID	Blockchain
Data Integrity	Medium	Low	High
Real-Time Visibility	Low	Medium	High
Transparency	Limited	Limited	Full
Interoperability	Medium	Medium	High
Decentralization	No	No	Yes
Immutability	No	Partial	Yes

With the completion of this literature review, it is evident that a critical study of the role of blockchain in SSCM is a necessary analysis that this chapter attempts to provide through the BSI framework and an integrated roadmap.

8.3 BLOCKCHAIN TECHNOLOGY: AN OVERVIEW

Blockchain is an online communication system where people can conduct transactions electronically without the presence of a central authority [14]. Like in normal databases, there is no connection between the transaction records in a blockchain, but they are interconnected using cryptography, and they form a chain that can hardly be altered [18]. Thanks to each block's hash of the previous one, timestamp and transaction information, there is no way to change data on earlier blocks without changing those that follow. Thanks to decentralization, blockchain does away with a central authority and lets each person on the network share control [19]. It stops the system from relying on a single weak point, which strengthens its resistance to disruptions—an important advantage in today's complex and worldwide supply chains [20].

Because it is transparent, blockchain stands out as a strong choice for SSCM. Stakeholders who are part of a permissioned blockchain can instantaneously view and approve transaction information, making it a useful single source of data [21]. Being clear about employees' actions makes organizations more accountable, encourages trust among groups and helps them obey laws and ethical rules [22]. Examples from the agricultural sector allow stakeholders to check the origin, certification and how products are handled at every part of the process, supporting food safety and sustainability. Because it is impossible to adjust previous records without agreement, immutability underlies the reliable function of blockchain [20]. This option concentrates on one of the main issues of supply chain management: data change protection. Any form of supply chain data change, whether planned or not, can lead to enormous issues. Since blockchain does not allow the modification of transaction records, we possess the correct evidence of every activity in the supply chain.

With smart contracts applied to blockchain, business processes can be automated by writing code into the system [23]. With such digital agreements, there are preprogrammed activities that occur during occurrence of certain events, and as such, less manual checks and paperwork will be required [24]. To save time and misunderstandings, a smart contract agreement between the supplier and the retailer will make sure that shipping is checked and automatically compensated by sensors. All these characteristics unite to eliminate the major issues in the traditional supply chain management, which include incomplete data, unstructured record keeping, slow reconciliation and inability to verify whether a product is authentic. Without compatibility between systems, different stakeholders in a conventional supply chain often find themselves working with disconnected data. A single, insuperable and always-updated ledger made available by blockchain allows everyone involved to share data openly [25]. Because blockchain provides uncensored and unalterable records, sectors like pharmaceuticals and electronics struggle far less with fraud and counterfeiting. The technology allows for each unit of a product to be followed from the beginning of its production to its final delivery [26].

Beyond those features, blockchain encompasses governance improvements by allowing participants to agree collectively and hold each other accountable. Various blockchain models such as public, private and consortium, may be used depending on what level of trust and privacy supply chain actors require. The broad range of uses for blockchain includes ethical fashion and controlling the safety and temperature of vaccines. In addition, connecting blockchain to other Industry 4.0 tools like AI and IoT makes it more useful. IoT devices help blockchain by providing current data on temperature, humidity and location automatically and trustfully. Anomalies, possible disruptions and best ways to manage routes and inventory can be discovered and predicted with analysis done by AI algorithms, all relying on blockchain for data security. Blockchain is already being used through industry-sponsored projects to tackle problems in the supply chain. IBM Food Trust applies blockchain to following the journey of food, allowing problems to be addressed and supply chains made safer. As part of MediLedger Project, drug companies use blockchain to confirm the legitimacy of send-outs and stop fake drugs from being shipped.

8.4 BLOCKCHAIN AND SSCM: CONCEPTUAL FRAMEWORK

In SSCM, blockchain helps by ensuring four points: traceability, transparency, efficiency and security. Because these problems affect constant challenges in traditional supply chains, blockchain can have a bigger effect on ESG performance.

8.4.1 Traceability

The term "traceability" in supply chains means being able to track products from where they are made to where they are sold. Blockchain makes it possible to follow any movement or change because every transaction is recorded in an unchangeable record. This is most important in fields such as agriculture and drug manufacturing, as what happens to the goods during handling can determine their safety, standard and legal status. As an illustration, producers of agricultural goods need carefully collected data on how their products are cultivated, handled with pesticides and stored in the cold chain. Also, pharmaceutical supply chains are expected to ensure that counterfeits do not make their way to consumers. Blockchain ensures that all documentation on sourcing, processing and transporting is irreversible. Giving each stakeholder access to the same truth helps simplify remembering facts, verifying accounts and creating reports [27].

8.4.2 Transparency

It issues when information about supply chain activities and transactions is easy for everyone involved to see and comprehend. Because blockchain uses a shared ledger, authorized people such as manufacturers, suppliers, distributors and regulators can access the same and most recent records. Access to data in the open decreases imbalances in knowledge, increases trust and encourages people to make decisions together. In these areas like fashion and electronics, where sourcing and labor rights are important, blockchain can record supplier licenses, labor behavior and information about sustainability. This gives consumers a way to check how environmentally responsible brands are, and it allows companies to demonstrate that they follow ESG demands [22].

8.4.3 Efficiency

Because most supply chain tasks are done manually and information is not shared well, traditional supply chains often become bogged down by bureaucratic processes. With smart contracts stored on the blockchain, blockchain resolves the need by automatically enforcing contracts and rules. Because of these contracts, there is less chance of delay, involvement of intermediaries or human mistakes. Thus, in logistics, it is possible to release funds following confirmation of delivery by IoT sensors. You can set inventory replenishment to happen automatically when thresholds are met in manufacturing. The changes made in production bring down expenses, speed up production and help save the environment [24].

8.4.4 Security

In digital supply chains, keeping data safe is very important. A centralized database can be easily changed, hacked or attacked by people inside the organization. Because blockchain is decentralized and uses cryptography, supply chain data is shielded from risks to confidentiality and integrity. Changes to transaction records in the blockchain are verified with consensus and the data is encrypted and timestamped, so altering transactions is unlikely. With this rigorous security framework, all sensitive data such as pricing, contract details and patents is kept safe from danger or sharing without permission all along the supply chain [18] (Table 8.2).

TABLE 8.2
Comparison of Blockchain Capabilities in SSCM

Dimension	Traditional Systems (ERP/RFID)	Blockchain-Based Systems
Traceability	Limited to internal records	End-to-end visibility across all stakeholders
Transparency	Selective access, potential data silos	Shared ledger ensures real-time access and updates
Efficiency	Manual processes, prone to errors	Automated via smart contracts, reduces paperwork
Security	Centralized, vulnerable to breaches	Decentralized, cryptographically secure

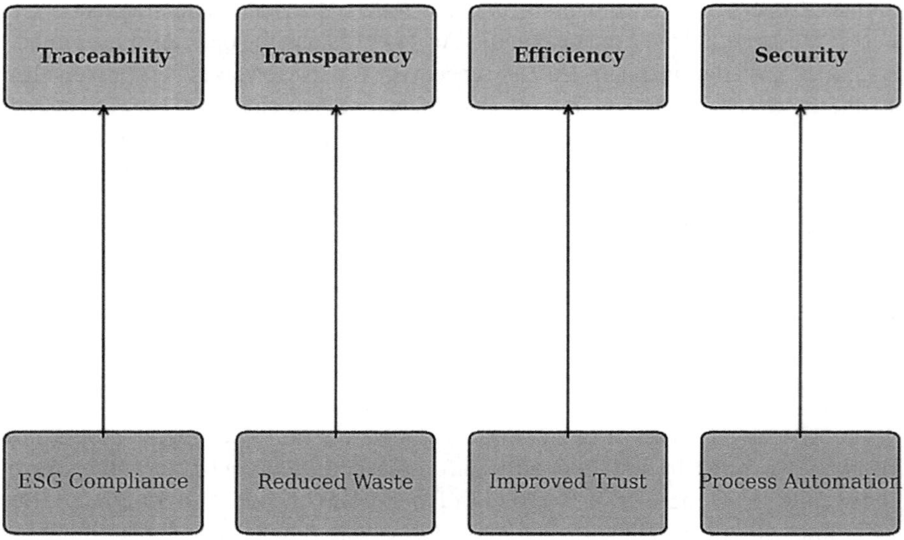

FIGURE 8.1 Blockchain integration in SSCM.

8.5 MULTI-SECTORAL ANALYSIS

The greatest power of blockchain in SSCM is seen in key industries facing issues related to transparency, tracking goods and data integrity. This part looks at five areas (Figure 8.1), agriculture, fashion, pharmaceuticals, logistics and electronics, that have their own sustainability issues and can gain from using blockchain.

8.5.1 Agriculture

Agriculture supply chains for items that go bad easily are affected by food fraud, inconsistent quality and not being able to track the products well. Consumers and regulators are demanding origin, safety and ethics verification in products. They are also not so good in presenting clear and up-to-date details of how and where produce is treated. Blockchain makes it possible to track every step of agricultural goods from the farm to the end consumer using a permanent record of every transaction. It makes it easier to find out about false food claims, allow less wastage and ensure security. With IBM Food Trust, everyone from farmers to retailers can keep track of produce in real time, which boosts clarity and accountability along the supply chain. As an example, Walmart applied this system and cut down the time it takes to trace mangoes, from seven days to just 2.2 seconds.

Each participant in the supply chain shares details on the blockchain, including those about harvesting, transportation and retail. As a result, trust among partners goes up, and regulators and consumers are provided with accurate information, which helps the food sector become more sustainable by cutting waste and improving resource usage and food delivery safety.

8.5.2 Fashion

The global fashion industry worth over $2.5 trillion is said to cause environmental harm, use unfair labor and grow fake products. Due to fast fashion, these problems have grown, which makes openness and responsibility in the supply chain more essential than ever. Blockchain creates a digital history of every step taken with a garment—from choosing the materials to making it and selling it. It helps to follow where each raw material and person involved in production comes from. Provenance and VeChain are among the startups that use blockchain to oversee the whole process of making clothes. Brands using Provenance can share transparent supply chain information that comes from sensor technology and blockchain data. Because of this openness, people who buy clothes are more confident that the textiles are not fake or illegally sourced, and it also appeals to consumers concerned with how their purchases affect the environment. Using blockchain means that organic and recycled resources can be validated and fair treatment of employees is insured, which helps sustain both the environment and society.

8.5.3 Pharmaceuticals

Because of counterfeit drugs, the pharmaceutical industry loses an estimated $200 billion every year and places many people at great health risk. Fraud like this becomes possible because supply chain issues and multi-layered distribution networks are common. All steps, from making the drug, packing it, moving it, to delivering it, are logged in an unchangeable ledger due to blockchain. A unique identifier is given to every batch and all transactions are checked and marked with the time they were done, so any attempt to change data would be immediately noticed. Medi Ledger, which sometimes works with Pfizer and Genentech, relies on blockchain to differentiate real drugs from fakes and prevent the market from becoming flooded with adulterated drugs. Blockchain technology helps maintain the quality and source of data to protect public health and also meet requirements set out in laws like the U.S. Drug Supply Chain Security Act (DSCSA).

8.5.4 Logistics

Logistics nowadays is carried out by linking carriers, freight brokers, customs and warehousing partners. When paperwork is ineffective, data is sent late and messages are misinterpreted, this usually adds to costs and to the total carbon emissions generated. By digitizing papers (like bills of lading) and automating workflow processes using smart contracts, blockchain simplifies shipping and gives real-time updates on the movement of goods. Using TradeLens from Maersk and IBM, different companies in the logistics chain can safely exchange their data in one place. With usage in more than 600 ports and terminals globally, TradeLens has given insights into 10 million weekly shipping happenings. Due to its openness and resistance to modifications, blockchain will minimize the chances of conflicts regarding delivery, reduce delivery times and decrease paperwork. With this kind of effort, less containers

TABLE 8.3
Blockchain Applications Across Sectors

Sector	Key Challenges	Blockchain Benefits
Agriculture	Food fraud, traceability	Real-time tracking, safety compliance
Fashion	Counterfeiting, unethical sourcing	Supply transparency, origin authentication
Pharmaceuticals	Drug counterfeiting	Tamper-proof tracking, trust verification
Logistics	Shipment delays, documentation	Paperless processes, real-time updates
Electronics	Conflict minerals, labor violations	Compliance tracking, digital audits

are shipped without any cargo, less emission and more partners around the world improve collaboration with each other toward a more sustainable logistics system.

8.5.5 Electronics

Because the electronics industry has complicated manufacturing and a long chain of suppliers, it is being checked for performing unethical practices in mining and employing workers. Complying with the Dodd-Frank Act and the EU Conflict Minerals Regulation is compulsory for firms to show their ethical sourcing. Each action involving making the components, from collecting raw materials to final assembly and delivery, is recorded by blockchain. It is because of this that suppliers can conduct audits remotely that demonstrate that the minerals are mined in a lawful manner.

Samsung Data System (SDS) which deals with IT solutions for Samsung is adding blockchain to help track the supply chain of their electronics. Their system provides a clear view of all the information required to report on ESG because they input data on numerous suppliers. Furthermore, blockchain technology and IoT sensors allow firms to control the temperature and humidity when transporting sensitive devices, thereby significantly reducing returns and wastage and greatly preventing quality problems (Table 8.3).

8.6 BLOCKCHAIN SUSTAINABILITY INDEX (BSI)

BSI is an additional new measure discussed in this chapter to evaluate the impact of blockchain on SSCM. The overall score provided by Blockchain Global ESG Index illustrates how blockchain is used in four key domains, namely efficiency, waste management, adherence to ESG principles and enhancing transparency. Following an extensive examination of a large volume of literature and case studies, the following dimensions were identified that provides a convenient framework for measuring the sustainability of blockchain in every place it is implemented.

8.6.1 Components of the Blockchain Sustainability Index (BSI)

The BSI is a weighted combination of four important parameters: Inclusion of Efficiency Gain (EG) indicates an increase in efficiency of 30%.

Blockchain ensures that operations are done more efficiently, redundancy is minimized and verification of transactions takes less time because of smart contracts and decentralized approval. It measures improved productivity, faster lead times and how smoothly operations are run.

$$\text{Waste Reduction (WR)} - 25\%.$$

It looks at whether blockchain can reduce the squandering of resources by allowing real-time observation, making predictions more accurate and controlling inventory better. When blockchain lowers overproduction and waste, it helps protect the environment.

25% of the performance score is based on ESG Compliance Improvement (EC).

Today, supply chains are depending more on ESG as a key requirement. It checks how effectively blockchain backs environmental standards, fair labor practices and ethical sourcing through easily auditable information.

$$\text{Transparency Score (TS)} - \text{contributing } 20\%.$$

Being clear about supply chain processes enables producers, manufacturers, regulators and consumers to monitor where the products come from and observe their transactions. It shows how much information can be accessed using blockchain on the network.

8.6.2 Mathematical Model

The BSI is worked out using a weighted linear approach.

$$\text{BSI} = 0.3 \times \text{EG} + 0.25 \times \text{WR} + 0.25 \times \text{EC} + 0.2 \times \text{TS} \quad (8.1)$$

It gives people freedom to adapt the formula as they see fit. For example, the system can be fine-tuned so that it stresses transparency in food or ESG standards in electronics.

8.6.3 Empirical Values and Calculation

Compiling information from case studies and latest research within various industries:

The efficiency gain (EG) is 60%.

Numerous organizations in logistics and agriculture using blockchain claim a 60% rise in process efficiency thanks to automation, fewer documents and faster reconciliation [28].

$$\text{Waste Reduction (WR)} = 50\%.$$

Having visible data on products and predictive analytics thanks to blockchain has cut material and process waste linked to perishable goods by 50% [29].

There was a 45% completion of work on Eco, Social and Governance Compliance (EC).

Since the process of ESG monitoring is based on fixed registers and decentralized audit, it is now much easier to become certified and to comply with government regulations, by approximately 45% [9].

The Transparency Score (TS) is 70%.

Due to the DLT, the supply chain visibility is significantly improved in comparison to legacy ERP, which increased the transparency 70 times [30].

Introducing the new values into the formula (8.1), we get,

$$BSI = 0.3 \times 60 + 0.25 \times 50 + 0.25 \times 45 + 0.2 \times 70 = 18 + 12.5 + 11.25 + 14 = 55.75$$

8.6.4 Interpretation of the BSI Score

The BSI score of blockchain in most industries is 55.75/100, which means moderately high demand to make supply chains more sustainable. Even though there is still much more to achieve, mainly in ESG compliance and efficiency, the results so far show that blockchain is able to transform supply chains that focus on sustainability [10].

It allows officials to compare and track the progress of blockchain efforts. It is possible for companies to benchmark their blockchain strategy against the sector's normal practices and notice where improvements could be made.

8.6.5 Comparative Insights

To clearly explain the impact of blockchain on the BSI, Table 8.4 shows what score each component achieved and its relative weight.

8.6.6 Sectoral Relevance of BSI

BSI is useful in many different sectors. Make sure that agriculture improves how perishable goods are managed and reduces waste. It puts ESG principles and the ability to trace products first to protect against counterfeit drugs.

TABLE 8.4
Weighted Contribution of Blockchain Parameters to the Blockchain Sustainability Index (BSI)

Parameter	Weight (%)	Sectoral Average (%)	Weighted Contribution
Efficiency Gain (EG)	30	60	18.00
Waste Reduction (WR)	25	50	12.50
ESG Compliance Improvement (EC)	25	45	11.25
Transparency Score (TS)	20	70	14.00
Total BSI Score	**100**		**55.75**

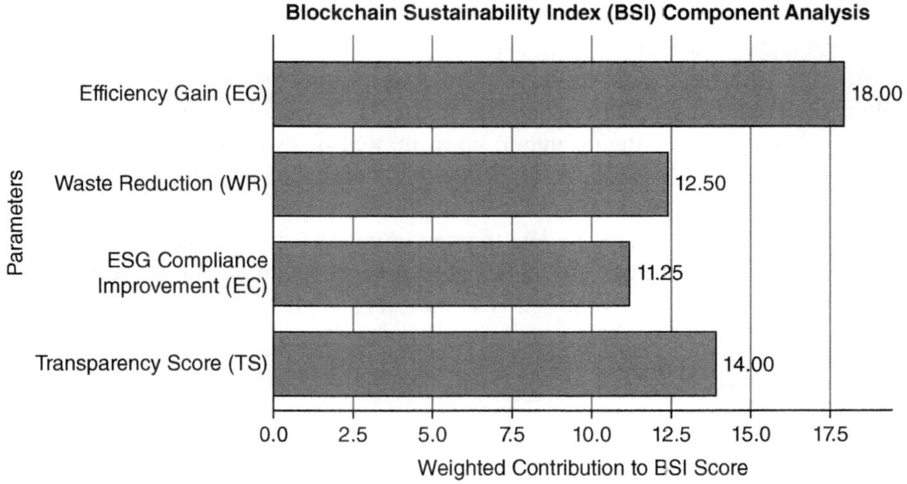

FIGURE 8.2 Component-wise analysis of the blockchain sustainability index (BSI).

Fashion: It concentrates on getting materials in an ethical manner and informing customers openly. At the stage of electronic production, it is necessary to have documentation about minerals and environmental compliance. It seeks different ways to work faster and safely to store documentation. Industries might find these parameters more or less important, and the BSI framework can be adapted to suit their needs for closer analysis (Figure 8.2).

8.7 COMPARATIVE ANALYSIS WITH ERP AND RFID

Supply chain management systems have relied on ERP and RFID technologies for a long time. They offer basic functions for logistics, planning resources, managing inventory and tracking products. Yet, because supply chains are moving toward being sustainable, transparent and strong in a more tightly regulated global economy, the weaknesses of traditional systems are more visible. Blockchain has appeared as a strong choice because it improves many supply chain problems and ensures safe, easy-to-follow and efficient procedures.

8.7.1 Limitations of ERP and RFID in Sustainable Supply Chains

ERP Systems: ERP platforms gather all essential data from every part of the business for planning. But having a central focus in their design makes them less flexible: while getting information related to one's business smooth and efficient, ERP does not easily connect with external partners. It complicates how the organizations can notice what the other is doing. ERP is poor at tracing products in their winding through numerous supply levels and processes.

The old ERP systems may not be flexible and may not be at all compatible with the new technology available at the exact moment that can be very expensive and can even increase the set-ups of the new systems [4]. No Real-Time Auditing: Although

ERP brands can trace the changes, they still do not generate entries that cannot be changed and can be viewed by everyone.

RFID Technology: RFID is the concept of identifying the tags attached to various physical objects using electromagnetic waves. RFID may be applied to give real-time updates and track the inventory; however, it also has its problems: RFID technology can give an item-level monitoring; however, it does not store the identity of the supplier or the information of their compliance.

RFID may be vulnerable to data tampering unless it is adequately connected to the back end. RFID captures the location of a product but does not provide any detail on its historical location, or the ability to trace its complete lifecycle.

8.7.2 Comparative Advantage of Blockchain Technology

It is a decentralized, encrypted and immutable record-keeping method. Every transaction is stored in a block, authenticated through the consensus system and linked safely to the block that came before it. Blockchain solves most of the key issues compared to ERP and RFID (Table 8.5).

8.7.3 Key Advantages of Blockchain Over ERP and RFID

In the context of supply chain management, blockchain technology provides various benefits over traditional systems such as ERP and RFID. First, its immutable character helps with the requirement to have records that can not be easily manipulated to improve audit trails and regulatory compliance, a shortcoming with ERP and RFID. Second, blockchain provides real end-to-end traceability of the track-and-trace of products, which in effect allows the delivery of visibility of the overall lifecycle of a product in the context of ethical sourcing and adherence to rules and regulations as well as environmental stewardship. Unlike ERP systems, which only connect records at the organizational level, blockchain

TABLE 8.5
Comparison of the ERP, RFID and Blockchain Within the Supply Chain Functions

Feature	ERP	RFID	Blockchain
Data immutability	Low	Medium	High
Real-time updates	Medium	High	High
Decentralization	No	No	Yes
Transparency	Limited	Limited	Full
Lifecycle tracking	Medium	Low	High
Security	Medium	Medium	High
Integration cost	Medium	Low	High
Auditability	Medium	Low	High
Automation via smart contracts	No	No	Yes

enables interoperability decentralization, which means that various stakeholders can view the same secure data without intermediaries, building trust. Last, the inherent security of blockchain, which incorporates encryption, timestamping and validation with a consensus-based protocol, reduces the risk of fraud and loss that RFID systems face with threats like signal spoofing. In addition, as outlined earlier, blockchain automatically coordinates supply chain processes using smart contracts, codified agreements with outcomes and consequences, to execute the contracts, without human involvement, rapidly reducing costs, inefficiencies and errors with outcomes that ERP and RFID don't automatically coordinate.

8.7.4 Addressing the Cost Barrier

Some of the major concerns with blockchain are the high charges to initially set up the system. To implement, companies must change their business procedures, train employees, link with older systems and maintain cybersecurity. Yet, the one-time cost should be reviewed with the potential future savings in mind: fewer cases of fraud and counterfeiting: this is extremely important in pharmaceuticals, luxury goods and electronics. Automation means that less labor is needed and paperwork decreases. Having more transparent and traceable processes aids companies in keeping up with rules and gaining investor and customer reliability. Competitive Advantage: Individuals and organizations looking at ethics tend to choose companies with transparent supply chain management.

8.7.5 Real-World Adoption

Global giants such as Maersk and IBM with its TradeLens platform use blockchain to help improve transparency and efficiency in logistics. Blockchain works the same way for Walmart, helping them trace a food product to its source immediately, much faster than waiting days or weeks with older approach. As can be seen, blockchain reduces waiting time, improves who is held accountable and makes better use of resources, even though it requires a start-up expense.

8.8 CHALLENGES AND LIMITATIONS

Blockchain technology can greatly improve the transparency, trackability and running of supply chains, but it has not been fully implemented everywhere because of several problems. Various studies and hands-on implementations have shown that the switch to blockchain-based systems is not without problems, which arise mainly from difficulties on both technical and non-technical sides. It is important for companies, regulators and technologists to be aware of these barriers when aiming to make blockchain work for SSCM.

8.8.1 Interoperability Issues

One of the biggest technical difficulties is making sure blockchain shares information easily with tools such as ERP, RFID and cloud-based logistics. Most of these systems are created on their own structures like Ethereum, Hyperledger Fabric and Corda, where every system has its own standards, protocols and coding languages. A lack of standardization stops information from transferring smoothly, which limits how well different supply chain parts can communicate and work together. Because legacy systems were not originally made for decentralized networks, it became costly and inefficient to try to integrate them. Trying to overcome interoperability challenges, people are working to establish blockchain-agnostic protocols and middleware options. Even so, adopting this model is still difficult in big, complex supply chains because there aren't any universally used frameworks [31].

8.8.2 It Is More Expensive to Implement CRM Systems

Setting up a blockchain project involves a hefty initial investment for building the system, setting up the infrastructure, protecting it from cyberattacks, connecting to current databases and maintenance afterward. These high one-off costs are too much for many small and medium enterprises (SMEs). In addition, scalability challenges, especially with public blockchain systems, can cause costs to go up. With more transactions taking place, more computing resources are needed, which reduces the speed at which transactions are processed and raises expenses. Such concerns have caught more attention when blockchain is used in areas where there is heavy traffic such as logistics and retail operations [32]. Private and consortium blockchains address certain issues, but they also add governance issues and managing trust among those involved. So, until more economical solutions are available, adopting blockchain may be limited mostly to large companies with the resources they need.

8.8.3 Regulatory and Legal Uncertainty

A major non-technical issue is that some rules are unclear in this area. The laws that control blockchain in supply chain data, trading and managing identity are not fully mature yet. As blockchain networks can be global and do not care about borders, laws in different locations on data privacy, trading and record keeping are directly contradictory to them. Let us take blockchain's property of never being able to change as an example, since it conflicts with General Data Protection Regulation (GDPR)'s requirement to delete personal data upon request. Similarly, the binding character of smart contracts is relative in nature with consistent controversies where multiple legal frameworks are involved. There is no single set of standards across the world, so companies are hesitant about blockchain. The regulators must also devise rules to ensure the businesses do not embark in a law suit spree, defame their name or risk of not acting to the order so that the decision-makers will be more cautious to invest [33].

8.8.4 Shortage of Skilled Workforce

Strong knowledge of cryptographic engineering, smart contract design, decentralized applications (dApps) and cybersecurity are needed to work with blockchain technology. The issue here is that there is no easy way to find talented leaders, primarily in the developing economies. Supply chain experts are sometimes unsure how to apply blockchain in business activities. Being separated by this knowledge gap, technologists and supply chain managers have trouble designing and carrying out effective and scaled solutions. A full and coordinated training approach is necessary, which must be led by academic institutions, industry and agencies. Joining blockchain technology with supply chain management in educational programs can address the shortage of people with these skills and encourage faster use of blockchain [34].

8.8.5 Organizational Resistance and Change Management

Introducing blockchain technology often means businesses have to alter their cultural habits, daily procedures and the way they communicate with others. Many people resist changes caused by blockchain when it breaks up traditional structures or challenges current business models. Besides, blockchain needs companies to cooperate and trust one another despite being rivals, for example, suppliers, manufacturers and logistics firms. In most cases, it is difficult to motivate large numbers of players to work on a shared ledger, as no central office can be sure that everyone is playing by the same rules. The methodologies of change management should be resilient and should engage stakeholders, test systems pilot and advantages and disadvantages of blockchain description. Blockchain-based projects that have not been carefully thought through their implementation or still do not have a distinct value can often struggle to scale, or even to survive [35].

8.8.6 Overcoming the Barriers

Such challenges require multi-stakeholder collaboration. Above all, governments will get an opportunity to build regulatory sandboxes, fund technology development through grants and open standards. Forming industry memberships can lead to interoperable platforms that all can utilize; and one way universities can contribute value is by exchanging how-to knowledge and training and curriculum development. Other groups, including the World Economic Forum project on redesigning trust and the Blockchain in Transport Alliance (BiTA), are facilitating the adoption of blockchain into mainstream international trade and logistics. Their goal is to align new technology and rules so that using blockchain is safe and easy for everyone.

8.9 INTEGRATION WITH AI AND IOT

Due to blockchain combining forces with AI and IoT, supply chain tracking has become more sustainable, transparent and efficient. Every technology plays a unique role in the supply chain, but when used together, they let the system automatically handle challenges like traceability, regular monitoring, predicting issues and following regulations much better. Having this type of digital triad, business organizations can develop new, innovative, fast and environmentally friendly supply chains.

8.9.1 Role of AI in Sustainable Supply Chains

AI enhances supply chain decisions, especially when it comes to relying on better data analytics, machine learning and cognitive computing. The significance of AI is that it operates predictive analytics on both past and present data before making a decision about what is likely to occur in the market and what the company should stock [12]. It enables companies to only produce what is necessary to save them the bother of resource and energy wastage. AI is also used to conduct anomaly-detection tasks that help detect delays, fraud or equipment malfunctions within a supply chain. They make a company more fit to stay in business since they assist in addressing the problems at an early stage and enable the individuals to handle them before they get into any serious trouble. Once something in the supply chain falls behind schedule or falls off track, the AI will be aware of the difference and give suggestions on what to do next. Demand prediction permits the scheduling of production, logistics and storage to achieve minimal or no wastage of goods and unwarranted use of energy. It is also easier to minimize resource wastage and to make the supply chain environmentally friendly with the help of AI-enabled optimization tools.

8.9.2 Role of IoT in Sustainable Supply Chains

By placing sensors and connected tools in the supply chain, IoT brings more real-time data to companies. These IoT devices are constantly gathering temperature, humidity, location and shock impact information on products and assets while in the supply chain. In the food, pharmaceuticals and high-tech manufacturing sectors, seeing all the conditions can be very important because they influence the safety and quality of what is made. By linking data from the IoT to blockchain, it gains security and can be verified, which improves how supply chains maintain proof and comply with rules. As an example, a cold-chain system sending vaccines relies on IoT sensors to keep an eye on the temperature during transportation. Recording the data on a blockchain creates a record that allows for checking whether the right environmental measures were taken and whether the product meets regulations. Also, monitoring assets and their conditions using IoT gadgets allows logistics providers to use their vehicles less, make fewer stops and choose more fuel-efficient routes, which lowers their carbon emissions.

8.9.3 Combined Impact: A Smarter and More Sustainable Supply Chain

The integration of AI, the IoT and blockchain technologies creates a resilient, intelligent and self-regulating supply chain system that repositions traditional logistics into a more open and agile supply chain. One of the most common outcomes of this effect is smart logistics. In smart logistics, the delivered condition of goods can be analyzed in real time using IoT sensors and the data is processed using AI algorithms so the best route is selected based on real-time delivery data such as location, traffic, fuel and time scheduling. Smart logistics ensures faster delivery, more dependable delivery of goods and less energy used in the delivery process.

Blockchain ensures accountability for every delivery and routing decision through a complete chain of custody and traceability. Another important benefit of these technologies in supply chain is predictive maintenance. IoT devices constantly collect data about an equipment or asset's metrics, including, but not limited to, vibration, temperature and utilization. The data is analyzed by AI and meaning is assigned to the data to help predict equipment failure before failure actually occurs. Predictive maintenance minimizes downtime, extends the life of an asset and reduces waste. Specific to responsible or sustainable supply chain practices, blockchain stores each equipment's historical repair and maintenance records as well as AI predictive information in a secure and tamper-proof format that is essential for audits and insurance claims.

In addition, the convergence enables Automated Compliance Monitoring, as environmental, health safety and labor regulations become stricter. The sensors deliver information to the AI systems, where the AI can then assess the real-time compliance (e.g., emissions, operational safety) for supply chains. Each time compliance is measured, it is recorded on the blockchain for verification by the public or regulators, which dramatically decrease the time required and the cost of inspections and even the ability to initiate mitigative action before being identified as non-compliant. The convergence of these technologies also generates consumer trust because it provides end-to-end transparency on where the product originated, how it was processed and if it was sustainably produced. Companies can show every movement of a material, and every transformation that material underwent, which enables consumers to make informed ethical choices and leverage their brand quality. Furthermore, the convergence of these technologies, including AI scenario planning, data via IoT systems and information stored on the blockchain, allows resilience and responsiveness when facing a crisis, such as a pandemic or war. Furthermore, when the merger of these technologies employs AI and uses data from IoTs, and information shared securely on the blockchain which allows the supply chain to quickly adapt to changes in disruptions, maintain operations in the new conditions and protect stakeholder trust. This merger of technologies builds a new base for safe supply chains that are future-proof, sustainable and resilient.

8.10 ROADMAP FOR FUTURE RESEARCH

While blockchain seems to aid transparency, trackability and responsibility in supply chains, its role in SSCM is not yet fully seen. It is necessary for several research fields to combine their efforts to drive the adoption of AI beyond pilot experiments and single areas of application. The next five categories list the main topics that should get priority attention to help blockchain support sustainability in global supply chains.

8.10.1 Developing Standardized and Validated Blockchain Sustainability Index (BSI) Metrics

One main issue that blocks sustainable blockchain evaluation is that there are not yet standard tools to measure its environmental and social effects. The way current assessments are done is often split up, and they use many different systems to rate environmental, social and economic outcomes. Thus, it becomes tough to understand differences in outcomes between industries or regions, and no clear system is available for finding best practices or accountability. Research should work on developing BSI measurements that are scientifically sound, applicable across all supply chains, able to quantify both the direct and indirect sustainability impacts. These measures should include reduction of carbon emissions, improved management of resources, reduction in wastes, improved use of energy in blockchain operations and improved labor conditions in the supply chain. The availability of standardized benchmarking tools will help policymakers, researchers and businesses select the most suitable methods of implementing blockchain in their operations. They can also be helpful to increase cooperation regarding the concept of sustainability concerning blockchain activity.

8.10.2 Development of Industry-Specific Sector-Blockchain Frameworks

The application of blockchain in different industries depends on legal regulations, the complexity of the industry, the durability of the products and their owners. To take an example, the pharmaceutical industry is concerned with the ability to monitor goods and eliminate cases of counterfeiting, but in food, the primary issue is how goods are stored and how long they have been stored and are safe to use. To become the most significant player in these domains, blockchain must be scaled by interlinking with existing systems; managing regulations and issues in particular sectors; providing templates and codes established to serve supply chains in agricultural, manufacturing, retail and energy sectors. They may include smart contract libraries, network runtime frameworks, pre-approved compliance features that accelerate development and provide less uncertainty. Furthermore, the Application Programming Interfaces (APIs) and middleware provided by companies should be customizable so that the systems can be easily integrated with ERP, AI and IoT tools.

8.10.3 Forging Global Policy Regimes of Blockchain Governance and Harmonization of Regulations

Due to the global nature of global supply chains, the application of blockchain technology creates problems. It can be problematic and can drag a new idea down because of different privacy laws and computer laws, trade regulations and the way a country is managed. Moreover, the fact that blockchain does not involve any central authority makes one ask whose duty it is, who owns the data and how conflicts can be resolved. Due to these issues, studies should offer constructs in international policies that are the following: establish common standards in applying blockchain and interoperability across countries, provide standards in the appropriate handling of data and protection of user privacy, determine regulations in responsibility in smart contract transactions. The people who design such frameworks should include representatives of the government, members of international organizations, academic researchers and people who work in the private sector. New regulation approaches like regulatory sandboxes, which could be used to safely test blockchain applications, should also be studied in order to keep pace with the aspirations of a more sustainable future.

8.10.4 Promoting Interdisciplinary Research Linking IT, Operations Management and Sustainability Sciences

The use of blockchain in green supply chain management must consider different ways of thinking, not only focusing on technology. In practice, the research done in blockchain and supply chain management often stays segregated, as technologists examine technology, business experts examine strategy and environmental experts assess environmental effects. The gaps can be closed by encouraging cooperation between the fields of information technology and blockchain engineering, operations and supply chain management, environmental science and sustainability assessment, Economics, law and public policy. By doing research from various fields, it is possible to make frameworks that address technical, financial, ethical and environmental aspects of a project. For example, a combined study could study how tracking carbon using blockchain tools helps people make decisions on what to buy or how decentralized governance makes the supply chain better able to handle environmental disasters. Schools, research groups and financing groups can help by offering special initiatives, seminars and articles that encourage scholars to cooperate across old discipline boundaries.

8.10.5 Piloting Blockchain Adoption in Underserved Sectors Such as Healthcare and Education

Blockchain technology is advancing in banking, manufacturing and logistics, but its potential in socially underprivileged or developing sectors remains untapped. Essentially important areas like healthcare and education, significant components of sustainable development, could benefit significantly from the way blockchain facilitates trust, traceability and accountability. It can help strengthen the visibility of medicine distribution, confirm the actual manufacturing of medical goods and securely keep and share patient health records using it in healthcare. Education can benefit from blockchain when checking credentials, building stronger safe learning environments as well as improving school programs and spending accountability. This pilot study can identify how plunging into blockchain would be able to solve non-ordinary issues in supply chains (such as vaccine or education distribution) and reveal particular challenges involved in marginalized regions. Pilots also enable us to quantify blockchain's impact on Sustainable Development Goals (SDGs) like quality education, good health and well-being and reducing inequalities.

8.11 CONCLUSION

Blockchain technology has revolutionized how supply chains can be managed, monitored and optimized for sustainability. Through having decentralization, immutability, transparency and security, it facilitates making the supply chains visible, structured, fast and responsive. By applying blockchain, different companies within a supply chain can exchange data securely that is verified without a central authority that minimizes dishonesty, inaccuracies and inefficiencies. The chapter examined the different means through which blockchain facilitates SSCM in industries such as agriculture, manufacturing, energy, retail and logistics. Case studies from different industries showed that blockchain is used effectively to enhance traceability of products, manage who supplies them, monitor their environmental impact and assure ethical sourcing. They illustrate how blockchain can contribute to various sustainability initiatives, such as reducing harm to the environment and providing equality for everyone.

The chapter introduces the Blockchain Sustainability Index (BSI), a tool designed to assess and quantify the extent to which blockchain projects are increasing supply chains' sustainability. By employing ESG metrics along with various technical measurements, the BSI provides a standardized means to quantify blockchain-based sustainability outcomes. Through the application of the BSI, stakeholders are able to base their decisions on evidence which allows them to invest, create and legislate with more confidence. While bringing several opportunities, making blockchain a part of sustainable supply chains is not problem-free. To make blockchain mature and extensively used, scalability issues, high-energy expenditure for certain consensus mechanisms, indistinct rules, weak link among blockchains and lack of standardization must be fixed. Furthermore, it requires an explicit image of the technical and primary activities and the local contexts in which they occur to get things done properly.

When blockchain is added to technologies like AI and the IoT, it becomes highly promising. With AI, predictions are made, decisions are assisted and processes optimized and IoT supplies real-time data from all supply chain assets. Applying blockchain to manage data securely supports these technologies that drives smart logistics, automated compliance, predictive maintenance and dynamic supply chain reconfiguration. Through convergence, supply chains are able to improve sustainability and work more intelligently. Convergence also allows them to respond to changes and survive major disruptions. In the future, making blockchain a big part of SSCM will depend on cooperation and joint efforts from many players. Private businesses need to spend resources on solutions that grow with the sector and fit its particular needs. Scholars should aim at novel case studies, develop informative metrics like the BSI and consolidate technology, operations and sustainability sciences. Governments and regulators, however, need to craft policies that enhance innovation in the sector and pay particular attention to data privacy, personal data and the environment.

REFERENCES

1. S. Seuring and M. Müller, "From a literature review to a conceptual framework for sustainable supply chain management," *J. Clean. Prod.*, vol. 16, no. 15, pp. 1699–1710, 2008.
2. P. Ahi and C. Searcy, "A comparative literature analysis of definitions for green and sustainable supply chain management," *J. Clean. Prod.*, vol. 52, pp. 329–341, 2013.
3. M. Pagell and Z. Wu, "Building a more complete theory of sustainable supply chain management using case studies of 10 exemplars," *J. Supply Chain Manag.*, vol. 47, no. 2, pp. 37–56, 2011.

4. A. Gunasekaran and E.W.T. Ngai, "Information systems in supply chain integration and management," *Eur. J. Oper. Res.*, vol. 159, no. 2, pp. 269–295, 2004.
5. S. Saberi, M. Kouhizadeh, J. Sarkis, and L. Shen, "Blockchain technology and its relationships to sustainable supply chain management," *Int. J. Prod. Res.*, vol. 57, no. 7, pp. 2117–2135, 2019.
6. K. Christidis and M. Devetsikiotis, "Blockchains and smart contracts for the Internet of Things," *IEEE Access*, vol. 4, pp. 2292–2303, 2016.
7. F. Casino, T. K. Dasaklis, and C. Patsakis, "A systematic literature review of blockchain-based applications: Current status, classification and open issues," *Telematics Inf.*, vol. 36, pp. 55–81, 2019.
8. V. Paliwal, S. Chandra, and S. Sharma, "Blockchain technology for sustainable supply chain management: A systematic literature review and a classification framework," *Sustainability*, vol. 12, no. 18, p. 7638, 2021, https://doi.org/10.3390/su12187638
9. A. Panigrahi, N. Vashisht, Shalini, A. V. Nair, S. Gopinath and D. Bhanot, "Enhancing Trust and Lightweight Security in Green IoT: Models for Sustainable Computing," *2025 2nd International Conference On Multidisciplinary Research and Innovations in Engineering (MRIE)*, Gurugram, India, pp. 280–284, 2025, https://doi.org/10.1109/MRIE66930.2025.11156263
10. A. Panigrahi, A. Pati, B. Sahu, B. B. Dash, S. Chowdhury and S. S. Patra, "Cluster-Driven CA Selection Space Optimization in Blockchain with POA for Trust Calculation," *2024 International Conference on IoT Based Control Networks and Intelligent Systems (ICICNIS)*, Bengaluru, India, pp. 251–256, 2024, https://doi.org/10.1109/ICICNIS64247.2024.10823131
11. A. Panigrahi, A. K. Nayak, and R. Paul, "Smart contract assisted blockchain based public key infrastructure system," *Transactions on Emerging Telecommunications Technologies*, 2022, https://doi.org/10.1002/ett.4655
12. A. Panigrahi, A. Pati, B. Sahu, B. B. Dash, S. Chowdhury and S. S. Patra, "Cluster-Driven CA Selection Space Optimization in Blockchain with POA for Trust Calculation," *2024 International Conference on IoT Based Control Networks and Intelligent Systems (ICICNIS)*, Bengaluru, India, pp. 251–256, 2024, https://doi.org/10.1109/ICICNIS64247.2024.10823131
13. A. Sharma, A. Sharma, R. K. Singh, and T. Bhatia, "Blockchain adoption in agri-food supply chain management: an empirical study of the main drivers using extended UTAUT," *Business Process Management Journal*, 2023, https://doi.org/10.1108/bpmj-10-2022-0543
14. S. Nakamoto, "Bitcoin: A peer-to-peer electronic cash system," 2008, https://assets.pubpub.org/d8wct41f/31611263538139.pdf
15. S.S. Kamble, A. Gunasekaran, and R. Sharma, "Modeling the blockchain-enabled traceability in agriculture supply chain," *Int. J. Inf. Manage.*, vol. 52, 2020.
16. R. Casado-Vara, J. Prieto, F. de la Fuente, and J.M. Corchado, "How blockchain improves the supply chain: Case study alimentary supply chain," *Procedia Comput. Sci.*, vol. 134, pp. 393–398, 2018.
17. T. Alladi, V. Chamola, R. M. Parizi and K. -K. R. Choo, "Blockchain Applications for Industry 4.0 and Industrial IoT: A Review," in *IEEE Access*, vol. 7, pp. 176935–176951, 2019, https://doi.org/10.1109/ACCESS.2019.2956748
18. O. Alphand *et al.*, "IoTChain: A blockchain security architecture for the Internet of Things," *2018 IEEE Wireless Communications and Networking Conference (WCNC)*, Barcelona, Spain, pp. 1–6, 2018, https://doi.org/10.1109/WCNC.2018.8377385
19. A. Dorri, S. S. Kanhere, R. Jurdak, and P. Gauravaram, "Blockchain for IoT security and privacy: The case study of a smart home," *IEEE International Conference on Pervasive Computing and Communications Workshops (PerCom Workshops)*, Kona, HI, USA, pp. 618–623, 2017, https://doi.org/10.1109/PERCOMW.2017.7917634.

20. E. Politou, F. Casino, E. Alepis and C. Patsakis, "Blockchain Mutability: Challenges and Proposed Solutions," in *IEEE Transactions on Emerging Topics in Computing*, vol. 9, no. 4, pp. 1972–1986, 2021, https://doi.org/10.1109/TETC.2019.2949510
21. M. Crosby, P. Pattanayak, S. Verma, and V. Kalyanaraman, "Blockchain technology: Beyond bitcoin," *Appl. Innov. Rev.*, vol. 2, no. 6–10, 2016.
22. E. C. Onukwulu, I. N. Dienagha, W. N. Digitemie, and P. I. Egbumokei, "Blockchain for transparent and secure supply chain management in renewable energy," *International Journal of Science and Technology Research Archive*, vol. 3, no. 1, pp. 251–272, 2022, https://doi.org/10.53771/ijstra.2022.3.1.0103
23. N. Szabo, "Smart contracts: Building blocks for digital markets," *Extropy*, vol. 16, 1996.
24. K. Christidis and M. Devetsikiotis, "Blockchains and Smart Contracts for the Internet of Things," in *IEEE Access*, vol. 4, pp. 2292–2303, 2016, https://doi.org/10.1109/ACCESS.2016.2566339
25. J. Yli-Huumo, D. Ko, S. Choi, S. Park, and K. Smolander, "Where is current research on blockchain technology?—A systematic review," *PLoS ONE*, vol. 11, no. 10, 2016.
26. H. Kim, Z. Xiao, X. Zhang, X. Fu, and Z. Qin, "Rethinking Blockchain Technologies for the Maritime Industry: An Overview of the Current Landscape," *Future Internet*, vol. 16, no. 12, p. 454, 2024, https://doi.org/10.3390/fi16120454
27. A. Kamilaris, A. Fonts, and F. X. Prenafeta-Boldú, "The rise of blockchain technology in agriculture and food supply chains," *Trends Food Sci. Technol.*, vol. 91, pp. 640–652, 2019.
28. A. Panigrahi, A. Pati, B. Dash, G. Sahoo, D. Singh, and M. Dash, "ASBlock:An Agricultural based Supply Chain Management using Blockchain Technology," *Procedia computer science*, vol. 235, pp. 1943–1952, 2024, https://doi.org/10.1016/j.procs.2024.04.184
29. Amrutanshu Panigrahi, B. Sahu, Satya Sobhan Panigrahi, S. Khan, and Ajay Kumar Jena, "Application of Blockchain as a Solution to the Real-World Issues in Health Care System," *Intelligent systems reference library*, pp. 135–149, 2021, https://doi.org/10.1007/978-3-030-69395-4_8
30. Amrutanshu Panigrahi, A. Pati, Santosh Reddy Addula, A. K. Pati, G. Sahoo, and M. Dash, "An Ensemble Machine Learning-Based Model for Blockchain Transactional Data Classification," *Learning and analytics in intelligent systems*, pp. 430–438, 2025, https://doi.org/10.1007/978-3-031-82706-8_44
31. A. Reyna, C. Martín, J. Chen, E. Soler, and M. Díaz, "On blockchain and its integration with IoT: Challenges and opportunities," *Future Gener. Comput. Syst.*, vol. 88, 2018.
32. N. Kshetri, "1 Blockchain's roles in meeting key supply chain management objectives," *Int. J. Inf. Manage.*, vol. 39, 2018.
33. K. Wüst and A. Gervais, "Do you need a blockchain?," *Crypto Valley Conference on Blockchain Technology (CVCBT)*, 2018, https://doi.org/10.1109/cvcbt.2018.00011
34. M. Crosby et al., "Blockchain technology: Beyond bitcoin," *Appl. Innov. Rev.*, vol. 2, 2016.
35. S. Madakam, R. Ramaswamy, and S. Tripathi, "Internet of Things (IoT): A Literature Review," *Journal of Computer and Communications*, vol. 03, no. 05, pp. 164–173, 2015, https://doi.org/10.4236/jcc.2015.35021

9 BASIS-IoT
Blockchain and AI-Integrated SDN-Based Framework for Smart Irrigation Systems in IoT Environments

Sasmita Parida, Tanmay Mukherjee, Ayushee Das, Sujit Bebortta, and Sruthi Balammagary

9.1 INTRODUCTION

Crop growing is the most important source of employment for people in India and has an extensive impact on the financial system of the country, and almost 70% of agriculturalists and general people depend on farming. But issues regarding cultivation have been repeatedly impeding the economy of India. So, in order to improve the productivity of smart farming by modernizing the existing outdated methods of agriculture, smart farming is established [1]. India is home to roughly 4% of the world's water resources and 18% of the world's population, out of which about 80% of the water is used in cultivation. So, increasing demand from an upward population, coupled with economic action, adds a burden on already stressed water resources. The scarcity of fresh water around the earth has engendered a necessity for minimum utilization [2]. An increase in population and modern lifestyles has augmented the necessity of water in both urban and rural regions. So, it is very challenging to improve plant growth and to reduce costs, which points to an inventive idea by using an irrigation management system that will offer automated services and promote better supervision of water and human resources in the future. The Internet of Things (IoT) technology can provide a better solution for a smart irrigation system [3]. The objective of the proposed work is to provide an IoT-based architecture with Distributed Sensor Network (DSN) and to address the basic challenges for a smart irrigation system.

In a large irrigation system, the major challenge is designing the network and the network complexity, which is costly. The network complexity is so complex that it requires lots of effort to manage the network. However, this issue could be solved by adopting software-defined networking (SDN) technology with minimal network

DOI: 10.1201/9781003658597-9

effort [4]. Monitoring of crop growth is an essential issue in agriculture; it is quite difficult to monitor each crop on a in large scale. Moreover, the monitoring, observation, and analysis for decision-making is now influenced by humans using past experience. The decision-making for the growth of the crop may be dangerous and damage the crop. With the advancement of technology, IoT can provide a better solution to the agriculture industry. Various IoT sensors have been developed for different purposes and can be used to solve current challenges in this sector. As an example, water irrigation is one of the essential problems that could be solved using IoT. In water irrigation, we generally use pumps running on electricity or petroleum products as fuel, and the irrigation may not be monitored properly; there are maximum chances of over-irrigation or under-irrigation, which may damage the crop. In such a situation, water and energy resources are wasted. To solve this problem, an IoT-based system is highly recommended.

IoT networks are embedded with sensors and software and exchange data with other systems. It appears as the ordinary selection for smart water management applications, where the main purpose is to reduce the labor cost, save water, and improve the productivity [5]. Some challenges arise in the current period to overcome the drawbacks of the existing IoT framework, i.e., development of efficient software for IoT-based innovative applications, advancement of all software in the IoT platform, and also advancement of sensors that require satisfactory principles and data models. Cloud computing is changing the computing world and provides various computing functionalities through the services [6].

With the rapid growth of IoT technologies, the demand for a variety of IoT applications such as smart healthcare, smart irrigation, and industrial automation has increased rapidly. The real-time processing of these applications demands essential computation properties, which lead to high energy consumption on resource-constrained IoT devices and is a complex task [7]. To avoid such situation, SDN technologies were developed. Clustering plays an important role in computing and networking and also in IoT [8]. In the traditional network model, both the control plane and the data plane are present for each network device or switch. The forwarding rules for the incoming packets are determined by the control plane, and the forwarding table is stored by the data plane, which is the arrangement of the forwarding rules resolved by the control plane; this system is very complex and requires modification [9]. SDN is a cutting-edge networking prototype designed to divide the control plane from the data plane and deliver network services in real time [9]. When using SDN, a single controller or a collection of controllers establishes the forwarding protocols and installs them in the switches. The switches then store the forwarding tables and forward incoming packets according to the entries in the relevant tables [10].

9.1.1 Motivation

In large-scale agricultural fields, the irrigation system is complex and requires physical intervention, which is not effective. The operation of the traditional irrigation system is purely based on observation and experience in operating the pump. The major problem is the improper supply of water to the crop without studying the soil parameters and the exact requirements of the crop, which may affect growth. It also leads to the wastage of a huge amount of water, fuel consumption, and human effort. Due to the rapid development of IoT and sensor technology, the above problem can be solved. The moisture is the major parameter to create protein, which helps the growth of the crop. Moisture sensors are developed to measure accurately, which helps in further analysis and decision-making. The major problem in an IoT system for a large network is network management. As several sensors are required to be deployed in the agricultural field, the network comprising the IoT became a complex one that requires lots of effort to manage. On the other hand, IoT with cloud computing provides resources with minimum cost and effort [11]. In this work, we motivate and suggest that the IoT network management effort can be reduced by SDN technology. It provides various functions to manage the network through a program in an effective way.

9.1.2 Contribution

This chapter discusses the need for IoT systems integrated with SDN, along with the blockchain framework for a smart irrigation system for large-scale agricultural land. We propose the architecture for an SDN-based IoT model for a smart irrigation system. We explain different SDN components and their importance in the usability of the smart irrigation system. Moreover, we state different issues and the possible solution approaches in an SDN-based IoT smart irrigation system. Finally, we present the network performance through the simulation.

The rest of the chapter is organized as follows. Section 9.2 portrays the related literature on SDN-based IoT smart irrigation systems. Section 9.3 discusses the need for an automatic irrigation system in smart farming. Section 9.4 provides the details about SDN and its characteristics. Section 9.5 presents the proposed architecture for the SDN-based IoT model. In Section 9.6, analysis of various important features is provided, and the issues along with possible solutions of SDN-based IoT systems are presented in Section 9.7. Finally, Section 9.8 provides the conclusion and future scope of the chapter.

9.2 LITERATURE SURVEY

By using humidity sensors, a smart irrigation system was designed based on IoT [12]. The sensors collect the moisture level data from the soil, and according to that data, irrigation-based decisions are taken by the system automatically, which can control the operation of the pump quickly [12]. In [13], the authors deliberated on the current efforts to integrate SDN and IoT and underlined the benefits of such integration on information acquisition, analysis, and decision-making in IoT. When compared to the uncontrolled drip irrigation approach, automatic drip irrigation scheduling is intended to save 16%–35% of irrigation water and boost crop production by an estimated 20%. The best results for managing water and fertilizer were obtained by scheduling irrigation based on climatological station data [14].

Broadly, researchers discussed various issues in the agriculture industry, such as crop growth, infection detection, application of fertilizers, irrigation, and smart greenhouses. These solutions are technology-based, such as edge computing, fog computing, cloud computing, blockchain, IoT, and robotics, to monitor, analyze, and make decisions for the growth of the production [1]. Generally, in an irrigation system, water pumps and pipes are used, but control of these pumps is required to reduce water and fuel waste. In [15], a smart irrigation system is suggested to control the water pumps through a mobile phone, which reduces the wastage of water. The system performs with less time and effort to monitor the growth of the crop. In [16], a wireless system that includes a soil moisture sensor and a temperature sensor is install under the soil wherever plant roots are extended, forming a distributed network. The evidence related to sensors that activate the actuators, and data is transferred using a Global System for Mobile Communications (GSM) module, is managed by a gateway unit. An effective automated irrigation system is established, which has the capacity to adjust the usage of water and other resources. This structure is scalable, low-maintenance, and could be familiar with several types of crops without much human exertion, and also using similar techniques. Other sections, in terms of the utility of the project, that is, a greenhouse or an open field, can be established and fulfilled [17].

In [18], a software-defined fog architecture was proposed to develop and enact an IoT network by distributing the fog nodes. The work emphasized the benefit of the SDN–fog relationship and showed the high flexibility and scalability in the network. In [19], a very simple model is established to help the farmers by lessening the cost of labor as well as the usage of water, and increasing productivity using IoT technology. The data collected is stored across servers, which can be retrieved by using the URL. One more algorithm is advanced by using a soil moisture sensor; the idea is to sense the temperature of the soil, and a programmed microcontroller monitors continuously and communicates through the gateway for the quality of water. This model contains photovoltaic panels, and it establishes communication using a duplex link to the cellular network that permits data assessment and irrigation planning to be automated over a web page [20]. For application in sensor networks, the authors in [21] suggested implementation rules that are displayed on a flow table called Sensor-OpenFlow. Two different flow-table rules, one based on ID and the other on value, are proposed. Before being promoted to other nodes in the network, the significance of the sensed information is compared and defined using a value-based approach. In contrast, the ID-based approach presents the sensed information to sink nodes in the network by matching the ID of the sensor node.

9.3 NEED FOR AUTOMATIC IRRIGATION

This section presents the need for automatic irrigation and is as follows.

- Farmers can designate the precise amount of water at the precise time by automating the irrigation process.
- Energy and resources are saved for future utilization in a proper and optimal way.
- Installing the automatic irrigation model is very simple and easy to configure.

- It saves time by eliminating human error in regulating available soil moisture levels in the land.
- By avoiding irrigation at the wrong time, you can lessen overspill from overwatering and soaking soils, which will improve crop performance.
- Reduce labor costs because it uses sensors to operate the pump motor, as IoT systems are enabled in it.
- The work is specific to a smart irrigation system for large-scale agricultural fields and an accurate and perfect technology-enabled system for moisture control for the growth of the crops.

9.4 SDN AND ITS CHARACTERISTICS

SDN is a network design methodology that facilitates the network to be efficiently and dynamically programmed or centrally controlled through software applications by open Application Programming Interfaces (APIs) in order to progress the network enactment. The control or network control functions are separated by this architecture. The main process in the network that requires the most effort is network control and control functions. The administrator incurs a lot of overhead to control the network by adopting the network decision rules. SDN provides the feature to program to control the specific network. network function virtualization (NFV) makes it feasible by separating network functions from particular hardware, which requires a lot more time to maintain. In a traditional network prototype, the control plane is combined with the data plane and is presented to each network device or switch. The control plane regulates the incoming packets using a forwarding table that is accumulated by the data plane. It defines a set of forwarding rules that are very intricate and entail amendments [9]. So, to overcome this approach, an innovative networking prototype was developed that splits up the control plane and separates it from the data plane to provide dynamic network services [9, 22]. The key characteristics of SDN are summarized in Table 9.1, and the major components are shown in Figure 9.1.

The SDN is mainly designed using three layers, i.e., data plane layer, control plane layer, and management plane layer, and is described as follows.

Data Plane Layer: The SDN-enabled devices that communicate with the network architecture module, which physically manages the network configurations sent from the control plane, comprise the data plane layer. The device data plane is not connected to the network intelligence. It moves to the SDN controller, which is centralized in the network. This plane has the capability to transfer data to and from the clients as well as supervise multiple conversations through multiple protocols, and also handle the conversations with remote peers. SDN devices based on the data plane or forwarding plane are merely basic forwarding devices with no control capabilities. SDN defines various functions to maintain quality of service (QoS) for the services, request processing to handle user requests, routing the packets, and filtering [4].

Control Plane Layer: In SDN, the control plane is a part of the software that designs and controls the data plane, and it also manages how data packets

TABLE 9.1
Key Characteristics of SDN

Decoupled architecture plane	• Distinct control plane and data plane. • Centralizes network astuteness. • Transfers programmable features from network devices to centralized application servers.
Network operability	• Centralized control system removes multiple device configurations. • SDN algorithms supervise the network to determine how to manage when network changes occur and also dynamic pattern changes. • Controllers communicate with network devices through APIs.
Openness and interoperability	• Handles organizational policies, systems, as well as different network applications. • Offers interoperability, vendor neutrality, and integration across the networks. • Handles common software environments for network setup. • Maintains standard communication protocols between devices from different users.

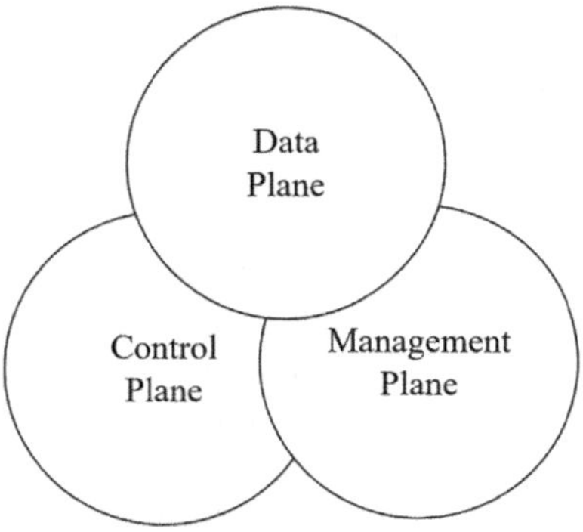

FIGURE 9.1 Major components of SDN.

are transferred from one location to another. The SDN approach offers a capability that enables device management by a controller. A single common API may be used to configure and manage the devices' many data planes. The decision on how to manage the packet routing tables can be taken by the control plane [4].

Management Layer: The Management plane manages all layers of the SDN architecture, and it can handle the wider network configuration and also monitor the management processes of different layers. It comprises network traffic used by the network administrator to manage the network.

9.5 SDN-BASED IOT METHODOLOGY FOR IRRIGATION

In this section, we suggest the proposed model architecture for a smart irrigation system and the implementation of SDN technology to reduce the network management effort. First, we discuss our proposed SDN architecture; then we briefly explain the IoT model for the irrigation system as follows.

i. SDN Architecture
ii. IoT Model

9.5.1 Designed SDN Architecture

The design involves the following:

- Centralized Network controller
- Programmable open APIs
- Standard communication interface (OpenFlow)

SDN is a virtual networking methodology which is software-based and programmable. It is an open interface and easy to program as required, and separates control planes from the data planes with low complexity and high extensibility. It permits the management process to use A low-cost device that results from simple and straightforward manufacture. Whereas the traditional Network is a closed interface and difficult to program, and replacing the old program as required is very costly and involves a multifarious management process.

There are two types of OpenFlow switches: OpenFlow-only and OpenFlow-Hybrid. Here, we consider an OpenFlow-only switch that supports only OpenFlow operations. In pipeline processing, a number of flow tables are used. Data packets are processed using two processes: ingress processing and egress processing. The packets are passed through the flow tables from 1 to n, then the selected tables are grouped. For outputting the packets, the ingress processing is performed as shown in Figure 9.2.

The major operation is matching the packet and putting the packet out in the proper port in SDN. Initially, the pipeline fields are initialized, and the packet in the ingress process passes through the flow table from the 1st. If not, we update the action set, packet header, match set fields, pipeline fields, check the table for missing flow entries, move on to the second flow table, and so on. If the match is found, then the packet goes for ingress processing; otherwise, the packet is dropped. In ingress processing, there are also multiple flow switches, and a similar process will be carried out.

The various processes and functions that specify the route taken by the packet or frame as it moves from one location to another are stated in the control plane. It carries out its function autonomously and is in charge of how packets are sent. It is also responsible for building and maintaining the IP routing table. Packets are administered by the router to update the routing table in the control plane. The control plane includes routing information protocol (RIP), spanning tree protocol (STP),

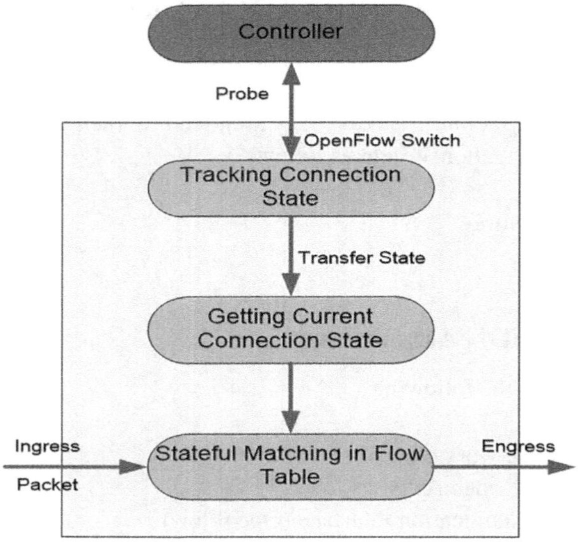

FIGURE 9.2 Connection-state processing mechanism.

address resolution protocol (ARP), dynamic host configuration protocol (DHCP), etc. Packets in the control plane originate from the router, and in the data forwarding control plane, it behaves as a decision-making system.

Forwarding packets from the source to the destination is the responsibility of the data plane. Data planes rely on control planes to do various tasks and are capable of forwarding IP packets. Packets based on the control plane's built-in logic are forwarded by the data plane. It performs switching and incorporates features like decrementing time to live (TTL), recalculating IP header checksum, and more. The data plane acts as a decision implementer in data forwarding.

9.5.2 IoT Model and Network for Smart Irrigation

In the agricultural irrigation system, water is absorbed by the soil, and most of the water is wasted because it goes to the lower level of the ground where the crop roots cannot be reached. The crop root is a maximum of one ft. from the ground. So it is essential to measure the moisture within one ft. of the ground. The moisture level can easily vary within this range. To measure the moisture level, soil moisture sensors are developed, which sense the moisture level, the presence of water, and the quantity. It uses the technique to measure the electric permittivity through the capacitance of the surroundings. It generates an electrical signal that is proportional to the water content in the soil. Here, we follow some assumptions based on the moisture specification. When the soil is dry from ½ to 1 in. from the top, the sensor can measure 8–10 in. in diameter. Generally, the crop root may grow to a maximum of 6–12 in.; it requires maximum irrigation on a regular basis. While the field is sandy, the water is absorbed rapidly and requires a water supplement, which means that when the soil is dry at a level of 2–4 in.

Plants absorb the water rapidly when the humidity content of the soil is higher. Humidity is an essential supplement for the growth of crops. Due to humidity, a huge amount of water is absorbed and forms a thin layer in the soil. The nutrients are formed from the salt and water available in the soil, which aids the growth of the plants. In an Automatic irrigation system, a sensor detects the moisture and temperature level variation near the crop area, and after that, the connected motor starts operating. The model automates the irrigation system and avoids human errors. It also checks the moisture level, and the IoT model provides the platform to control and manage through the monitoring mechanism to make decisions over the internet from remote locations [2, 17].

Moisture sensors are used as nodes in the agriculture field and deployed in clusters. The clusters are formed depending upon the hardness and moisture of the soil. The label of the agriculture field also matters while making the clusters. Here, we ignore the labels and the land situation of the agricultural field and consider labelled lands. The access point and several nodes make up the clusters. Data forwarding to the gateway is the responsibility of the access point. The clusters are communicating with each other using these gateways. The SDN module is present in the next layer of the node layer. SDN architecture contains an access point, the SDN controller, and the data server. We suggest the wireless communication system through the access point, as portrayed in Figure 9.3.

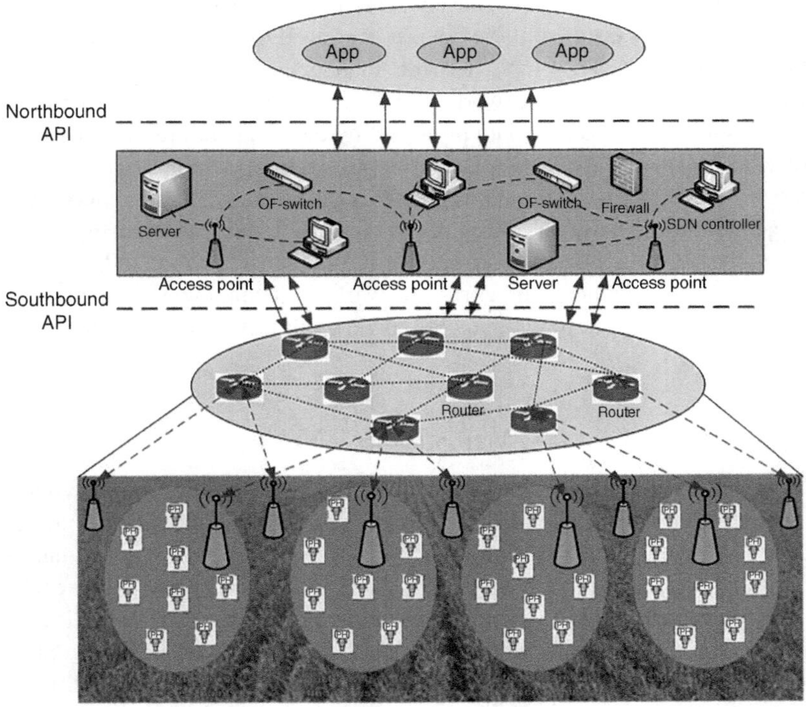

FIGURE 9.3 Proposed SDN-based irrigation system architecture.

The OpenFlow switch is one of the most important components in the SDN model. OpenFlow is used to directly access and manipulate the switches and routers, whether these are physical or virtual, using the hypervisor. The OpenFlow protocol is used for communicating between the OpenFlow switch and the SDN controller. The protocol can manage the OpenFlow switch from the OpenFlow controller remotely. The Flow Tables are maintained inside the OpenFlow switch and are controlled by the OpenFlow channels. Rather than the standard ports, OpenFlow ports are also used as the network interfaces to pass packets. One OpenFlow switch can communicate with another through the output port. Besides these ports, logical ports are responsible for a higher-level abstraction of the switch in the architecture. The SDN architecture uses two APIs: the northbound API, which is depicted in Figure 9.3, is used to communicate the SDN network with the application layer, while the southbound API is used to talk to the cluster network node.

9.6 IMPORTANT FEATURES ANALYSIS

This section provides certain important features of SDN.

9.6.1 Network Management

It is predicted that a large number of items will be in use globally in the near future due to IoT mechanization [23]. Consequently, it is noticeable that a massive amount of data will be produced from the devices that need to be managed in a timely and well-organized way. Therefore, network management is an essential feature for supervising such a massive network, which is embedded with a number of devices and the enormous amount of data produced by them. Therefore, in order to accomplish load balancing and network delay optimization, it is necessary to have the necessary skills to distribute and regulate traffic management and network device management in the network. These needs could be met by SDN technology, which changes the network's overall perspective to one that is centralized. Hence, it is a suitable technology among the currently available technologies to manage the IoT network with respect to load balancing, bandwidth utilization, and network traffic management [24].

9.6.2 Network Function Virtualization (NFV)

The traditional network technologies with predefined programming types do not permit the devices to accomplish multifarious tasks, even though they are capable of doing so. Thus, virtualizing the functions of the devices and modifying them in real time is needed. The new approach, which has been termed NFV, enables the devices to perform a variety of functions while modifying their capabilities in real-time based on the needs of individual applications [25]. Because NFV in SDN technology separates the control plane from the physical devices, it makes things easier for Internet service providers. Therefore, SDN-based methods play an imperative role in recognizing the importance of NFV in IoT networks [26].

9.6.3 Accessing Information from Anywhere

This refers to the idea that a large number of devices will be connected to the IoT, and that suppliers will be able to access them at any time and from any location. That is why the vendor should be capable of governing and changing the utilities of their devices, according to the necessities, and in a unified manner [27]. Through the SDN technology, the physical and virtual devices can be accessed and controlled through a program in the network [28].

9.6.4 Resource Utilization

The network's performance may suffer from increased or decreased resource utilization, which progressively reduces a system's usefulness. As a result, efficient planning of user needs is necessary for improved resource use to boost network effectiveness [29]. In SDN technology, flow rule–based traffic forwarding aids in improving the use of network resources. Multiple user requests can therefore be promoted through the selected path in accordance with the flow rules that are determined by the SDN controller [30].

9.6.5 Energy Management

A significant amount of energy will be utilized by the data centers in the IoT to handle the vast amounts of data that are gathered from numerous devices [27, 31]. Therefore, smart energy management techniques must also be guaranteed for energy-efficient data center networking. With SDN-based data center networking, network traffic may be effectively routed to the necessary servers. As a result, the data center's gadgets can be turned on and off dynamically based on needs [32], which starts an organized, energy-efficient data center network. From the perspective of an IoT network, this capability can be utilized [28].

9.6.6 Privacy and Security

Lastly, one of the most important tasks is securing the devices and network to allow multiple devices, vendors, as well as the users to play a part in a solitary platform [33, 34]. As a result, numerous devices are linked to a specific service provider. As a result, only the specific service provider can manage the devices that are linked to it. Additionally, even though they have the data, other service providers are unable to access the data that the devices have initiated. At the same time, one of the biggest concerns for users in an IoT network is privacy. The integration of numerous devices into a single platform compromises user privacy since multiple specialists may know information about other devices, such as what kind of operation is being carried out at the moment and who is doing what. Therefore, in order to protect user privacy, professionals must consider such scenarios while integrating various devices into a single platform. Network traffic is more secure and private when flows are controlled with SDN in an organized manner [35].

9.7 CHALLENGES AND PROPOSED SOLUTIONS

SDN-based IoT suffers from many challenges, as a growing technology, which is more challenging in the field of agriculture. The fundamental issues with SDN in IoT, specifically with regard to irrigation systems in agriculture, are covered in this section. The challenges need discussion to make the system reliable and suitable for the domain in real time.

9.7.1 Module Implementation

It describes how to implement the proposed model so that communication reliability can be achieved. Communication reliability includes three modules: connection state processing, intra-domain communication reliability, and inter-domain communication reliability. The connection processing module is generally the stateful match field in an OpenFlow switch. It mainly involves how packets will match according to the state of the controller, with the help of a state jump function implemented using a finite state machine. Mainly, there are four states: CONNECT, ACTIVE, IDLE, and DISCONNECT. The states CONNECT and DISCONNECT signify that the switches or gateways have not connected for packet transmission. Similarly, the states IDLE and ACTIVE represent the connection that has been made, and the controller is available. The states are communicated among them in a system using an echo and a timeout message. The challenge is that, as the data are sensed quickly, they must be transmitted to the system through different states. OpenFlow and its API are responsible for a self-learning mechanism for intra-domain communication reliability. If the controller is not available and the packet is transmitted, then what should happen, is that the self-learning mechanism will be enabled.

When a packet enters the gateway, it indicates that the SDN controller is ready and able to forward it to a nearby gateway in the cluster for system processing. But when the controller is not available, the entry must be valid and start to work, which is the challenging one. In the event that the packet header does not match, the ARP module is necessary and must be used to guarantee that the packet is appropriately altered and sent to the intended location [36]. The mechanism we discuss for inter-domain communication is shown in Figure 9.4 and can be implemented as a solution approach.

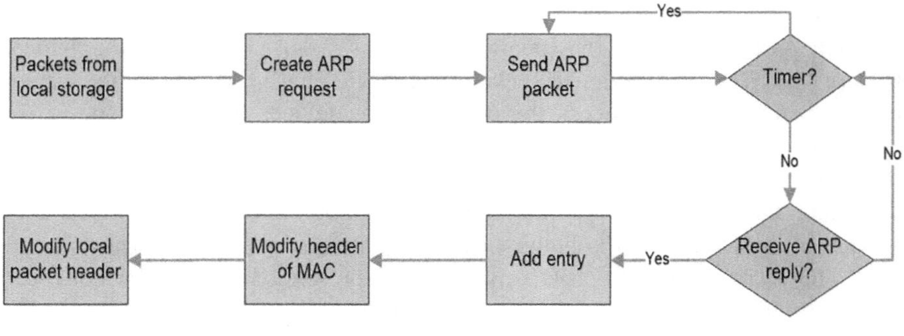

FIGURE 9.4 Proposed implementation module to achieve inter-domain communication reliability.

9.7.2 Failure of SDN Controller

While sensing the data in an agricultural field and forwarding the data packets to the system for processing, there is the chance of failure of the SDN controller, which causes a challenge for the system. For this, various methods have been suggested in the literature, such as having another SDN controller take responsibility and act as the primary SDN controller. This SDN controller must be reconnected to the switches and gateways to manage the network. It is very important in agriculture, as many disasters happen. Generally, information updating is one of the solution approaches to quickly recover the network. But the topology might change, which is the bottleneck.

9.7.3 Routing and Communication

Protocol is responsible for communication in the network, whereas routing is the mechanism to send the packets to the destination. Routing Protocol for Low-Power and Lossy Networks (RPL) is a very common protocol that runs with IPv6 and follows distance vector routing based on directed acyclic graph (DAG). RPL's primary feature is its objective function, which may be altered in response to network demands. RPL constructs the tree depending on the network and pushes the packets in the best path to reach the destination. Rather than RPL, there is no suitable routing protocol competing; it is a big challenge. With the rapid development of communication protocols, a number of protocols are available, but these have not been studied for the agriculture sector. Wi-Fi, Bluetooth, LoRa WAN, ZigBee, Z-Wave, and Sigfox are some of the existing protocols that have their own significance. Some specification parameters of these protocols are given in Table 9.2.

9.7.4 Security

Information technology security is a big problem, and it gets worse with cloud, fog, edge, and IoT technologies. Similar security issues must be resolved because cloud, fog, and edge computing are all used in the development of IoT technologies [37–39]. Moreover, in the SDN model, it is challenging for the SDN controller to provide

TABLE 9.2
Commonly Used Communication Protocols with Specifications

Protocols	Standard	Cost	Data Rates	Power Consumption	Frequency	Range
WiFi	IEEE 802.11n	L	54 Mb/s	M	2.4, 5 GHz	50 m
Bluetooth	IEEE 802.15.1	L	1 Mb/s	L	2.4 GHz	50–150 m
LoRa	LoRaWAN	M	50 kb/s	L	sub-GHz	<15 km
ZigBee	IEEE 802.15.4	M	250 kb/s	L	2.4 GHz	100 m
Z-Wave	ZAD 12837	M	100 kb/s	L	900 MHz	30 m
Sigfox	Sigfox	M	1000 b/s	L	900 MHz	10 m, 50 km

authorization and authentication. The OpenFlow switch requires special security measures to maintain the security of the network. There are three levels of security issues: lower-level security, intermediate security, and high-level security. So it is challenging to detect the defective SDN controller or OpenFlow switch. Different solution approaches for this can be to implement a recovery and backup mechanism [40, 41].

9.7.5 Mobility

It is a crucial aspect in IoT and SDN networks; the data and information must be delivered to the moving user. Different mobility support systems and mechanisms have been proposed in IoT, but there is a big question of whether these are effectively working in SDN-based IoT or not. Message Queuing Telemetry Transport (MQTT) is a well-known protocol to maintain mobility in IoT, which is supported by Transmission Control Protocol/Internet Protocol (TCP/IP). Constrained Application Protocol (CoAP) is one of the schemes widely supported in mobile WSN networks. Quantum Lifecycle Management (QLM) is one of the techniques suggested by researchers for SDN-based IoT applications.

9.7.6 Reliability

It is highly essential in an IoT-based agriculture system to measure the accuracy and precision while sensing and processing data to perform action. Reliability is important at both the hardware and software levels in agriculture. As we are adopting and suggesting IoT-based techniques for the growth of crops, reliability must be considered. Incomplete or corrupted data may lead to wrong decisions and actions for the crops, which is very dangerous. The crops may be damaged by excess irrigation and the supply of fertilizers. As the crops go through different stages with a limited time period, the proper decision is essential, which could be possible through high reliability in the proposed system. Moreover, energy management is a major concern in IoT-based technology. Due to a large number of node deployments in the network, it is challenging to manage energy for the sensing node and network components. Solar energy is one of the solutions for energy management in agricultural IoT, but it requires more studies.

9.7.7 Quality of Services (QoSs)

The measurement of service performance in terms of packet loss, availability, bit rate, delay, etc. is called QoS. Service delivery as per the requirement is the major objective of the QoS. It is very important in an IoT system; otherwise, the service and application may not provide the service as per the requirements [42]. As the user requirement changes on demand, the QoS must be maintained. In agriculture, it is quite difficult to achieve. In a year, seasonal crops are cultivated; moreover, various types of crops have different requirements. Hence, the QoS may also change according to the requirements of crops. So, some agriculture-based QoS is required for the IoT-based system. Agriculture and crops are also human-influenced, so it is very challenging to maintain QoS. Moreover, the crops also have environmental influences, so the system requires some QoS management parameters by considering these.

9.7.8 Mobile Computing Generation

In IoT-based systems, the application layer has multiple applications for monitoring, decision-making, and analysis as per the requirements of the user. These applications are generally developed as mobile applications. Through mobile computing, the applications interact with the IoT-based system. Mobile computing is a rapidly growing industry that has expanded its usability to various fields. Along with the growth of usability, the technology is also changing from generation to generation. Currently, 5G networks are widely used in mobile computing. With the successful development of 5G, most countries have adopted it. Most of the applications have been migrated to 5G networks. However, SDN is a newly developed computing technology, and it has not yet reached the desired level. Most SDN-based applications have yet to be studied in the context of the 4G network. Moreover, considering both 4G and 5G networks, it is common for the propagating signal to face various interferers over the propagation medium, leading to degradation in signal quality commonly referred to as wireless fading [43, 44]. It is crucial to model the propagation channel accurately [45–47] in order to dynamically manage signal variations while maintaining QoS. In this context, it is quite challenging for researchers to propose an SDN-based system utilizing a 5G network, while also managing fading conditions.

9.7.9 Integration of AI and Blockchain in Smart Agriculture

With the evolution of increasingly intelligent, secure, and programmable infrastructure, the combination of artificial intelligence (AI), blockchain, and SDN is transforming traditional farming practices in the rapidly evolving field of smart agriculture. For vital functions including supply chain logistics, crop monitoring, and irrigation systems, this threefold infrastructure ensures transparent data management, real-time decision-making, and dynamic control [48].

By providing a decentralized, immutable ledger for documenting agricultural operations, such as soil moisture levels, weather, fertilizer application, and irrigation schedules, blockchain acts as the basic layer. It guarantees data integrity, accountability, and traceability for various parties associated with the agricultural supply chain. Blockchain allows for intelligent action in addition to data storage when combined with AI-based decision frameworks. AI systems are able to estimate the best time and amount of irrigation by analyzing environmental data, including crop type, soil moisture, and weather forecasts. To ensure straightforwardness and auditability, these AI-driven insights are recorded on the blockchain after verification. When AI and blockchain are involved, SDN becomes very important for overseeing AI-controlled irrigation systems. With SDN, the whole network used in the smart farm is centrally managed and programmed by keeping its control and data functions separate. By using SDN controllers, the network can route real-time soil moisture data first, manage bandwidth based on needs, and send traffic elsewhere when faults occur. Because of this, there is reliable and flexible communication among blockchain nodes, AI, and field-deployed sensors, which makes it possible to control irrigation in real time [49].

For smart irrigation practices, the AI mechanism examines sensor information to work out the precise water requirements for each area in an agricultural setting. It is possible to start or stop irrigation equipment by sending the relevant decision through the SDN-managed network. Every activity on the blockchain is noted, along with details such as time, how much water was used, and the kind of crop grown. By integrating AI inference in smart contracts on the blockchain, financial transactions for irrigation can be carried out automatically. For instance, as soon as some conditions met by AI and communicated through the SDN have been verified, contracts will begin paying for agricultural water or equipment hire. Such agreements make sure farming work is done according to schedule, help lower charges, and reduce manual labor costs.

9.8 CONCLUSION AND FUTURE SCOPE

IoT is the next generation of technology that allows things to connect to people through the Internet. It has a wide range of applications from home to industry for the betterment of human lifestyle. It is also applied to agriculture for different purposes and crop cultivation. Generally, sensors have been developed according to the agricultural environment and requirements. Different sensors are deployed as nodes, and the network is configured for processing data and decision-making. Irrigation system management is highly essential for the growth of the crops. In this chapter, an irrigation system based on IoT, blockchain, and an SDN framework for large-scale agricultural fields is portrayed. SDN is the new network management mechanism to provide a robust network with minimal network management effort. We suggest an SDN-based architecture for an IoT irrigation system. We discussed and analyzed the architecture and its components along with its applications. Finally, we present different challenges and possible solutions that majorly occur in SDN-based IoT systems for agriculture. The discussion will give an idea of how to handle the issues to design a reliable and robust system for agriculture. Moreover, the design architecture can be studied by considering multiple sensing parameters, and the fault tolerance mechanism could be regarded as a potential future research.

REFERENCES

1. S. Y. Liu, "Artificial Intelligence (AI) in Agriculture," in *IT Professional*, vol. 22, no. 3, pp. 14–15, 1 May-June 2020, doi: 10.1109/MITP.2020.2986121.
2. S. Velmurugan, V. Balaji, T. M. Bharathi, and K. Saravanan, "An IoT Based Smart Irrigation System using Soil Moisture and Weather Prediction," *International Journal of Engineering Research and Technology*, vol. 8, no. 7, May 2020.
3. R. N. Rao and B. Sridhar, "IoT based smart crop-field monitoring and automation irrigation system," *2018 2nd International Conference on Inventive Systems and Control (ICISC)*, Jan. 2018, doi: https://doi.org/10.1109/icisc.2018.8399118.

4. I. Deva Priya and S. Silas, "A Survey on Research Challenges and Applications in Empowering the SDN-Based Internet of Things," *Advances in Intelligent Systems and Computing*, vol. 750, pp. 457–467, Dec. 2018, doi: https://doi.org/10.1007/978-981-13-1882-5_39.
5. C. Kamienski *et al.*, "Smart Water Management Platform: IoT-Based Precision Irrigation for Agriculture," *Sensors*, vol. 19, no. 2, p. 276, Jan. 2019, doi: https://doi.org/10.3390/s19020276.
6. S. C. Nayak, S. Parida, C. Tripathy, B. Pati, and C. R. Panigrahi, "Multicriteria Decision-Making Techniques for Avoiding Similar Task Scheduling Conflict in Cloud Computing," *International Journal of Communication Systems*, p. e4126, Aug. 2019, doi: https://doi.org/10.1002/dac.4126.
7. S. Misra and N. Saha, "Detour: Dynamic Task Offloading in Software-Defined Fog for IoT Applications," *IEEE Journal on Selected Areas in Communications*, vol. 37, no. 5, pp. 1159–1166, May 2019, doi: https://doi.org/10.1109/jsac.2019.2906793.
8. A. Banerjee, A. K. Pujari, C. Rani Panigrahi, B. Pati, S. Chandan Nayak, and T.-H. Weng, "A New Method for Weighted Ensemble Clustering and Coupled Ensemble Selection," *Connection Science*, vol. 33, no. 3, pp. 623–644, Jan. 2021, doi: https://doi.org/10.1080/09540091.2020.1866496.
9. C. Metter, M. Seufert, F. Wamser, T. Zinner, and P. Tran-Gia, "Analytical Model for SDN Signaling Traffic and Flow Table Occupancy and Its Application for Various Types of Traffic," *IEEE Transactions on Network and Service Management*, vol. 14, no. 3, pp. 603–615, Sep. 2017, doi: https://doi.org/10.1109/tnsm.2017.2714758.
10. K. Yang, D. Guo, B. Zhang, and B. Zhao, "Multi-Controller Placement for Load Balancing in SDWAN," *IEEE Access*, vol. 7, pp. 167278–167289, 2019, doi: https://doi.org/10.1109/access.2019.2953723.
11. S. C. Nayak, S. Parida, C. Tripathy, and P. K. Pattnaik, "Modeling of Task Scheduling Algorithm Using Petri-Net in Cloud Computing," *Advances in Intelligent Systems and Computing*, vol. 563, pp. 633–643, Jan. 2018, doi: https://doi.org/10.1007/978-981-10-6872-0_61.
12. D. Mishra, A. Khan, R. Tiwari, and S. Upadhay, "Automated Irrigation System-IoT Based Approach," *IEEE Xplore*, Feb. 01, 2018. https://ieeexplore.ieee.org/document/8519886
13. M. M. Raikar, M. S M, and M. M. Mulla, "Software Defined Internet of Things Using Lightweight Protocol," *Procedia Computer Science*, vol. 171, pp. 1409–1418, Jan. 2020, doi: https://doi.org/10.1016/j.procs.2020.04.151.
14. S. A. Wahba, A. M. El-Gindy, K. F. El-Bagouri, and M. A. Marwa, "Response of Green Peas to Irrigation Automatic Scheduling and Potassium Fertigation," *International Journal of ChemTech Research*, vol. 9, no. 3, pp. 228–237, 2016.
15. M. E. Karar, M. F. Al-Rasheed, A. F. Al-Rasheed, and O. Reyad, "IoT and Neural Network-Based Water Pumping Control System for Smart Irrigation," *Information Sciences Letters*, vol. 9, no. 2, p. 7, Jan. 2020, doi: https://doi.org/10.48550/arXiv.2005.04158.
16. N. G and J. Megala, "Wireless sensor Network based automated irrigation and crop field monitoring system," *2014 Sixth International Conference on Advanced Computing (ICoAC)*, Chennai, India, pp. 189–194, Dec. 2014, doi: https://doi.org/10.1109/icoac.2014.7229707.
17. K. Taneja and S. Bhatia, "Automatic irrigation system using Arduino UNO," *2017 International Conference on Intelligent Computing and Control Systems (ICICCS)*, pp. 132–135, Jun. 2017, doi: https://doi.org/10.1109/iccons.2017.8250693.
18. S. Tomovic, K. Yoshigoe, I. Maljevic, and I. Radusinovic, "Software-Defined Fog Network Architecture for IoT," *Wireless Personal Communications*, vol. 92, no. 1, pp. 181–196, Oct. 2016, doi: https://doi.org/10.1007/s11277-016-3845-0.

19. S. Anitha, P.V.V. Hymavathi, and E. Brumancia, "Smart irrigation automation system using IoT," *2018 2nd International Conference on Trends in Electronics and Informatics (ICOEI)*, pp. 397–402, May 2018, doi: https://doi.org/10.1109/icoei.2018.8553725.
20. J. Gutiérrez, J. F. Villa-Medina, A. Nieto-Garibay, and M. Á. Porta-Gándara, "Automated Irrigation System Using a Wireless Sensor Network and GPRS Module," *IEEE Transactions on Instrumentation and Measurement*, vol. 63, no. 1, pp. 166–176, Jan. 2014, doi: https://doi.org/10.1109/TIM.2013.2276487.
21. T. Luo, H.-P. Tan, and T. Q. S. Quek, "Sensor OpenFlow: Enabling Software-Defined Wireless Sensor Networks," *IEEE Communications Letters*, vol. 16, no. 11, pp. 1896–1899, Nov. 2012, doi: https://doi.org/10.1109/lcomm.2012.092812.121712.
22. G. Raja and A. Thomas, "SAFER: Crowdsourcing Based Disaster Monitoring System Using Software Defined Fog Computing," *Mobile Networks and Applications*, vol. 24, pp. 1414–1424, May 2019, doi: https://doi.org/10.1007/s11036-019-01267-x.
23. J. Gubbi, R. Buyya, S. Marusic, and M. Palaniswami, "Internet of Things (IoT): A Vision, Architectural Elements, and Future Directions," *Future Generation Computer Systems*, vol. 29, no. 7, pp. 1645–1660, Sep. 2013, doi: https://doi.org/10.1016/j.future.2013.01.010.
24. X. Huang, R. Yu, N. Wang, S. Maharjan, and Y. Zhang, "Software Defined Networking with Pseudonym Systems for Secure Vehicular Clouds," *IEEE Access*, vol. 4, pp. 3522–3534, Jan. 2016, doi: https://doi.org/10.1109/access.2016.2560902.
25. N. Omnes, M. Bouillon, G. Fromentoux, and O. L. Grand, "A Programmable and Virtualized Network & IT Infrastructure for the Internet of Things: How Can NFV & SDN Help for Facing the Upcoming Challenges," *IEEE Xplore*, Feb. 01, 2015. https://ieeexplore.ieee.org/stamp/stamp.jsp?tp=&arnumber=7073808 (accessed Jun. 02, 2022).
26. T. Wood, K. K. Ramakrishnan, J. Hwang, G. Liu, and W. Zhang, "Toward a Software-Based Network: Integrating Software Defined Networking and Network Function Virtualization," *IEEE Network*, vol. 29, no. 3, pp. 36–41, May 2015, doi: https://doi.org/10.1109/mnet.2015.7113223.
27. L. Atzori, A. Iera, and G. Morabito, "The Internet of Things: A Survey," *Computer Networks*, vol. 54, no. 15, pp. 2787–2805, Oct. 2010, doi: https://doi.org/10.1016/j.comnet.2010.05.010.
28. S. Bera, S. Misra, and A. V. Vasilakos, "Software-Defined Networking for Internet of Things: A Survey," *IEEE Internet of Things Journal*, vol. 4, no. 6, pp. 1994–2008, Dec. 2017, doi: https://doi.org/10.1109/jiot.2017.2746186.
29. M. Nkomo, G. P. Hancke, A. M. Abu-Mahfouz, S. Sinha, and A. J. Onumanyi, "Overlay Virtualized Wireless Sensor Networks for Application in Industrial Internet of Things: A Review," *Sensors*, vol. 18, no. 10, p. 3215, Sep. 2018, doi: https://doi.org/10.3390/s18103215.
30. R. C. A. Alves, D. A. G. Oliveira, G. C. C. F. Pereira, B. C. Albertini, and C. B. Margi, "WS3N: Wireless Secure SDN-Based Communication for Sensor Networks," *Security and Communication Networks*, vol. 2018, pp. 1–14, Aug. 2018, doi: https://doi.org/10.1155/2018/8734389.
31. C. C. Aggarwal, N. Ashish, and A. Sheth, "The Internet of Things: A Survey from the Data-Centric Perspective," *Managing and Mining Sensor Data*, pp. 383–428, Dec. 2012, doi: https://doi.org/10.1007/978-1-4614-6309-2_12.
32. M. Dayarathna, Y. Wen, and R. Fan, "Data Center Energy Consumption Modeling: A Survey," *IEEE Communications Surveys & Tutorials*, vol. 18, no. 1, pp. 732–794, 2016, doi: https://doi.org/10.1109/comst.2015.2481183.
33. Q. Jing, A. V. Vasilakos, J. Wan, J. Lu, and D. Qiu, "Security of the Internet of Things: Perspectives and Challenges," *Wireless Networks*, vol. 20, no. 8, pp. 2481–2501, Jun. 2014, doi: https://doi.org/10.1007/s11276-014-0761-7.
34. Z. Yan, P. Zhang, and A. V. Vasilakos, "A Survey on Trust Management for Internet of Things," *Journal of Network and Computer Applications*, vol. 42, pp. 120–134, Jun. 2014, doi: https://doi.org/10.1016/j.jnca.2014.01.014.

35. R. Vilalta *et al.*, "Improving security in Internet of Things with software defined networking," *2016 IEEE Global Communications Conference (GLOBECOM)*, Dec. 2016, doi: https://doi.org/10.1109/glocom.2016.7841889.
36. T. Huang, S. Yan, F. Yang, and J. Liu, "Multi-Domain SDN Survivability for Agricultural Wireless Sensor Networks," *Sensors*, vol. 16, no. 11, p. 1861, Nov. 2016, doi: https://doi.org/10.3390/s16111861.
37. A. Panigrahi, A. K. Nayak, R. Paul, B. Sahu, and S. Kant, "CTB-PKI: Clustering and Trust Enabled Blockchain Based PKI System for Efficient Communication in P2P Network," *IEEE Access*, vol. 10, pp. 124277–124290, 2022, doi: https://doi.org/10.1109/access.2022.3222807.
38. A. Panigrahi, A. K. Nayak, and R. Paul, "Smart Contract Assisted Blockchain Based Public Key Infrastructure System," *Transactions on Emerging Telecommunications Technologies*, Oct. 2022, doi: https://doi.org/10.1002/ett.4655.
39. A. Panigrahi, A. K. Nayak, and R. Paul, "HealthCare EHR," *International Journal of Information Systems and Supply Chain Management*, vol. 15, no. 3, pp. 1–15, Jul. 2022, doi: https://doi.org/10.4018/ijisscm.290017.
40. A. Panigrahi, A. K. Nayak, and R. Paul, "A Blockchain Based PKI System for Peer to Peer Network," *Lecture Notes in Networks and Systems*, pp. 81–88, 2022, doi: https://doi.org/10.1007/978-981-16-4807-6_9.
41. A. Panigrahi, A. K. Nayak, and R. Paul, "Impact of Clustering Technique in Enhancing the Blockchain Network Performance," *2022 International Conference on Machine Learning, Computer Systems and Security (MLCSS)*, pp. 363–367, Aug. 2022, doi: https://doi.org/10.1109/mlcss57186.2022.00072.
42. S. Parida, S. C. Nayak, P. K. Pattnaik, S. A. Siddique, S. Keshri, and P. Priyadarshi, "Design Model of Smart 'Anganwadi Center' for Health Monitoring," *Intelligent Systems Reference Library*, vol. 178, pp. 67–76, Jan. 2020, doi: https://doi.org/10.1007/978-3-030-37551-5_4.
43. T. Mukherjee, A. K. Singh, and D. Senapati, "Performance Evaluation of Wireless Communication Systems over Weibull/q-Lognormal Shadowed Fading Using Tsallis' Entropy Framework," *Wireless Personal Communications*, vol. 106, no. 2, pp. 789–803, Feb. 2019, doi: https://doi.org/10.1007/s11277-019-06190-8.
44. T. Mukherjee, S. Bebortta, and D. Senapati, "Stochastic Modeling of q-Lognormal Fading Channels over Tsallis' Entropy: Evaluation of Channel Capacity and Higher Order Moments," *Digital Signal Processing*, vol. 133, pp. 103856–103856, Mar. 2023, doi: https://doi.org/10.1016/j.dsp.2022.103856.
45. T. Mukherjee and D. Senapati, "An Adaptive q-Lognormal Model Towards the Computation of Average Channel Capacity in Slow Fading Channels," *Telecommunication Systems*, vol. 79, no. 3, pp. 341–355, Jan. 2022, doi: https://doi.org/10.1007/s11235-021-00843-5.
46. S. Samal, T. Mukherjee, S. Bebortta, and S. Chakravarty, "Intelligent characterization of wireless fading channels using a single statistical q-weibull distribution," *2022 IEEE 2nd International Symposium on Sustainable Energy, Signal Processing and Cyber Security (iSSSC)*, Feb. 2023, doi: https://doi.org/10.1109/isssc56467.2022.10051241.
47. T. Mukherjee and D. Senapati, "A Tight Approximation Towards the SEP Computation Over Nakagami-m Fading Channels," *National Academy Science Letters*, vol. 45, no. 5, pp. 423–426, Aug. 2022, doi: https://doi.org/10.1007/s40009-022-01162-2.
48. A. Panigrahi, B. Sahu, S. S. Panigrahi, S. Khan, and A. K. Jena, "Application of Blockchain as a Solution to the Real-World Issues in Health Care System," *Intelligent Systems Reference Library*, pp. 135–149, Jan. 2021, doi: https://doi.org/10.1007/978-3-030-69395-4_8.
49. A. Panigrahi, A. Pati, B. Dash, G. Sahoo, D. Singh, and M. Dash, "ASBlock: An Agricultural Based Supply Chain Management Using Blockchain Technology," *Procedia Computer Science*, vol. 235, pp. 1943–1952, Jan. 2024, doi: https://doi.org/10.1016/j.procs.2024.04.184.

10 Decentralized Identity and AI-Powered Identity Management

Madhumita Mahapatra, Debabrata Singh, Seema Verma, and Rachana Sharma

10.1 INTRODUCTION

10.1.1 Background and Motivation

The rapid adoption of "artificial intelligence (AI) and blockchain" is fueling a profound transformation taking place in the healthcare industry. The combination of these technologies has introduced a data-driven modern paradigm of delivery, efficiency, security, and personalization that has redefined the apparatus of generation, processing, exchange, and security of healthcare data [1]. Long plagued by data silos in an antiquated healthcare system, inefficient administrative processes, and growing operational costs, intelligent and decentralized digital solutions offer a way to boost the industry. Currently, AI which mimics human cognition is being used for a host of applications, including early disease detection, medical imaging, personalizing treatment recommendations, and drug discovery [2]. Clinical data is stored by electronic health records (EHRs) and comprises a vast amount of information. "Natural language processing (NLP)" and deep learning (DL) techniques are also being applied to allow the abstraction of unstructured data from EHRs, thus delivering actionable information to the clinician in real time [3]. Simultaneously, blockchain technology, initially devised to be the foundation to underpin cryptocurrencies, is also becoming popular in the healthcare field for its natural properties with decentralization, immutability, and transparency [4]. Through the implementation of secure and verifiable data exchange without centralized intermediaries, blockchain provides new ways to secure health data, manage digital identities, and make pharmaceuticals traceable. For example, patient data can be stored on a blockchain to ensure data integrity, and smart contracts can automate claims handling and billing. Figure 10.1 shows the application of NLP.

The reason to investigate the real-world applications of AI and blockchain in healthcare is driven by the utmost necessity to fix systemic inefficiencies and offer data-driven, patient-centered care. The COVID-19 pandemic has made it clear that real-time analytics, secure data sharing, and strong digital infrastructure can help support public health responses and continuity of care [5]. Given this scenario, it

DOI: 10.1201/9781003658597-10

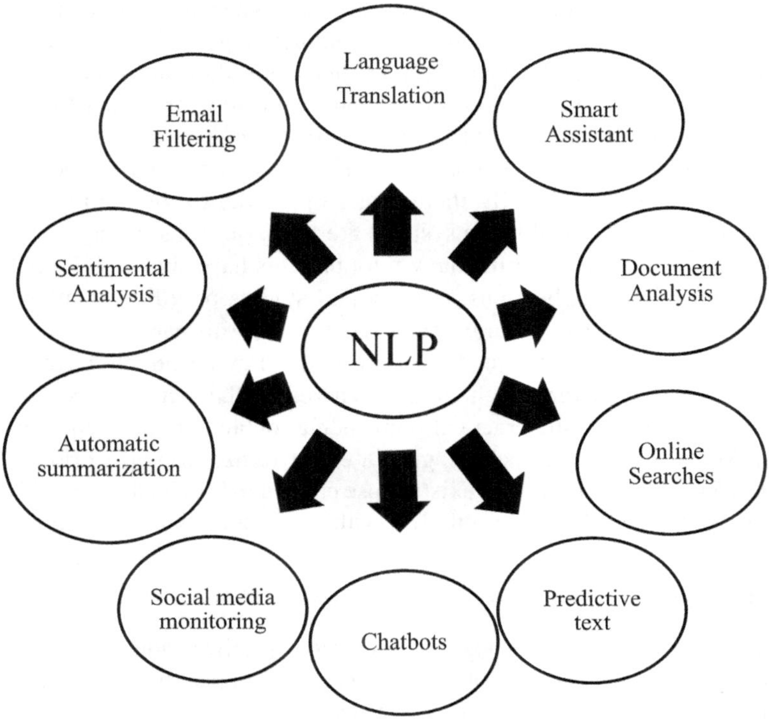

FIGURE 10.1 Application of NLP.

is important to consider the actual application of these technologies in the specific healthcare context, and what is still unclear that hampers their wider uptake.

10.1.2 Problem Statement

The practical application of AI and blockchain technologies in transforming the healthcare system is full of troubles. Due to the lack of interoperability between current healthcare systems and new digital platforms, scalability is a major issue. Health data is usually spread over different systems and organizations, which makes it made difficult to access. This results in a failure to duplicate efforts, and it exposes frequent medical errors [2]. Incorporating AI tools and blockchain frameworks into these legacy systems requires large quantities of technical, financial, and organizational investments. Also, the issues related to data privacy and the compliance with the regulations like Health Insurance Portability and Accountability Act (HIPAA) and General Data Protection Regulation (GDPR) are another roadblock. However, data sharing in healthcare is restricted by ethical and legal constraints, and therefore, such models rely on large volumes of high-quality data. It doesn't mean we release our data ownership to anyone, or we have no clue that our data has been leaked or stolen, all we do is that we encrypt and decentralize [1]. As it relates to clinicians, there is worry around the interpretability and reliability of that AI, of what it's recommending. Without providing a clear rationale on how the results were obtained, black box algorithms rely on black box algorithms to generate diagnostic suggestions, which doctors find difficult to trust and validate. Consequently, just like blockchain's immutability, which is normally viewed as a good thing, also becomes a problem if there is genuine need to change or delete patients' data. Finally, there is lack of standardization of the technology implementation since healthcare systems are heterogeneous throughout different regions and institutions. While many pilot projects have shown the feasibility of AI and blockchain applications, longitudinal studies or full evaluation of their true-world effectiveness remains sparse. As a result, this gap prevents healthcare providers from making informed decisions and policy formulation, causing them to be hesitant to scale these technologies. Therefore, the focus of this chapter is to solve the gap between the practical implementation and the theoretical possibilities of AI and blockchain technologies in effective use for real-world healthcare systems. Systematic analysis of existing use cases needs to be done quickly to find out best practices and strategies to deal with implementation bottlenecks.

10.1.3 Research Objectives

An effort is made to try and bridge this knowledge gap by conducting a comprehensive study of the practical uses of AI and blockchain in healthcare. Specifically, the research is guided by the following objectives.

1. This chapter throws light on how far AI and blockchain have been accepted in the healthcare sector. It also investigates worldwide trends in the use of these technologies for certain clinical and administrative functions.
2. The purpose of the case study is to identify and categorize real-world examples of AI and blockchain integration. The focus areas include diagnostics EHRs drugs supply chain management clinical trials insurance automation.
3. The analysis of the benefits and the limitations observed in these applications will consider the improvements in efficiency, patient outcomes, and in security of the data, as well as technical, ethical, and organizational challenges.
4. It would analyze the supporting and obstructing forces for large-scale implementation. This means assessing the regulatory framework, infrastructure readiness, stakeholder engagement, and interoperability standards.
5. This will help in developing a roadmap for future research and development. With the findings of the chapter, directions for innovation, policy-making, and strategic planning will be suggested on how to enhance sustainable technology adoption in healthcare.

This aims to achieve this by addressing the objectives of becoming sufficiently acquainted with how the practical application of AI and blockchain technologies are transforming healthcare delivery.

10.1.4 Contribution

This particular chapter presents a unique contribution, which is not encountered in the rest of the literature on emerging technologies. It offers a holistic perspective which is backed by real-world application and data. Furthermore, this chapter studies the convergence of AI and blockchain in the domain of healthcare. Finding framework of above-mentioned technologies (architecture, code/circuits, data, application) can greatly help in creating an efficient solution to blockchain-based ecosystem and digital currencies which address most of the use cases. This chapter can be an invaluable source for learning for the academic and professional audience. The chapter provides an overview of contemporary developments that may also interest researchers, to the extent they indicate gaps that deserve future investigation. It offers a practical guidance for the practitioners to understand use of these technologies to enhance patient outcomes, minimize operational workflows, and deliver healthcare. The chapter looks at key ethical and regulatory issues that will be helpful for policy makers and legal scholars studying data governance and health equity. The socio-technical components of digital transformation are explored and emphasize collaboration between technologist, healthcare professional, and patient. This chapter becomes a brick in the wall of the wider narrative of the book that shows how tangible outcomes from the very slippery, young technologies like AI and blockchain can help in solving complex real-life problems. Their emphasis is on weaving in these emerging technologies in use not just as playthings but as necessary supports of systemic change within the vast area of social healthcare.

10.2 IMPORTANCE OF DIGITAL TRANSFORMATION IN HEALTHCARE

The healthcare sector has always been perceived as slow-moving, but the current buzzword in the industry is digital. Because of the fast-evolving technology, the government, hospitals, insurance companies, and also patients are thinking out-of-the-box for the delivery, management, and also experiencing of healthcare service. Digital transformation in healthcare refers to the strategic implementation of technologies in the healthcare ecosystem to enhance operational efficiency, clinical outcomes, and increase patient engagement. Such technologies include big data, cloud computing, AI, Internet of Things (IoT), and blockchain [6].

Changes in this environment are being driven extremely fast because of the accelerating global growth in the total population, rising costs of the burden of chronic disease, rising overall annual expenditure on healthcare, and increasing demands for personalization. Surface systems can no longer meet the increasing demands. The global pandemic of COVID-19 has unexpectedly hastened this shift and brought out the gaps in the healthcare system. Following the pandemic, it was a stark reminder that healthcare must be leveraging digital solutions, including telemedicine, remote patient monitoring, contactless data interchange, and more to bring the world closer with the technology of tomorrow. Digital transformation not only automates the workflow but also changes the patient caregiving relationship by delivering services through look-through as well as accessible and data-driven. Because of this shift, healthcare is quickly changing from a reactive, illness-driven model to a proactive, wellness-driven model. The integration of AI with blockchain capabilities can work together synergistically to provide a robust solution to the big problems of the healthcare delivery and management system.

10.2.1 Challenges in Traditional Healthcare Systems

It is important to know the shortcomings of the key features of a traditional healthcare system before understanding AI and blockchain's capabilities. These limitations have limited-service quality, accessibility, and sustainability for a long time, particularly in low resource settings.

1. Fragmented Data Silos: Fragmentation of patient data across different providers and departments is one of the most critical challenges. Arguably, information stored in EHRs are trapped within their systems and almost never have interaction with other systems, and consequently leading to information duplication, delays in making diagnoses, and missing and incomplete medical histories [7]. Fragmentation of such sort not only disrupts continuity of care but also comes at an unnecessary administrative cost. Figure 10.2 shows the EHR of a patient.
2. Lack of Interoperability: One of the current issues in healthcare IT infrastructure is that it lacks interoperability. Because different systems often

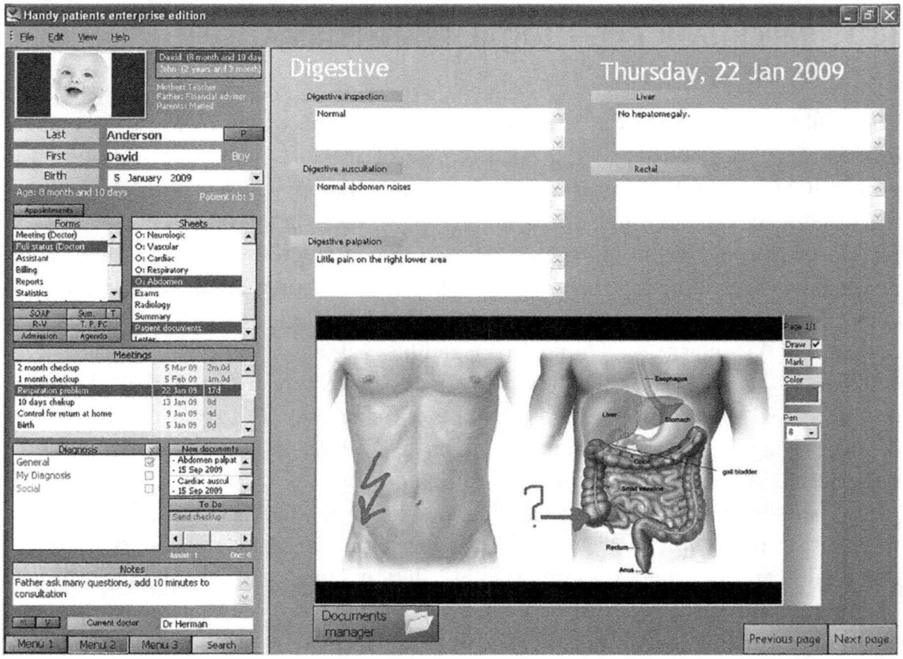

FIGURE 10.2 Electronic health records (EHRs).

work on its own incompatible standards and data formats, data exchange is cumbersome and prone to errors [8]. The absence of standardization impedes collaboration among healthcare providers, insurers, and researchers.
3. Inefficiency and Bureaucracy: In developing countries, healthcare is still very burdened with manual, paper-based processes. Even in appointments scheduling, billing, insurance claims, and managing prescription, there are many time-consuming administrative tasks that hinder the clinical productivity and increase patient wait time [9].
4. People living in rural and un-developed areas often face difficulties in availing quality healthcare services. Poor infrastructure, a shortage of trained professionals, and high service costs lead to unequal health outcomes. This gap is a concern for traditional models that depend on service delivery that is expensive and based on centralized models.
5. Nonetheless, digital records of health information are prone to breaches and cyber-attacks. Overall, the risk of hackers is another problem. Since health data is by their very nature sensitive, it needs a high level of privacy and security. However, the existing system finds it difficult to provide such privacy [1].
6. The standardization of techniques in the conventional healthcare practice provides little scope for personalization in treatment. Unfortunately, this strategy often fails to deliver good results as it does not completely fulfill the needs of each patient. By contrast, anti-China policies deal with features that are explicitly related to the pool and which have no international legal status. These two technologies possess complementary capabilities that can effectively mitigate their respective limitations.

10.2.2 Brief Overview of AI and Blockchain Technologies

AI refers to the simulation of human intelligence by machines. In the context of healthcare, AI encompasses a range of subfields, including:

- *Machine Learning (ML)*: Enables computers to learn from historical data and make predictions without being explicitly programmed.
- *DL*: A subset of ML involving neural networks that can process unstructured data like images or text.
- *Natural Language Processing (NLP)*: Allows machines to understand and interpret human language, useful in summarizing clinical notes or extracting information from patient records.
- *Computer Vision*: Facilitates automated analysis of medical images like X-rays and MRIs.

These capabilities have already shown remarkable success in diagnostics, drug discovery, robotic surgery, and personalized treatment planning [3, 10].

Blockchain is a decentralized, distributed ledger technology that ensures data immutability and transparency. Each block contains a timestamp and a link to the previous block, creating a chain that cannot be tampered with. Key features include:

- *Decentralization*: No single authority controls the data.
- *Immutability*: Once recorded, data cannot be altered.
- *Smart Contracts*: Self-executing contracts with the terms directly written into code.
- *Consensus Mechanisms*: Ensure agreement among nodes before data is added.
- In healthcare, blockchain has applications in maintaining accurate medical records, ensuring drug traceability, managing clinical trial data, and automating administrative processes [4].

10.2.3 Objective and Significance of Integrating AI and Blockchain

Individually, AI and blockchain are on the pedestal, but when used in conjunction then this framework brings a synergistic outcome to a lot of pain points of healthcare.

The joint application creates a secure, intelligent, and transparent ecosystem for benefitting clinical and operational domains.

1. The primary purpose of blockchain in italics is to enable the tamper-proof and transparent sharing of all health records to authorized stakeholders. The outcomes produced by AI systems that have been trained on blockchain-verified data are however extremely reliable. Thus, this integration helps health professional, patient, and regulator to build trust [11].
2. Privacy concerns restrict access to it. AI thrives on large datasets. Data sharing in a secured manner is possible through access control and audit trail with blockchain. Patients can maintain data ownership as permissioned blockchain platforms selectively allow sharing of such data [12].
3. The ownership of blockchain-based smart contracts automates a process like insurance claims, billing, or a clinical workflow, and thus, we make them transparent. Contracts available on the platform are enhanced with adaptive decision-making supported by AI. A smart contract can then execute payment automatically after it's determined by AI that the user is eligible for treatment.
4. Fraud detection and risk management is the fourth popular use of AI and blockchain technology. The blockchain provides a way of storing and publishing transaction histories, which are significantly immutable and auditable. On the other hand, AI can sniff out billing or prescription pattern anomalies. This combination reduces the incidence of fraud and compliance to regulations.
5. AI has a much bigger role in developing medicines: it can help scientists speed up clinical trials and find the right experimental drugs much earlier, thus speeding up the pipeline for drug development. The dual-layer implementation prevents counterfeit drugs, ensures timely delivery, and reduces wastage in comparison to single-layer approaches [13].
6. AI assists in the selection of subjects and generation of hypotheses in clinical trials conducted. This is ensured by the blockchain: trial protocols, results, and data sharing transparency are all ensured by the blockchain.

This creates an environment that fosters the shared responsibility and reduces the chances of skewing or falsifying results [14].

7. AI has the ability to analyze patients' data and identify risk factors and recommendation for intervention. This blockchain data is secure and tamper-proof for long-term studies and continuity of care.
8. Harnessing AI's analytical power with blockchain traceability enables greater auditability and regulatory compliance, for example, GDPR or HIPAA. With smart contracts, you can dynamically communicate and manage consent with your patients.
9. Blockchain-based digital identity systems enable patients to take control of their healthcare data and allow them to determine who they want to provide access to their health records. AI Chatbots and virtual assistants can help patients to allow them to follow self-care, appoint themselves, and also track their own symptoms to boost engagement and adherence.
10. The impact of mobile blockchain and AI solutions can be significant in developing countries. In such countries where various infrastructure is wanting, important functionalities like diagnostics, remote monitoring, and epidemic support can all be executed well. Combined, AI and blockchain will change the way of treating people from reactive (to say the least sloppy) to proactive, preventative, and personalized care. It serves the larger goal of value-based care and focuses on results over volume.

Healthcare organizations must take the bull by the horns and put concerted effort into digital solutions to prevent further disasters. In fact, healthcare digital transformation can no longer be a dream of the future, it is the present. The state of the world and technological innovation has made it so. By merging AI with blockchain technology, we can build future healthcare systems/solutions that lend the powerful and smart safe, and equitable health solution. The combination of these technologies will not only solve existing inefficiencies but also enable secure, data-driven decision-making with the potential to revolutionize healthcare for generations to come.

10.3 FUNDAMENTALS OF AI AND BLOCKCHAIN

AI and blockchain are especially transformative technologies, which the global healthcare ecosystem is undergoing its digital transformation. Both technologies are standalone in their areas of applications but have been integrated together in healthcare setting resulting in innovative models of diagnostics, patient management, clinical research, as well as data governance. The scope of AI and blockchain foundational concepts, subfields, and healthcare applications are discussed in this section, to establish a basis for grasping their real synergy in a world setting.

10.3.1 Artificial Intelligence in Healthcare

Definition and types as per the dictionary definition, AI is the capacity of computer systems to do things which are typical (human intelligence). They can be decision-making, pattern recognition, natural language understanding, problem solving, etc.

AI systems have been designed to be used in healthcare that analyzes complex clinical data, aids in the diagnostic, predicts the disease outcome, and improves operation efficiency [3].

AI in healthcare can be broadly classified into several subtypes:

- *Machine Learning (ML)*: The most important subfield of AI is ML. In ML, we train systems to identify patterns from data. After that, we use those patterns to make predictions and decisions. The most common paradigms used in health analytics and disease modelling are supervised, unsupervised, and reinforcement learning [15].
- *DL*: It is a type of ML that uses multilayer neural networks, or deep networks, to analyze large amounts of unstructured data like medical images, genetic codes, and other sensor readings. DL has the capacity to recognize very small correlations in data. As such, it will prove useful in radiology, pathology, and genomics [16].
- Natural language processing (NLP), a subfield of AI, enables a machine to interpret and respond to human languages. NLP is leveraged in the healthcare industry to extract interesting information from clinical notes, automate documentation, and analyze patients' feedback or health forum.
- Computer vision refers to analysis of visual data automatically. This technology plays a vital role in the interpretation of diagnostic images like X-rays, CT scans, and MRIs, typically achieving a diagnostic accuracy level similar to human experts [17].
- Each of these AI types helps to resolve a unique aspect of healthcare delivery, thereby promising enhanced accuracy, speed, and personalization.

10.3.1.1 Current Use Cases in Healthcare

In such a short time, AI has invaded different layers of healthcare practice and specifically has brought real-world benefits in clinical, administrative, and research domains.

1. *Medical Diagnostics*: Aide for detecting diseases at early stage are successfully deployed by AI algorithms. To further illustrate, DeepMind based on the idea of an AI model is able to diagnose over 50 eye diseases in the equal degree as the best ophthalmologists [18]. Like other image detection problems, convolutional neural networks (CNNs) are utilized to precisely identify skin cancer through images, diabetic retinopathy, and breast cancer.
2. *Radiology and Medical Imaging*: Large image datasets are being trained in DL models into which the abnormality is to be recognized, localized tumor, and to quantify disease progress. Moreover, AI is used today to improve the image quality, determine which ones are prioritize based on urgency, and help radiologists interpret results fast [19].
3. *Predictive Analytics and Risk Stratification*: EHR data can also be used by AI systems to make predictions such as prediction of patient deterioration, readmission risk, or predicting likelihood of complications. These

predictive insights help clinicians to make the proactive decisions, particularly those in intensive care units and emergency departments [20].

4. *Drug Discovery and Development*: AI is changing drug discovery, identifying drug candidates, predicting toxicity, and repurposing already approved medications. For instance, in the AI platform Atomwise DL is used to screen the billions of molecular structures for potential interactions with biological targets [21].
5. *Virtual Health Assistants*: NLP–based chatbots and voice-based assistants are taught to guide patients through the self-care routines, medication adherence, and symptom checking. Bickmore and colleagues [22] describe these tools as reducing administrative burden and improving patient engagement.
6. *"Clinical Decision Support Systems (CDSS)"*: CDSS driven by AI take a patient data and medical literature synthesis to provide evidence-based recommendations for the physician. These systems will help significantly in the processes of making complex decisions in care delivery, and they will help reduce variability in care delivery and decrease diagnostic errors. However, despite its potential, AI penetration in healthcare is still in its infancy, as algorithm transparency, regulatory approval, and clinician trust still present formidable obstacles.

10.3.2 Blockchain Technology in Healthcare

Initially designed for cryptocurrency, blockchain technology is now being used in a variety of fields, including healthcare. A blockchain definition tells us that blockchains are decentralized, immutable, and transparent, which make them ideal for many blockchain applications. A blockchain is a record of the transactions of a cryptocurrency which is shared by a group of computers network. Manipulation of a block in a blockchain or alteration of any type is not possible as each block has the cryptographic hash of the previous block along with a timestamp and data of the transaction. Some characteristic features of blockchain that could be relevant and useful from the healthcare perspective are decentralization, immutability, consensus, smart contracts, and crypto-security. One of the great things about the system is that it is decentralized. No single entity can own the data in such a system, it belongs to everyone. This function helps to limit transparency and ensure that nothing is a single point failure.

When we speak of cryptographic security, the meaning that consensus has more than likely to be understood the way it has just been outlined. Consensus algorithms are notably Proof-of-Work or PoW and Proof-of-Stake or PoS in action that validate the transactions while smart contracts will be the management of functions like insurance claims, request for consent automatically. Hospitals, Health Information Exchanges (HIEs), and others have successfully implemented interoperable electronic records to make patient information easily accessible.

Blockchain technology empowers patients to have authority over who can view and edit their data. This helps to secure the information, thereby improving patient's effectiveness. The blockchain can act as a global protocol layer facilitating unrelated systems to communicate and interact or pass information to each other.

Another useful application is consent management. According to the expert, blockchain technology has made it possible for people to manage their own data like creating data consents and granting privacy permissions like patient consent. "The blockchain enables dynamic and auditable patient consent where individuals get to grant revoke access to their data". Data integrity will not be tampered with and will be transparently accessible on the internet. This way, the origin, and movement of drugs in the pharmaceutical supply can be tracked. Overall, it will prevent harm because of counterfeit drugs and ensures compliance. Smart contracts can help in automating claims and payments in the insurance and billing industry and help in controlling frauds. Data collected and used to conduct clinical trials is stored on an immutable blockchain. Thus, it ensures that the outcome of the experiment cannot be manipulated. Verification phase will be followed by user support for patients and healthcare professionals. While blockchain technology can offer many possibilities when adopted, it does have challenges of scalability. Regulatory ambiguity and a huge piece infrastructure are also there. The role of healthcare is very important for the lives of people around the world. The potential of AI and blockchain is massive and massive. When used in isolation, AI will have its downsides, and blockchain will have its downfalls. They rectify each other's errors when they work together. ML with blockchain technology enhances the power of each other. You can think of it as creating a strong ecosystem. Blockchain enables decision-making and interpretation AI.

10.4 SYNERGISTIC APPLICATIONS IN HEALTHCARE

A giant step in the resolution of the most arduous in the business of healthcare—that are integrated with AI and blockchain. While AI possesses exceptional capabilities to intelligently process data and conduct analytics, and blockchain has the ability to safely and transparently operate data, but if we combine these two technologies together, they create an excellent synergy. Combined, they promise to make the healthcare system secure and trustworthy as well as efficient and personalized. This convergence is affecting multiple areas, but the most affected areas are patient data management and security. This section describes how a combination of AI and blockchain would be beneficial by changing all this.

10.4.1 Patient Data Management

Monitoring and protecting patient data clinical records, diagnostic imaging, test results, prescriptions, and wearable device data are just a few of the many pieces of data that contemporary healthcare gathers on a daily basis. This information must be kept private, accessible, and secure in order to provide the proper treatment. However, outdated IT systems, data breaches, and disconnected data silos are issues faced by conventional healthcare institutions. Blockchain and AI work together to address these issues by enabling intelligent analysis and data security. By automating data entry, identifying abnormal data, and converting both structured and unstructured data into immediately useful insights, AI aids in the management of patient data. Clinical notes can be examined by ML algorithms to locate pertinent information,

FIGURE 10.3 Cybersecurity threats in healthcare.

such as correcting errors in patient records or identifying duplicate entries [3]. Because of this, AI systems are more adept at managing the unstructured portions of a large portion of the input they get, particularly when it comes to unstructured data like medical notes or discharge summaries, where crucial information is frequently beyond the scope of standard fields. The operation of cybersecurity in the medical industry is described in Figure 10.3.

Additionally, AI-powered predictive analytics helps healthcare products to imagine the demand of their patients and react before the need arises. Through analyzing longitudinal patient data, AI can suggest preventive interventions, and identify high risk individuals as well as support decision-making for healthcare. AI is used for example by hospitals to forecast patients' admissions, to optimize staffing, and to manage the resources allocation better [20]. Moreover, practitioners are aided by AI-powered decision support systems in terms of evaluating treatment options using similar case histories and evidence-based guidelines. But when it comes to AI, its success rests on the data that it has, and it must be quality, available, and clean. Here, blockchain comes in with tremendous value. Patient data contained in the ledger is recorded everywhere with blockchain technology, and can be accessed only by designated parties. Electronically viewed patient data is timestamped and verified through a consensus mechanism, resulting into an auditable trail of who, when, and how did a person access and modify data of a patient [4]. It acts as a prevention to tampering, unauthorized alteration, and data loss and improves the trust between stakeholders. One of the unique features of blockchain is that it is decentralized. While traditional databases are managed by a single authority, blockchain's data is distributed across various nodes, which mitigates the risk of failure or breach of data in a centralized server [7].

In addition, smart contracts also allow automated consent management where patients can give, modify, and withdraw their consents any time as basis for giving, modifying, or withdrawing their consent to data sharing is recorded in the blockchain [23]. Blockchain-based systems also provide other added benefits into data privacy and compliance. Zero-knowledge proofs and private blockchains using technologies such as them guarantee that dedicated health information is confidential but authenticable by other legalized users. In the "U.S. and Europe, meeting regulatory requirements (HIPAA and GDPR respectively)" requires this the most. Blockchain allows for second possible kind of access control—enabling ethical data usage and legal responsibility [1]. It also supports data provenance and integrity across the multi-stakeholder environment of clinical research as well as insurance. In research blockchain provides certainty to patient-reported outcomes and trial data authentications, and AI accelerates data analysis and cohort variable picking. In insurance, AI identifies fraudulent claims based on patterns in historical data, and blockchain makes sure to use immutable and transparent billing transactions [22]. Additionally, AI and blockchain synergy strengthens the patient's empowerment. Individual can own and handle their health records, deciding who to share with, and when and what for. The AI-enabled dashboards summarize the trends in personal health data using blockchain, such that no third party can misuse or manipulate the data [11].

To sum, AI blockchain integration in patient data protection and management has the unhealthy by solving the information generation and data protection, which remain glaring trashes. Speed, scalability, and intelligence are provided by AI, while blockchain provides security, transparency, and decentralization. By combining use, the static patient records can become dynamic, intelligent systems able to provide personalized, secure, and efficient healthcare.

10.4.2 Drug Supply Chain Transparency

AI and blockchain technology together can handle major problems in the health sector. Therefore, a significant advancement in surmounting obstacles. Through intelligent data processing and prediction extrapolation, AI and predictive analytics, and blockchain as a safe and transparent data management system are all powerful technology by themselves. Together, however, they synergize into one powerful thing. They are capable of laying the foundation for healthcare systems that are protocol-efficient and personalized as well as secure and trustworthy. The convergence of ground-breaking technologies will also really impact patient data management and data security. Due to this, the following section discusses how the two technologies are creating a change in the functionality. Health systems create immense data on a daily basis through their AI systems. Data from clinical records, diagnostic images, lab reports, wearable devices, and prescriptions are included in this list. The information used in the delivery of care services is legitimate, which affects confidentiality, integrity, or availability. Nevertheless, the provision of high-quality care does not work in isolation. Sadly, old school healthcare systems are often full of data silos, legacy IT, and vulnerable to data breaches. Solutions like intelligent analysis will be leveraged from AI and blockchain technology to tackle such problems. AI assists in patient data management. The technology facilitates automated entry of data, flags anomalies, and provides real-time insights on both structured and unstructured data. The software can group and feature and extract relevant information in clinical notes; Can find duplicate entries and identify inconsistencies in entries across patients. Together, this enables the use of AI systems for free-text data, such as physician notes or discharge summaries. The documents capture information that is missing in the standardized fields.

AI integrated with predictive analytics helps healthcare professionals in predicting a patient's needs and intervening accordingly. Longitudinal patient data can be analyzed using AI to identify high-risk ones, provide preventive interventions and help in clinical decision-making. This is, for instance, how [20], hospitals use AI to predict patient admissions, plan labor, and other resource allocation. AI-powered decision support systems also allow physicians to review treatment options and choose based on similar case histories and evidence-based guidelines. Though, AI is strong, but the usage of same depends on how good data is, accessible, and reliable. That is where blockchain gives some big value. Depending on where we are in the blockchain value chain, blockchain technology helps us achieve several things—we prevent patient data from being recorded or removed, and we make sure it gets recorded only to those with the most appropriate authority. Every patient's medical history transaction or update is timestamped and verified via a consensus mechanism and provides an auditable trail of data access as well as modification [4]. The features add the confidence among the stakeholders and make this tampering, unauthorized alteration, or data loss impossible which guarantees their trust. One of major benefits of blockchain comes due to its decentralized nature. Compared with typical centralized databased managed by one authority, blockchain spans data across different nodes, thus reducing the risk of the centralized failures and data breaches. To describe healthcare, this can be thought of as patient records no longer being be restricted to silos but able to be used freely between institutions; with patients able to dictate who may view or edit their data [7]. In real-world terms, blockchain renders interoperability of different health systems neat and secure. Healthcare providers exchange information using techniques based on standardized protocols and smart contracts that have no impact on data security. To use a clinical example, if a patient visits a specialist, his/her medical history can be accessed immediately from blockchain with a permission granted by the patient, skipping redundant tests and helping to speed up diagnosis. The automation of giving, changing, and removing, consent, and knowing when each action takes place via the blockchain [23].

In addition to data privacy and compliance, benefit of blockchain-based systems includes reducing errors, promoting integrity and transparency of transactions, discouraging fraudulent activity, and enhancing security of network, among others. Zero knowledge proofs and private blockchains also maintain the privacy of sensitive health information while it is still being made verifiable by authorized users. This is especially important when it comes to satisfying the regulatory under HIPAA in the United States and GDPR in Europe. This is because blockchain facilitates fine-grained access control and transparent audit logs to establish both ethical use of data in society and legal accountability [1]. In multi-stakeholder environments such as clinical research and the insurance industries, AI and blockchains also jointly provide data provenance and integrity. In research, blockchain guarantees authenticity patient-reported outcomes as well as trial data, whilst AI speeds data analysis and cohort selection. In insurance, AI identifies frauds in claims through historical data patterns, and blockchain is implemented to make billing transactions transparent and immutable [22]. Furthermore, AI and blockchain projects produce synergy and help patients become empowered. With digital health wallets or decentralized identifiers (DIDs), individuals can own and determine which providers receive copies of their health records, and under what circumstances. The interactions with personal health data are secure with blockchain, and no third party is allowed to misuse or manipulate the data, and AI-enabled dashboards summarize trends in these data [11]. Finally, it is summed up that AI and blockchain can be combined to provide insight generation and data protection for patient data management. As we know, speed, scalability, and intelligence are the qualities that AI possesses, while blockchain provides security, transparency, and decentralization. Combining these technologies makes static patient records into dynamic, intelligent systems that provide personalized, secure, and efficient healthcare.

10.4.2.1 Blockchain for Tracking and Verification

The global pharma supply chain, comprising stakeholders, forms a complex network of manufacturer, distributor, pharmacies, and government regulators. The traditional drug supply chain suffers from counterfeits, lack of transparency, and inefficient forecasting. Nevertheless, the primary pillars are authenticity, safety, and on-time delivery. By implementing AI and blockchain, predictive analytics, real-time tracking, and verifiable authenticity, a strong solution to these problems can be achieved. The effectiveness of the drug supply chain can be improved by predictive analytics and demand forecasting, and AI plays a key role in that. Research indicates that ML models that evaluate past sales figures, trend lines, and predictive epidemiology can estimate future demand for specified medicines. By having this knowledge, manufacturers are able to organize their production effectively in a way that also helps to avoid both stock-outs at pharmacies and overstock that causes waste [24]. The use of AI enables the appropriate measurement and modeling of disease spread and ultimately predicts the amount of drug, vaccine, or medical supply needed in various places. AI supports real-time monitoring of supply chain performance along with forecasting. Sensor-equipped packaging or vehicles, or IoT-equipped packaging—these IoT devices relay information about temperature, humidity, and location, which are analyzed by an AI system that looks for deviations from optimum environmental conditions. Cold chain management, which means temperature-sensitive items, includes pharmaceutical drugs such as insulin or certain vaccines. Stakeholders will be informed of any threat of spoilage through that. It holds significant value for quality assessment and adherence to safety regulations. The integrity and traceability of the movement of drugs is ensured through blockchain technology. On the other hand, the transference and supervision of drugs is brought through AI. The manufacturing of the drug up to the patient's usage through drug trading is captured in an immutable ledger, creating a transparent, end-to-end view of the drug. This initiative will help thwart counterfeit drugs entering the supply chain. Counterfeit drugs are responsible for the deaths of hundreds of thousands of people worldwide every year, particularly in developing nations, which is more significant.

Every drug package can be given a unique digital identity or QR code associated with a blockchain entry. Each time there is a transfer, it is recorded with a timestamp, the batch number, and the conditions of handling at every point of transfer: manufacturer, distributor, wholesaler, and retailer. Therefore, a product's origin and authenticity can be verified instantly by authorized stakeholders (i.e., regulators and consumers) through scanning the code [25]. It encourages trust and removes the work of manual documentation and audit. Additionally, blockchain offers regulatory compliance as it provides a verifiable audit trail. This also allows governments and health authorities to track drug distribution in real time, to better identify lines of bottlenecks, and to enforce recalls more quickly. When contamination or mislabeling occurs, blockchain enables fast first situation determination, characterized by narrowing down of the sets of bars that may become exposed to obligation, and likewise decreases the danger of extended damage. Blockchain platforms can bootstrap the compliance checks using smart contracts that alert the authorities when deviations from the norm occur. This further enhances security and responsiveness with an integrated AI blockchain ecosystem. For instance, when AI feels a dramatic uptick in drug demand in a specific place, it can issue alerts and start smart contracts to ship emergency supplies. Every step of the transaction, from dispatch to delivery, is recorded on blockchain and traceable and accountable fully. In addition, blockchain helps proving suppliers and transport partners legitimacy. In global supply chains, the intermediaries are made to meet that certification and the quality standards. This enables organizations to conduct faster and more reliable due diligence [26] by storing the credentials and performance histories on a blockchain. However, its true potential lies in the combination of AI and blockchain in the trucking and delivery of drugs in the case of more complex logistics such as is that of vaccine distribution. During the COVID-19 pandemic, countries used blockchain to track vaccine shipments, AI suggested regions of high need, and illuminated how to deliver; in other words, AI and blockchain powered experimental vaccine distribution, based on experiments with a situation COVID-19 established. The applications not only lowered losses, but also increased trust in the healthcare system of the public.

The clear advantages still persist despite implementation. The interoperability with existing enterprise system, scalability of blockchain networks, and standardized protocols are some of these. Also, small pharmaceutical companies and healthcare service providers may find the cost of engaging in AI and blockchain infrastructure high. With the global supply chains becoming digitized, not only the AI blockchain integration be essential to be safekeeping the distribution systems of drugs more transparent and dispatch. This not only addresses long-standing vulnerabilities; it opens up a new era in pharmaceutical logistics that is intelligent, trusted, and accountable.

10.4.2.2 Benefits of AI and Blockchain Integration

The integration of AI and blockchain technologies is enabling delivery, management, and improvement in health services integration. We are advancing toward a new frontier of healthcare innovation. Utilizing these technologies together will yield an even greater impact than utilizing them separately. Essentially, AI will value massive datasets, while blockchain will provide you with secure, tamper-proof, and suitably shared underlying datasets. Through collaboration, improvements to operational efficiency along with increased data integrity will help deliver a more personalized and tailored approach to care. We now set forth the four biggest advantages likely spurred by this technology convergence. Includes assured data security, greater diagnostic accuracy, fraud prevention and process automation, and better consumer engagement through personalized care.

10.4.2.3 Enhanced Data Security

Modern healthcare has one of the most pressing concerns related to data security. As it continues to become more digitized, it becomes all the more susceptible to cyberattacks, data breaches, and the unauthorized access of sensitive patient information. Combining AI and blockchain jointly provides a two-layered approach to protect healthcare data. By using blockchain, data security is improved as patient records are stored on a decentralized and immutable ledger. By not relying on a centralized database, blockchain transmits encrypted data across a peer-to-peer network. Data integrity and non-repudiation are ensured through the mechanism of consensus algorithms and recorded with a timestamp [4]. It is very difficult for unauthorized parties to tamper with the medical data without being detected. At the same time, AI improves security as it scans threats in real time. Access patterns are a useful problem for ML algorithms to help train to detect unusual patterns, flag possible breaches, and alert administrators prior to significant loss. For instance, if AI detects that an unauthorized user is trying multiple times to get access to confidential files or the data transferred suddenly increases abnormally [27]. The combination of AI and blockchain works together to ensure that the health data is safe from attack from the outside and is monitored for any middle internal anomalies.

To maintain the trust and legitimacy of patients, while complying with stringent data privacy regulations such as HIPAA and GDPR, a dual protection framework is crucial. AI is helping medical professionals diagnose diseases more accurately, thanks to the ability of ML algorithms to quickly analyze data for patterns. AI can also use the ML and DL techniques to analyze large amount of both structured and unstructured data such as medical images, lab results, and clinical notes with equally high precision. It helps clinicians in earlier and more accurate disease identification. For example, "convolutional neural networks (CNNs)", a type of DL algorithm, can achieve cancerous lesion detection accuracy comparable to or higher than that of human radiologists on radiological scans [15]. As with, AI models are used to predict diabetic retinopathy, pneumonia, and various cardiovascular anomalies. The diagnostic insights are provided by AI, and blockchain provides the validity and originality of the diagnostic data. All diagnostic records can be securely logged on a blockchain, enabling status of data generation and access and trusted audit trail. This is particularly valuable in environments where specialists in different locations need to confer over the same case. With blockchain, everyone starts from the same authenticated dataset to minimize the errors and increase the diagnostic confidence [23]. In addition, the risk of model bias or mislearning caused by contaminated input data is significantly decreased when diagnostic models are trained on blockchain-verified data. It provides better informed decisions, more reliable clinical outcomes.

10.4.2.3.1 Fraud Prevention and Process Automation

Fraud involving the Health Care Crisis greatly impacts healthcare costs and damages services to the most vulnerable people, like the elderly. As these dishonest activities are costing the system billions of dollars every year not only are they ruining the system but public trust is wearing thin. AI helps in developing anomaly-detecting models that spot frauds. These models can also study the past data to help find patterns of the legitimate ones that can be reachable and the outliers. And the outliers can be a suspected sign of fraud behavior. For example, AI may similarly alert and examine any provider that bills for procedures that are statistically inconsistent with the service user's demographic [28]. Blockchain keeps track of buyers and sellers with accuracy. All diagnosis tests, treatment delivery, as well as treatment insurance claim, happen on tamper-resistant screen. Once they are recorded, they cannot be adjusted or deleted; it is a straightforward chain of evidence and accountability. Smart contracts built on the blockchain can automate the claims process by checking eligibility and cross-verifying the documents, although the payment will only be released when the criteria for payment are met [22]. The integrated approach minimizes and often eliminates vast opportunities for fraud, which simultaneously enhances operational efficiency. It takes the administrative strain away from health professionals and insurers, freeing up resources to be used on patients.

10.4.2.3.2 Better Patient Engagement and Personalized Care

The shift from reactive to proactive healthcare seeks to empower patients to become active agents. Expect to see AI and blockchain play a significant role in this paradigm shift. They, along with IoT, will allow the real-time monitoring of patients and predictive modelling. Additionally, they will also help in securely owning the data. These include the genomic profile, wearable metrics, lifestyle information, and medical history. Using these methods creates personalized treatment plans that are more effective and better suited to a patient's particular needs. AI-based tools are capable of providing all-time health assessments and recommendations for lifestyle changes, medication alterations, and specialist referral for chronic disease management. A virtual health assistant is a software program created using NLP and powered through an AI system. The Virtual AI Healthcare System (VAHS) enables straightforward interaction between patients and AI systems. Additionally, it provides responses to queries related to health, scheduling appointments, and monitoring symptoms. These tools help people get involved with their health. It also restricts unnecessary hospital visits. Furthermore, patients get to participate more [22]. Patients may get ownership of this health data through the blockchain technology involved in these efforts. Using DIDs, patients can tell who can see the information, and under what conditions. A doctor, researcher, or insurer can be granted permission with complete transparency, which can be revoked at any time [11]. In fact, digital trust enhances privacy as well. The convergence of AI combined with the blockchain creates a responsive healthcare environment that puts the patient first, responds to their needs, and respects an individual's rights as much as possible. Patients now feel active in their care journey, securely sharing their own data and receiving insightful feedback driven by AI. The amalgamation of "Artificial Intelligence and Blockchain technologies" is transforming Healthcare around its key aspects security: accuracy, transparency, and personalization. We have made our data protection better to ensure it complies with laws and patient trust. The use of AI-powered diagnosis allows better clinical outcomes, whereas confirmed data using blockchain technology prevents data manipulation and enhances reliability. Streamlining healthcare services to prevent fraud and allowing for automatic administrative work is helping build efficiencies. For the first time, long-term health engagement and patient satisfaction are improved through the use of AI and blockchain. Even if blockchain and AI can generate huge benefits in the long run, it still has to overcome certain challenges such as health authorities' regulatory consistency, infrastructure interconnectivity, and technological literacy in healthcare. As a result, these technologies not only make healthcare smarter but also (re)humanize it to make it more equitable and reliable.

10.5 CHALLENGES AND LIMITATIONS

AI and blockchain integration in healthcare has become omnipresent because of their disruptive power. Nevertheless, the implementation of the Action Bias is not without difficulties. It includes all the legal, technical, ethical, and financial barriers. According to experts, the healthcare sector must tackle four challenges before it can be able to enjoy the benefits of Emerging Digital Technologies (EDTs). These are interoperability, privacy compliance of data, ethical implications of AI-based decision-making, and high cost of implementation. In this section, these obstacles are explored in depth. Interoperability issues One of the major draws back of implementing the integrated AI and blockchain solutions is interoperability, or seamless exchange of information across different healthcare systems. However, inconsistent models of the health data and the use of various EHR systems prevent sharing and integration of information efficiently from spreading across different institutions [29]. While blockchain provides a transparent and immutable record, its true use case lays in how it can be integrated with the existing healthcare IT infrastructures that were not built around decentralized technologies. In a similar vein, AI systems to operate in a way that can be trusted, that means in so standardized and clean data. The disparate datasets hamper ML model's ability to achieve consistent performance, biasing or giving misinterpretations [30]. Additionally, there is no way of having uniform data formats, uniform way to invoke Application Programming Interfaces (APIs), and uniform security protocols that all the components can agree on, which only adds to the problem of improper data format and a lack of "hooks". Although Fast Healthcare Interoperability Resources (FHIR) from HL7 have had some progress, they are insufficient for the widespread AI blockchain integration [31]. Thus, to address this, reaching the policy level needs to put efforts on enforcing interoperability rules, providing open-source frameworks, and organizing industry collaboration. Such as establishing common data governance protocols (which can make it easy to do data interchange without losing accuracy, security, or system performance). Figure 10.4 shows the healthcare interoperability resources.

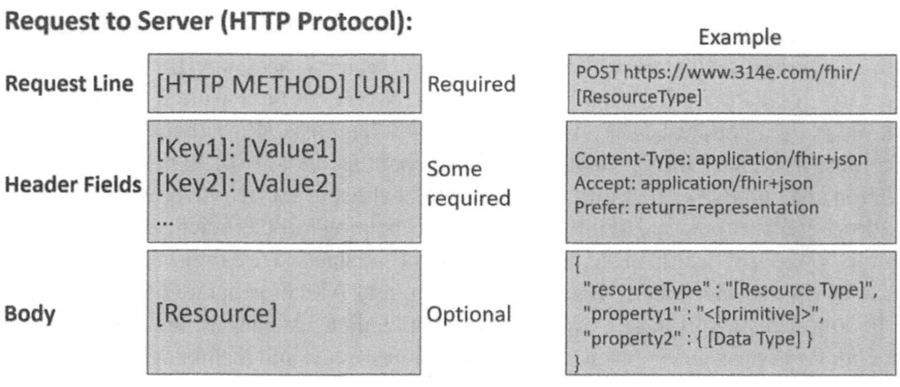

FIGURE 10.4 Healthcare interoperability resources (FHIR).

10.5.1 Data Privacy and Compliance (HIPAA, GDPR)

Healthcare data is so sensitive, it has to comply with strict regulations tied to privacy, including "Health Insurance Portability and Accountability Act (HIPAA)" in the U.S. or "General Data Protection Regulation (GDPR)" in the European Union. In fact, these laws stipulate very strict regulations regarding the collecting, storing, processing, and sharing of personal data [32]. Blockchain, by its nature, poses unique challenges to these regulations. However, its immutability does not agree with GDPR's "right to be forgotten": a person's ability to delete his/her personal data [18]. Furthermore, accountability and consent management for a decentralized environment become more difficult to determine in terms of data controllers and processors. Having said that, AI brings in its own privacy problems. Usually, a large volume of personal health information (PHI) is needed to train ML models properly. Therefore, incorrect data anonymization has the risk of re-identification, especially when combining several datasets [33]. Privacy compliance can be enhanced, however, by emerging solutions such as federated learning, differential privacy, and zero-knowledge proofs, which allow for data-driven insights. However, there are still some countermeasures; however, these methods have not yet entered the implementation phase in an industrial scale. While AI and blockchain offers great benefits to healthcare organizations, the data governance strategy has to be robust enough to meet the privacy regulations. Data flows are continuously monitored and include encryption, access controls, and consent auditing. The application of AI and blockchain in the healthcare sector requires substantial cost and complex technical collaboration. There was an effort made to procure sophisticated computing systems, train the staff, and integrate them with legacy systems while ensuring compliance with all legal and ethical requirements [3].

Due to their heavy computational requirements, PoW networks use a lot of energy. Alternative energy-efficient options, such as PoS, have not been adopted. Apart from that, in high-transaction cases, like real-time healthcare, blockchain scaling may face a technical barrier. Unlike humans, AI systems need large, high-quality datasets and data science, software engineering, and clinical expertise [20]. Integrating AI models into clinical workflows without disrupting processes is a challenging task. Obviously, they need to be properly integrated into the workflow. The technical complexity and high resource requirements of the transparency and explainability of models, especially in critical care situations. Many smaller and medium-sized healthcare institutions do not have sufficient financial and technical capacity to do so on their own [34]. By utilizing government incentives, cloud models, and Public-Private Partnerships (PPPs), technology adoption barriers can be reduced, resulting in lower upfront and subsidy costs.

10.5.2 Ethical Concerns in Decision-Making AI Models

There is an inherent ethical question posed by the role AI can play in medical decision-making from diagnosis and treatment recommendations to allocation of resources. Specifically, these include algorithmic bias, transparency, accountability, and dehumanizing care. AI trained on non-representative datasets may propagates the biases which will disadvantage some population. To give an example, when a model has been trained in the primary using the data from the urban hospitals, the model may not do as well as expected on the patients from the rural or minority communities [35]. Not only that, this can increase or impedes the access to care or affect positively or negatively the treatment outcomes. This makes ethical use of many AI algorithms even more complicated, with the "black box" nature of many of them. The fact that we are unaware of the decisions made or are unaware of our own decision affects the clinicians' willingness to trust in systems that they cannot understand or explain to the patients. Without interpretability this lack can break the trust and is not suitable for clinical adoption [36]. Despite some of these ethical challenges being resolved by blockchain, it does not solve them inherently. But it can still contribute to adopting ethical AI usage if it keeps transparent logs of processes of decision-making and the data provenance.

10.6 FUTURE SCOPE AND RESEARCH DIRECTIONS

The possibilities for AI and blockchain in health are growing exponentially as these technologies develop. Current applications have already improved communication, data security, and operational efficiency among the applications. The future will offer much more wide variety and new possibilities. This section further examines some of the most important areas for future exploration such as possibility of integration with IoT and wireless devices, advanced development of federated learning and decentralized AI models, need for strong legislation and regulatory framework, and finally global scalability and adoption.

Access to comprehensive and high-quality data will determine the success of AI in healthcare. The inability to centralize data owing to privacy norms and ethical issues. Federated learning, with the help of decentralized learning of AI in various devices or institutions provides a solution to the problem of raw data not being transferred [37]. Through federated learning, AI models learn locally on dispersed data sources, which only share model updates rather than data that is aggregated. This better respects privacy, supports local data, and helps enable collaboration between organizations. In the hospital's home country, a model can be trained on the patient data before being contributed to a globally accepted model for the region. In case of blockchain technology, we can record model updates immutably and reach consensus on model versions in the context of federated learning [38]. Ownership, incentive, and auditing of data can be governed by smart contracts that will rule the rules of cooperation. The incorporation of Federated Learning with blockchain facilitates to creation of decentralized and privacy-aware AI healthcare ecosystems [39]. Researchers in the future should look forward to building ethical frameworks for data and model governance, and for communication efficiency trade-offs in federated networks against adversarial attacks. The future of decentralized AI will be enabled by edge computing and 5G. Even so, the healthcare industry's adoption of AI and blockchain is largely impeded by scalability. Typically, blockchain networks face limitations when it comes to the speed and capacity of transactions, but more often, it's public networks that do. An instance of this is the capability of Bitcoin just to process seven transactions per second, while Ethereum can only handle 30 transactions. This capacity is insufficient to drive a healthcare system at the required scale [37]. This can be minimized by exploring new consensus mechanisms like Proof of Authority (PoA), sharding, Layer-2 solutions like state channels and sidechains in future. Subsequently, these technological solutions are meant to increase throughput without compromising security or decentralization.

The challenge of AI is to scale the models so that they can take on different multilingual heterogeneous healthcare data from various countries. Potential improvements to scalability and generalizability to the global population include transfer learning, self-supervised learning, and synthetic data generation [10]. In addition, bridging the digital divides of infrastructure, literacy, and affordability is critical to enabling a more equitable global adoption. Without technical resources to deploy cutting-edge AI–blockchain systems, the "Low- and middle-income countries (LMICs) may not be able to implement". Unlike many digital health ecosystems where one domain is owned by an entity, in this case, there is no single domain owner so necessity to work with global partners and request help from funding sources. Information from case studies and pilot projects from around the world is worth taking as we scale responsibly and sustainably Estonia's blockchain-based eHealth system and India's AI-powered diagnostics. These projects are the opposite of generic tech solutions. Whether it's the farmer who uses drones to improve his yields or the community that improves its health prospects using an app, they matter.

10.7 CONCLUSION

The application of AI and blockchain technology in the healthcare domain is a key step toward intelligent, secure, and patient-centric solutions. The technologies discussed in this chapter can help to secure data better, make more accurate diagnoses, improve business processes, detect fraud, make the supply chain process more efficient, and ultimately provide patients with the best treatment. Together, both AI and blockchain will not only address the issues hampering the smooth functioning of the healthcare sector, but also will create new opportunities for equity and innovation. However, there are barriers that hinder individuals from utilizing such technologies. These include issues related to interoperability, concerns about data privacy, high implementation costs, and unresolved ethical dilemmas. The issue with blockchain is its immutable nature. The rules that go along with it need to be in sync with it first, like the GDPR for instance. Strong policy framework and cooperation across sectors are required in both the cases. We can envisage the future of healthcare with AI and blockchain technology through the lines of a futuristic hospital. The use of federated learning, edge computing, and IoT integration can make it possible to manage healthcare in a real-time, decentralized manner without compromising on the privacy of human beings. For access to expand and standards to align globally, infrastructure should develop, and there should be public policy to enable global rules, standards on a sustainable basis. Ultimately, the effective application of AI and blockchain in healthcare is achievable with a balanced approach that brings together new technology and ethical vision along with flexibility to accommodate the new rules. Technically, it does not need to be rock solid but should be something that is socially acceptable and available to all. If this does not happen, stakeholders will not receive a return on their investment to create them. The health industry is now prepared for a new era of digital resilience, where care will become smarter, more personalized, and available for all.

REFERENCES

1. P. Esmaeilzadeh and T. Mirzaei, "The potential of blockchain technology for health information exchange: Experimental study from patients' perspectives," J. Med. Internet Res., vol. 21, no. 6, p. e14184, 2019, doi: 10.2196/14184.
2. P. Zhang, J. White, D. C. Schmidt, G. Lenz, and S. T. Rosenbloom, "FHIRChain: Applying blockchain to securely and scalably share clinical data," Comput. Biol. Med., vol. 101, pp. 103–111, 2018, doi: https://doi.org/10.1016/j.csbj.2018.07.004.
3. F. Jiang et al., "Artificial intelligence in healthcare: Past, present and future," Stroke Vasc. Neurol., vol. 2, no. 4, pp. 230–243, 2017, doi: 10.1136/svn-2017-000101.
4. T. T. Kuo, H. E. Kim, and L. Ohno-Machado, "Blockchain distributed ledger technologies for biomedical and health care applications," J. Am. Med. Inform. Assoc., vol. 24, no. 6, pp. 1211–1220, 2017, doi: 10.1093/jamia/ocx068.
5. A. Roehrs, C. A. da Costa, R. da Rosa Righi, and K. S. F. de Oliveira, "Personal health records: A systematic literature review," J. Biomed. Inform., vol. 84, pp. 68–82, 2018, doi: 10.1016/j.jbi.2018.06.006.
6. A. Shuaib, "Transforming Healthcare with AI: Promises, Pitfalls, and Pathways Forward," *International journal of general medicine*, vol. 17, pp. 1765–1771, May 2024, doi: https://doi.org/10.2147/ijgm.s449598.
7. J. Adler-Milstein and A. K. Jha, "HITECH Act drove large gains in hospital electronic health record adoption," Health Affairs, vol. 36, no. 8, pp. 1416–1422, 2017, doi: 10.1377/hlthaff.2016.1651.
8. A. Torab-Miandoab, T. Samad-Soltani, A. Jodati, and P. Rezaei-Hachesu, "Interoperability of heterogeneous health information systems: A systematic literature review," *BMC Medical Informatics and Decision Making*, vol. 23, no. 1, 2023, doi: https://doi.org/10.1186/s12911-023-02115-5.
9. Y. Wang, L. Kung, W. Y. C. Wang, and C. G. Cegielski, "An integrated big data analytics-enabled transformation model: Application to health care," Inf. Manage., vol. 57, no. 1, p. 103141, 2020, doi: 10.1016/j.im.2019.01.001.
10. E. Topol, Deep Medicine: How Artificial Intelligence Can Make Healthcare Human Again. New York: Basic Books, 2019.
11. A. Sharma, Sarishma, R. Tomar, N. Chilamkurti, and B.-G. Kim, "Blockchain Based Smart Contracts for Internet of Medical Things in e-Healthcare," *Electronics*, vol. 9, no. 10, p. 1609, Oct. 2020, doi: https://doi.org/10.3390/electronics9101609.
12. G. G. Dagher, J. Mohler, M. Milojkovic, and P. B. Marella, "Ancile: Privacy-preserving framework for access control and interoperability of electronic health records using blockchain technology," Sustain. Cities Soc., vol. 39, pp. 283–297, 2018, doi: 10.1016/j.scs.2018.02.014.
13. A. Musamih *et al.*, "A Blockchain-Based Approach for Drug Traceability in Healthcare Supply Chain," in *IEEE Access*, vol. 9, pp. 9728–9743, 2021, doi: 10.1109/ACCESS.2021.3049920. Proc. IEEE.
14. M. Benchoufi and P. Ravaud, "Blockchain technology for improving clinical research quality," Trials, vol. 18, p. 335, 2017, doi: 10.1186/s13063-017-2035-z.
15. A. Esteva et al., "Dermatologist-level classification of skin cancer with deep neural networks," Nature, vol. 542, no. 7639, pp. 115–118, 2017, doi: 10.1038/nature21056.

16. A. Panigrahi, A. K. Nayak, R. Paul, B. Sahu and S. Kant, "CTB-PKI: Clustering and trust enabled blockchain based PKI system for efficient communication in P2P network," in IEEE Access, vol. 10, pp. 124277–124290, 2022, doi: 10.1109/ACCESS.2022.3222807.
17. A. Panigrahi et al., "Enhancing blockchain transaction classification with ensemble learning approaches," Sci. Rep., vol. 15, no. 1, Jul. 2025, doi: 10.1038/s41598-025-04072-7.
18. M. Finck, "Blockchain and the General Data Protection Regulation: Can Distributed Ledgers Be Squared with European Data Protection Law?" European Parliamentary Research Service, 2018.
19. T. W. Bickmore et al., "Patient and consumer safety risks when using conversational assistants for medical information: An observational study," J. Med. Internet Res., vol. 20, no. 9, p. e11510, 2018, doi: 10.2196/11510.
20. A. Rajkomar, M. Hardt, M. D. Howell, G. Corrado, and M. H. Chin, "Ensuring fairness in machine learning to advance health equity," Ann. Intern. Med., vol. 169, no. 12, pp. 866–872, 2019, doi: 10.7326/M18-1990.
21. B. Mesko, G. Hetényi, and Z. Győrffy, "Will artificial intelligence solve the human resource crisis in healthcare?," BMC Health Serv. Res., vol. 20, p. 59, 2020, doi: 10.1186/s12913-018-3359-4.
22. S. Angraal, H. M. Krumholz, and W. L. Schulz, "Blockchain technology: Applications in health care," Circ.: Cardiovasc. Qual. Outcomes, vol. 10, no. 9, p. e003800, 2017, doi: 10.1161/CIRCOUTCOMES.117.003800.
23. L. Tan, K. Yu, N. Shi, C. Yang, W. Wei and H. Lu, "Towards Secure and Privacy-Preserving Data Sharing for COVID-19 Medical Records: A Blockchain-Empowered Approach," in *IEEE Transactions on Network Science and Engineering*, vol. 9, no. 1, pp. 271–281, 1 Jan.-Feb. 2022, doi: 10.1109/TNSE.2021.3101842.
24. G. Radhakrishnan, P. P. Gaikwad, V. Pimplapure, I. A. Mohammed, A. D. Todmal and S. H. Vardhan Sanne, "AI-Based Demand Forecasting System for Supply Chain Optimization," *2025 Second International Conference on Intelligent Technologies for Sustainable Electric and Communications Systems (iTech SECOM)*, Coimbatore, India, 2025, pp. 1–7, doi: 10.1109/iTechSECOM64750.2025.11307472
25. M. Mettler, "Blockchain technology in healthcare: The revolution starts here," in *2016 IEEE 18th International Conference on e-Health Networking, Applications and Services*, 2016, doi: 10.1109/HealthCom.2016.7749510.
26. N. Kshetri, "Blockchain's roles in meeting key supply chain management objectives," Int. J. Inf. Manage., vol. 39, pp. 80–89, 2018, doi: 10.1016/j.ijinfomgt.2017.12.005.
27. World Health Organization, "A study on the public health and socioeconomic impact of substandard and falsified medical products," 2017. [Online]. Available: https://www.who.int/publications/i/item/9789241513432.
28. A. J. King et al., "Using machine learning to selectively highlight patient information," J. Biomed. Inform., vol. 100, p. 103327, 2019, doi: 10.1016/j.jbi.2019.103327.
29. G. S. Birkhead, M. Klompas, and N. R. Shah, "Uses of electronic health records for public health surveillance to advance public health," Annu. Rev. Public Health, vol. 36, pp. 345–359, 2015, doi: 10.1146/annurev-publhealth-032013-182458.
30. C. Krittanawong et al., "Deep learning for cardiovascular medicine: A practical primer," Eur. Heart J., vol. 40, no. 25, pp. 2058–2073, 2020, doi: 10.1093/eurheartj/ehz904.
31. J. C. Mandel, D. A. Kreda, K. D. Mandl, I. S. Kohane, and R. B. Ramoni, "SMART on FHIR: A standards-based, interoperable apps platform for electronic health records," J. Am. Med. Inform. Assoc., vol. 23, no. 5, pp. 899–908, 2016, doi: 10.1093/jamia/ocv189.
32. D. McGraw, "Building public trust in uses of Health Insurance Portability and Accountability Act de-identified data," J. Am. Med. Inform. Assoc., vol. 20, no. 1, pp. 29–34, 2013, doi: 10.1136/amiajnl-2012-000936.

33. R. Shokri and V. Shmatikov, "Privacy-preserving deep learning," in *22nd ACM SIGSAC Conference on Computer and Communications Security – CCS*, 2015, pp. 1310–1321, doi: 10.1145/2810103.2813687.
34. X. Yue, H. Wang, D. Jin, M. Li, and W. Jiang, "Healthcare data gateways: Found healthcare intelligence on Blockchain with novel privacy risk control," J. Med. Syst., vol. 40, no. 10, p. 218, 2016, doi: 10.1007/s10916-016-0574-6.
35. Z. Obermeyer, B. Powers, C. Vogeli, and S. Mullainathan, "Dissecting racial bias in an algorithm used to manage the health of populations," Science, vol. 366, no. 6464, pp. 447–453, 2019, doi: 10.1126/science.aax2342.
36. F. Doshi-Velez and B. Kim, "Towards a rigorous science of interpretable machine learning," arXiv preprint arXiv:1702.08608, 2017.
37. T. Li, A. K. Sahu, A. Talwalkar, and V. Smith, "Federated learning: Challenges, methods, and future directions," IEEE Signal Process. Mag., vol. 37, no. 3, pp. 50–60, 2020, doi: 10.1109/MSP.2020.2975749.
38. A. Panigrahi, A. K. Nayak, and R. Paul, "Smart contract assisted blockchain based public key infrastructure system," Trans. Emer. Telecommun. Technol., Oct. 2022, doi: 10.1002/ett.4655.
39. N. Rieke et al., "The future of digital health with federated learning," npj Digit. Med., vol. 3, p. 119, 2020, doi: 10.1038/s41746-020-00323-1.

11 IMBM
Integrating Metaverse, Blockchain, and Machine Learning Models for Effective Disease Diagnosis

Amrutanshu Panigrahi, Vinutha Ragavaiah Sethupathy Sarma, Abhilash Pati, Bibhuprasad Sahu, Sambit Ranjan Pattanayak, and Ahmed A. Elngar

11.1 INTRODUCTION

Over the last several years, a significant level of interest has been expressed in the metaverse by the business world and the academic world to a considerable degree. In the science fiction book Snow Crash, published in 1992, the phrase "metaverse" was first presented to the market for the first time. The Oxford English Dictionary, the first language to include the phrase in its list of definitions in 2008, defines a metaverse as a computer-generated environment where users can interact with one another and their surroundings. This definition was included in the dictionary for the first time. To put it another way, a metaverse is a virtual environment. Now we are here. Even though the definition is straightforward, it is not feasible to adequately capture the breadth and complexity of this ever-evolving idea within it [1].

Many people have the misconception that the metaverse is nothing more than an extension of computer games and social networking. This is a popular misconception about what the metaverse is. For the most part, the terms "augmented reality" and "virtual reality" are used interchangeably to refer to virtual reality (VR) and augmented reality (AR), respectively. To realize the benefits that have been widely promised, the metaverse needs to integrate the full capabilities of supporting technologies such as VR, AR, extended reality (XR), mixed reality (MR) haptics, digital twins, holography, and artificial intelligence (AI) on a massive scale. This is necessary to realize the benefits that have been promised. To make good on the promises made in the past is something that has to be done. The ability to speak with one another will be available to everyone. In addition, people will be able to interact with avatars, agents of AI, algorithms, medical facilities, and equipment [2].

DOI: 10.1201/9781003658597-11

While other areas are anticipated to have a prosperous future in the metaverse, the medical industry is also expected to have a bright future. With its exceptional qualities, the metaverse can revolutionize the healthcare industry by offering digital healthcare services via an immersive experience. So, the healthcare market is ripe, and the metaverse has an opportunity to cash in. There was a dramatic uptick in the demand for remote, internet-based therapy during the COVID-19 pandemic. Because of the outbreak, this became necessary. Not to mention that it has affected life choices in some manner. Avatars like National Health Service (NHS) and Sensely encourage users to complete extensive personal and health background forms [3]. These models, powered by blockchain technology and AI, are responsible for data analysis. For physicians to be able to deliver therapy to patients, input generated by AI-powered models is sent to them. The involvement of various technological fields is necessary for developing the healthcare ecosystem based on the metaverse. The internet of the fifth generation (5G), AI, digital twins, blockchain, and other users' privacy are posed by the possibility of collecting technologies analogous to these, some of the critical components that make up metaverse ecosystems.

The possibility of collecting sensitive data in metaverse systems poses a substantial threat to the users' privacy, which is far more significant than that of conventional systems. When it comes to the domain of the virtual environment, the metaverse platform, there is a substantial potential that sensitive information may be altered or leaked. The information that users supply should not be put in jeopardy since this would compromise the confidentiality and safety of the information. Introducing blockchain technology into the metaverse system is one of the ways we are working to find solutions to this challenge to guarantee the confidentiality of medical records [4].

The use of the metaverse in the area of medicine might likely result in a variety of potential benefits. The first benefit is that patients can get medical care without leaving the convenience of their homes. In addition, individuals can participate in virtual exams, which include an immersive experience that simulates the sensation of being in the same room with each other. An increase in benefits available to patients who cannot leave their homes or are incapacitated would occur. Furthermore, the metaverse offers rapid access to various healthcare information and services, which is the second advantage of using it. Because of this, the mortality rate of patients who are delayed in seeking emergency medical aid would, therefore, be reduced. As a third point of interest, patients who reside in remote areas with a scarcity of medical professionals and doctors are entitled to benefits regardless of the distance that separates them and the challenges they confront while going. In fourth place, it reduces the number of patients who visit the clinic, minimizes the carbon footprint produced by transportation, and helps avoid infectious diseases and pandemics like the one caused by the COVID-19 virus. Additionally, it comes with the advantage of reducing the costs associated with medical services. Medical professionals and surgeons use it to practice complex operations and model surgeries before attempting to execute them on actual patients. This is done with the aim of training for complex operations and modeling surgeries. In addition, metaverse technology can detect many types of diseases, including chronic diseases, phobias, and mental health difficulties [5].

This work aims to create an immersive framework using the metaverse, blockchain, and machine learning (ML) for effective disease diagnosis. The objectives of this research work can be summarized as follows:

- To develop an immersive, virtual healthcare system in the metaverse for real-time patient interactions, data collection, and diagnosis.
- Implement blockchain to store health-related data securely.
- To apply the ML classifiers for effectively predicting the healthcare status of the patient

11.1.1 Literature Survey

When it comes to various dental and medical treatments, determining a person's developmental status is an essential component [6, 7]. Both of these treatments are available. More specifically, one of the critical factors that must be reviewed before a patient undergoes jaw surgery, the installation, or the acquisition of a dental crown is whether or not the patient has reached their maximal development potential. This is one of the most critical concerns that must be evaluated. The evaluation of skeletal markers has been employed extensively [8], even though a variety of ways may be used to determine the development state of a person.

The amount of skeletal development may be determined by using several methods, one of which is examining wrist X-rays. In contrast, lateral cephalometric radiographs also include landmarks that may be utilized to determine the skeletal maturity stage. These radiographs are used to diagnose orthodontic conditions. By doing away with the necessity for wrist X-ray measurements, lateral cephalometric radiographs provide a way to reduce unnecessary radiation exposure. The elimination of the need for the measurements accomplishes this. The developed approach, which is defined by the careful examination of changes in the cervical vertebrae's morphology, may be used to achieve this outcome [9]. Computer science is a subject of research that emphasizes the creation of computer systems capable of carrying out tasks that need cognition equivalent to that of humans. AI is a subfield of computer science that may be regarded as an area of study [10].

In AI, the focus is on teaching computers to do specific tasks automatically via data. One of the mathematical models inspired by the way the human brain analyzes data is the artificial neural network (ANN) [11]. This approach would be a part of a mathematical model. Problems requiring cognitive abilities comparable to those of a human are the driving force behind the development of what is often known as an ANN. The functional components of this structure consist of an input layer, two intermediary levels that are concealed from view, and an output layer. The two basic methods for training AI models are supervised learning and unsupervised learning. Supervised learning involves trained people identifying or extracting features from data, whereas unsupervised learning involves computers doing all feature extraction and classification tasks on their own.

The COVID-19 pandemic and the start of the Industrial Revolution have given rise to a digital civilization that is both fresh and more advanced than its predecessor.

Businesses are the connecting tissue between individuals and their communities in modern society [12, 13]. The traditional method of doing business face-to-face has been supplanted by a method of conducting business with little contact, and the use of the internet for commercial transactions is becoming more ubiquitous across all sectors of the economy. This shift has had a tremendous influence on several different businesses, one of which is the healthcare industry. Through smart technology, the healthcare sector has provided services in a manner that does not need physical touch. This is a result of the fact that the use of smart services has risen, as well as the fact that the purposes for which these services are utilized have greatly expanded [14, 15].

The goal of creating a digital twin is to connect the physical and digital worlds. The assets included in this virtual realm may be represented by digital twins. By relocating assets, goods, and diseases like cancer to this virtual arena, patients may make use of the metaverse's potential capabilities [16]. One of the most important reasons blockchain technology is beneficial to the healthcare and metaverse industries is that it can create secure, decentralized, and transparent systems. It is possible to construct a virtual economy in the metaverse with its assistance, and it may also be used in the healthcare business to safeguard the confidentiality and security of data, track down the origin of medications, and simplify the process of conducting clinical trials. To illustrate this point, consider the architects who ensured the safe transfer and storage of data by using robust encryption techniques like the Rivest-Shamir-Adleman (RSA) and Advanced Encryption Standard (AES) algorithms; this system also safeguards the privacy and autonomy of patients receiving medical treatment. Considering the rapid development of blockchain technology, the suggested approach was designed [17].

The author in [18] looked at the potential and constraints of using the metaverse for education within their study. They broke the metaverse road plan into four sections: lifelogging, VR, AR, and mirror worlds. Each of these areas was partitioned off from the others. Compared to more traditional forms of medical education, they found that students who wore AR T-shirts learned more about the human body. It turned out that this was true. Nevertheless, a few drawbacks are associated with metaverse application use, including concerns about privacy and decreased social relationships. The usage of applications in the metaverse is related to these downsides. In a virtual classroom, students employed the metaverse model developed by the authors in [19]. This architecture includes infrastructure, VR and AR systems, cloud-based apps, and avatars. AR is also a part of this system. The authors examined the metaverse's technological road map in [20]. The fundamental technologies and procedures that are used in a metaverse were the subject of a lengthy discussion between the two of them. Besides, it entered the extraordinarily vast and exciting world of medicine, where many possibilities that the metaverse would bring about were checked line by line, so it was ascertained through thorough analysis that the latter significantly upgraded general healthcare service systems.

The development of blockchain technology was made possible by Syed Badruddoja and his colleagues [21] by using AI software. The Ethereum blockchain serves as the platform for carrying out intelligent contracts. They achieved a level of accuracy of 95% using their AI model. In addition to this, they provided an overview of the challenges involved in the formation of the metaverse for smart contracts that make use of AI. Based on blockchain technology, Ayesha Shahnaz and colleagues presented the cornerstone for the electronic health record (EHR) [22]. The implementation of granular access limitations is something that they do to guarantee that the electronic documents that are saved inside their suggested framework are safely stored. They analyzed to see whether the architecture they described allowed for scalability and security.

11.2 BACKGROUND STUDY

This section describes the topics that are most concerning in this research work. This includes the concepts of the metaverse and blockchain.

11.2.1 Metaverse

The metaverse is a shared online digital platform allowing users to connect via VR and AR environments. No single vendor owns it and is not dependent on technological equipment. The decentralized metaverse is made possible by digital currencies and non-fungible tokens (NFTs), which are backed by cutting-edge technology like AI, VR, computer vision, blockchain, and other similar technologies [23]. Through the combination of various technologies, users can create digital representations of themselves or of themselves to investigate their environment. In addition, users have access to all of the same elements available in the actual world, such as the opportunity to get a job, shop, and other similar activities [24]. Many virtual businesses and organizations can be discovered inside it, and many intriguing use cases and applications are connected [25].

The metaverse concept has recently acquired popularity due to the increased use of technologies such as VR and AR and the rapid development of 5G networks. Because the COVID-19 epidemic compelled many individuals to work from home, people have developed a greater awareness of how it may impact their day-to-day lives. All of this has been brought to the attention of investors and regular internet users all around the globe, in addition to Facebook's recent foray into the market above [26]. The use cases of the metaverse can be depicted in Figure 11.1.

Increasing one's level of immersion in the metaverse requires the presence of natural interaction. Its ability to duplicate the faces of friends and celebrities enables users to engage in more lifelike conversations. It gives the impression that they are in familiar and well-known locations. The interaction takes advantage of feelings of control, curiosity, and intrinsic desire, as well as temporary detachment, focus, and increased pleasure. These are all significant components of the interaction. The contract is primarily directed toward human beings, and hands are an essential component of this contract. Because a field of vision encompassing 360 degrees is employed as the receptive field for spatial recognition, many pictures and distortion corrections are necessary to ensure that video processing is carried out effectively. Visual and physical sensory collisions and an alternate sensory approach are required to lessen the likelihood of an individual experiencing motion sickness and weariness. In addition, multimodal sensory awareness is needed to account for voice, gestures, and the flow of dialogue [27].

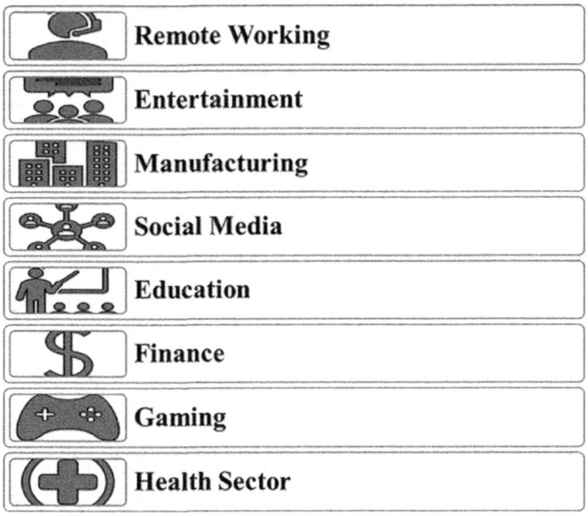

FIGURE 11.1 Use cases of metaverse.

Introducing the metaverse is classified clearly into four distinct phases: the design phase, the model training phase, the operation phase, and finally, the assessment phase. During the design phase, it critically looks upon certain vital aspects, specifically at the very aims and the overall design of that concept, as well as at the amount of time and money resources that are likely to be required during its development processes. During that phase, it prepares an estimate of the risks available, identifies a limitation, makes probes at the user scenarios, and gets a detailed understanding of what the scope or requirement would entail. It further analyzes the probability of how the execution and the succeeding assessment would go on accordingly. Data analysis, user modeling, a scientific approach, learning iteration, and parameter fine-tuning in the model training procedure. Simulations, task scheduling, network setup, and prototype demonstration of the system will occur during the running phase. Questions that include content integrity, authenticity in interaction, implementation possibility, and failure will arise during the assessment phase.

11.2.2 Blockchain

Blockchain technology is a groundbreaking idea that evolved with the introduction of cryptocurrencies, the most prominent of which is Bitcoin. Blockchains are used to record transactions. The blockchain functions on a peer-to-peer network of nodes, each with a copy of the whole blockchain. This characteristic of blockchain makes possible an agreement among the nodes over the correctness of the transactions and then permits them to enter the ledger. It's among the most vital components of this technology. The best-known consensus technique is the Proof of Work (PoW) consensus technique applied with Bitcoin. In this system, nodes, often called miners, compete to solve complex mathematical problems to append a new block. The Proof of Stake (PoS) consensus technique is widely used to achieve agreement. Depending on the number of stakes the node has, it is selected to create new blocks in the network [28].

One of the most important ones is security using blockchain technology. It is done based on cryptographic methods. Participants in the network have pair keys, which are public and almost like an address. A private key is used for identification when any transaction is made. Only he who owns can have control over the management of these assets, and access, in this case, is secured only by the right of using a private key. As soon as a block is added to the blockchain, it becomes impossible to alter the information contained inside it. This is because the blockchain is connected by cryptographic linkages between blocks, guaranteeing that the ledger cannot be changed [29].

In addition to its original use in cryptocurrencies, blockchain technology has evolved to include smart contracts. Smart contracts are bits of code that are capable of executing themselves and have terms that have been established. They commit themselves automatically when specific criteria are satisfied.

In a public blockchain that does not need permission, anybody can join the network, take part in the process of reaching consensus, and read the ledger. Blockchains that are accessible to the public include Bitcoin and Ethereum. This limits entry and participation to only a few registered organizations in permissioned or private blockchains. This level of control exercised on the network is higher in this case. This would be critical in the business environment because of the need to keep some information confidential and comply with relevant regulations [30].

The many applications of blockchain technology have resulted in its widespread acceptance across various sectors. One use of blockchain technology is supply chain management, which may benefit from its ability to offer a transparent and verifiable inventory of items from manufacturing to delivery. This helps to reduce instances of fraud and improve accountability. Therefore, this can be one of the areas whereby blockchain technology may be exploited for healthcare industries so that patient data may be saved securely, ensuring data integrity and easy access to those authorized. Some of these actors are the voting systems and several financial services, who started investigating possibilities opened by blockchain technology to improve the operation process or even the security level [31].

Although the advantages of blockchain are multifaceted, no advantage comes without its challenges. In research and development, scalability, specifically power-of-will-based energy consumption, and regulatory uncertainty constitute ongoing hot-topic challenges. Researchers and developers have undertaken these challenges because technology is constantly advancing to create more possible and applicable blockchain technologies in this technological age. The features of blockchain include decentralization, which helps to remove the single-point failure, a potential drawback of the conventional system, by introducing the decentralization concept in the network for any communication. Distributed ledger technology (DLT) aims to provide transparency in blockchain communication. The immutability feature of blockchain ensures the integrity of the data within the network. The features mentioned above make implementing the blockchain in various sectors possible. The use cases of blockchain are shown in Figure 11.2.

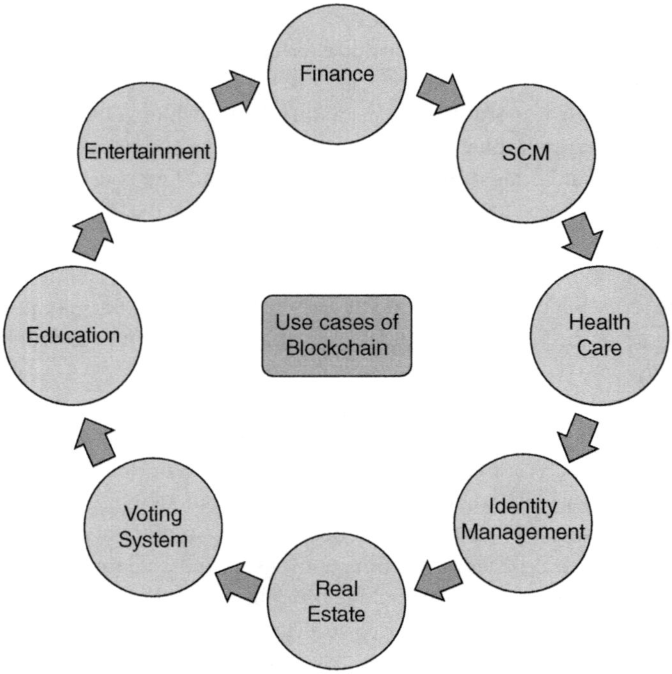

FIGURE 11.2 Use cases of blockchain.

11.2.3 Building Blocks of Blockchain

Major building blocks of a blockchain include the hash function, blocks, decentralized networks, mechanisms of achieving consensus, smart contracts, and so on. All of these lead to ensuring that the blockchain network retains all features, such as transparency, decentralization, and immutability [32]. The building blocks of blockchain may be put together into this list:

- *Hash Function*: Blockchain is a vital component to maintain the integrity of the data stored in the block. Hash functions convert the data into a fixed-size hashed value. When the hash function is applied, tampering with the input data is challenging. The blockchain supports various types of hash functions, including SHA-256, SHA-3, Ethash, Scrypt, and Keccak-256.
- *Blocks*: Blocks store the processed data in the network. When the transaction is initiated in the network, the block is created, and each block will be connected to the previous block by keeping the hash.
- *Consensus Mechanism*: To facilitate the process of nodes reaching an agreement about the validity of transactions and the present status of those transactions, the goal of consensus mechanisms is to offer a way by which this may be accomplished. Methods such as PoW, PoS, Delegated PoS (DPoS), and Practical Byzantine Fault Tolerance (PBFT) are all examples of procedures that allow for the establishment of consensus. Every one of these approaches for reaching a consensus addresses a particular purpose. Since

these mechanisms ensure that all nodes will reach a consensus, there is no need for a central authority since it is already guaranteed that they will.

- *Cryptography Key*: Cryptographic keys provide secure authentication, authorization, and verification of ownership. The function of this system is to produce public and private keys for every individual. Public keys are used as addresses for receiving payments, but private keys are kept secret and used to sign transactions to demonstrate ownership. The purpose of intelligent contracts is that they are contracts that can execute themselves and have established rules written in code.
- *Smart Contract*: The function of smart contracts is to automate and enforce the terms of agreements, removing the need for intermediaries and guaranteeing that transactions are executed without trust as much as possible.
- *Peer-to-Peer Network*: Blockchain uses a peer-to-peer network to facilitate direct node communication. Because information is distributed directly among members, this decentralized network structure contributes to the increased resilience and efficiency of the blockchain.
- *Merkle Trees*: Merkle trees are a data structure used to summarize and validate large amounts of data efficiently. The transactions inside a block are organized using a Merkle tree, and the tree's root is included in the block's header. This tree is used to organize the transactions. Furthermore, as a consequence, it is now feasible to check in a time-efficient way whether or not a particular transaction is included in a block.

11.2.4 Working of Blockchain

A blockchain is a series of blocks. A blockchain may contain the total information or details regarding the transaction, the contract, or other similar types of transactions. All blocks hold data to at least some level. Figure 11.3 shows the working of

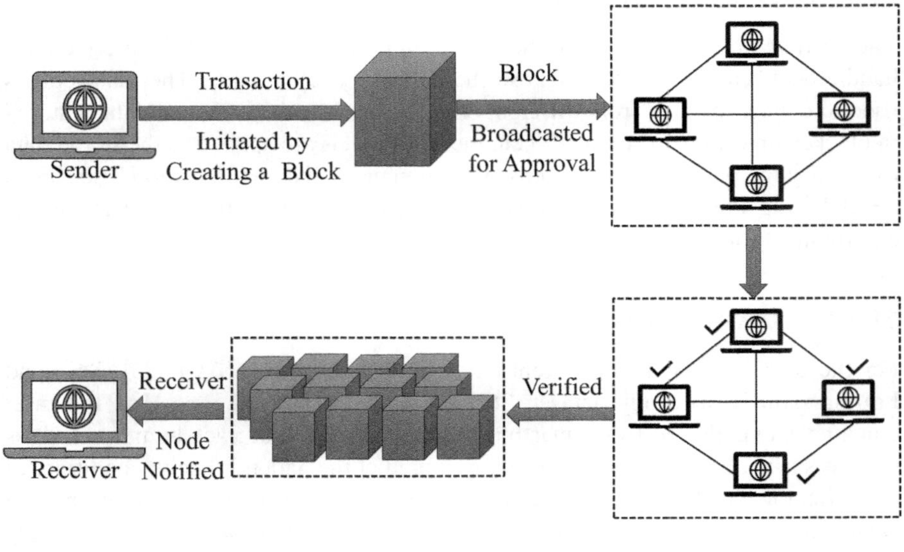

FIGURE 11.3 Working of blockchain.

blockchain. For example, a blockchain can be used as a distributed database stored in numerous computers called nodes. Getting an identical replica of that database on each node is possible. Once a record has been added to the database, also called the blockchain, it becomes nearly impossible to make any alterations or fiddle with the records [33]. It will check each copy in any of the nodes where the databases are stored to guarantee that all the entries must agree with one another and, thus, that the records stored within the database do not change. A technical term for this distributed database system accessed over a network is a distributed ledger [34]. This database in networked form is otherwise known as a distributed ledger system, and the term that describes it is decentralized. Therefore, one could term a blockchain as a decentralized distributed ledger system. The lowest level of a database comprises entries grouped in some "blocks," added in sequential order onto the "chain." The main components present in a block are the following:

- *Data*: Any information process inside a blockchain network from the source to the destination address.
- *Hash*: A string value calculated using the data and the cryptographic hash functions such as SHA-256. Once generated, it is shared with every participant node in the network. A simple change in the data will directly affect the hash value. So it helps maintain data integrity.
- *Hash of the Previous Block*: Each block contains a link to the last block, so the chain is constructed correctly and consistently. That, therefore, means modifying something in any block changes this hash value, impacting not only the block from whence it came but the succeeding block as well. This would be the finality of the entire chain. Being the head of this series, and since no such thing as "prior" exists from which it would be coming, no prior block's hash recorded in this chain is the Genesis block – it is the first.

11.3 PROPOSED METHODOLOGY

The current work integrates the metaverse with blockchain and ML to effectively handle healthcare data and diagnose the patient's health status. The metaverse is used to collect the data from different clinics, and then the collected data is stored in blockchain off-chain storage. Then, the ML models are applied to the stored data to identify the patient's health status. The Human Activity and Postural Transitions (HAPT) and Framingham Heart Study datasets are considered in the metaverse environment for the current work.

11.3.1 Dataset Description

For the current work, two different datasets, including the HAPT [35] (DS_1) and Framingham Heart Study dataset [36] (DS_2), are considered. The HAPT dataset contains data collected from smartphone-based sensors that track human activities such as sitting, lying down, and walking to predict the patient's health condition. In this case, the health condition is related to mobility and rehabilitation. Framingham Heart Study dataset consists of longitudinal data with health-related parameters such

TABLE 11.1
Dataset Description

Dataset	Number of Instances	Number of Features	Number of Class
HAPT (DS_1)	10,299	563	6
Framingham Heart Study dataset (DS_2)	4240	16	2

as cholesterol level, smoking status, blood pressure, etc. DS_1 contains 10299 numbers of instances and 563 numbers of features with six different classes. DS_2 contains 4240 cases and 16 features, with two classes, 0 for non-heart disease and 1 for heart disease. Table 11.1 shows the dataset description for the current work. Figures 11.4 and 11.5 show the class distribution of DS_1 and DS_2, respectively.

11.3.2 Mutual Information (MI)

Mutual information (MI) is a feature selection method that calculates the dependency between the features (F) [37]. In this, the idea is to quantify the number of features that contribute most toward the class variable (C). In other words, the features that contribute more to accurate prediction are selected. MI is calculated using the entropy (H), which measures the uncertainty of the feature. Equation (11.1) shows the entropy of the feature F_i.

$$H(F) = -\sum_{f \in F} p(f)\log(p(f)) \tag{11.1}$$

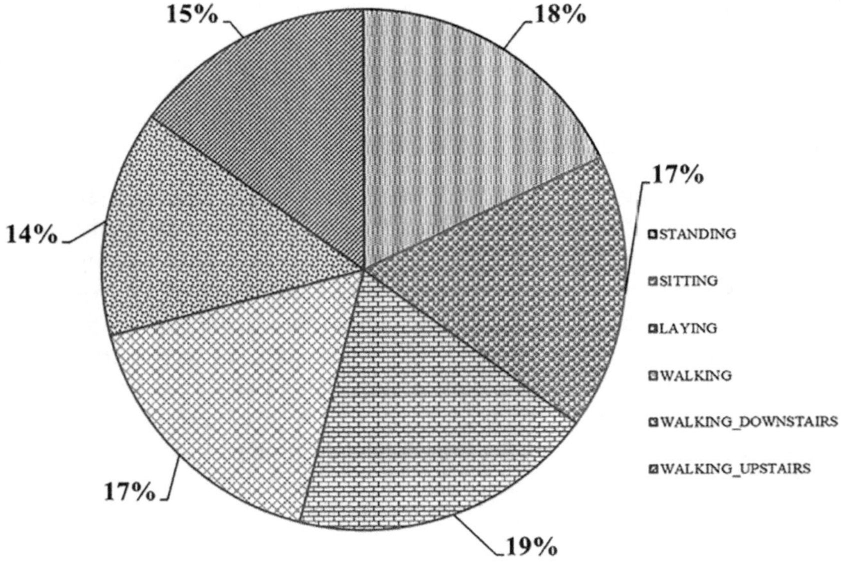

FIGURE 11.4 Class distribution of DS_1.

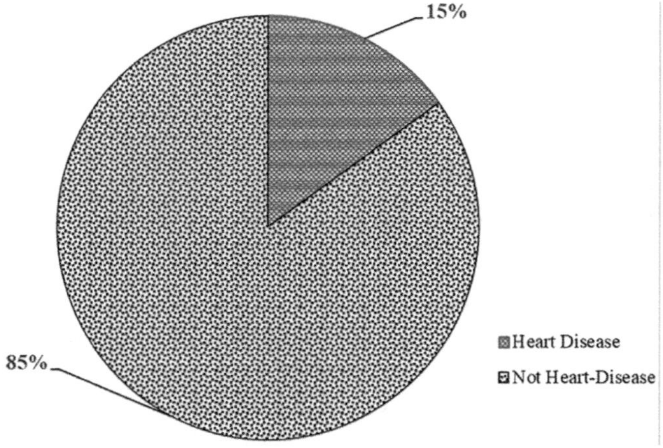

FIGURE 11.5 Class distribution of DS_2.

$p(f)$ is the probability of the value of f of F. A higher value of $H(F_i)$ represents the high uncertainty. Equation (11.2) shows the joint probability H (F_i, C) with $p(f,c)$ as the joint probability of f and c.

$$H(F,C) = -\sum_{c \in C} \sum_{f \in F} p(f,c) \log(p(f,c)) \tag{11.2}$$

The MI can be calculated using Equations (11.1) and (11.2). A higher MI value represents a higher dependency between the feature and the target variable. The features with high MI values are selected as they contribute more to accurate prediction.

$$MI(F;C) = H(F) + H(C) - H(F,C) \tag{11.3}$$

11.4 MACHINE LEARNING CLASSIFIERS

For the current work, four different ML classifiers, including support vector machine (SVM), random forest (RF), ELM (extreme learning machine), and multi-layer perceptron (MLP), are used to classify the health status of the patient using the given dataset. SVM is a supervised ML classifier used to find the optimal hyperplane to separate classes in the feature space to maximize the margin between the features of different classes. RF is an ensemble ML-based classifier with multiple trees to improve classification accuracy. ELM is a single-layer feed-forward neural network that can be used for accurate classification. MLP is a type of neural network with one or more hidden layers capable of learning complex non-linear feature space [38–40].

11.4.1 Workflow of IMBM

The current work involves three different phases. Phase I is a metaverse environment where the health records are collected from the clinics and test reports using various

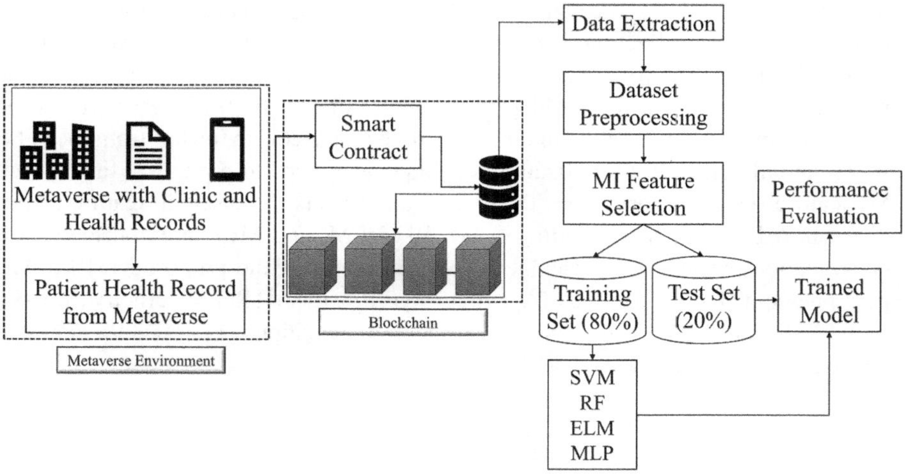

FIGURE 11.6 Workflow of the proposed IMBM.

sensors and mobile phones. The generated data is stored off-chain on a blockchain-based IPFS server. In Phase III, the data is extracted from the blockchain. Then, the data is pre-processed, followed by the MI-feature selection algorithm. Figure 11.6 shows the workflow of the proposed work. The detailed workflow of the proposed IMBM can be summarized as follows:

Step 1: Process the clinical records
Step 2: Store the patient's test results to form a dataset
Step 3: Implement the smart contract to store the dataset in the IPFS server
Step 4: Implement SHA-256 to create the hash to store the data in terms of blocks
Step 5: From IPFS, extract the dataset
Step 6: Initialize the dataset preprocessing using Min-Max normalization
Step 7: Initialize the MI feature selection algorithm to select the appropriate number of features
Step 8: Split the dataset into training and test sets with a distribution ratio of 0.2
Step 9: Apply classifiers to training set
  i. SVM
  ii. RF
  iii. ELM
  iv. MLP
Step 10: Apply test data to the trained model
Step 11: Performance calculation

11.5 RESULTS AND DISCUSSION

The current work is implemented in a system with Ubuntu 22. 04 LTS, 16 GB of RAB, 1 TB of SSD, and an Intel i7 processor with a 4.1 GHz clock speed. Initially, the datasets DS_1 and DS_2 are considered the metaverse environment output due to the restriction of data collection from the different clinics. Then, the Ethereum blockchain (GETH) is used to implement the smart contracts to store the dataset from the metaverse environment. In the blockchain environment, the IPFS server stores the dataset in an off-chain storage manner. Then, the dataset is extracted from the IPFS server, and the dataset normalization technique is applied to normalize the dataset. MI feature selection normalizes the dataset and selects the essential features. Four different ML classifiers, including SVM, RF, ELM, and MLP, are considered for classification purposes. To calculate the performance of the proposed IMBM ML parameters, including accuracy (A_Y), precision (P_N), recall (R_L), specificity (S_Y), F-1 score (F_1S), and F-2 score (F_2S) are considered. Equations (11.4)–(11.9) show the above-mentioned parameter calculation.

$$A_Y = \frac{t_1 + t_2}{t_1 + f_1 + t_2 + f_2} \tag{11.4}$$

$$P_N = \frac{t_1}{t_1 + f_1} \tag{11.5}$$

$$R_L = \frac{t_1}{t_1 + f_2} \tag{11.6}$$

$$S_Y = \frac{t_2}{t_1 + f_2} \tag{11.7}$$

$$F_1S = \frac{2 * \dfrac{t_1}{t_1 + f_1} * \dfrac{t_1}{t_1 + t_2}}{\dfrac{t_1}{t_1 + f_1} + \dfrac{t_1}{t_1 + f_2}} \tag{11.8}$$

$$F_2S = \frac{5 * \dfrac{t_1}{t_1 + f_1} * \dfrac{t_1}{t_1 + f_2}}{\left(4 * \dfrac{t_1}{t_1 + f_1}\right) + \dfrac{t_1}{t_1 + f_2}} \tag{11.9}$$

where t_1 and f_1 represent the true positive and false positive, respectively. Similarly, t_1 and f_1 represent the actual negative and false negative, respectively. Table 11.2 shows the performance analysis of ML-based models over DS_1 and DS_2.

From the analysis, it can be clearly stated that the ELM classifier outperforms all other classifiers in both datasets. For $DS_{1,}$ ELM shows an accuracy of 92.2%, and for $DS_{2,}$ the accuracy is 92%. However, to improve the performance level, the MI feature selection technique is applied to enhance the result. Table 11.3 shows the performance analysis of the proposed IMBM model.

TABLE 11.2
Performance Analysis of Different Classifiers over DS_1 and DS_2

Dataset	Classifier	A_Y	P_N	R_L	S_Y	F_1S	F_2S
DS_1	SVM	91.8	95	94.2	83.7	94.63	94.4
	RF	91	93.7	94.6	79.9	94.1	94.37
	ELM	92.2	93.5	96	82.5	94.7	95.46
	MLP	91.7	94.6	94.6	82.7	94.58	94.58
DS_2	SVM	91.5	94.2	94.6	81.4	94.4	94.51
	RF	90	92.3	94.4	77.1	93.35	94.01
	ELM	92	95.2	94.3	84.2	94.76	94.49
	MLP	91.4	94	94.8	80.2	94.37	94.62

TABLE 11.3
Performance Analysis of Proposed IMBM with Different Classifiers over DS_1 and DS_2

Dataset	Proposed IMBM	A_Y	P_N	R_L	S_Y	F_1S	F_2S
DS_1	SVM	95.73	97.51	96.60	93.37	97.05	96.78
	RF	97.09	98.60	97.42	96.15	98.01	97.65
	ELM	98.06	98.73	98.60	96.61	98.66	98.63
	MLP	96.07	97.45	97.13	93.25	97.29	97.19
DS_2	SVM	95.28	97.19	96.24	92.80	96.72	96.43
	RF	96.46	97.93	97.31	93.98	97.62	97.43
	ELM	98.94	99.36	99.20	98.21	99.28	99.23
	MLP	96.82	98.18	97.38	95.36	97.78	97.54

Figures 11.7 and 11.8 show the performance analysis of the proposed IMBM with different classifiers for datasets DS_1 and DS_2, respectively. From the study, it can be observed that the proposed IMBM with ELM classifier shows an accuracy of 98.1% for DS_1. The other parameters, including precision, recall, specificity, F_1S, and F_2S, become 98.73%, 98.60%, 96.61%, 98.66%, and 98.63%, respectively.

Similarly, for DS_2, the proposed IMBM with ELM classifier shows the highest accuracy of 98.9% with precision, recall, specificity, F_1S, and F_2S as 99.36%, 99.20%, 98.21%, 99.28%, and 99.23%, respectively. Figure 11.9 shows the gas utilization by the smart contract for storing the data and for extracting the data.

11.6 CONCLUSION

In the current era, the metaverse, blockchain, and ML are becoming pivotal technologies for transforming real-world scenarios, and the healthcare sector is one of them. The number of patients is also increasing, and doing manual tests through humans

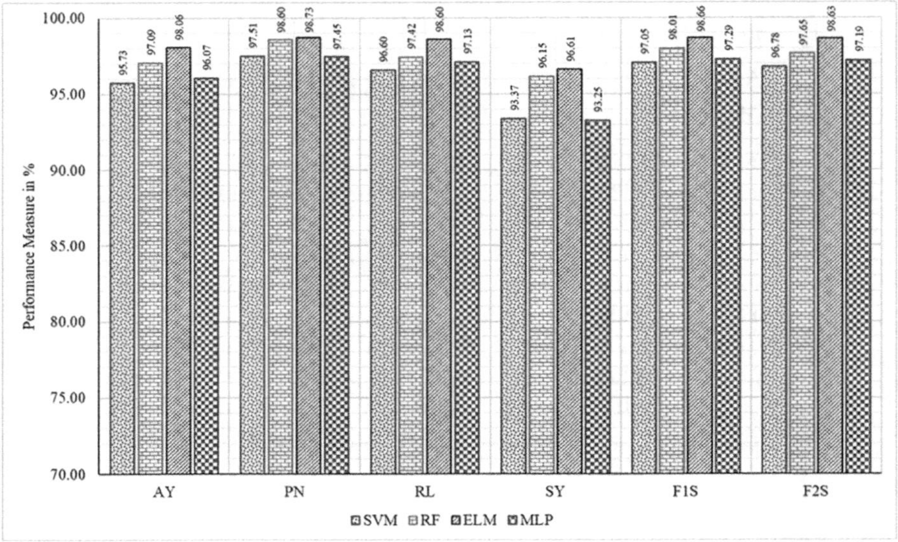

FIGURE 11.7 Performance analysis of proposed IMBM for DS_1.

is becoming difficult. Hence, the metaverse can emerge as a potential solution in this section, including smartphones and sensors like gadgets for the patient to collect data directly from the human body. These reports can be stored in a system for further use. The healthcare sector is a crucial sector in which the number of health records is increasing on a daily basis, which creates an issue of efficient storage in a

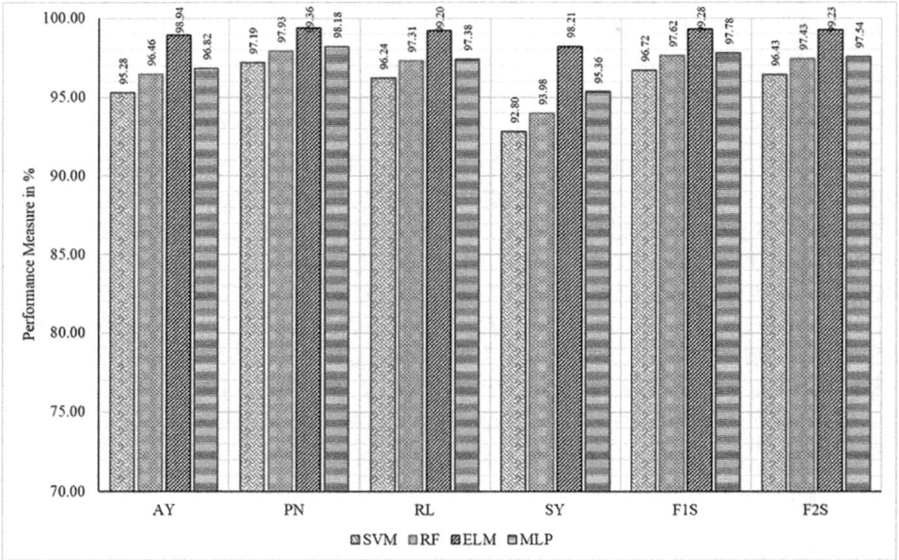

FIGURE 11.8 Performance analysis of proposed IMBM for DS_2.

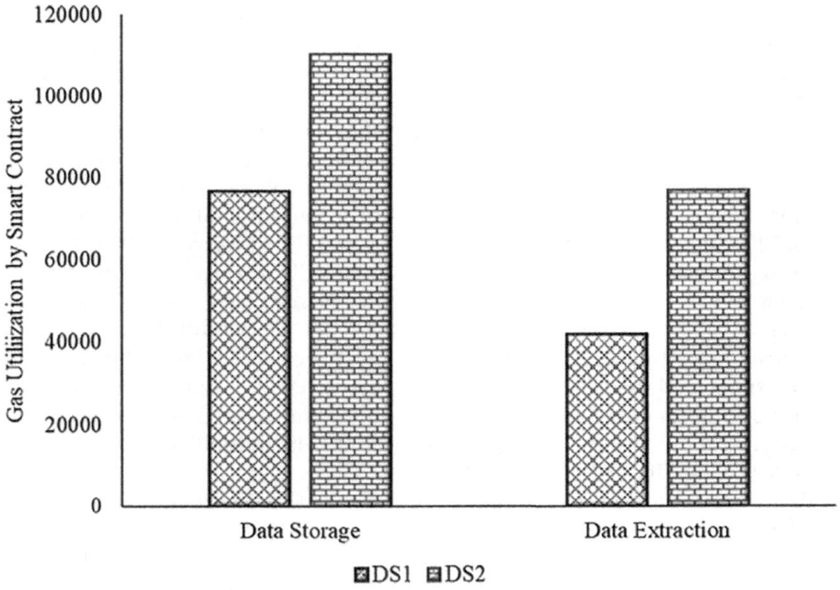

FIGURE 11.9 Performance analysis of proposed IMBM for DS_1 and DS_2.

secure manner. Blockchain technology can become an emerging technology for this service due to its pervasive technology. The stored data can be analyzed using ML models for efficient disease diagnosis. The current work proposes a hybrid approach to IMBM, integrating the metaverse, blockchain, and ML to handle different diseases effectively. In the current work, the metaverse is used to collect data from the sensors, the blockchain is used to store the data securely, and the ML is used to diagnose diseases. The current work employs two types of disease datasets to show the efficacy. The empirical analysis shows that the proposed model has the highest accuracy of 98.94%. The future scope of this work is to test the effectiveness of the proposed model with the real-time sensor-based dataset, which will be collected from the real-world scenario.

REFERENCES

1. Mystakidis, Stylianos. "Metaverse." Encyclopedia 2, no. 1 (2022): 486–497, doi: 10.3390/encyclopedia2010031.
2. Wang, Yuntao, Zhou Su, Ning Zhang, Rui Xing, Dongxiao Liu, Tom H. Luan, and Xuemin Shen. "A survey on metaverse: Fundamentals, security, and privacy." IEEE Communications Surveys & Tutorials 25, no. 1 (2022): 1, doi: 10.1109/comst.2022.3202047.
3. Ning, Huansheng, Hang Wang, Yujia Lin, Wenxi Wang, Sahraoui Dhelim, Fadi Farha, Jianguo Ding, and Mahmoud Daneshmand. "A survey on the metaverse: The state-of-the-art, technologies, applications, and challenges." IEEE Internet of Things Journal 10, no. 16 (2023): 1, doi: 10.1109/JIOT.2023.3278329.
4. Buchholz, Florian, Leif Oppermann, and Wolfgang Prinz. "There's more than one metaverse." I-Com 21, no. 3) (2022): 313–324, doi: 10.1515/icom-2022-0034.

5. Huynh-The, Thien, Thippa Reddy Gadekallu, Weizheng Wang, Gokul Yenduri, Pasika Ranaweera, Quoc-Viet Pham, Daniel Benevides da Costa, and Madhusanka Liyanage. "Blockchain for the metaverse: A review." Future Generation Computer Systems 143 (June 2023): 401–419, doi: 10.1016/j.future.2023.02.008.
6. Korde, Swapnil J., Pallavi Daigavane, and Sunita Shrivastav. "Skeletal maturity indicators – Review article." International Journal of Scientific Research 6 (2015): 361–370.
7. Rolland-Cachera, Marie-Françoise, and Sandrine Péneau. Assessment of growth: Variations according to references and growth parameters used. The American Journal of Clinical Nutrition 94 (2011): S1794–S1798, doi: 10.3945/ajcn.110.000703.
8. Fang, Dongdong, Zhangbiao Long, and Jun Hou. "Clinical application of concentrated growth factor fibrin combined with bone repair materials in jaw defects." Journal of Oral and Maxillofacial Surgery 78, no. 6 (2020): 882–892, doi: 10.1016/j.joms.2020.01.037.
9. Ferrillo, Martina, Claudio Curci, Andrea Roccuzzo, Mario Migliario, Marco Invernizzi, and Alessandro De Sire. "Reliability of cervical vertebral maturation compared to hand-wrist for skeletal maturation assessment in growing subjects: A systematic review." Journal of Back and Musculoskeletal Rehabilitation 34, no. 6 (2021): 925–936, doi: 10.3233/bmr-210003.
10. Hamet, Pavel, and Johanne Tremblay. Artificial intelligence in medicine. Metabolism, 69 (Apr. 2017): S36–S40, doi: 10.1016/j.metabol.2017.01.011.
11. Jamshidi, Mohammad Behdad, and Fatemeh Daneshfar. "A hybrid echo state network for hypercomplex pattern recognition, classification, and big data analysis." In 2 022 12th International Conference on Computer and Knowledge Engineering (ICCKE), pp. 007–012. IEEE, 2022, doi: 10.1109/ICCKE57176.2022.9960125.
12. Jamshidi, Mohammad Behdad, Mohsen Ebadpour, and Mona Malekzadeh Moghani. "Cancer digital twins in metaverse." In 2022 20th International Conference on Mechatronics-Mechatronika (ME), pp. 1–6. IEEE, 2022, doi: 10.1109/ME54704.2022.9983328.
13. Kerdvibulvech, Chutisant. "Exploring the impacts of COVID-19 on digital and metaverse games." In International Conference on Human-Computer Interaction, pp. 561–565. Cham: Springer International Publishing, 2022, doi: 10.1007/978-3-031-06391-6_69.
14. Jamshidi, Mohammad, Ali Lalbakhsh, Jakub Talla, Zdeněk Peroutka, Farimah Hadjilooei, Pedram Lalbakhsh, Morteza Jamshidi et al. "Artificial intelligence and COVID-19: Deep learning approaches for diagnosis and treatment." IEEE Access 8 (2020): 109581–109595, doi: 10.1109/ACCESS.2020.3001973.
15. Jamshidi, Mohammad Behdad, Jakub Talla, Ali Lalbakhsh, Maryam S. Sharifi-Atashgah, Asal Sabet, and Zdeněk Peroutka. "A conceptual deep learning framework for COVID-19 drug discovery." In 2021 IEEE 12th Annual Ubiquitous Computing, Electronics & Mobile Communication Conference (UEMCON), pp. 00030–00034. IEEE, 2021, doi: 10.1109/UEMCON53757.2021.9666715.
16. Nguyen, Tam N. "Toward human digital twins for cybersecurity simulations on the metaverse: Ontological and network science approach." JMIRx Med 3, no. 2 (2022): e33502, doi: 10.2196/33502.
17. de Moraes Rossetto, Anubis Graciela, Christofer Sega, and Valderi Reis Quietinho Leithardt. "An architecture for managing data privacy in healthcare with blockchain." Sensors 22, no. 21 (2022): 8292, doi: 10.3390/s22218292.
18. Kye, Bokyung, Nara Han, Eunji Kim, Yeonjeong Park, and Soyoung Jo. "Educational applications of metaverse: Possibilities and limitations." Journal of Educational Evaluation for Health Professions 18 (Dec. 2021), doi: 10.3352/jeehp.2021.18.32.
19. Dahan, Neama A., Muna Al-Razgan, Ali Al-Laith, Muaadh A. Alsoufi, Mahfoudh S. Al-Asaly, and Taha Alfakih. "Metaverse framework: A case study on E-learning environment (ELEM)." Electronics 11, no. 10 (2022): 1616, doi: 10.3390/electronics11101616.

20. Mozumder, Md Ariful Islam, Muhammad Mohsan Sheeraz, Ali Athar, Satyabrata Aich, and Hee-Cheol Kim. "Overview: Technology roadmap of the future trend of metaverse based on IoT, blockchain, AI technique, and medical domain metaverse activity." In 2022 24th International Conference on Advanced Communication Technology (ICACT), pp. 256–261. IEEE, 2022, doi: 10.23919/ICACT53585.2022.9728808.
21. Badruddoja, Syed, Ram Dantu, Yanyan He, Mark Thompson, Abiola Salau, and Kritagya Upadhyay. "Trusted AI with blockchain to empower metaverse." In 2022 Fourth International Conference on Blockchain Computing and Applications (BCCA), pp. 237–244. IEEE, 2022, doi: 10.1109/BCCA55292.2022.9922027.
22. Shahnaz, Ayesha, Usman Qamar, and Ayesha Khalid. "Using blockchain for electronic health records." IEEE access 7 (2019): 147782–147795, doi: 10.1109/ACCESS.2019.2946373.
23. Aswin, BG Sai, S. Vishnubala, D. Dhinakaran, N. Jagadish Kumar, SM Udhaya Sankar, and AM Mohamed Al Faisal. "A research on metaverse and its application." In 2023 World Conference on Communication & Computing (WCONF), pp. 1–6. IEEE, 2023, doi: 10.1109/WCONF58270.2023.10235216.
24. Thien Huynh-The, Quoc-Viet Pham, Xuan-Qui Pham, Thanh Thi Nguyen, Zhu Han, and Dong-Seong Kim. "Artificial intelligence for the metaverse: A survey." Engineering Applications of Artificial Intelligence. 117, (2023):105581. doi: https://doi.org/10.1016/j.engappai.2022.105581.
25. Chengoden, Rajeswari, Nancy Victor, Thien Huynh-The, Gokul Yenduri, Rutvij H. Jhaveri, Mamoun Alazab, Sweta Bhattacharya, Pawan Hegde, Praveen Kumar Reddy Maddikunta, and Thippa Reddy Gadekallu. 2023. "Metaverse for healthcare: A survey on potential applications, challenges and future directions." IEEE Access 11: 1, doi: 10.1109/ACCESS.2023.3241628.
26. Musamih, Ahmad, Ibrar Yaqoob, Khaled Salah, Raja Jayaraman, Yousof Al-Hammadi, Mohammed Omar, and Samer Ellahham. "Metaverse in healthcare: Applications, challenges, and future directions." IEEE Consumer Electronics Magazine 12, no. 4 (2022): 33–46, doi: 10.1109/MCE.2022.3223522.
27. Sahu, Bibhuprasad, Amrutanshu Panigrahi, Bibhu Dash, Pawan Kumar Sharma, and Abhilash Pati. "A hybrid wrapper spider monkey optimization-simulated annealing model for optimal feature selection." International Journal of Reconfigurable and Embedded Systems 12, no. 3 (2023): 361. doi: 10.11591/ijres.v12.i3.pp360-375
28. Panigrahi, Amrutanshu, Ajit Kumar Nayak, Rourab Paul, Bibhuprasad Sahu, and Shashi Kant. "CTB-PKI: Clustering and trust enabled blockchain based PKI system for efficient communication in P2P network." IEEE Access 10 (2022): 124277–124290, doi: 10.1109/ACCESS.2022.3222807.
29. Panigrahi, Amrutanshu, Ajit Kumar Nayak, and Rourab Paul. "A blockchain based PKI system for peer to peer network." In Advances in Distributed Computing and Machine Learning: Proceedings of ICADCML 2021, pp. 81–88. Singapore: Springer, 2022, doi: 10.1007/978-981-16-4807-6_9.
30. Panigrahi, Amrutanshu, Ajit Kumar Nayak, and Rourab Paul. "Impact of clustering technique in enhancing the blockchain network performance." In 2022 International Conference on Machine Learning, Computer Systems and Security (MLCSS), pp. 363–367. IEEE, 2022, doi: 10.1109/MLCSS57186.2022.00072.
31. Panigrahi, Amrutanshu, Abhilash Pati, Bibhu Dash, Ghanashyam Sahoo, Debabrata Singh, and Manoranjan Dash. "ASBlock: An agricultural based supply chain management using blockchain technology." Procedia Computer Science 235 (2024): 1943–1952, doi: 10.1016/j.procs.2024.04.184.

32. Panigrahi, Amrutanshu, Ajit Kumar Nayak, and Rourab Paul. "Healthcare EHR: A blockchain-based decentralized application." International Journal of Information Systems and Supply Chain Management (IJISSCM) 15, no. 3 (2022): 1–15, doi: 10.4018/ijisscm.290017.
33. Panigrahi, Amrutanshu, Ajit Kumar Nayak, and Rourab Paul. "Smart contract assisted blockchain based public key infrastructure system." Transactions on Emerging Telecommunications Technologies 34, no. 1 (2023): e4655, doi: 10.1002/ett.4655.
34. Panigrahi, Amrutanshu, Bibhuprasad Sahu, Satya Sobhan Panigrahi, Md Sahil Khan, and Ajay Kumar Jena. "Application of blockchain as a solution to the real-world issues in health care system." In Blockchain Technology: Applications and Challenges, pp. 135–149. Cham: Springer International Publishing, 2021, doi: 10.1007/978-3-030-69395-4_8.
35. Reyes-Ortiz, Jorge, Davide Anguita, Alessandro Ghio, Luca Oneto, and Xavier Parra. 2013. Human Activity Recognition Using Smartphones. UCI Machine Learning Repository, doi: 10.24432/C54S4K.
36. "Framingham Heart Study Dataset." n.d. www.kaggle.com. https://www.kaggle.com/datasets/aasheesh200/framingham-heart-study-dataset.
37. Estévez, Pablo A., Michel Tesmer, Claudio A. Perez, and Jacek M. Zurada. "Normalized mutual information feature selection." IEEE Transactions on Neural Networks 20, no. 2 (2009): 189–201, doi: 10.1109/TNN.2008.2005601.
38. Panigrahi, Amrutanshu, Abhilash Pati, Bibhuprasad Sahu, Manmath Nath Das, Debasish Swapnesh Kumar Nayak, Ghanashyam Sahoo, and Shashi Kant. "En-MinWhale: An ensemble approach based on MRMR and whale optimization for cancer diagnosis." IEEE Access 11 (2023): 113526–113542, doi: 10.1109/ACCESS.2023.3318261.
39. Panigrahi, Amrutanshu, Manoranjan Dash, Bibhuprasad Sahu, Abhilash Pati, and Sachi Nandan Mohanty. "Machine learning-based integrated approach for cancer microarray data analysis." In Machine Learning for Healthcare Systems, pp. 149–168. Bhubaneswar: River Publishers, 2023.
40. Pati, Abhilash, Amrutanshu Panigrahi, Manoranjan Parhi, Niranjan Panda, Umang Kumar Agrawal, and Sambit Ranjan Pattanayak. "Enhancing the heart diseases prediction based on a novel hybrid model." In 2023 2nd International Conference on Ambient Intelligence in Health Care (ICAIHC), pp. 1–6. IEEE, 2023, doi: 10.1109/ICAIHC59020.2023.10431464.

12 Modeling Herding and Contagion Effects in Digital Currencies

A Comparative Study of Holt–Winters and Deep Learning Approaches

Nrusingha Tripathy, Gobinda Chandra Das, Subrat Kumar Nayak, Amrutanshu Panigrahi, Abhilash Pati, and Janmejaya Mishra

12.1 INTRODUCTION

The emergence of cryptocurrencies as a means of digital dialogue has led to a radical change in the world monetary system, especially in developing countries. In contrast to traditional fiat currencies, cryptocurrencies utilize blockchain technology, which is an unassailable, peer-enabled ledger system for secure and transparent transactions without the need for intermediaries [1]. Their partnership with financial institutions has made them sophisticated payment mechanisms, as well as attractive (but speculative) asset devices. Due to the exciting volatility, sudden price fluctuations, and huge number of unknown factors surrounding the cryptocurrency market, accurate prediction remains challenging. It is one of the toughest tasks in time-series forecasting to forecast cryptocurrencies' prices due to the dynamics that cause disproportionate temporal compulsions. It is essential for market participants, government representatives, and scholars 3 to understand how cryptocurrencies behave, as digital payment systems continue to develop due to consumer demand for decentralization and efficiency [2].

Currency that exists only in electronic form and is organically stored, moved, and exchanged via digital systems and time periods is identified as digital currency. Digital currencies, in disparity to conventional physical money, are not distributed in notes or coins and lack a physical form. They can be autonomous, like cryptocurrencies that rely on blockchain technology without a central expert, or federal, like those provided by governments or central banks. Digital currencies provide a number of rewards, such as increased convenience, reduced prices, faster transaction times, and

DOI: 10.1201/9781003658597-12

more opportunities. Digital currencies are playing an upward role in financial innovation, assets, and international trade as the world economy becomes more digitalized. However, they also raise new concerns about monetary policy, security, and regulation. Over the past eight years, the price of Bitcoin has consistently increased because of its positive outlook for the foreseeable future of cryptocurrencies. Compared to the well-known banking system, Bitcoin has certain advantages that investors have seen. The fact that Bitcoin allows for decentralized banking, which means that large banks cannot control it, is one of these advantages. The market limit of 21 million Bitcoins prevents an overabundance from being created, which would drive prices to skyrocket. The issue of transaction security is addressed by Bitcoin by facilitating a blockchain, sometimes called a ledger, which aggregates the history of any transactions into a single, long hexadecimal chain of anonymized transactions, maintaining the anonymity of transaction history. Bitcoin has thus turned into a very hopeful investment vehicle. This chapter attempts to assist investors in making conclusions by providing contribution projections for the price of the cryptocurrency, given the dangerous volatility of the Bitcoin market price.

With a market value of over $584 trillion, Bitcoin is the most valuable cryptocurrency out of the more than 26,000 recognized ones. It was created in 2009 by Satoshi Nakamoto, an unidentified individual or organization. Numerous more cryptocurrencies, including Ethereum, Binance Coin, and Dogecoin, have arisen since then. Bitcoin is the most extensively used cryptocurrency, despite the mounting opposition. One important indicator of risk is volatility, which increases the amount of variation in the price of a financial instrument. Stockholders must comprehend and measure volatility in order to assess possible risks and returns. Bitcoin's extreme volatility is one of its main censures, since many believe it is inappropriate as a stable medium of trade. Research has shown that compared to conventional fiat currencies like the nation's dollar, British pound, euro, or Japanese yen, Bitcoin is charismatically more unstable [3].

With the emergence of cryptocurrencies as effective digital assets, the networks of the global financial bionetwork have been reinstated. Blockchain technologies are making these currencies go from a geeky gadget to something that is both mainstream and convenient to use. The peer-to-peer consensus makes sure that they are secure, valid, and immutable. The use of cryptocurrencies provides us with alternative methods of payment that are not derived from supporting systems. This is particularly useful in developing economies. Their assistance, however, comes with unmatched volatility and fast-changing markets with a complicated behavioral blueprint. The price movements of cryptocurrency often diverge from the time series forecasts, and this causes severe assessment problems. It is becoming more essential to understand the fundamental behavior of the digital financial markets, especially cryptocurrencies, in order to make better assessments and design policies.

The existence of herding and contagion in the cryptocurrency market suggests that there are elements that drive the market and price movements, influencing strategic behavior. When investors act like one another rather than independently, it is herding. Investors often follow each other when purchasing or selling assets, even when the fundamentals disagree, according to an economist. Hype behavior is often seen within cryptocurrency markets due to their extreme volatility and low regulation, alongside a speculative stance. The meaning of contagion is a market shock that passes from one digital strength to another or from one digital strength-related market to another. The price of Bitcoin can collapse and cause a mini panic event, which can lead to the liquidation of other crypto regardless of whether they are performing well independently or not. Market inefficiencies and rising volatility affecting investors are due to herding and contagion. The law-making, monetary, finance-oriented will have a phenomenal impact on Euro and other currencies' viability and survivability as well.

The deep learning models with broad geometrical capabilities, particularly long short-term memory (LSTM) and gated recurrent unit (GRU), are studied to observe whether they can exhibit herding (when investors imitate other investors) and contagion (when shocks in one asset class spill over to another). It does this by also comparing the results with the classic Holt–Winters exponential smoothing. The results imply that the Holt–Winters technique is able to filter out large stable mass in the market. But it is unable to capture hasty behavioral change during heavy volatility. The precision of LSTM and other deep learning models is higher than traditional models. Similarly, the models' agents could capture complex nonlinear relationships involving investor sentiment and inter-asset linkages. This study showed that the use of powerful, data-driven models for risk pricing and decision-making in very hypothetical situations has been accomplished and has also yielded valuable lessons about the behavioral exteriors of cryptocurrency markets.

One of the most significant challenges in forecasting and risk assessment is the volatility of Bitcoin markets. Specifically, cryptocurrencies are a problematic asset class to predict due to price declines instigated by both speculative and market fundamental causes. Numerous deep learning algorithms have improved their capacity to represent nonlinear, temporal behaviors in complicated financial time-series data in response to these assessments. While GRUs show computational aptitude and responsiveness to short-term tasks, LSTM networks are excellent at addressing long-term dependencies. These designs may be combined to create a hybrid LSTM-GRU model, which stimulates the strengths of each and provides an extra framework for good prognosis. In this study, we evaluate the efficiency of a few deep learning models and their mutually valuable forms in predicting the movements of the Bitcoin price. According to our research, the LSTM-GRU hybrid offers investors who want to improve their entry and exit strategies in a highly volatile market better forecasting accuracy and value regulation.

12.2 LITERATURE REVIEW

Cryptocurrencies are a group of virtual currencies that use cryptographic techniques to ensure secure and provable transactions. As decentralized and open-source systems, they operate on a peer-to-peer basis without reliance on central authorities. Their functionality is initiated through complex encryption algorithms, which necessitate extensive computational power distribution across a network of connected nodes. Due to their low transaction costs, global user-friendliness, and pseudonymous nature, cryptocurrencies have permitted the appearance of alternative digital economies and novel financial ecologies. It has been more difficult for investors to use prediction models to make suitable investment decisions due to the extreme volatility of the market price of cryptocurrencies like Bitcoin. When considering a stock market investment, the Fibonacci retracement is a common method that many investors would use as an estimate metric. Fibonacci retracement aids traders in determining when it is best to purchase or sell stocks. The two extreme trends in a graph are identified using Fibonacci retracement, which makes use of the stock's volatility. The figured vertical distance is then divided by important Fibonacci ratios, most frequently the golden ratio of 0.618. The most prominent degrees of support and resistance are then identified with the aid of these values.

According to Yasir et al. [1], business intelligence (BI) has prolonged momentous purchase in recent years, allowing managers to make more informed and planned decisions. The cryptocurrency market, recognized for its rapid growth and exciting price volatility, is mainly sensitive to global actions and online sentiment. In this case, BI agendas are trained in order to estimate the values of the top five cryptocurrencies. Deep learning models are being used in conjunction with Support Vector Regression (SVR) and Linear Regression. The predictive accuracy of these models is improved by incorporating sentiment scrutiny related to major global events. The findings reveal that deep learning and SVR models, when combined with BI techniques, outperform traditional methods in terms of forecasting performance.

As per Moni et al. [2], one-way data flow from the crypto market to the Indian stock market fits well with Information Transfer and Causality Philosophy. According to this theory, money markets will incorporate information that comes from stocks. Utilizing Granger causality and transfer entropy techniques driven by wavelet analysis, one can identify the information flow patterns evolving between financial markets. According to this theory, the traders in the stock market may change their positions because of the news or price signals in the crypto market, which may impact the stock market behavior. According to Seabe et al. [3], there is no unpredictability in the cryptocurrency market. Thus, the forecast system developed for the project alludes to this. The capability to recognize and take advantage of quick price movements gives investors a valuable advantage. The establishment of a forecast framework is still being carried out for digital assets. Nonetheless, existing evidence indicates that models based on a range of signals have exciting prospects.

According to Rao et al. [4], AI should be incorporated in financial forecasting and portfolio optimization. It is important that prediction systems be as precise as possible because of sudden price fluctuations impacting crypto markets. This study uses ensemble deep learning techniques such as stacking, bagging, and averaging in order to predict the fluctuation of major cryptocurrencies. Will Ensemble Deep Learning Models help in building AI-based investment strategies for fund managers, which could result in better risk-adjusted returns being obtained in a consistently transparent manner? The Liu et al. [5] study shows machine learning can predict using more than 3700 cryptocurrencies. Thus, machine learning is already evolving as a good model. Studies find that a more general theory of AI-enhanced financial innovation holds that econometric models designed to complement or replace data-driven methods capable of analysis of large-scale, high-frequency data are becoming even more popular. The machine learning model can capture hidden structures within complex financial contexts, as indicated by its relatively strong out-of-sample R^2 performance.

The computer-intensive method of Artificial Neural Network (ANN) optimization for crypto price prediction was proposed by Behera et al. [6]. Optimization theory teaches us that finding the global optimum is hard in high-dimensional parameter spaces. The standard backpropagation algorithm is not the most efficient algorithm for ANN models, which require heavy computing resources for training purposes without any domain knowledge. The research chapter reconstructs a broad view of complementary model quality and processing dimensions in financial time series forecasting.

Digital currencies exhibit herding and contagion behaviors, which are observed through Holt–Winters and deep learning conventions. It is a great insight. Mainstream finance's adoption of crypto is growing. However, investors, regulators, and other policymakers are quickly adapting to this new trend. All of them need to be aware of the behavior driving this market. A better understanding of herding behavior can lead to more appropriate judgments on speculation and risk-reducing interventions through the identification of episodes of irrational euphoria or panic. Alternatively, modeling taint enables early identification of systemic risk when shocks to Bitcoin present a spillover to Altcoins or to conventional assets. According to the research, which claims to make use of an ever-increasing number of sources, it is necessary to employ contemporary AI technologies that are nonlinear and high-frequency (and other things) and that have volatile data characteristics. This research analyzes the benefits and merits of a few of the old statistical schemes and non-traditional systems with contemporary AI devices, such as LSTM and GRU. Among the very helpful models are those that can improve forecasting and establish systems that can endure negative shocks for years in digital transformations. Only external financial institutions like banks are necessary for unadventurous economic systems to process cash or electronic payments. During intricate money transfers, these services come into play as intermediaries and have full control. While it has a practical purpose when making financial transactions, it is not flexible, secure, or transparent, nor is it inevitable, and it can only send a small amount of money. To solve these problems, we use a system that removes intermediaries "trustfully" from financial transactions, i.e., enables both parties to move funds conservatively to one another, and varying how the economy turns.

There is a network of computers which are connected in such a way that they are on A11, which means anyone takes control over the mining process as there are non-competitors.

The Deep Learning efficiency and optimization theory allows for the implicit integration of LSTM and GRU models. According to this theory, hybrid models such as the LSTM-GRU alliance recover the trade-off between learning ability and computational complexity. GRU units speed up model training while sustaining LSTM's capacity to classify long-term relationships because of its more straightforward strategy. When working with enormous datasets, the mixture of these two models rallies performance and speeds up merging in time-series estimating trades.

12.3 MATERIAL AND METHODS

Understanding the patterns and structural aspects of these markets has received a lot of attention as a result of the rapid emergence and expansion of digital currencies, especially currencies like Bitcoin, Ethereum, and others. Herding and contagious holdings are two of the main anomalies seen in Bitcoin markets; both contribute to price hiccups and excessive market volatility. This learning aims to compare the efficiency of traditional time series models, precisely the Holt–Winters exponential smoothing method, with progressive deep learning models in modeling and forecasting the herding and contagion dynamics of digital currencies. Cryptocurrencies are virtual money that may be traded among people or organizations. They are a type of network-based exchange medium that facilitates transactions via cryptographic techniques. As cryptocurrencies are contingent on blockchain technology, they obtain the properties of blockchain, i.e., decentralization, security, and immutability. Cryptocurrency transactions are not ruled by a single entity, in contrast to traditional schemes. Therefore, consensus trials are required to validate or approve the transaction, resolving trust issues among system participants.

12.3.1 Data Collection

The purpose of this study is to utilize complex deep learning architectures to forecast the price of Bitcoin with time. I have collected minute-wise OHLC data with the transaction volumes in BTC and fiat, and adjusted closing prices from historical data available on Kaggle, which ranges from Jan 2012 to Jul 2020. These historical data represent live trading on select interactions. Based on data from the years 2012–21, we conduct an impartial assessment of several models. Investors' herd behavior refers to the inclination of investors to mimic the actions of others rather than their own values. It makes the trends more impactful and effective. Contagion is the term for when a shock to one market results in a shock to others, usually in times of stress. Grasping these phenomena both theoretically and empirically is imperative for prediction, risk assessment, and policy design.

12.3.2 Methodology

Due to the fast pace of increase and adoption of the digital currency (cryptocurrency) like Bitcoin, Ethereum, and others, there has been substantial attention toward understanding the behavioral and structural dynamics of these markets. Contamination effects and herding behavior are two of the most important phenomena seen in the markets for digital currencies. Both lead to price abnormality as well as a high level of market volatility. Cryptocurrency derives its name from the fact that they are all in some way "encrypted." In this work, we explore a unified forecasting model to influence trading strategies across a range of cryptocurrencies. Nascent research shows that effective Bitcoin price prediction enhance price discovery while also reducing information asymmetries, both of which help improve market efficiency. When more market players use analytical forecasting methods in their strategies, divergences in the market can be stabilized more quickly, and this creates a more liquid and controllable trading environment.

12.3.3 Forecasting Methods

By counting courtesy mechanisms, deep learning models can meet key variable quantities and time edges that evocatively influence forecast outcomes. This insight

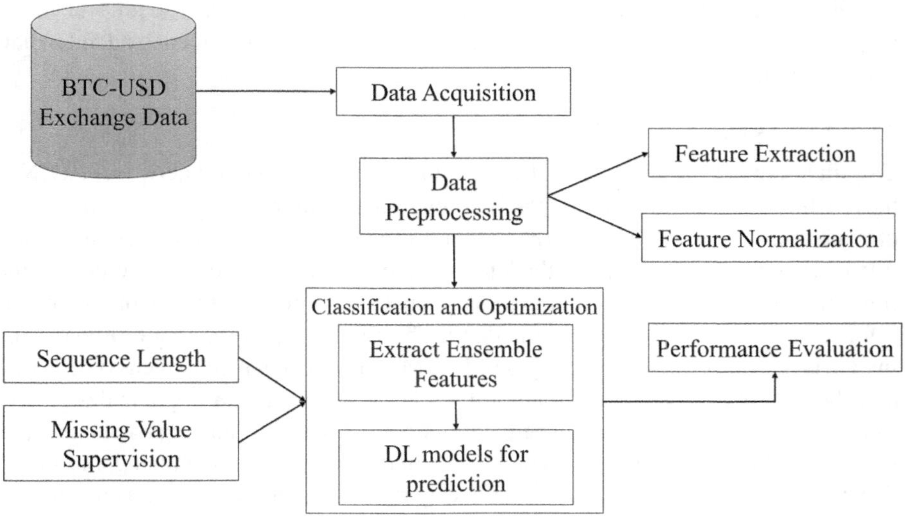

FIGURE 12.1 Proposed workflow diagram.

contributes to a better clench of the drivers of Bitcoin price volatility and aids in producing robust trading algorithms [7]. The wide-ranging procedural flow is portrayed in Figure 12.1. Herding refers to the practice of investors copying the actions of others instead than relying on their own research, which frequently reinforces substantial market trends. On the other hand, infection states refer to the spread of financial shocks among markets or properties, typically during times of amplified unpredictability or disaster. To increase forecasting accuracy, control investment risk, and guide financial policy, it is essential to comprehend and analyze these behavior's both theoretically and practically. In order to capture and predict the herding and contagion effects seen in digital currency markets, this study examines and contrasts the capabilities of state-of-the-art deep learning models, such as LSTM networks, with those of conventional time series procedures, particularly the Holt–Winters smoothing exponential method.

The parallel processing power of modern hardware strategies can help deep learning models by improving the efficiency of training and inference on large datasets. Because of its scalability, models that can process mammoth amounts of past market information have grown, producing predictions that are more accurate. Predicting the price of digital currencies offers a variety of tools to help investors, banks, and legislators navigate the incredibly unstable and quickly developing cryptocurrency market. By using specific estimation models, investors may minimize risks and exploit profits by making informed decisions about whether to purchase, sell, or keep assets. Prognostic analytics helps financial organizations with risk assessment, portfolio management, and the creation of cutting-edge financial products based on cryptocurrency. Prophecy technologies also help recognize market anomalies and conceivable booms gaining of time, which promotes more stable trading conditions. Furthermore, extrapolative insights may be used by controllers and regulators to identify universal dangers and create prompt responses to safeguard market integrity. As digital currencies convert more widely accepted, trustworthy prediction models particularly those based on machine learning and deep learning become increasingly important for guaranteeing both planned advancement and financial stability in the digital economy.

12.3.3.1 LSTM

To gain lessons from subsequent efforts, common recurrent neural networks (RNNs) have a hidden state that stores past memory information. Nonetheless, the back-propagation vanishing gradient issue often causes RNNs to lose important information from previous time steps as the length of the system increases. To overcome this limitation, the LSTM model learns to use a special memory cell that can remember information for a long period of time [8, 9]. The ability to capture long-term patterns in data is one of the major advantages of LSTM. The filtering mechanisms of LSTMs and their ability to work with temporal evidence make them a popular design for time series forecasting and other sequential data problems. "This represents a major step forward for deep learning." The LSTM model is capable of capturing long-term dependencies within the sequence that is why it is used to forecast digital currencies. Cryptocurrency markets often exhibit extreme volatility and nonlinear movements, making it hard to model them with traditional models. Through their gated architecture, LSTM networks control the flow of information over time, enabling them to remember substantial price shifts and trends occurring in the financial market. The model also discards irrelevant noise. LSTM is thus suitable for forecasting cryptocurrency values, detecting hidden trends, attracting familiar with abrupt market changes. Ultimately, the uncertainties of the cryptocurrency market can be traversed with the help of LSTM models that aid in more accurate and timely predictions for better investment decisions, risk management, and programmed trading strategies. Equations (12.1)–(12.5) show the basic LSTM structure.

$$i_t = \sigma\left(W_i.\left[h_{t-1}, x_t\right] + b_i\right) \tag{12.1}$$

$$\widetilde{C}_t = tanh\left(W_C\left[h_{t-1}, x_t\right] + b_C\right) \tag{12.2}$$

$$f_t = \sigma \tag{12.3}$$

$$o_t = \sigma\left(W_o.\left[h_{t-1}, x_t\right] + b_o\right) \tag{12.4}$$

$$h_t = o_t * tanh\left(C_t\right) \tag{12.5}$$

where σ is the sigmoid activation function, h_{t-1} is the former state, X_t is the input state, *Tanh* is the activation layer occupation, C_{t-1}, C_t are cell state, $W_{C,}$ W_i are weight matrix of input allied with hidden state, and b_c, b_i are the biases. Researchers from all over the world have been fascinated in the cryptocurrency's pricing. Cryptocurrency values alter founded on a number of variables, counting transaction costs, mining difficulty, market trends, popularity, other coin prices, stock markets, feelings, and some legal considerations. The said elements contribute to the volatility of cryptocurrency values, which fluctuate quickly over time and are hard to forecast. For the scholars, predicting has therefore been an extremely trying and vital endeavor.

12.3.3.2 Bi-LSTM

Bi-LSTM networks are designed to overcome vanishing gradient problems and seize long-term dependencies for time-series data. Due to their ability to learn complex temporal trend styles, they are well suited for Bitcoin price prediction [10]. Input–output pairs contain the data, as each input sequence is a window of past price data and each output contains the price to be predicted. Following the training process, the Bi-LSTM can take the recent historical observation data in order to predict one or more future-time steps [10, 11]. The Bi-LSTM model is advantageous in predicting the price of digital currency due to the actor's ability to easily learn complex, consecutive patterns. Unlike LSTM models which deal with the past time series data for the current time stamp and only one direction, Bi-LSTM (bidirectional LSTM) networks deal with the past as well as the future price series data, thus can learns the respective relations between the interrelated relationships better than LSTM or unidirectional models can. This bidirectional split structure fits well with cryptocurrency markets, characterized by fast price differentials and nonlinear demands. Bidirectional LSTM (Bi-LSTM) models can effectively learn the long-term dependencies and subtle trends present in the time series data. Consequently, they are highly efficient in forecasting future prices or identifying early indications of market shifts, enhancing the accuracy of trading signals. Because the Bi-LSTM is noise-resistant and versatile across time ranges, it can be a valuable tool for investors, algorithmic traders in crypto, and financial analysts seeking a competitive edge. The Bi-LSTM architecture shows the basic architecture.

$$i_t = \sigma\left(Y_i\left[p_{t-1}, x_t\right] + z_i\right) \tag{12.6}$$

$$f_t = \sigma\left(Y_f\left[p_{t-1}, x_t\right] + z_t\right) \tag{12.7}$$

$$c_t = f_t \times c_{t-1} + i_t \times tanp\left(Y_c\left[p_{t-1}, x_t\right] + z_c\right) \tag{12.8}$$

$$o_t = \sigma\left(Y_o\left[p_{t-1}, x_t\right] + z_o\right) \tag{12.9}$$

$$h_t = o_t \times \text{tanp}\left(c_t\right) \tag{12.10}$$

In this setting, where the contribution at time step t is denoted as z_t, the hidden state as p_t, and the cell state as c_t, the Bi-LSTM model extends the standard LSTM by processing input sequences in both forward and backward directions. This bidirectional approach enables the model to capture temporal dependencies from both past and future contexts simultaneously. Bitcoin prices are influenced by past market trends, external shocks, and investor sentiment. Traditional LSTMs only consider past data (unidirectional). Bi-LSTM uses both past and future contextual information within a given sequence window to improve prediction accuracy [12].

12.3.3.3 Fb-Prophet Model with Holt–Winters Method

Exponential smoothing can effectively forecast time series data with a trend and/or seasonal component. It is a popular technique. Experts often use exponential smoothing in order to determine smoother curve-fitting methods. This approach is very effective with non-stationary data, which shows seasonal patterns or designs that tend to fluctuate over time [13]. The Fb-Prophet model for predicting digital currencies helps us with a lot of benefits. All the benefits revolve around the issues found in the crypto world. These may include high volatility and irregular seasonality. Facebook designed Prophet for time series forecasting. Furthermore, it is powerful for historical data that contains strong seasonal effects and missing values.

Prophet is a white box model which means it traces patterns. The sudden change or anomaly in cryptocurrency will help analysts and investors predict the future price. Other than that, Prophet just might be the complete opposite of a black box model like ARIMA. It is usually great for capturing behavior that is affected by the mood of the market and any world event since it can model holidays and unique seasonality. When you leverage Prophet, you can conduct risk management, algorithmic trading, and strategic decision-making within the cryptocurrency field. This is thanks to the tool's intuitive interface as well as fast performance. Both those with technical skills and those without can create accurate forecasts thanks to this. Equation (12.11)–(12.16) shows the basic Fb-Prophet model structure,

$$F_t = \alpha Y_{t-1} + (1-\alpha) F_{t-1} \tag{12.11}$$

$$L_t = \alpha Y_t + (1-\alpha)(L_{t-1} + T_{t-1}) \tag{12.12}$$

$$T_t = \beta (L_t - L_{t-1}) + (1-\beta) T_{t-1} \tag{12.13}$$

$$F_t = L_{t-1} + T_{t-1} \tag{12.14}$$

$$S_t = \gamma (Y_t - L_{t-1} - T_{t-1}) + (1-\gamma) S_{t-m} \tag{12.15}$$

$$F_t = (L_{t-1} + T_{t-1}) + S_{t-m+1} \tag{12.16}$$

In the given scenario, m represents the length of the cycle, while γ is the pressing parameter. The value of α is chosen based on the fundamental characteristics of the data set. open-source forecasting tool created by Meta, allows novice users to access time series forecasting in a simplified manner. It also submission advanced structures suitable for specialists [14]. It invariably claims seasonal data on a daily, weekly, and yearly basis. In addition, Prophet allows users to incorporate domain knowledge by allowing them to specify unique holiday or outlier events that may affect the time series. Furthermore, the model generates indecision ranges around its assumptions that provide insight into how resolute they are. Prophet successfully handles outliers and uses symmetric strategies and shifts in seasons that are often present in historical data from the real world to ensure robust performance [15, 16].

12.3.3.4 LSTM-CNN

The LSTM-CNN (convolutional neural network) hybrid framework utilizes the benefits of both models when analyzing repetitive data with latitudinal structures such as Bitcoin price actions. To cut down on extra geographic areas and increase processing efficiency, convolution is followed by max-pooling after feature extraction in the convolution layers. The model's output layer generates the final forecast, which can produce multiple outputs in classification situations or a single outcome for regression-based jobs, such as price forecast [17]. The basic LSTM-CNN architecture is illustrated in Equations (12.17)–(12.21).

$$i_t = \sigma\left(W_i.\left[h_{t-1}, x_t\right] + b_i\right) \tag{12.17}$$

$$f_t = \sigma\left(W_f.\left[h_{t-1}, x_t\right] + b_f\right) \tag{12.18}$$

$$o_t = \sigma\left(o.\left[h_{t-1}, x_t\right] + b_o\right) \tag{12.19}$$

$$\widetilde{C}_t = \tanh\left(W_c.\left[h_{t-1}, x_t\right] + b_c\right) \tag{12.20}$$

$$s_{i,j} = \sum_{m=0}^{M-1} \sum_{n=0}^{N-1} x_i + m, j + n.w_{m,n} + b \tag{12.21}$$

where x_t is the effort at time t, h_{t-1} is the former hidden state, $s_{i,j}$ is the output ingress map value at site (i, j). $x_i + m, j + n$ is the spur chin map rate at spot (i + m, j + n). $w_{m,n}$ is the weight censure of the filter at spot (m, n). The arrival of digital currencies, chiefly in very volatile markets such as Ethereum and Bitcoin, has escalated the requirement of understanding behavioral phenomena like contagion and herding. Investors tend to imitate the actions of other investors due to fear, uncertainty, and abstract goals. This phenomenon is called herding. On the other hand, one asset or region's volatility, which then transmits through other assets, is known as infection. The GARCH, VAR, CSAD, and other conventional econometric methods have been regularly used to measure these characteristics [18, 19]. Nonetheless, they often assume linear relationships and fail to account for the complex nonlinear relationships and temporally variable nature of stakeholder in the cryptocurrency sector. Deep learning model designs such as hybrid LSTM-CNN should be able to investigate and model these characteristics with reasonable success. The use of CNNs is efficient in classifying different patterns such as price clusters, volatility spikes, and other discontinuities in time series. The patterns often indicate signs of group action or academic waves, which are often linked to herding behavior. LSTM networks, however, can assimilate longer durations and temporal links. As a result, they effectively demonstrate the evolution of these local shapes over time and the curling of initial market shocks that are useful for classifying defect attributes [20, 21].

12.3.3.5 LSTM-GRU

The hybrid LSTM-GRU strategy is suitable for the Bitcoin price forecast as it can effectively capture complex temporal dependencies in sequential data. Both GRUs and LSTMs have memory units and gating mechanisms that allow the models to save some inputs and reject others, selectively, over periods of time. This function assists the model in eliminating noise and focusing on useful patterns. The structure papers for cryptocurrencies show the volatile short and long-term drifts of these coins. These models can be adjusted to forecast across different time levels by changing the input order sizes and the design of the network layers. Equations (12.22) and (12.23) show the structure of the LSTM-GRU model.

$$\widetilde{h_t} = \tanh\left(W_{r\cdot}\left[r_t \odot h_{t-1}, x_t\right] + b_h\right) \tag{12.22}$$

$$h_t = \left(\left(1 - z_t\right) \odot h_{t-1} + z_t \odot \widetilde{h_t}\right) \tag{12.23}$$

where z_t is the explain gate output, r_t is the reset gate output, $\widetilde{h_t}$ is the candidate hidden state, h_t is the hidden state output, x_t is the input at time stage t. The volatile and notional landscape of the digital currency market has made it mainly vulnerable to behavioral phenomena such as herding and contagion. Herding ensues when investors trail the actions of the majority, often ignoring their private indication or fundamental signals, while contagion imitates the hasty transmission of shocks or catastrophes from one asset or market to others. Traditional financial models, such as the GARCH family, VAR, or CSAD-based tests, have been broadly applied to enumerate these belongings. These models' ability to capture the high-dimensional, dynamic, and nonlinear dynamics that express stakeholder behavior and inter-asset linkages in cryptocurrency markets is frequently inhibited, albeit [22].

Because RNNs are good at modeling consecutive relationships in time-series data, such as LSTM and GRU designs, researchers have gradually contained deep learning models to get around these confines. An LSTM-GRU hybrid model combines the rewards of both architectures. With the help of its memory cell function and GRU's more straightforward gating structure, LSTM can disrupt long-term temporal routines, permitting faster training and clever memory use. When combined, these networks provide a very realistic way to observe and simulate how multi-currency price shocks spread and how shared investor behavior changes over time [23]. The LSTM-GRU hybrid model can organize types of synchronized stakeholder behaviors in the context of herding expose by means of previous price data, trading volume, and mood cues. This is particularly beneficial during times of speculative bubbles or dangerous volatility. While GRU layers more effectively filter and transmit information, LSTM layers retain the context of past investor behavior's, making the simulation more agreeable to abrupt behavioral vicissitudes or structural disruptions in the data. This is essential for identifying contagion effects, in which a significant shift in the value of one cryptocurrency may cause properties to spread across other currencies as a result of communal market processes or emotional responses.

12.3.4 Exploratory Data Analysis

Developing an Effective Strategy for Website Development EDA is a necessary first step in the investigation of Bitcoin data. Retrieve historical Bitcoin data from various sources, such as Application Program Interfaces (APIs), blockchain explorers, and links. To ensure correct styling and timestamps, eliminate excess data, rectify any missing numbers, and clean up the data. By helping forecasters better understand the structure, trends, and anomalies within the data, EDA is a crucial process in ensuring the correctness and reliability of digital currency guesses. With the assistance of correlation study, summary statistics, infographics, and other methods, EDA will enable researchers to identify patterns, variations in volatility, and anomalies in the Bitcoin price movements. This in-depth understanding will help in choosing relevant features, classifying data quality problems, and determining the overall modeling strategy. When it comes to forecasting digital currencies, EDA aids in identifying, concealed correlations between variables such as trade volume, market sentiment, macroeconomic data, and pricing behavior. By helping better selection of models and preprocessing stages, EDA improves analytic performance, enhances data-driven decision making and decreases the risk of model bias or overfitting in highly volatile crypto markets.

12.3.4.1 Visualizing the Weighted Price

In Bitcoin space where technological changes are frequently happening, time-series data visualization can be useful. Traders may identify major events or anomalies by marking significant areas within the data. Investors often use weighted price charts to help them decide the optimal time to enter and exit a trade in cryptocurrencies, which are notoriously volatile and decentralized in nature. According to Figure 12.2, weighted price data covers years [24]. In addition to assistance in everyday trading, accurate price prediction is critical for portfolio optimization, allowing investors to better allocate and rebalance their assets for favorable returns. Through prognostic models, investors can create different portfolios that suit their investment objective and risk tolerance level for a better long-term return. Besides, these predictions are implemented in algorithmic trading systems which perform trades on behalf of traders taking advantage of arbitrage opportunities, inefficiencies in the market, and trends while reducing emotional elements from decision-making [25].

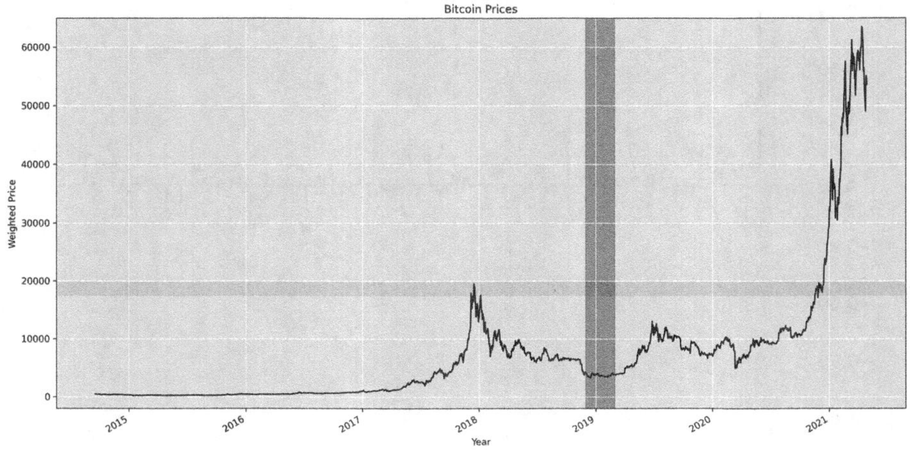

FIGURE 12.2 Weighted price of cryptocurrency.

12.3.4.2 Pre-Processing

Cryptocurrency market data is frequently quite noisy (that is, it might have anomalies, missing values, outliers, etc.) which may distort basic trends and reduce forecasting accuracy. Methods of data preparation include outlier identification, interpolation of missing values, and smoothing. By using such methods, unwanted noise is removed from the data making it usable for analysis. In addition, normalization and scaling techniques, including min–max scaling, variance scaling, and robust scaling, must be applied due to the varying scales and shapes in the cryptocurrency data set [26]. This is to make sure that all the features are equivalent and have a uniform magnitude. Subsequently, model convergence will improve when such processes are done. The presence of trending, seasonal, and structural breaks in the prices of cryptocurrencies makes them nonstationary, which causes issues with many models. To enhance model performance in the presence of dependency (seasonality or trends), preprocessing methods must be attempted (deseasonalizing, seasonal adjusting, time series decomposition) [27, 28].

12.3.4.3 Partial Auto-Correlation Function (PACF)

The Partial Auto-Correlation Function (PACF) is used in time series analysis to measure the relationship between a value and a lag of itself, considering the intervening lags. On the other hand, the Autocorrelation Function (ACF) investigates the relationship between an observation and its lagged values without taking into account the intermediate lags, whereas PACF deals with only the direct relationship between a value and the lagged outcome [29]. The PACF shown in Figure 12.3 helps in bringing out the relationship between the time series at a given lag and its previous delayed values. It shows how these values are related when the intermediate lags are removed or adjusted for [30, 31].

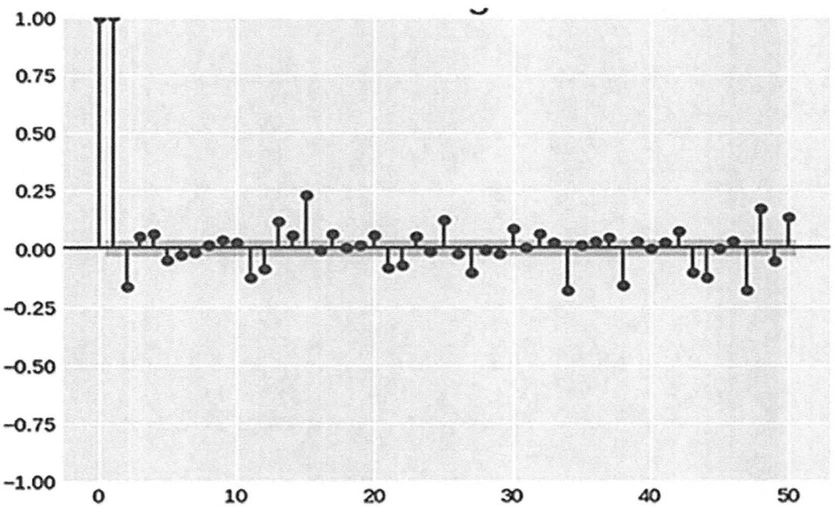

FIGURE 12.3 Partial Auto-Correlation Function (PACF) plot.

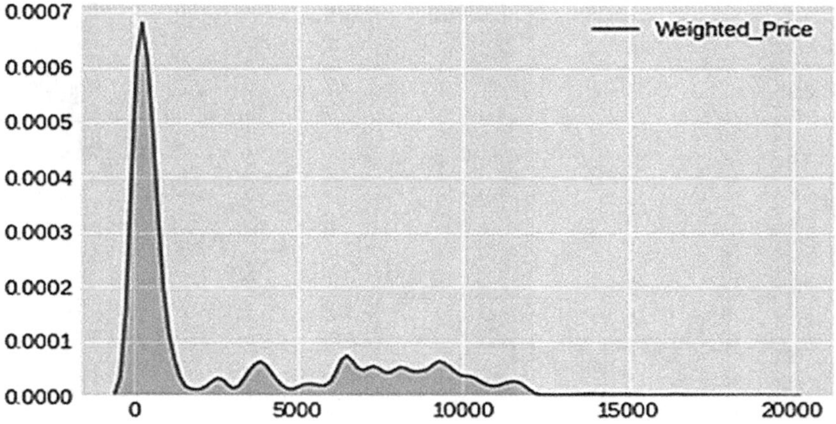

FIGURE 12.4 KPSS statistical analysis plot.

12.3.4.4 Kwiatkowski–Phillips–Schmidt–Shin (KPSS) Statistical Analysis

The Kwiatkowski–Phillips–Schmidt–Shin (KPSS) test is a test that has been developed to determine whether a time series is stationary [32]. The KPSS test looks for a deterministic trend in the data, unlike the Dickey–Fuller (ADF) test, which looks for the presence of a unit root. A fixed time series has a constant variance, mean, and autocovariance over time. Stationarity is an important concept in time series analysis The KPSS test statistic applies the residuals from a regression model, which examines the difference between the fitted trend and the observed time series [33, 34]. Studying cryptocurrency price movements statistically helps to identify unfolding patterns like seasonality, cycles, and interrelation with other assets. By understanding the statistical properties of Bitcoin return, investors can make better decisions, and this will help them in portfolio diversification and managing risk. Important metrics like fluctuation, skeweness, and kurtosis give information about the complete distribution of returns [35]. The KPSS statistical test plot is shown in Figure 12.4.

12.4 RESULT ANALYSIS

To measure the magnitude of herding and contagion effects, it is necessary to evaluate particular occurrence or episodes of crisis. These might include regulatory announcements, technological changes, security breaches, or macroeconomic changes that affect other financial markets [36]. LSTM models are perfect for modeling and predicting cryptocurrency price fluctuations because price data is sequential, with each observation dependent on the prior one. The erratic nature of crypto markets can affect the way those markets trend and behave. LSTM networks can effectively adjust their functioning in the dynamic stock market by continuously adapting their predictions as they learn from incoming data. LSTMs reduce the level of manual feature engineering in situations where they can automatically determine the relevant structures from the raw input data. In Bitcoin price prediction, the relevant factors may not be obvious, and may also change over time. Cheed LSTMs can

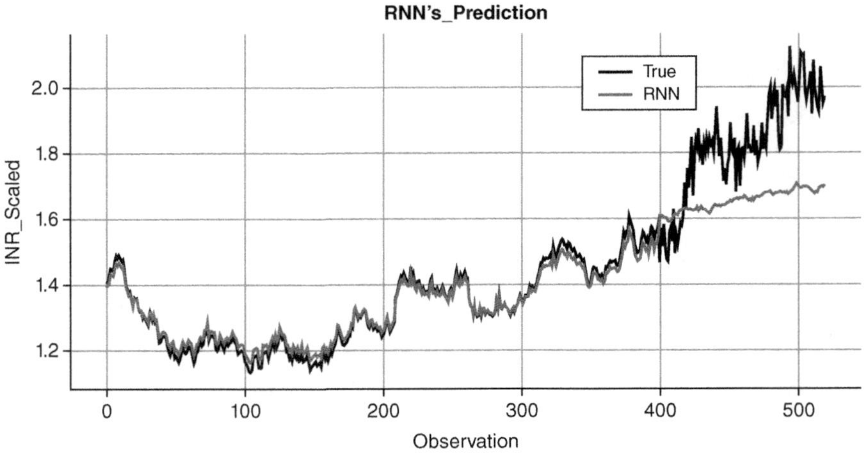

FIGURE 12.5 LSTM predicted BTC-USD exchange price.

improve prediction accuracy by using past price data. The LSTM model predicted the BTC-USD exchange price as shown in Figure 12.5.

Cryptocurrency price data frequently exhibits long-term dependencies, where movements in one asset's price can impact others over time. Bi-LSTM models are precisely designed to overcome the vanishing gradient issue usually faced by traditional RNNs, allowing them to better seizure these extended progressive relationships. Equipped with memory cells, Bi-LSTMs retain crucial information across longer sequences, making them well-suited for modeling complex patterns in cryptocurrency markets. This characteristic allows them to retain key insights from past price movements, market trends, and trading behaviors, which helps them predict future cryptocurrency prices. Figure 12.6 displays the Bi-LSTM-predicted

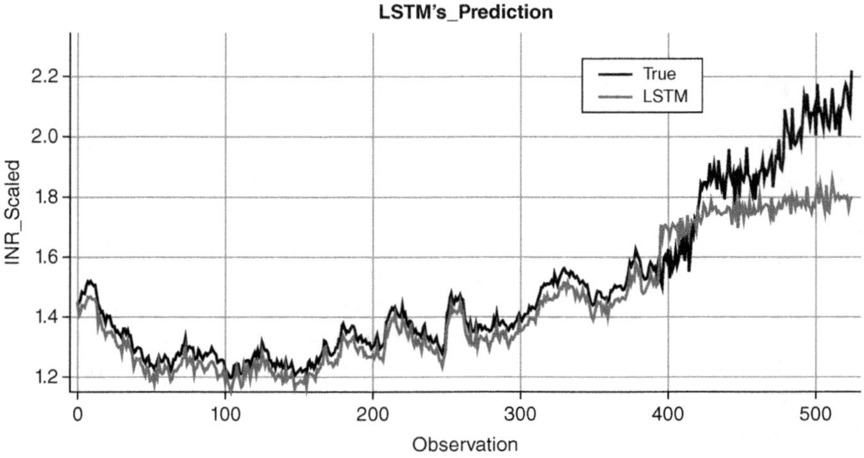

FIGURE 12.6 Bi-LSTM predicted BTC-USD exchange price.

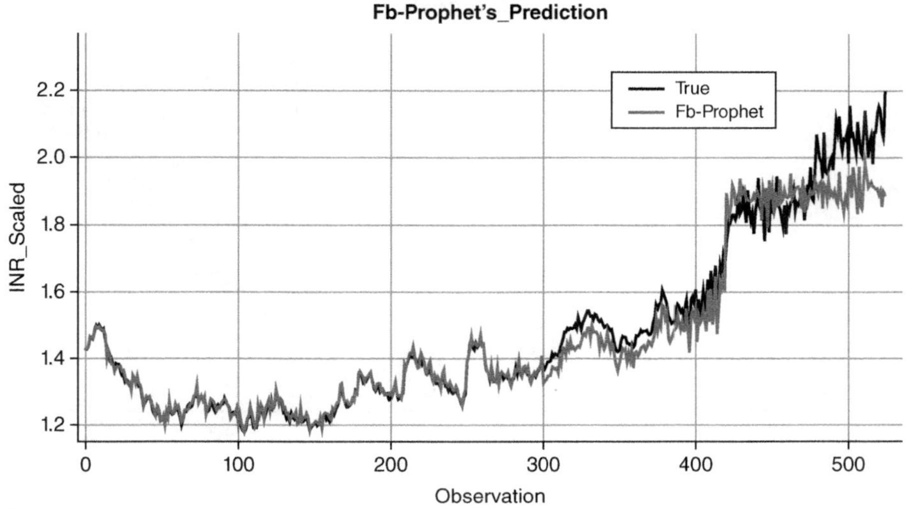

FIGURE 12.7 Fb-Prophet model with Holt–Winters method predicted BTC-USD exchange price.

BTC-USD exchange price. To adapt to varying forecasting horizons, LSTMs can handle input sequences of different lengths, making them appropriate for both short-term and long-term estimate tasks.

Prophet makes forecasts with uncertainty intervals and automatically accounts for demand fluctuations, trend changes, and data outages. Consequently, a similar analysis is performed using the Holt–Winters technique for the Bitcoin price historical data in order to derive the trend, seasonality, and level components.

This method estimates seasonal, trend, and level through constant weighted moving average. By putting together the prediction from the Holt–Winters method and Prophet, a final prediction can be made. The forecasts may be averaged or weighted according to performance to achieve this purpose through using ensemble strategies. The fit() function is fitted to the historical Bitcoin price data, during which estimation of the components and parameters of the Prophet predictive model takes place. The forecasted BTC-USD exchange rate price utilizing the Holt–Winters method via the Fb-Prophet model can be seen in Figure 12.7.

We harness the capabilities of LSTM and CNN neural architectures for Bitcoin (BTC) value prediction. The procedure involves extracting sequences of past Bitcoin prices with features, as the CNN and LSTM models rely on these sequences. A sequence length is chosen to enable the building of overlapping or non-overlapping sequences, depending on the structure of the data. The loss meaning, optimizer, and LSTM-CNN model are then different. The model performs well on the drill dataset, and its performance is evaluated through the validation dataset. We confirmed the functionality of various buildings and hyper-parameters to retrieve model recital. The BTC-USD exchange price prediction achieved by the LSTM-CNN model has been depicted in Figure 12.8.

The blend of LSTM and GRU architecture striking strengths is influenced by the hybrid model. Though suitable to model long-term dependencies with progressive

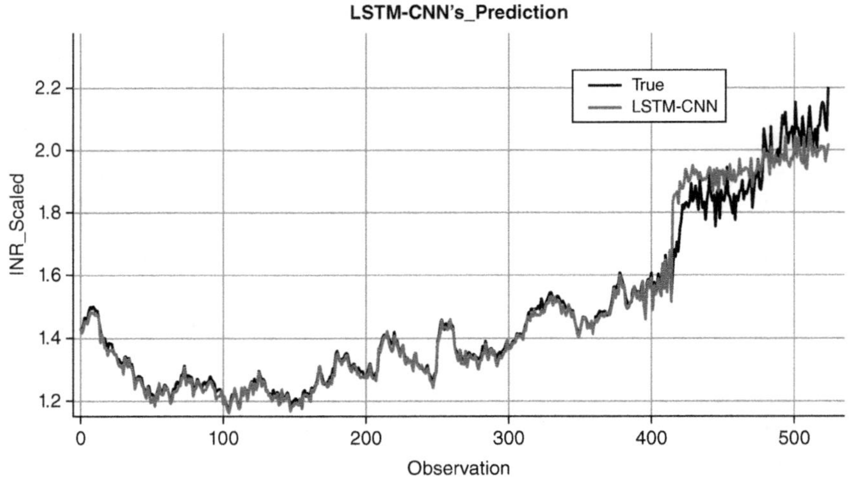

FIGURE 12.8 LSTM-CNN predicted BTC-USD exchange price.

memory process, GRU is known for efficiency and effectiveness to model short-term pattern. By combining the two techniques, the hybrid model learns short-term fluctuations as well as long-term patterns in Bitcoin price data, providing it with a more robust and comprehensive predictive power. The combination ensures better comprehension of the factors of the change of the price of Bitcoin. By analyzing the contributions of the LSTM and GRU components, the model and market dynamics can be further understood by the analysts. The extent to which the hybrid LSTM-GRU model can scale is dependent on the availability of computational resources and the nature of the forecasting task, making it flexible for both research and application. The LSTM-GRU model has predicted a parabolic delivery from BTC-USD. Figure 12.9 parades the foretold BTC-USD exchange price from the LSTM-GRU model.

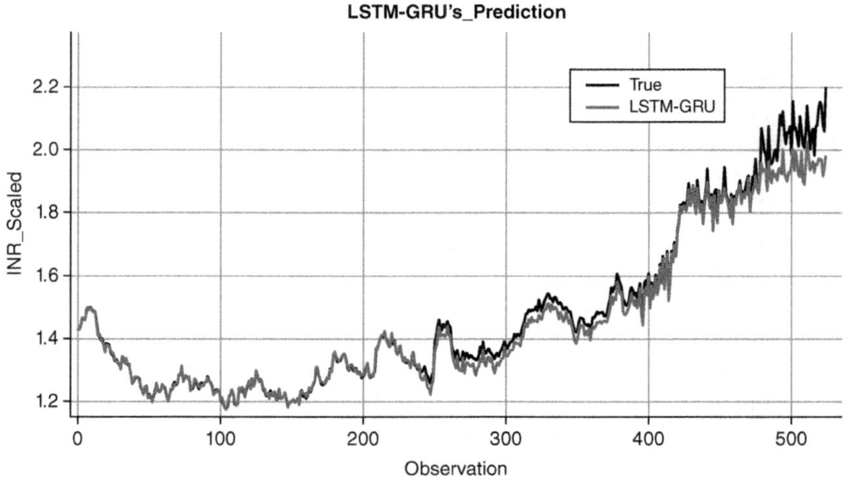

FIGURE 12.9 LSTM-GRU predicted BTC-USD exchange price.

12.5 ASSESSMENT OF PERFORMANCE AND MODEL VALIDATION

Cryptocurrencies, especially in recent years, have quickly become a disruptive technology and financial force changing the financial industry. Since its inception, Bitcoin, the pioneer of cryptocurrencies, has the potential to tackle significant challenges of the financial system. By integrating various forecasting techniques, hybrid models provide the benefit of enhancing extrapolative accuracy beyond individual models. These models capture the intricate dynamics of the Bitcoin market, producing more accurate predictions. In this chapter, the hybrid LSTM-GRU model demonstrates a value of 0.933, 0.054, and 0.074, respectively for R2, Mean Absolute Error (MAE), and RMSE. Flexibility in model assortment and integration policies is offered by the hybrid models. Using blockchain technology, Bitcoin peer-to-peer transacts without peacekeepers and essential third parties like banks that have always been part of all financial systems. Table 12.1 provides a summary of the R2, MAE, and RMSE scores for each model.

Deep learning models can reduce the reliance on manual feature engineering by allowing machines to autolearn and remove useful structures from unprocessed Bitcoin price data. It is especially advantageous for Bitcoin price prediction since the essence of key features may not be overtly visible and may evolve over time. Deep learning models can adapt to changing market conditions through direct experience with the data. LSTM architecture captures long-term dependencies well, but Bi-LSTM can capture temporal relationships better due to its dual attention mechanism. LSTM networks are faster and handle shorter sequences very well, while bi-LSTM architectures are efficient at remembering over longer period of time. The benefit of ensemble models is that they will incorporate the strengths of both architecture, thereby complementing each other's characteristics. A graph in a bar chart comparing performances of various models is shown in Figure 12.10.

The unpredictable currency trading of the sector and the reliability of forecast models keeps the Bitcoin mechanics market evolving. To fully understand the similarities and differences among different financial institutions with cryptocurrencies, a comparison study is necessary. This chapter takes the help of numerous deep-learning prediction methods to estimate cryptocurrency market activities.

TABLE 12.1
Assessment of R^2, MAE, RMSE Result

Model Name	R^2 Score	MAE	RMSE
LSTM	0.659	0.139	0.191
Bi-LSTM	0.876	0.106	0.141
Fb-Prophet	0.906	0.071	0.093
LSTM-CNN	0.920	0.060	0.078
LSTM-GRU	0.933	0.054	0.074

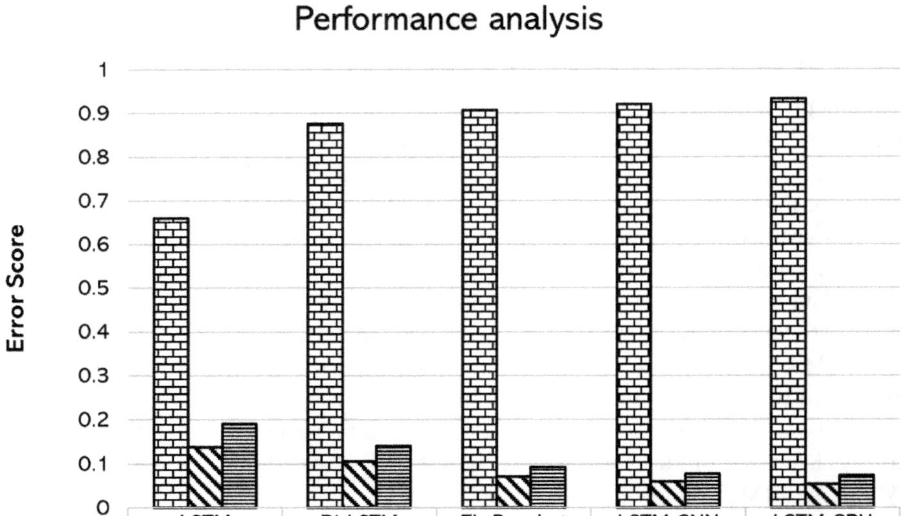

	LSTM	Bi-LSTM	Fb-Prophet	LSTM-CNN	LSTM-GRU
R2 Score	0.659	0.876	0.906	0.92	0.933
MAE	0.139	0.106	0.071	0.06	0.054
RMSE	0.191	0.141	0.093	0.078	0.074

FIGURE 12.10 Bar chart illustrating R^2, MAE, RMSE scores for each model.

12.6 CONCLUSION

Deep learning models are especially useful in cryptocurrency prediction because they learn from the data itself. This allows auto-adaptation of the model based on market conditions. It is important because some key factors impact the market but may not always be evident and may act over time. Herding behavior among investors is when they follow the crowd rather than make their own independent analysis. Various methods such as the net flow of capital into cryptocurrencies, correlation, and the cross-sectional variance of returns can detect herding behavior. Ensemble models can capture a wider range of patterns from the Bitcoin market, due to the presence of diverse forecasting methods, resulting in accurate and powerful forecasts. In this study, the hybrid model of LSTM-GRU beats other deep learning models. Due to the unique structure of both LSTM and GRU architectures, the representation of the data is learnt differently by LSTM … In the future, quantum computing has the potential to transform cryptocurrency forecasting as it will be able to generate large data sets and solve complex optimization problems. This will enhance predictions in terms of speed and accuracy.

REFERENCES

1. M. Yasir, M. Attique, K. Latif, G. M. Chaudhary, S. Afzal, K. Ahmed, and F. Shahzad, "Deep-learning-assisted business intelligence model for cryptocurrency forecasting using social media sentiment," *J. Enterprise Inf. Manage.*, vol. 36, no. 3, pp. 718–733, Apr. 2023.

2. M. Moni, V. Sreeraj, and S. Sankararaman, "Unveiling the interdependency of cryptocurrency and Indian stocks through wavelet and nonlinear time series analysis: An Econophysics approach," *Physica A Stat. Mech. Appl.*, vol. 634, p. 130643, May 2025.
3. P. L. Seabe, C. R. Moutsinga, and E. Pindza, "Forecasting cryptocurrency prices using LSTM, GRU, and bi-directional LSTM: A deep learning approach," *Fractal Fract.*, vol. 7, no. 2, p. 203, Feb. 2023.
4. K. R. Rao, M. L. Prasad, G. R. Kumar, R. Natchadalingam, M. M. Hussain, and P. C. Reddy, "Time-series cryptocurrency forecasting using ensemble deep learning," in *Proc. Int. Conf. Circuit Power Comput. Technol. (ICCPCT)*, Aug. 2023, pp. 1446–1451.
5. Y. Liu, Z. Li, R. Nekhili, and J. Sultan, "Forecasting cryptocurrency returns with machine learning," *Res. Int. Bus. Finance*, vol. 64, p. 101905, Jan. 2023.
6. S. Behera, S. C. Nayak, and A. P. Kumar, "Evaluating the performance of metaheuristic based artificial neural networks for cryptocurrency forecasting," *Comput. Econ.*, vol. 64, pp. 1219–1258, 2024.
7. N. Tripathy, S. Hota, D. Singh, B. M. Acharya, and S. K. Nayak, "A comprehensive analysis of Bitcoin volatility forecasting using time-series econometric models," *Appl. Soft Comput.*, p. 113339, May 2025.
8. M. Almasarweh and S. Alwadi, "ARIMA model in predicting banking stock market data," *Mod. Appl. Sci.*, vol. 12, no. 11, pp. 309, Oct. 2018.
9. Y. Wei, Y. Wang, B. M. Lucey, and S. A. Vigne, "Cryptocurrency uncertainty and volatility forecasting of precious metal futures markets," *J. Commodity Markets*, vol. 29, p. 100305, Mar. 2023.
10. Q. Dai, Z. Ma, and Q. Xie, "A two-phased and Ensemble scheme integrated Backpropagation algorithm," *Appl. Soft Comput.*, vol. 24, pp. 1124–1135, Nov. 2014.
11. N. Tripathy, S. K. Nayak, and S. Prusty, "A comparative analysis of Silverkite and interdependent deep learning models for bitcoin price prediction," *Front. Blockchain*, vol. 7, p. 1346410, May 2024.
12. A. Panigrahi, A. K. Nayak, and R. Paul, "A blockchain based PKI system for peer to peer network," in *Advances in Distributed Computing and Machine Learning: Proc. ICADCML 2021*, Singapore: Springer, 2022, pp. 81–88.
13. S. Galeshchuk, "Neural networks performance in exchange rate prediction," *Neurocomputing*, vol. 172, pp. 446–452, Jan. 2016.
14. C. Li and T. W. Chiang, "Complex neurofuzzy ARIMA forecasting—A new approach using complex fuzzy sets," *IEEE Trans. Fuzzy Syst.*, vol. 21, no. 3, pp. 567–584, Nov. 2012.
15. A. Panigrahi, A. K. Nayak, and R. Paul, "Impact of clustering technique in enhancing the blockchain network performance," in *Proc. Int. Conf. Mach. Learn., Comput. Syst. Secur. (MLCSS)*, Aug. 2022, pp. 363–367.
16. N. Tripathy, S. Hota, and D. Mishra, "Performance analysis of bitcoin forecasting using deep learning techniques," *Indones. J. Electr. Eng. Comput. Sci.*, vol. 31, no. 3, pp. 1515–1522, Sep. 2023.
17. H. Ismail Fawaz, G. Forestier, J. Weber, L. Idoumghar, and P. A. Muller, "Deep learning for time series classification: a review," *Data Min. Knowl. Discov.*, vol. 33, no. 4, pp. 917–963, Jul. 2019.
18. S. Hochreiter and J. Schmidhuber, "Long short-term memory," *Neural Comput.*, vol. 9, no. 8, pp. 1735–1780, Nov. 1997.
19. N. Liu and X. Zhong, "Cloud-based overall design of sculptural public art in commercial neighborhoods," *EAI Endorsed Trans. Scalable Inf. Syst.*, vol. 10, no. 6, Aug. 2023.
20. A. Panigrahi, B. Sahu, S. S. Panigrahi, M. S. Khan, and A. K. Jena, "Application of Blockchain as a solution to the real-world issues in health care system," in *Blockchain Technology: Applications and Challenges*, Cham: Springer, 2021, pp. 135–149.

21. F. A. Gers, J. Schmidhuber, and F. Cummins, "Learning to forget: Continual prediction with LSTM," *Neural Comput.*, vol. 12, no. 10, pp. 2451–2471, Oct. 2000.
22. N. Tripathy, S. Hota, D. Mishra, P. Satapathy, and S. K. Nayak, "Empirical forecasting analysis of bitcoin prices: A comparison of machine learning, deep learning, and ensemble learning models," *Int. J. Electr. Comput. Eng. Syst.*, vol. 15, no. 1, pp. 21–29, Jan. 2024.
23. S. J. Taylor and B. Letham, "Forecasting at scale," *Am. Stat.*, vol. 72, no. 1, pp. 37–45, Jan. 2018.
24. N. Tripathy, S. Hota, S. Prusty, and S. K. Nayak, "Performance analysis of deep learning techniques for time series forecasting," in *Proc. Int. Conf. Adv. Power, Signal, Inf. Technol. (APSIT)*, Jun. 2023, pp. 639–644.
25. A. Panigrahi, A. Pati, B. Dash, G. Sahoo, D. Singh, and M. Dash, "ASBlock: an agricultural based supply chain management using blockchain technology," *Procedia Comput. Sci.*, vol. 235, pp. 1943–1952, 2024.
26. M. Iqbal, M. Iqbal, F. Jaskani, K. Iqbal, and A. Hassan, "Time-series prediction of cryptocurrency market using machine learning techniques," *EAI Endorsed Trans. Creative Technol.*, vol. 8, no. 28, Jul. 2021.
27. A. Panigrahi, A. Pati, B. Sahu, B. B. Dash, S. Chowdhury, and S. S. Patra, "Cluster-driven CA selection space optimization in blockchain with POA for trust calculation," in *Proc. Int. Conf. IoT Based Control Netw. Intell. Syst. (ICICNIS)*, Dec. 2024, pp. 251–256.
28. N. Tripathy, S. Hota, D. Mishra, B. Dash, S. K. Nayak, and J. Tripathy, "Empirical analysis of digital currency herding and contagion effect using deep learning approaches," in *Proc. Odisha Int. Conf. Electr. Power Eng., Commun. Comput. Technol. (ODICON)*, Nov. 2024, pp. 1–6.
29. S. K. Nayak, A. K. Nayak, S. Mishra, P. Mohanty, N. Tripathy, and S. Prusty, "Improving Kui digit recognition through machine learning and data augmentation techniques," *Indones. J. Electr. Eng. Comput. Sci.*, vol. 35, no. 2, pp. 867–877, Aug. 2024.
30. A. Panigrahi, A. K. Nayak, and R. Paul, "Smart contract assisted blockchain based public key infrastructure system," *Trans. Emerg. Telecommun. Technol.*, vol. 34, no. 1, p. e4655, Jan. 2023.
31. N. Tripathy, D. Mishra, S. Hota, M. P. Behera, G. C. Das, S. S. Dalai, and S. K. Nayak, "A comparative analysis of exponential smoothing method and deep learning models for bitcoin price prediction," *Int. J. Artif. Intell.*, vol. 14, no. 2, pp. 1401–1409, Apr. 2025.
32. P. K. Bhowmik, F. R. Chowdhury, M. Sumsuzzaman, R. K. Ray, M. M. Khan, C. A. Gomes, M. A. Al Helal, M. A. Siam, and C. A. Gomes, "AI-driven sentiment analysis for Bitcoin market trends: A predictive approach to crypto volatility," *J. Ecohumanism*, vol. 4, no. 4, pp. 266–288, 2025.
33. A. Mishra and A. K. Dash, "Return volatility of Asian stock exchanges; a GARCH DCC analysis with reference of Bitcoin and global crude oil price movement," *J. Chin. Econ. Foreign Trade Stud.*, vol. 17, no. 1, pp. 29–48, Jun. 2024.
34. A. Brini and J. Lenz, "A comparison of cryptocurrency volatility-benchmarking new and mature asset classes," *Financial Innov.*, vol. 10, no. 1, p. 122, Jun. 2024.
35. T. Conlon, S. Corbet, and R. J. McGee, "The Bitcoin volume-volatility relationship: A high frequency analysis of futures and spot exchanges," *Int. Rev. Financ. Anal.*, vol. 91, p. 103013, Jan. 2024.
36. Y. Fang, Q. Tang, and Y. Wang, "Geopolitical risk and cryptocurrency market volatility," *Emerg. Mark. Finance Trade*, vol. 60, no. 14, pp. 3254–3270, Nov. 2024.

13 Privacy-Preserving AI Through Blockchain and Federated Learning

Pooja CS and Sathish Babu B

13.1 INTRODUCTION

As artificial intelligence (AI) becomes increasingly paramount, the significance of addressing data privacy concerns has become more pronounced in vital sectors such as healthcare, finance, education, and public services. AI architectures that are centralized aggregate data and optimize models effectively. Consequently, they present an imminent danger to privacy, ethics, and regulation. This section describes the inherent limitations of centralized AI systems and the need for privacy-preserving AI.

13.1.1 Need for Privacy-Preserving AI

Privacy-preserving AI is the set of intelligent systems that are able to process and analyze information without the loss of individual or organizational privacy. The existence of such systems must take into account a few main factors:

- *Protection for Sensitive Information:* AI models continually deal with large volumes of private or sensitive information, including financial transactions or medical records. Preserving the confidentiality of these data is essential.
- *Regulatory Compliance:* The General Data Protection Regulation (GDPR) in the European Union and the Health Insurance Portability and Accountability Act (HIPAA) in the United States are two examples of laws governing global data protection that are in place. Data use, storage, and distribution are subject to strict limits under these rules. As long as these rules are followed, AI systems remain legal.
- *Ethical Considerations:* AI addresses the moral standards and ideals that ought to guide the creation, application, and use of AI systems, especially when handling personal information. Fairness, accountability, and transparency are therefore encouraged by integrating privacy into the AI systems themselves, which is necessary for responsible AI use in terms of user autonomy and privacy.
- *User Trust and Adoption:* The degree to which AI systems protect personal data is directly related to public trust in these technologies. Encouragement

DOI: 10.1201/9781003658597-13

is available for both increased adoption and cooperation. Improvements have been made to privacy protections.

- *Data Ownership and Control:* Techniques for protecting privacy provide individuals and organizations with greater authority and control over their data, thereby reducing the likelihood of abuse or illegal exploitation.

13.1.2 Limitations of Centralized AI

Typically, numerous sources of data are gathered by centralized AI systems and compiled on a central server for inference and training. This method streamlines administration and model training, but it has multiple drawbacks.

- *Data Privacy Risks:* Centralized data storage creates a large attack surface. Sensitive data can be exposed in large quantities in a single breach.
- *Single Point of Failure:* The network as a whole may be compromised by disruptions, hacking, or technological issues that affect centralized systems.
- *Scalability Challenges:* Scalability is challenging when transferring enormous volumes of information to a single location, as it requires a significant amount of bandwidth and computing power.
- *Legal and Ethical Barriers:* Due to contractual requirements or privacy restrictions, institutions may be legally prohibited from sharing data, which would limit the variety of datasets available for model training.
- *Data Silos:* Data is often kept within organizational boundaries, resulting in fragmented insights and suboptimal model performance.
- *Limited Personalization:* Centralized models are designed to generalize across users; they are less capable of generating results tailored to the specific demands and circumstances of individual users.
- *High Latency in Real-Time Applications:* Centralized AI is not suitable for time-sensitive applications, as it requires data transmission to and from a central server, which can increase latency.

13.1.3 Learning Objectives

- Describing the need for privacy preservation in AI and the limitations of centralized AI.
- Introduction to the federated learning (FL) concept, components, architecture, pros, and cons.
- Integration of FL with blockchain
- To provide various privacy-preserving techniques in the blockchain-FL system.
- To exemplify various use cases and applications of the blockchain-FL system.
- To discuss various challenges in the development of the blockchain-FL system.

13.2 FEDERATED LEARNING

FL is a cooperative, decentralized machine learning approach in which a central server coordinates model training across several client devices or organizations. Each client trains a locally shared model on a privately owned dataset rather than sending raw data to a single location. The central server, also known as the aggregator or coordinator, continuously exchanges model parameters with clients after initializing a global model. Data privacy is protected by this process, as only model changes (weights or gradients) are provided, not the raw data.

For example, in 2016, Google added FL to its Android keyboard. However, no individual text messages were ever transmitted to Google's servers.

13.2.1 Federated Learning Components

- *Central Server (Aggregator/Coordinator):* The central server is the heart of the FL system. Initializing, distributing, and updating the global model are its responsibilities, and it usually operates on a powerful computer or cloud service. The server initializes a global model (typically a neural network or other machine learning model) using either pre-trained or randomly generated parameters at the start of training. A selected group of clients (devices or organizations) that will participate in the present training session is then provided with this model.
- *Clients:* Clients are the entities that maintain private information and participate in FL. These could range from organizational servers (such as those used by hospitals, banks, and factories) to personal gadgets (including smartphones, IoT sensors, and wearable devices). Every client has their local datasets, which are never shared. For example, a hospital client may hold patient records, but a smartphone client may have a user's typing history or photo collection. For privacy and legal reasons, each client's data must stay on-device or on-premises.

13.2.2 Communication Flow between Server and Clients

FL involves iterative, bidirectional communication. The steps included in the communication flow are

a. *Model Broadcast:* The most recent global model is made available to some or all of the clients via the central server. When a request is ready, clients can pull it, or the server can push it to them. The server may send the model along with training parameters, such as the learning rate and the number of local epochs.
b. *Local Training:* After receiving the model, each client utilizes it to initialize its own local model. Subsequently, as previously stated, the client uses its private data for training. This step is executed separately on each client's device using local computation.
c. *Update Upload:* Each client returns its modified model to the server after training is complete. The client does not submit the raw data; instead, they

only send the gradients, or trained parameters (the changes in weights). To protect privacy and reduce traffic, some updates may be encrypted or compressed; confidentiality is guaranteed.

d. *Aggregation Wait:* In synchronous FL, the server waits until all chosen clients have sent updates, whereas in asynchronous FL, it processes updates as they arrive. For scalability, a small percentage of customers are typically used per round, with participants switching between rounds.

Network connectivity is restricted to model parameters during this phase. Compared to transferring datasets, this significantly lowers bandwidth use and privacy risk. Sending the weight matrix of a model is often less computationally intensive than sending all the raw data samples. Additionally, secure aggregation techniques can ensure that the server only sees an aggregated update, rather than the individual weights of each client. Until the global model is stable or satisfied, these processes will be repeated (Figure 13.1).

13.2.3 Types of Federated Learning

There are various variations of FL (see Figure 13.2), each tailored to fit distinct organizational configurations and data dissemination scenarios. Knowing these FL types will enable us to choose the best possible ways for our infrastructure, privacy, and teamwork objectives [1, 2].

- *Horizontal Federated Learning*: This approach is applied when participants have datasets with distinct user samples but the same feature space. For instance, two hospitals may serve different patient groups while gathering the same kinds of patient data (diagnosis, age, and symptoms). Without exchanging personal information, they can work together to train a model.
- *Vertical Federated Learning:* This approach is applied when participants have information about the same users, but their feature sets differ. For example, an e-commerce platform and a bank may serve the same clients, yet one may have purchase history and the other financial data. Vertical FL facilitates cooperative model training by securely aligning data across everyday users.
- *Federated Transfer Learning*: This approach is applied when participants have datasets with different samples and attributes, yet they wish to benefit from one another's expertise.
- *Cross-Device vs. Cross-Silo:* The cross-device strategy is used when scalability is a crucial factor; participants have millions of edge devices, such as wearables and smartphones, that provide small quantities of data. For example, a recommendation engine can be trained using user data from multiple devices to provide more personalized product recommendations. Conversely, a cross-silo method is used when a dimension, such as trust, is significant and more dependable participants, such as banks, hospitals, or companies, have larger datasets and more reliable infrastructure.

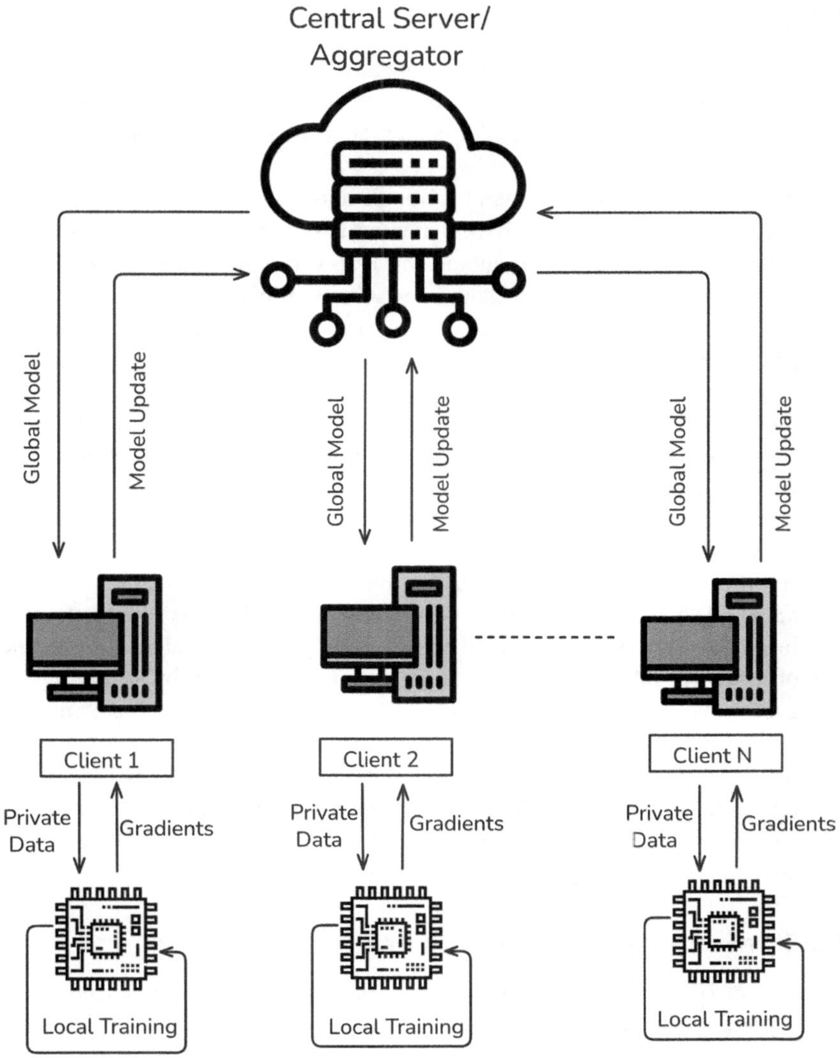

FIGURE 13.1 Federated learning.

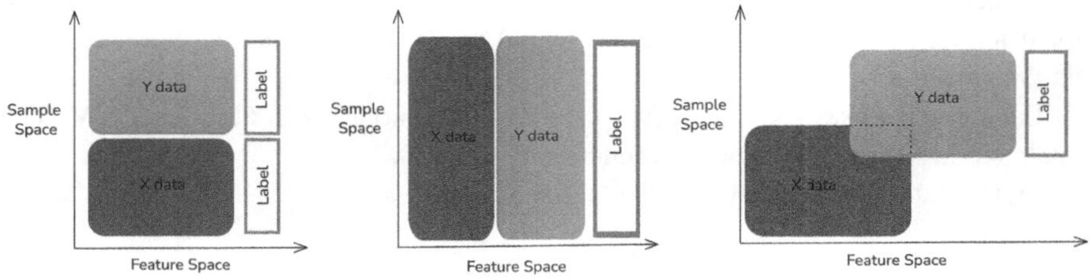

FIGURE 13.2 Types of federated learning.

13.2.4 Federated Learning Algorithms

FL algorithms regulate how local model updates are merged and optimized among distributed clients. They must account for data heterogeneity, restricted communication capacity, and potentially unreliable clients. Here are some of the ones widely used:

1. *FedAvg:* It was first suggested by Google and is currently the most popular aggregation algorithm. FedAvg's method is based on selecting a group of clients to participate in FL and a central server to act as an orchestrator. It entails weighting the local models' gradients or parameters by the size of the regional datasets. This ensures that devices with larger datasets have a greater impact on the global model. It strikes a balance between effective communication and optimal performance.
2. *FedProx:* To manage data heterogeneity and prevent local updates from significantly deviating from the global model, FedProx, an extension of FedAvg, incorporates a regularization term. In situations where client datasets differ significantly, this improves convergence. This helps to stabilize the training process and enhance convergence, especially when there are significant variations in the data distributions between devices.
3. *Secure Aggregation:* This is a cryptography method that is frequently used in conjunction with other methods; it is not a training algorithm in and of itself. An additional degree of anonymity is provided by secure aggregation, which enables the server to calculate the average of local changes without knowing the updates of any specific participant.
4. *Adaptive Federated Optimization:* By incorporating adaptive learning rates (such as Adam or Yogi) into the federated environment, these more advanced algorithms enhance performance and manage non-IID (non-independent and identically distributed) data across clients.

13.2.5 Mathematical Formulations of Federated Learning

Local Model Training (LMT): Local training measures the discrepancy between the model's predictions and the actual data. The local loss function (which shows which direction the error increases) varies depending on the type of learning job and is unique to each client. The local loss function, for instance, could refer to the cross-entropy loss in a classification or the mean squared error in a regression. Local model training refers to the process by which each client uses gradient descent to modify its model, thereby lowering prediction error based on its data. The more precise the local model is, the more accurate the global model becomes when combining the updates from all clients.

Each client i uses its dataset D_i to train a local model with parameters W_i. The goal is to minimize the local loss function F_i (W_i, D_i).

Mathematically, the update rule can be expressed as

$$W_i(t+1) = W_i(t) - \eta * \nabla F_i(W_i(t), D_i) \tag{13.1}$$

where the model parameters at iteration t are denoted by $\mathbf{W}_i$ **(t)**.

η is the learning rate,

$\nabla F_i (W_i (t), D_i)$ is the local loss function for the model parameters.

Until the local model converges to a good solution, this process is repeated a predetermined number of times.

Global Aggregation: The server aggregates the local model updates to compute a new global model W.

Federated Averaging (FedAvg) is one of the most used aggregation algorithms. A weighted average of the local models makes up the global model in FedAvg.

$$W = \Sigma\left(n_i / n\right) * W_i \tag{13.2}$$

where n_i is the dataset D_i**'s** size.

n is the total dataset size.

This aggregation stage combines data from all participating clients. Machine learning models produced through this iterative process are more reliable and broadly applicable. This allows the global model to learn from the combined experience of all clients progressively. Because the aggregation process is carefully designed, FL permits collaborative learning without compromising data privacy.

Convergence Analysis: Analyzing the convergence of FL algorithms involves demonstrating that the global model reaches the stationary point of the global loss function. The number of clients, the selection of optimization algorithms, and data heterogeneity are some of the variables that affect convergence rates. The performance and constraints of FL are frequently revealed via theoretical study.

Data heterogeneity, which occurs when the statistical distributions of data differ significantly among clients, can hinder convergence and lead to divergence if not effectively addressed. The number of clients also affects convergence, as more customers can introduce more noise into the aggregation process. The optimization algorithm used, for example, FedAvg or FedProx, is important in the determination of the convergence rate.

13.2.6 Federated Learning Pros and Cons

Pros

- *Efficiency:* FL eliminates the need to access or transfer big datasets. This leads to better latency and less bandwidth used to train machine learning models.
- *Better Data Privacy:* Due to the privacy-preserving framework of FL systems, private information does not leave a device. There is less opportunity for data leaks or cyber-attacks [3].
- *Better Compliance:* FL can help organizations comply with data protection regulations since data is stored and processed locally. Compliance is key for industries that deal with private data such as finance and healthcare.

Cons

FL is a game changer in the training of AI models, but there are also downsides.

- *Adversarial Attacks:* FL can be vulnerable to data poisoning attacks. An adversary can introduce bad data during the local training process or add malicious changes to the model updates that are sent to alter or corrupt the central model.
- *Communication Overhead:* There may be significant bottlenecks from the regular communication between client nodes and the central server.
- *Heterogeneity:* The decentralized model of FL has been able to increase the variety of data, which can reduce bias. This implies that the data may not be evenly distributed and might not be balanced. The global model may be significantly biased toward nodes that have more data to contribute because the data amounts may not be equal between devices. Varying computational capacities from device to device creates another problem called system heterogeneity. Adaptive local training can allow for training the local model around a node's capacity.

13.3 LITERATURE SURVEY

Research on blockchain technology and FL as a field is critical to addressing the challenges of scalability, privacy, and trust in decentralized AI systems. The survey does not intend to be exhaustive—it identifies important contributions, emphasizes core principles, architectural combinations, privacy protections, and deployments.

- *Comparative Studies*

  Several studies have been made to compare centralized, decentralized, and federated approaches. FL has large personalization and privacy benefits (Abhishek et al. [4]; Garst et al. [5]), but these also come with strong communication protocols and fault-tolerance methods. In some situations, centralized training is inferior to decentralized parallel stochastic gradient descent (SGD) as shown by Lian et al. [6].
- *Foundational and Evolving Views on FL*

  In the past few years, FL evolved substantially from a conceptual notion for privacy-preserving purposes to a fully-fledged distributed AI paradigm. Bharathi et al. [7] also chronologically tracked the evolution of FL in terms of origin, key developments, and expansion of applications. The authors emphasized modern challenges like
  - Model drift due to non-IID data,
  - Scalability of client participation,
  - Trade-offs between personalization and generalization.

    Their insights underscore the need for hybrid privacy techniques and blockchain-based auditability in future FL deployments, aligning well with the direction proposed in this chapter.

- *Blockchain Integration Techniques*

  Jain and Chaudhari [8] and Liu et al. [9] both examined blockchain-based financial ledger (BCFL) systems using both decoupled and coupled strategies. Al Asqah and Moulahi [10] examined the trade-off between computing complexity and degree of decentralization within BCFL systems. Their findings highlight how significant secure model aggregation and lightweight consensus protocols are within BCFL systems.

  Kang et al. [11] proposed an incentive-aware BCFL system that can handle incentives and penalties according to the behavior of the client. By using blockchain technology, this partially addresses a significant gap in FL, which is the sustainability of client involvement. Kim et al. [12] investigated how using permissioned blockchains such as Hyperledger Fabric can reduce latency within FL systems without sacrificing throughput. The system can support consensus methods that are energy-efficient and suitable for edge computing conditions.
- *Privacy-Preserving Federated Learning Systems*

  Only recently have researchers advanced privacy-preserving approaches, with distributed learning processes based on blockchain, for FL systems. In their literature review of BCFL frameworks, Sameera et al. [13] identified verifiable update trails and trustless collaboration as key concepts. Awan et al. [14] had also developed an integrated blockchain FL system focused on participant verification and permanent logging. Sharma et al. [15] contributed to the discussion by emphasizing the importance of blockchain and trusted execution environments (TEEs) for secure aggregation in FL, and proposing a method to limit attack surfaces during model updates, thereby enhancing data integrity. To avoid attacks involving gradient leakage and collusion, Dai et al. [16] proposed a decentralized privacy-preserving FL architecture, which hides model updates before they are deposited to the blockchain. Homomorphic encryption, secure multiparty computation (SMPC), and differential privacy (DP) are frequent tools employed to improve privacy in FL. Nagar [17] suggested methods to implement blockchain and DP techniques for preserving privacy during data exchange. Sen et al. [18] subsequently identified the privacy vulnerabilities due to adversaries and further amended their exposure with the issue of gradient leakage. Goryczka and Xiong [19] performed a thorough study comparing secure multiparty addition protocols with DP for distributed data aggregation with new efficient and fault-tolerant encryption schemes and a distributed Laplace noise mechanism, then experimentally verified their performance and scalability in real environments. Firdaus and Rhee [20] proposed a FL framework for health data sharing utilizing blockchain and homomorphic encryption to secure data aggregation while minimally relying on a central server, improving privacy and decentralization in regard to medical applications.
- *Domain-Specific Applications*

  One notable use of BCFL (blockchain-enabled FL) is competent healthcare. A blockchain-integrated FL framework designed for smart healthcare was created by Van et al. [21], with a focus on regulatory compliance with standards such as GDPR and HIPAA. Byzantine-robust FL algorithms that utilize blockchain technology to counter malicious clients were presented by Miao et al. [3].

- *Systematic Reviews and Surveys*

  Comprehensive reviews of the state-of-the-art are given by Qammar et al. [22] and Ning et al. [23], who assess the model accuracy, communication overhead, and scalability of BCFL systems. These assessments highlight the need for compatible frameworks and the absence of standardization.
- *Cross-Domain Use Cases*
  - BCFL has proven to influence IoT, financial, and automotive networks. Lu et al. [24] used FL and blockchain to demonstrate privacy-preserving data exchange in industrial IoT (IIoT) applications.
  - Otoum et al. [25] presented a reliable vehicular network with blockchain-enabled update validation for FL-based intrusion detection.
  - A safe FL system architecture for decentralized applications was created by Yu et al. [26], who also discussed the significance of smart contracts for incentive systems.
  - Cherukuri et al. [27] put out a paradigm that improves trust, transparency, and client motivation by handling model aggregation and client incentives on-chain. Their method addresses the primary issue of incentivization in collaborative learning by utilizing smart contracts to compensate participants who provide accurate updates.

13.4 BLOCKCHAIN-EMPOWERED FEDERATED LEARNING (BCFL) SYSTEM

FL, a distributed machine learning technique, permits multiple clients to work together to generate a shared model without the clients ever having to share their original data. FL protects privacy because all models are trained on the clients' own data in the clients' local environment. Nevertheless, the original FL method operates using a form of aggregator, a central server. A central server used as an aggregator raises issues about trust and data security. For instance, if malicious clients send corrupt or dishonest model updates, the central server might easily become a point of attack or total failure, and there are few ways to stop malicious clients from sending corrupt model updates. Blockchain could mitigate these issues.

BCFL systems could be categorized into three main architectural models, which are decoupled, coupled, and overlapped. These categories identify the different uses of blockchain technology within a BCFL system to increase the security, efficiency, and transparency of FL processes. Understanding the high-level architecture of these differences is essential to create and implement BCFL systems meeting the unique applications and concerns of each application.

1. **Decoupled systems** are the simplest type of integration. Under this concept, the FL process uses blockchain for small, independent tasks such as aggregating models or algorithmically creating incentive structures. In this

model, blockchain is considered an additional module that functions for narrow purposes for specific problems, while the FL process, itself is a mostly independent process. Blockchain is being used, for instance, to maintain secure, tamper-proof records of model updates. Also, clients who have contributed to the global model can use smart contracts to be automatically compensated. The value of decoupled systems is that it is an easy concept to implement as it requires few changes to existing FL processes. However, the primary challenges with this use-case of integration are that it does not maximize the range of synergies possible because of FL and blockchain functions. Lastly, decoupled systems would not necessarily address their own security concerns from a separate both FL and blockchain project.

2. **Coupled systems**, on the other hand, hinted at a stronger relationship, with FL and blockchain having a closer coupling in that data and model aggregation occurs on the blockchain. This method enables data provenance for the entire FL process by recording the blockchain as the single source of Truth for all model changes and training data. The model aggregation was performed through smart contracts, which ensured that only valid and accepted updates were added to the global model. A blockchain identity and access management system enhances data management and security by allowing data owners to selectively allow others to use their data for training. Coupled systems had a higher overhead and complexity than decoupled systems; however, this increases its transparency and security.
3. **Overlapped systems** are the most integrated model of blockchain and FL—the discrete purposes of blockchain and FL have been integrated together into one function. In this design, the blockchain not only manages data and model changes but also actively takes part in training. For example, blockchain nodes can be utilized as compute nodes for local model training, leveraging the distributed processing power of the blockchain network. Sensitive data about the local datasets can be kept confidential while the global model is being updated by utilizing smart contracts to develop privacy-preserving aggregation algorithms. While overlapping systems offer the highest levels of security, privacy, and transparency, they can be challenging to implement and require significant modifications to the FL and blockchain frameworks.

13.4.1 Integrated Architecture

The elements of both technologies are combined in a BCFL system. A blockchain network, client nodes (devices or organizations with local data), and optional aggregator or coordinator roles—often represented by smart contracts—are all components of a typical architecture. Key components are as follows:

- *Smart Contracts:* The FL process is coordinated by the on-chain code. By publishing training tasks, verifying submitted model updates, and enforcing rules for contributions and rewards, for instance, a smart contract can take the position of the central server. When updates are received, it can even initiate aggregation and retain the current global model state. The FL procedure (registration, training rounds, evaluation, etc.) becomes transparent and less vulnerable since contracts run on the blockchain.

- *Incentive Mechanisms:* Blockchain-based tokens can be used as incentives to reward clients in the FL process for contributing their data and computational resources. This motivates clients to contribute high-quality data and actively engage in FL. However, with FL, reputation management systems offer a way to incentivize honesty and discourage dishonest behavior. The reputation of mobile devices is one approach to determine how reliable and trustworthy they are.
- *Consensus Mechanism:* The blockchain's consensus process ensures that only legitimate transactions (model modifications) are appended to the ledger. In practice, this means that a model update received by a client is verified by the blockchain's node network and added to a new block. A single node cannot arbitrarily alter the training data or the outcomes. Decentralization eliminates the single point of failure, which is crucial.
- *Immutable Ledger (Data Provenance and Auditability):* All training transactions are permanently recorded in the blockchain ledger itself. Hashes or pointers to the clients' local model updates are usually included in each block. The system obtains complete provenance since each item is timestamped and cryptographically linked, allowing one to determine precisely which client generated which update and when. For instance, the community can replay the ledger to identify and remove a client's contributions if they attempt to change their previous updates or if a malicious update is discovered.

13.4.2 Workflow of an Integrated System

Regular training steps are as follows:

1. *Local Training:* Every client uses its local data to train the current global model after downloading or obtaining it. After training, the client has a new regional model or gradient.
2. *Update Submission:* Every client sends a transaction to the blockchain network with its local model changes. Sending the model (hash or pointer) to a smart contract is a common step in this process. For instance, client nodes may use a contract function to register the changed information and broadcast their updates to peers.
3. *Consensus and Recording:* Blockchain peers agree to incorporate each submitted update in a new block after validating it (verifying signatures, data format, etc.). The change is added to the immutable ledger after the block has been mined or committed. Every committed update is copied to every honest node.
4. *Model Aggregation:* A designated aggregator, which might be a smart contract or a selected node, receives the verified blockchain-based updates and determines the new global model (for example, by averaging weights). Once all (or a sufficient number of) updates for the round have been recorded. In

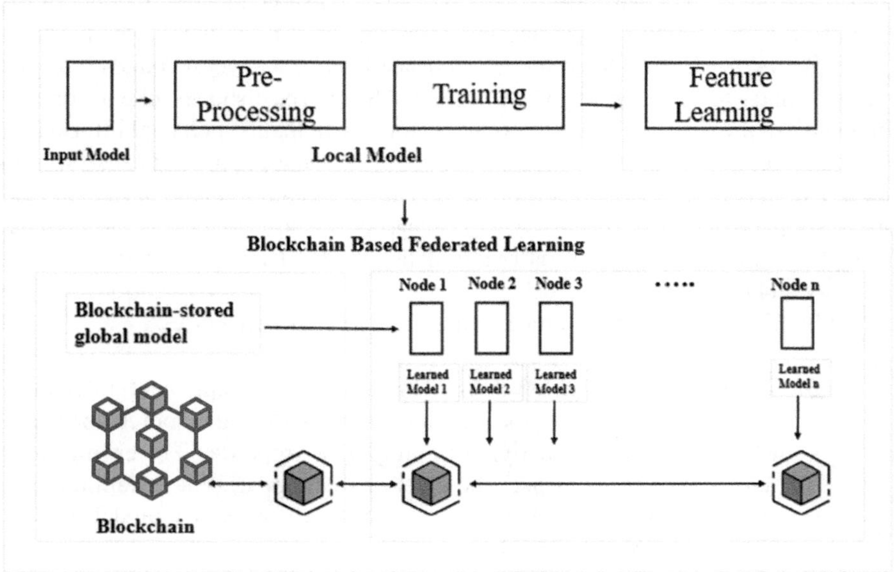

FIGURE 13.3 Blockchain-empowered federated learning (BCFL) system.

specific designs (like FL Chain), the blockchain network agrees on and carries out this aggregation.

5. *Global Model Distribution:* One way to publish the new global model (or its hash/pointer) is to write it to the blockchain or to an off-chain storage system that is referenced on-chain. For the following round, each client can then retrieve the most recent global model from the blockchain or associated storage.
6. *Iteration:* The model converges when steps 1 through 5 are repeated several times. External auditing of the process is facilitated by the blockchain log, which maintains an exhaustive record of all submissions, verifications, and global updates.

Example: Healthcare Federated Learning

Each hospital in the group uses private patient information to train a disease-prediction model locally (Figure 13.3). In a permissioned blockchain, hospitals upload encrypted model changes rather than raw data. Only authorized participants can contribute, as smart contracts verify and log these adjustments. The blockchain begins safe aggregation (similar to averaging) once all updates have been gathered, creating a new global model that is distributed to all hospitals. By providing auditability and traceability, the blockchain preserves confidentiality, integrity, and trust in the collaborative training process.

13.4.3 Privacy Threats in Blockchain-Enabled FL

Numerous studies have demonstrated that despite FL's intrinsic decentralization and privacy-focused architecture, FL systems are vulnerable to various privacy risks, particularly when paired with blockchain technology. Malicious entities could be present among participating clients as well as at the server level. For example, by examining local model modifications over several rounds, a central server can try to deduce sensitive information. Similarly, dishonest clients (or staff) may utilize provided information to infer other participants' personal information.

The capacity to retrieve private training information using gradient analysis presents a serious flaw in FL. According to recent studies, profound leakage can result from simply detecting gradients, which enables adversaries to recreate original data samples. This poses a significant risk to data confidentiality, potentially leading to privacy violations and data breaches.

In BCFL systems, privacy attacks fall into three main categories:

1. *Background Knowledge Attacks:* This involves an opponent inferring private information about the training data from outside sources or past knowledge to deduce underlying training data properties. For example, a participant who receives periodic global model updates may examine the changes. Such attacks exploit disparities between successive model states, leading to privacy compromise.
2. *Collusion Attacks:* It is a type of background knowledge attack in which several malicious actors (either clients or servers) join together to compromise system privacy. These actors can use collective inference methods and communicate internal updates or gradients to determine whether a certain sample is present in the training data (membership inference) or to rebuild individual data samples (model inversion).
3. *Inference Attacks:* These attacks aim to extract sensitive attributes from the FL model by analyzing its outputs.
4. *Reconstruction Attacks:* Adversaries attempt to reconstruct data samples or their attributes based on shared gradients. An example is the gradient inversion attack, where the attacker uses gradients to recover original training inputs.
5. *Tracing Attacks:* In this scenario, the attacker wants to know if a specific data record was part of the training set. For example, Shen et al. proposed a technique where a server finds participants with specific data qualities by using unintentional information leakage.

Unlike collusion attacks, inference attacks typically occur via passive scrutiny of the model's prediction or output, rather than by working together as collaborators.

13.5 PRIVACY PRESERVATION TECHNIQUES FOR BLOCKCHAIN-ENABLED FEDERATED LEARNING (BCFL)

In this section, we will focus on some stronger defense strategies against threats, especially within BCFL contexts, which include cryptography and privacy protection mechanisms that facilitate secure model training and are consistent with the cooperative idea behind FL. We will discuss the most commonly used techniques:

13.5.1 Differential Privacy (DP)

DP is the most widely used means of protecting private information in FL contexts (including in blockchain-enabled FL (BCFL) systems). By adding random noise to the local model parameters, attackers will not be able to identify individual or personal information. The major advantage of DP rather than cryptographic approaches is the reduction in computational resources and transmission.

13.5.1.1 Mathematical Formulation of Differential Privacy

DP is a well-defined mathematical concept that states that merely changing the input data by a small amount will not change the output of the algorithm. The main idea is to reduce the effect of any single record on the output by incorporating appropriately calibrated noise into the data or analytical output. A randomized algorithm A is said to satisfy ε-DP mathematically if, for any subset of possible outputs S and any two adjacent datasets D1 and D2, the following condition holds:

$$\boldsymbol{Pr}\left[A(\boldsymbol{D1}) \in S\right] \leq \boldsymbol{exp}(\varepsilon) * \boldsymbol{Pr}\left[A(\boldsymbol{D2}) \in S\right] \tag{13.3}$$

where:

- A(D) represents the application of the randomized algorithm in dataset D.
- S is any subset of the algorithm's potential outputs.
- Pr[A(D) ∈ S] represents the probability that the results of algorithm A on dataset D fall inside set S.
- The privacy metric that gauges how successfully privacy is secured is called ε (epsilon). Smaller ε provides stronger privacy safeguards.

According to this criterion, the likelihood of observing a particular result is broadly consistent regardless of whether a person's data is part of the dataset. The parameter ε controls the trade-off between accuracy and privacy. DP can be achieved through several methods, including the Gaussian and Laplace mechanisms.

13.5.1.2 Applying DP in BCFL

To achieve DP in FL, two key methods are local DP (LDP) and global (or central) DP (GDP/CDP). However, because blockchain integration eliminates the need for a central server, BCFL uses local DP (LDP).

Local Differential Privacy (LDP): DP can be used to protect the privacy of client-shared model updates by adding noise to the data before sending model updates to the central aggregator.

The process can be represented as follows:

1. *Local Model Training:* Each client i trains a local model on their dataset Di, resulting in a model update Δwi.
2. **Noise Addition** Each client adds noise to their model update using a DP mechanism:

$$\Delta \boldsymbol{w'i} = \Delta \boldsymbol{wi} + \boldsymbol{Noise}(\varepsilon \boldsymbol{i}) \tag{13.4}$$

where noise (εi) is noise that has been calibrated to provide εi-DP by using a Laplace or Gaussian technique.

3. *Aggregation:* The central server compiles the noisy model updates

$$\Delta w\_g = \sum \Delta w'i \tag{13.5}$$

The global model is then updated using the aggregated update **Δw_g**. The choice of DP mechanism and the calibration of the privacy parameter ε depend on the specific application and the desired trade-off between privacy and accuracy.

Note: The insertion of DP often degrades model usability, with studies citing a reduction in accuracy of 1%–5% by tightening privacy budgets with sensitive data [19].

13.5.2 Homomorphic Encryption (HE)

It is a kind of encryption that enables operations on ciphertext to be performed in a way that, upon decryption, produces results that are exactly the same as those of similar operations on plaintext. It makes it possible to do calculations on encrypted data without decrypting it and makes sure that client data is protected and out of the reach of prying eyes. This is particularly useful in BCFL when it is necessary to merge data from multiple sources without revealing the underlying data.

13.5.2.1 Mathematical Formulation of Homomorphic Encryption

The fundamental characteristic of HE is that, given two encrypted values, Enc(x) and Enc(y), we can conduct specific operations on them so that, upon decryption, the outcome is identical to that of operating on the original values, x and y. Mathematically, it is homomorphic if an encryption scheme meets the following criteria:

- *Additive Homomorphic*: Given Enc(x) and Enc(y), there exists an operation ⊕ such that:

$$\mathrm{Dec}\big(\mathrm{Enc}(x) \oplus \mathrm{Enc}(y)\big) = x + y$$

- *Multiplicative Homomorphic:* Given Enc(x) and Enc(y), there exists an operation ⊗ such that:

$$\mathrm{Dec}\big(\mathrm{Enc}(x) \otimes \mathrm{Enc}(y)\big) = x * y$$

where Enc(x) indicates that value x is encrypted.
Dec(x) indicates that value x has been decrypted.
⊕ and ⊗ are, respectively, homomorphic addition and multiplication operations.

HE systems can be additively homomorphic if they only support addition, or fully homomorphic if they support both addition and multiplication. There are many different HE systems, and each has its own mathematical properties and security assumptions. Examples include RSA, ElGamal, the Paillier cryptosystem, an additively homomorphic data encryption technique, and others.

13.5.2.2 Applying HE in BCFL

HE can be used to encrypt model changes before they are transmitted to the central server in BCFL. The server can then use the encrypted updates to do calculations without ever seeing the plaintext data.

The process can be mathematically represented as follows:

- *Local Model Training:* Every client i uses their dataset Di to train a local model, which yields a model update Δwi.
- *Encryption:* Every client i uses a HE technique to encrypt their model update:

$$\text{Enc}\left(\Delta \text{wi}\right)$$

- *Aggregation*: The encrypted model updates undergo homomorphic aggregation on the central server:

$$\boldsymbol{Enc}\left(\Delta \boldsymbol{w\_g}\right) = \oplus \boldsymbol{Enc}\left(\Delta \boldsymbol{wi}\right) \quad (13.6)$$

  where ⊕ is the homomorphic addition operation.
- *Decryption (Optional)*: The aggregated update can be decoded by the clients or a reliable third party:

$$\Delta \boldsymbol{w\_g} = \boldsymbol{Dec}\left(\boldsymbol{Enc}\left(\Delta \boldsymbol{w\_g}\right)\right) \quad (13.7)$$

  HE in BCFL protects data throughout the aggregation process, improving privacy and creating a safe, decentralized framework for data management and exchange.

  Note: Field studies suggest fully homomorphic encryption could increase overall execution time by upwards of 100× compared to plaintext, which makes it impractical for large-scale real-time AI applications in most environments [20].

13.5.3 Secure Multiparty Computation (SMPC)

This cryptographic technique preserves the privacy of each individual's input while allowing a group of parties to compute a function together. SMPC allows a series of parties to compute a function collaboratively while maintaining the privacy of their inputs.

13.5.3.1 Mathematical Formulation of SMPC

SMPC's objective is to permit a set of n clients, $C_1, C_2, \ldots, C_n$, each with a private input $x_1, x_2, \ldots, x_n$, to compute a function $f(x_1, x_2, \ldots, x_n)$ such that:

1. *Correctness:* The computation's result is the accurate value of $f(x_1, x_2, \ldots, x_n)$.
2. *Privacy:* Beyond what can be inferred from the computation's input and outcome, no client is given any further information about the inputs of the other clients.

SMPC is made possible by several protocols. Two well-known examples are secret sharing, which divides a secret into several shares and distributes each share to a distinct participant, and Shamir's secret sharing, which divides a secret into several shares and distributes each share to a distinct participant. Garbled circuits enable two people to safely calculate any function without revealing their inputs, and combining enough shares is the only way to reassemble the secret. A "garbled" version of the circuit that represents the function is created, and it is then safely evaluated.

13.5.3.2 Applying SMPC in BCFL

In BCFL, SMPC can be used to compile model updates from several participants without disclosing the specific revisions to the central server or each other.

The following is a mathematical representation of the process:

1. *Local Model Training*: Every client i generates a model update Δwi after training a local model on their dataset Di.
2. *Secret Sharing/Garbling*: Each client either scrambles the circuit that represents the aggregation function or employs a secret sharing mechanism to share their model update.
3. *Secure Aggregation*: The aggregator model performs secure aggregation by using secret shares or the garbled circuit.
4. *Output Reconstruction:* The composite model update is reproduced without revealing the individual changes.

Note: SMPC protocols often incur high costs to both communication and computation, which has resulted in total increases in training latency attributable to SMPC of between 3× and 10×, let alone any potential scalability issues, due to high dimensionality of the resulting data [19].

13.5.4 Hybrid Approaches Combining DP, HE, and SMPC

In some BCFL systems, DP, HE, and SMPC are integrated to provide multiple levels of privacy protection (Table 13.1). To further preserve privacy, model updates, for instance, can be aggregated using SMPC, encrypted using HE, and then subjected to DP.

The following is a mathematical representation of the combination of these techniques:

1. *Local Model Training:* Every client i generates a model update Δwi after training a local model on their dataset Di.
2. *Homomorphic Encryption:* Every participant uses HE: Enc(Δwi) using Equation (13.6) to encrypt their model update.
3. *Secure Multiparty Computation*: Using SMPC, the participants securely aggregate the encrypted model updates:

$$\text{SMPC}\left(\text{Enc}\left(\Delta \text{w1}\right),\text{Enc}\left(\Delta \text{w2}\right),\ldots,\text{Enc}\left(\Delta \text{wn}\right)\right) = \text{Enc}\left(\Delta \text{w\_g}\right)$$

TABLE 13.1
Comparative Description of Privacy-Preserving Techniques

Technique	Pros	Cons	Computational Costs
Differential privacy (DP)	• Easy to implement	• Over-protection reduces data fidelity	Low to medium (Based on noise level and data size)
	• Defends against attribute inference	• Hard to achieve optimal configuration	
	• Autonomous privacy preservation	• Not applicable for all models	
Homomorphic encryption (HE)	• Supports processing of ciphertexts	• Extreme computational overhead	High (Compare to plaintext)
	• High-end privacy	• Not suitable for large-scale AI	
	• Enhanced protection in hostile environment	• Selective support for certain models	
Secure multiparty computation (SMPC)	• End-to-End privacy	• Complex agreement	High (based on number of parties)
	• Semi-trusted part tolerance	• High data transmission	
	• Enables secure federated learning	• Expanding issues	
Hybrid approaches (SMPC + DP, HE + DP)	• Combined cryptographic composition	• Aggregated system load	Very high (more individual method cost)
	• Can achieve privacy amplification	• High protocol complexity	
	• Modular system configuration	• Combination challenges	

4. *Differential Privacy:* DP is used to add noise to the aggregated update using Equations (13.4) and (13.7)

$$\Delta w'\_g = Dec\left(Enc\left(\Delta w\_g\right)\right) + Noise\left(\varepsilon\right) \tag{13.8}$$

This hybrid approach provides a high degree of privacy protection, ensuring that data remains secure and private at all times. Thus, BCFL provides a strong framework for privacy-preserving AI in distributed environments by combining the trustless security and tamper-proof coordination of blockchain with the data-local training of FL.

Note: Hybrid methods are expected to produce stronger privacy assurances but are compounded by reductions in performance measures. Hybrid frameworks provided performance measures that stated energy costs increased by 10×, plus additional predictive accuracy loss from standard hybrid design [20].

13.6 USE CASES AND APPLICATION OF BCFL

BCFL has been presented in various application fields where trust or incentives are issues, and multiple parties need to train shared models without disclosing their sensitive data (Figure 13.4).

Healthcare: In the fields of medicine and health, the privacy of patient data is of utmost importance. Without exchanging raw data, BCFL enables multiple clinics, hospitals, or wearable device owners to collaborate on developing predictive or disease-detection models. For instance, a blockchain tracks each hospital's model updates and ensures provenance, enabling the federated training of a COVID-19 diagnosis model across hospitals. Current technologies target medical imaging and electronic health data. Collaboration can be strengthened by paying participants (such as hospitals or research labs) properly for their local data through the use of smart contracts to coordinate payments and verify contributions.

Finance: Despite holding sensitive customer data (credit histories, transactions), financial institutions (banks, insurers) can gain from a standard

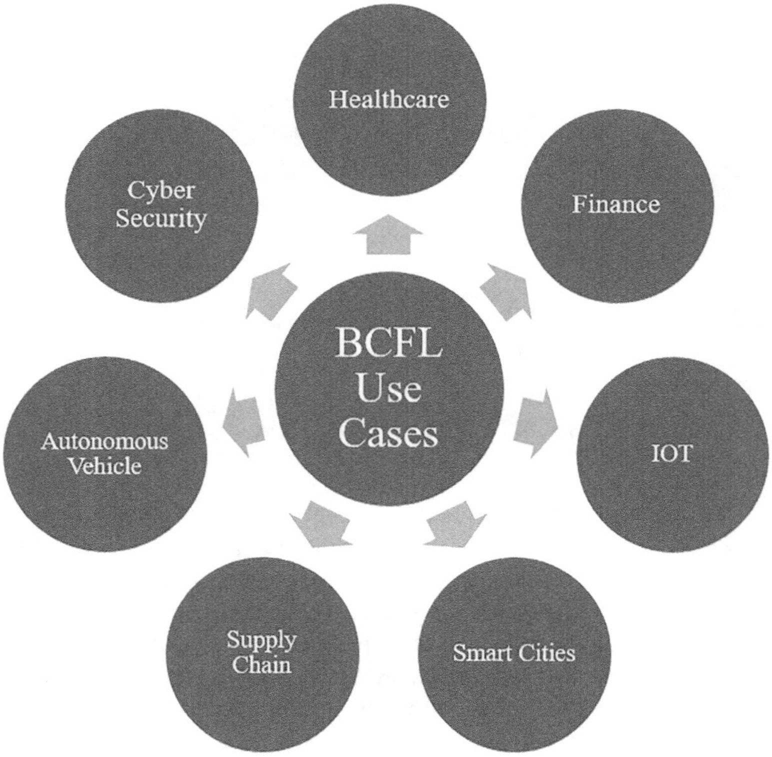

FIGURE 13.4 Use cases of the BCFL system.

model for risk modelling, credit scoring, and fraud detection. These banks served as FL nodes in one study, training a shared credit card fraud detector. The blockchain-federated system guaranteed privacy and equity while each bank trained locally and returned model updates. Blockchain can automate auditable rewards or penalties and provide tamper-proof logging, which stops a malware server from distorting outcomes. According to one analysis, incorporating blockchain technology into FL can "improve transparency, trustworthiness, and decentralization" in the financial services industry, assisting in the resolution of issues such as automatic compliance and safe data sharing. Federated models could potentially learn across exchanges or trading platforms in decentralized finance (DeFi) scenarios, with blockchain guaranteeing the precision of the knowledge acquired.

Internet of Things (IoT) and Industry 4.0: In IIoT networks, thousands of sensors and edge devices collect data (e.g., manufacturing process metrics, machinery vibration). For instance, FL can locally create a model to forecast equipment failures on devices within each plant. Through blockchain integration, these factory-edge nodes are assured to join a dependable, decentralized FL. For example, BCFL has been utilized to verify the integrity of sensor data and reliably disseminate model parameters in IIoT, thereby avoiding single points of failure and data tampering. Every IIoT node can function as both a blockchain miner and an FL participant, ensuring that any irregularities in inputs or changes are permanently documented and recorded. Smart contracts enable the management of reputation rankings and the identification and penalization of devices that submit incorrect updates (for example, by comparing contributions using on-chain reasoning). This strategy is particularly effective for grid or smart factory applications.

Smart Cities: Numerous public or private Internet of Things (IoT) networks, including utility meters, environmental sensors, and traffic cameras, provide data to innovative city platforms. Centralizing all citizen data is not necessary for FL to train city-wide models (such as traffic flow prediction and energy demand forecasting). The "BFLIoT" framework, for instance, combines FL and blockchain to facilitate IoT in smart cities. Before coordinating aggregation via a blockchain ledger, the system gathers real-time data streams (such as those from traffic or air quality sensors) and trains local models on city-edge nodes. By spreading computation throughout the network, BCFL in smart cities guarantees real-time processing and improves data privacy (raw camera or personal data never leaves its source). Additionally, it enables secure anomaly detection. For instance, if one sensor network notices an attack or equipment malfunction, it can record the alarm on-chain for the entire city.

Supply Chain: In supply chain management, companies can collaborate to create models for demand forecasting, inventory optimization, and fraud detection without revealing sensitive data. The addition of FL allows each business (supplier, distributor, and retailer) to train on its private data, while blockchain already offers product traceability; for example, manufacturers may collaborate to develop a quality-control model. Every model update is based on local sensor data, and a blockchain guarantees that only genuine (unaltered) models are accepted. Players who improve the global model's accuracy may receive token-based rewards. Although specific BCFL implementations in supply chains are still in their infancy, the combined strategy may help avoid collusion and single-firm bottlenecks, as federated analytics protects corporate data confidentiality and the shared ledger guarantees the provenance of data and models.

Autonomous Vehicles and Vehicular Networks: A large amount of data, like driving behavior and sensors data, are collected by cars and other automated vehicles. Using FL, which preserves the privacy of location and unprocessed video data, cars can collaborate to build perception or driving models. BCFL framework helps create prototypes for automotive networks, in which one system creates a decentralized vehicular network where the blockchain gathers all updates, and each vehicle trains locally. These technologies offer accountability (a smart contract can record which car supplied which update) and improve data integrity (location or sensor data cannot be fabricated on the ledger). According to the mentioned vehicular investigation, even when malicious vehicles were present, their blockchain-enhanced FL maintained a high prediction accuracy. In a broader sense, BCFL can facilitate the exchange of learned models for traffic management or navigation among fleets of drones or autonomous vehicles, as long as the chain ensures that updates originate from verified vehicles.

Cybersecurity: Collaborative threat detection is a logical step. To train an intrusion-detection model, for instance, several companies (or networked edge devices) can federate, and a blockchain logs the anomaly scores or model changes of every node. A new system for IIoT intrusion detection called FL-BCID combines blockchain update verification with FL across edge devices. By logging model updates and anomaly reports on-chain via smart contracts, it produces an impenetrable proof of attacks. Since no raw traffic data leaves the network, the system achieves high detection accuracy and accountability, enabling participants to protect their local privacy in this manner. Supply networks for secure software patches or threat signatures are another area where BCFL excels. Federated models are one way to send updates, and they are anchored in the blockchain to prevent manipulation.

Each area has the same fundamental benefits: tamper-resistant coordination combined with privacy-preserving collaboration. While distributed sensors in IoT and smart cities often do not require a trustworthy hub, sensitive personal data in healthcare and finance remains local. In every use scenario, the blockchain serves as a decentralized glue, allowing audit trails, transparent rewards, and trustless FL.

13.7 CHALLENGES OF BCFL

Despite its potential, BCFL faces numerous obstacles. In theory, combining two robust systems increases the demand for resources. In contrast to a centralized server that could process hundreds of model updates per second, the Bitcoin network can only process about seven transactions per second and takes several minutes to complete updates due to the latency and throughput limitations imposed by blockchain consensus. Training time and communication overhead are increased in a BCFL context, as every FL round now includes on-chain validation, consensus messaging, and possibly proof-of-work. Likewise, the need to retain even hashed references or smart contract logs of model updates across all nodes increases storage requirements. BCFL "introduces additional demands on network, computing, and storage resources," according to the analysis. For cross-device FL on mobile or IoT hardware, these overheads are particularly troublesome because edge clients may have limited CPU, memory, and energy resources, making full blockchain participation (mining and storing) taxing.

Trade-offs between privacy and security still exist. Unless additional safeguards are implemented, conventional FL still exposes certain information through model gradients, even though blockchain stops tampering with registered updates. It may be necessary to utilize methods such as safe aggregation or DP on top of the blockchain layer. Strong on-chain and in-model defenses are necessary because federated systems are still susceptible to Sybil or poisoning attacks, which involve an adversary fabricating numerous blockchain identities to distort the model. Long-term deployments will require quantum resilience, as blockchains typically rely on cryptographic keys for authentication; future quantum computers may be able to crack current ECDSA signatures.

Non-technical obstacles come from interoperability and regulatory concerns. Data protection rules restrict the processing and transfer of personal data. FL itself maintains data locally, but if any personally identifiable information leaks into the chain, blockchain's immutability may clash with "right to be forgotten" regulations. For example, if model updates from one country are placed on a global ledger, it may be challenging to guarantee conformance across jurisdictions. Furthermore, there is a lack of standardization; present BCFL solutions are incompatible with other blockchain platforms (e.g., Ethereum, Hyperledger, etc.) and FL frameworks. There are fragmentation issues that can lead to integration problems when many companies are all using different technologies.

Lastly, there is still the scalability issue of the number of participants. More clients can imply more consensus load, but they can also enhance model accuracy. While peer-to-peer BC-FL with hundreds of nodes is still quasi-experimental, some systems are already having this issue by employing a layered architecture or permissioned (private) blockchains. Overall, the area needs to find a balance in trade-offs for complexity, efficiency, and security.

13.8 CONCLUSION

This section looks at the partnership of blockchain and FL to provide privacy-preserving AI in a decentralized ecosystem. It shows how privacy issues with centralized AI come from aggregating confidential data: this is resolved through FL, in which multiple users build models locally, without exchanging raw data. Blockchain will provide a secure, immutable ledger of model updates and, with smart contracts, will help to validate models and incentives, while providing transparency and trust. Some of the main privacy-enhancing techniques that are discussed include DP (which mitigates risk in data-sharing by adding noise to data), homomorphic encryption (which performs computation in a secure manner), and secure multiparty computation (which processes data without revealing the data itself). A modular approach is suggested, which incorporates smart contracts, blockchain, and FL clients, to create a secure and transparent AI process. Example use cases include IIoT, smart cities, and healthcare, which require local governance over data. Finally, by discussing latency, adversarial attacks, and potential blockchain scalability in the context of FL, the benefits and challenges of combining FL with blockchain for next-generation AI will be articulated.

13.9 FUTURE WORK

- BCFL protocols can be standardized across platforms (e.g., Hyperledger, Ethereum).
- It can address security issues such as gradient leaks, Sybil attacks, and model inversion.
- It can overcome the computational overhead of blockchain consensus, which slows down FL training cycles.
- Quantum-resistant cryptography can be incorporated into future deployments.

This chapter brought together the technological, regulatory, and security perspectives within a single unified reference. Therefore, the novelty of this work lies in its double function as a research contribution and textbook, which can provide a foundation for future research and teaching around privacy-preserving AI.

REFERENCES

1. T. Yang, G. Andrew, H. Eichner, H. Sun, W. Li, N. Kong, D. Ramage, and F. Beaufays, "Applied Federated Learning: Improving Google Keyboard Query Suggestions," arXiv preprint arXiv:1812.02903, 2018. [Online]. Available: https://arxiv.org/abs/1812.02903
2. H. Ludwig et al., "IBM Federated Learning: An Enterprise Framework White Paper V0.1," arXiv preprint arXiv:2007.10987, 2020. [Online]. Available: https://arxiv.org/abs/2007.10987
3. Y. Miao, Z. Liu, H. Li, K.-K. R. Choo, and R. H. Deng, "Privacy-Preserving Byzantine-Robust Federated Learning via Blockchain Systems," IEEE Transactions on Information Forensics and Security, vol. 17, pp. 3366–3381, 2022, doi: 10.1109/TIFS.2022.3196274.
4. A. V. Abhishek, B. S., J. T. R., N. Raj, and V. Thomas, "Federated Learning: Collaborative Machine Learning without Centralized Training Data," International Journal of Engineering Technology and Management Sciences, vol. 6, no. 5, pp. 70–79, 2022, doi: 10.46647/ijetms.2022.v06i05.052.
5. S. Garst, J. Dekker, and M. Reinders, "A Comprehensive Experimental Comparison Between Federated and Centralized Learning," bioRxiv, 2023. [Online]. Available: https://doi.org/10.1101/2023.07.26.550615
6. X. Lian, C. Zhang, H. Zhang, C.-J. Hsieh, W. Zhang, and J. Liu, "Can Decentralized Algorithms Outperform Centralized Algorithms? A Case Study for Decentralized Parallel Stochastic Gradient Descent," in Proc. 31st Conf. Neural Inf. Process. Syst. (NeurIPS), 2017, pp. 5330–5340.

7. M. Bharathi, T. A. S. Srinivas, and M. Bhuvaneswari, "Federated Learning: From Origins to Modern Applications and Challenges," Journal of Information Technology and Cryptography, vol. 1, no. 1, pp. 29–38, 2024, doi: 10.48001/joitc.2024.1229-38.
8. C. Jain and P. Chaudhari, "Blockchain-Aided Privacy Preserving Framework for Federated Learning," in Proc. 2024 Int. Conf. Intelligent and Innovative Technologies in Computing, Electrical and Electronics (IITCEE), 2024, pp. 1–6, doi: 10.1109/IITCEE59897.2024.10467294.
9. J. Liu, Jack Goetz, S. Sen, and Ambuj Tewari. "Learning From Others Without Sacrificing Privacy: Simulation Comparing Centralized and Federated Machine Learning on Mobile Health Data." JMIR mHealth and uHealth, 2021.
10. M. Al Asqah and T. Moulahi, "Federated Learning and Blockchain Integration for Privacy Protection in the Internet of Things: Challenges and Solutions," Future Internet, vol. 15, no. 6, p. 203, Jun. 2023, doi: 10.3390/fi15060203.
11. M. A. Rasheed, S. Uddin, H. A. Tanweer, M. A. Rasheed, M. Ahmed, and H. Murtaza, "Data Privacy Issue in Federated Learning Resolution Using Blockchain," VFAST Transactions on Software Engineering, vol. 9, no. 4, pp. 1–12, 2021, doi: 10.21015/vtse.v9i4.726.
12. D. Naik and N. Naik, "The Changing Landscape of Machine Learning: A Comparative Analysis of Centralized Machine Learning, Distributed Machine Learning and Federated Machine Learning," in Proc. UK Workshop on Computational Intelligence, 2023, pp. 15–26, doi: 10.1007/978-3-031-47508-5_2.
13. K. M. Sameera, S. Nicolazzo, M. Arazzi, A. Nocera, R. R. K. A., V. P., and M. Conti, "Privacy-Preserving in Blockchain-based Federated Learning Systems," Computer Communications, vol. 223, 2024, doi: 10.1016/j.comcom.2024.04.024.
14. S. Awan, F. Li, B. Luo, and M. Liu, "A Reliable and Accountable Privacy-Preserving Federated Learning Framework using the Blockchain," in Proc. ACM SIGSAC Conf. Computer and Communications Security (CCS), 2019, pp. 1605–1607, doi: 10.1145/3319535.3363256.
15. S. Sharma, A. Pandey, V. Sharma, S. Mishra, and A. Alkhayyat, "Federated Learning and Blockchain: A Cross-Domain Convergence," in Proc. 2023 3rd International Conference on Technological Advancements in Computational Sciences (ICTACS), 2023, pp. 1–6, doi: 10.1109/ICTACS59847.2023.10390227.
16. W. Dai, Z. Liang, Y. Huang, R. Jiang, M. Qin, and B. Han, "Blockchain Combined with Federated Learning Technology Research," in Proc. 2023 IEEE 7th Information Technology and Mechatronics Engineering Conference (ITOEC), 2023, pp. 1–5, doi: 10.1109/ITOEC57671.2023.10291185.
17. A. Nagar, "Privacy-Preserving Blockchain-Based Federated Learning with Differential Data Sharing," doi: 10.48550/arXiv.1912.04859, 2019. [Online]. Available: https://arxiv.org/abs/1906.02562
18. J. Sen, H. Waghela, and S. Rakshit, "Privacy in Federated Learning," arXiv preprint arXiv:2408.08904, 2024. [Online]. Available: https://doi.org/10.48550/arXiv.2408.08904
19. S. Goryczka and L. Xiong, "A comprehensive comparison of multiparty secure additions with differential privacy," IEEE Trans. Dependable Secure Comput., vol. 14, no. 4, pp. 409–422, 2017, doi: 10.1109/TDSC.2015.2484326.
20. M. Firdaus and K.-H. Rhee, "Secure Federated Learning with Blockchain and Homomorphic Encryption for Healthcare Data Sharing," in Proc. Int. Conf. on Cyberworlds, 2024, doi: 10.1109/CW64301.2024.00036.
21. L. N. Van, A. H. Tuan, D. T. Phan, T.-K. Vo, and V. Pham, "A Privacy-Preserving Approach for Building Learning Models in Smart Healthcare using Blockchain and Federated Learning," in Proc. 11th Int. Symp. on Information and Communication Technology (SoICT), 2022, pp. 233–240, doi: 10.1145/3568562.3568665.
22. A. Qammar, A. Karim, H. Ning, and J. Ding, "Securing Federated Learning with Blockchain: A Systematic Literature Review," Artificial Intelligence Review, vol. 55, no. 7, pp. 5807–5843, Jul. 2022, doi: 10.1007/s10462-022-10271-9.

23. W. Ning, Y. Zhu, C. Song, H. Li, L. Zhu, J. Xie, T. Chen, T. Xu, X. Xu, and J. Gao, "Blockchain-Based Federated Learning: A Survey and New Perspectives," Applied Sciences, vol. 14, no. 20, p. 9459, Oct. 2024, doi: 10.3390/app14209459.
24. Y. Lu, X. Huang, Y. Dai, S. Maharjan, and Y. Zhang, "Blockchain and Federated Learning for Privacy-Preserved Data Sharing in Industrial IoT," IEEE Transactions on Industrial Informatics, vol. 16, no. 6, pp. 4177–4186, Jun. 2020, doi: 10.1109/TII.2019.2942190.
25. S. Otoum, I. A. Ridhawi, and H. Mouftah, "Blockchain-Supported Federated Learning for Trustworthy Vehicular Networks," in Proc. 2020 IEEE Global Communications Conference (GLOBECOM), 2020, pp. 1–6, doi: 10.1109/GLOBECOM42002.2020.9322159.
26. F. Yu, H. Lin, X. Wang, A. Yassine, and M. S. Hossain, "Blockchain-Empowered Secure Federated Learning System: Architecture and Applications," Computer Communications, vol. 189, pp. 58–67, 2022, doi: 10.1016/j.comcom.2022.09.008.
27. R. V. Cherukuri, G. L. Devi, and N. Ramesh, "Federated Learning with Blockchain-Based Model Aggregation and Incentives," International Journal of Computer Applications, vol. 46, no. 2, pp. 1–10, 2024, doi: 10.1080/1206212X.2024.2328492.

14 Blockchain-Based Intelligent Transportation Management System

*Dileep Kumar Murala, Sukanta Das, and Sandeep Kumar Panda**

14.1 INTRODUCTION

Blockchain was established as a Bitcoin distributed ledger to avoid double-spending [1]. Because blockchain technology is unchangeable, transacting parties and stakeholders can generate decentralised trust among untrustworthy actors. Because of the success of Bitcoin, academics' attention has been drawn to blockchain technology. Blockchain was the foundation of cryptocurrencies, but it has now become a distributed system technology that has accelerated the shift from centralised to dynamic systems [2]. Blockchain-based architecture is decentralised and open because nodes store cryptographically linked Bitcoin transaction records in blocks according to consensus rules. Blockchain is immutable due to cryptographic block chaining and the distributed consensus method. Blockchain's transparency and immutability allow anybody to inspect Bitcoin transaction history, preventing tampering without detection. Thus, decentralised trust between untrustworthy entities is possible. Once added to the chain, records cannot be altered [3]. The blockchain is distributed, transparent, and verifiable by the public in addition to being decentralised, open, and unchangeable. Blockchain architecture naturally addresses a single point of failure because records are replicated among several dispersed nodes. To capitalise on its alluring features, blockchain technology is being considered by numerous applications [4]. Nonetheless, automobile technology, cyber physical systems (CPS), and satellite communications make cars smarter and more autonomous or semi-autonomous. The blockchain intelligent transportation management systems (BBITMS) concept [2] will enable future intelligent transportation systems (ITS) with more smart vehicles connected to the Internet. BBITMS should enable ITS within a decade. ERTICO-ITS Europe [5] and CityVerve Manchester [6] are two initiatives promoting ITS development in smart cities. BBITMS also facilitates seamless interaction between smart cars, roadside infrastructures, and pedestrians to address ITS's growing functional needs and support the V2X paradigm. Cloud computing, edge computing, AI, and enhanced vehicle communication are also advancing BBITMS. BBITMS's ultimate goal is a unified, seamless, and integrated smart vehicle data and resource exchange platform. Applications for cars such as smart parking, entertainment, traffic efficiency, road safety, and driving safety are made possible by these

* Corresponding Author: sandeeppanda@ifheindia.org

DOI: 10.1201/9781003658597-14

data and resource transfers [7]. Network traffic management will be necessary as more smart cars produce and exchange enormous amounts of data due to the expanding automotive applications and services. The context complexity, heterogeneity, low latency, and high mobility of BBITMS will make cloud-based storage and management challenging. It's hard to keep BBITMS entities from multiple service providers compatible. Thus, BBITMS' data exchange and storage architecture must be decentralised, dispersed, interoperable, flexible, and scalable to support expansion and leverage ITS potential. Since the platform is decentralised, it is more vulnerable to cyberattacks, making BBITMS data security, privacy, and trustworthiness crucial. Thus, blockchain technology, sophisticated cryptography, and edge computing have opened up several BBITMS applications [8].

14.1.1 Blockchain Concept and Logic

Cryptography mail group member "Satoshi Nakamoto" introduced the blockchain concept in his 2008 essay "Bitcoin: a peer-to-peer electronic cash system" [9]. Blockchain stores verified and synchronised data in chronological, encrypted, linked chunks over a P2P network. Blockchain is a new paradigm for distributed computing and decentralised architecture. Distributed consensus is used to generate the data, which is then stored in encrypted chained blocks and modified via smart contracts [10].

Currently, other cryptocurrencies rely on blockchain technology, with Bitcoin being the first and most successful "killer use case." The concept behind every blockchain system is the same, but consensus techniques differ. Full client nodes store blockchain data in a decentralised peer-to-peer network, and they utilise the consensus mechanism to log and validate it. Proof-of-Work (PoW) is a technique used by Bitcoin in which distant nodes pool their processing power to solve a mathematical puzzle with dynamic impediments [11]. The node that finds the solution gets to compile all of the transaction data from a given time frame 10 minutes, for example into a new block and upload it chronologically to the main blockchain. The winning node will automatically receive a certain number of coins. Every node solves a new challenge and competes to create the next block as this process is repeated. This process will hash and encrypt blockchain data to safeguard it [12].

Blockchain solves cryptocurrency's "Byzantine generals" and "double spending" issues, making it crucial for decentralised ITSs. Blockchain's distributed consensus algorithms and digital encryption answer "how to reach consensus and establish trusted cooperation in a distributed system without trusted central nodes," the preceding problem [13]. In decentralised autonomous transportation systems, this is crucial for reliable communication and collaboration between cars, roadside equipment, and pedestrians (smartphones). Lastly, multiple uses for digital currency. An irreversible, irrevocable, and traceable blockchain ledger is created by the consensus-based, distributed data verification method, enabling complete decentralisation and double spending prevention in the absence of reliable central authorities. This capability allows for the exchange of digital assets or point-to-point money transactions without the need for middlemen, hence establishing a niche financial system within the ITS environment. Finally, blockchain technology can offer a decentralised, reliable, and secure ITS [14].

14.2 LITERATURE REVIEW

Blockchain-based Bitcoin leverages distributed data storage, point-to-point transmission, encryption, consensus, and intelligent contracts. Hash references create a linked ledger on the blockchain by connecting data blocks with digital signatures and timestamps. Blockchain's distributed storage makes data exchange easier, and digital signatures on data records have the potential to self-verify accuracy. Blocks are connected by hash pointers, which stop hackers from fabricating data and tracking it down. Blockchain is special because it allows users to agree on the ledger's authenticity without an intermediary [15]. Data interchange, tamper-proof, trustworthy, and traceability make the blockchain suited for a multiparty collaborative business information system. Our study created a government-led transport consortium blockchain that maximises road network carrying capacity, addresses traffic issues, and improves traffic safety and the environment using blockchain technology. This study examined the system's economic, social, and environmental aspects using triple bottom line theory. The environmental, social, and economic sides consider blockchain-based intelligent transportation's environmental benefits, societal issues, and costs. The intelligent transportation blockchain application system uses blockchain and IoT. There are 15 prerequisites and three aspects [16].

14.2.1 Economics of Blockchain-Intelligent Transportation

We start with a cost analysis to see how blockchain-based intelligent transportation influences government and commercial budgets. Transaction, managerial, infrastructure construction, and financial costs are considered. Well-thought-out opportunism might disappear thanks to blockchain's tamper-proof technology and permanent transaction record. Low transaction costs are encouraged by trustworthy ledgers, which increases wealth and economic efficiency [17]. Sharing of information and intelligent contracts can boost trust and lower transaction uncertainty. The decentralised and distributed accounting system of blockchain reduces middleman costs. These qualities lower government and corporate transaction costs [18].

Automatic data uploading and traceability solutions reduce cash flow monitoring, administration, and approval expenses, minimising fraud and boosting control. For governments and enterprises, immutable and distributed bookkeeping reduces data analysis, monitoring, and management labour [19]. Sharing datasets and using smart contracts can save administration workload, paper use, and debate time [20]. Blockchain traffic data may be used to design urban traffic network layout, logistics, transportation, road planning, road building, bus station construction, and supporting infrastructure development scheme optimisation, which affects infrastructure construction costs. Enterprise electronic bill administration is simplified by automated data uploading and traceability. Blockchain helps governments and auditors assess corporate data, manage earnings and taxes, and reduce tax fraud. According to Coyne and McMickle [17], blockchain-based digital currency only lives inside the network while economic transactions occur outside of it, making the blockchain paradigm unsuitable for transaction verification. Blockchain and IoT connectivity can fix this and enable transportation blockchain accounting.

14.2.2 Smart Transportation on Blockchain: Social

14.2.2.1 Blockchain Features Affect Society

Blockchain creates a distributed ledger and database by utilising computer programming, cryptography, the Internet, and mathematics, among other areas. It facilitates transparency, community upkeep, and whole-process tracking and is decentralised, tamper-proof, traceable, and open [21]. These components ensure blockchain trustworthiness. Blockchain and IoT technology automatically input and update data, establishing smart contracts quickly and speeding up transactions [22]. Thus, we classify blockchain properties as reliability and timeliness.

14.2.2.2 Management Issues

This section focusses on the following five criteria: utilising the blockchain, internet-based traffic management, congestion control, parking, convenient travel, and urban space optimisation may all be used to improve traffic solutions, reduce traffic congestion, and encourage urban development. Blockchain technology allows an aggregate signature approach to connect channels under the chain, creating a safe, large-scale, real-time payment system and increasing blockchain capacity [20]. Drivers' basic personal information and credit ratings are public, but blockchain-stored internet-based traffic data makes them liable for accidents. By monitoring Internet traffic transaction data and analysing circumstances, the government can more effectively collect and manage taxes. With "smart contracts" and blockchain technology, the traffic control department distributes a limited number of mobile permits to all users and allows free market exchange [21].

High fares are allocated to emergency vehicles on all routes. Data exchange between automobiles and the Bet-Regional industrial agglomeration facilitates sustainable city expansion, urban form and space optimisation, and transportation network optimisation in the context of the "Internet of vehicles" [22]. Blockchain users are encouraged to exchange traffic information and enhance navigation for comfortable travel. Reducing traffic congestion and enhancing public transport will simplify travel. Free parking can be swapped on the blockchain, earning cash for owners and solving parking issues.

14.2.2.3 Superior System Design

The reward and punishment system, credit evaluation system, and top-level system architecture are all part of the framework for the blockchain-based intelligent traffic index. For blockchain users who actively participate and publish genuine data, there are rewards and penalties in the form of virtual currency. Blockchain technology assures data integrity and non-repudiation, assesses user trust based on behaviour, service, and task trust, and creates a safe database for many timestamp analytical queries in credit assessment systems. The article in [22] described a blockchain-based decentralised automobile network trust management system.

14.2.3 Blockchain-Enabled Intelligent Transportation: Environmental Impact

Automotive exhaust emissions are the worst part of urban traffic pollution. Blockchain can reduce urban traffic pollution by optimising routes, controlling speed, preventing acceleration and idling, and promoting or requiring heavy truck lines to reduce air resistance and fuel usage. Electric vehicle use has increased due to vehicle-to-grid (V2G) energy transactions between charging stations and automobiles. A more thorough system has raised public transport rates. A good urban greening plan based on transportation consortium blockchain data improves urban environmental governance.

14.3 INTELLIGENT TRANSPORT MANAGEMENT SYSTEMS USING BLOCKCHAIN TECHNOLOGY

Safe, transparent, and efficient blockchain solutions can change intelligent transportation management systems (ITMS). Some primary areas where blockchain can be integrated into IT management systems:

1. *Privacy and Data Security:*
    - *Immutable Records:* Blockchain's decentralised ledger prevents data changes. This is essential for transportation data integrity.
    - *Data Privacy:* Blockchain technology can protect user privacy and data integrity from transportation sensors and gadgets.
2. *Live Data Sharing:*
    - *Decentralised Data Exchange:* Blockchain allows government agencies, transportation businesses, and users to communicate real-time data without a central authority.
    - *Smart Contracts:* Automating data transfers and transactions reduces delays and improves transport networks.
3. *Vehicle and Fleet Management:*
    - *Tracking and Maintenance:* Blockchain can track vehicle maintenance, usage, and ownership changes, reducing fraud and maintaining transparency.
    - *Asset Management:* Fleet managers can track vehicle usage, improve routes, and better manage resources with blockchain technology.
4. *Tolls and Payment:*
    - Blockchain can automate toll payments, parking fees, and other transportation transactions using cryptocurrencies or digital tokens.
    - Blockchain reduces payment system fraud by recording transactions on an immutable ledger.
5. *Logistics and Supply Chain:*
    - *Transparent Supply Chains:* Blockchain technology can track things in transit in real time.
    - *Efficiency:* Smart contracts can automate cargo monitoring and delivery confirmation, reducing administrative costs and enhancing productivity.

6. *Management of Traffic:*
   - *Decentralised Traffic Control:* Blockchain can help decentralised traffic management systems combine and evaluate data from multiple sources to optimise traffic flow and reduce congestion.
   - Rewards from blockchain-based incentive schemes can encourage carpooling, public travel, and other green practices.
7. *Transportation and Ridesharing:*
   - Blockchain can enable decentralised ride-sharing services, reducing consumer costs and intermediaries.
   - Blockchain can improve ride-sharing trust and reputation systems, ensuring drivers and passengers have correct information.
8. *Compliance with Regulations:*
   - Blockchain technology allows transparent and efficient reporting to regulatory organisations, ensuring transportation standards compliance.
   - *Audit Trails:* Blockchain's immutable records make regulatory audits and investigations easier.

Blockchain technology in ITMS can help cities and transportation companies create more secure, efficient, and transparent transportation networks, improving user experience and promoting sustainable mobility.

14.4 TRUCK TRANSPORTATION BLOCKCHAIN

Blockchain improves logistics and scheduling by verifying data faster. Companies can track fleets, find alternative routes, and monitor road conditions. Many companies use the global supply chain to serve clients worldwide. Only recently has this dependency expanded. Trucking is vital to the supply chain. They deliver and fulfil orders for several industries. Blockchain could simplify trucking processes. Security checks, commodities validation, and cross-border freight and transit taxes and tariffs are simply met. Blockchain can be utilised with facial recognition and automation. These sophisticated solutions secure data management, storage, and access. Without any effort, it can automate your activities and transactions.

14.5 PUBLIC TRANSPORTATION AND BLOCKCHAIN

Blockchain can also improve public transit. It might dramatically reduce corporate expenses, hazards, and waste. It provides a clear audit trail for public transport companies to ensure regulatory compliance and contract management. Blockchain automates data and information storage, reducing paperwork. All parties' privacy is protected when sensitive data is hack-proof. Blockchain enhances insurance, brokerage, and settlement firms. Modern transport networks involve various stakeholders working together to serve the public. Support systems like signalling and ticketing, which handle data quickly, link them. Blockchain technology could streamline communications, inspections, approvals, and revenue clearances due to this partnership. It secures all data layers. Real-time evaluations boost network availability and system fault tolerance. This dramatically cuts costs and boosts efficiency. Many operators can partner with various organisations to ensure smooth transportation services using blockchain technology.

14.6 NON-EMERGENCY MEDICAL TRANSPORT (NEMT) BLOCKCHAIN

Non-emergency medical transport (NEMT) can plan and manage transportation using blockchain technology. They can streamline healthcare services for patients and clients. Medical transportation spending will increase by 2023 under US public health initiatives. The business insurance market spends about $2 billion on NEMT. The medical transportation industry will grow in 2023 and beyond. NEMT providers provide many healthcare services. Thus, the sector has seen many client-assistance methods. Blockchain technology improves efficiency and savings. NEMT providers working with government-funded schemes and private insurers may be affected. RouteGenie, a cutting-edge NEMT software provider, leverages innovative tech. It records scheduled healthcare provider or facility visits. This saves time, money, and resources. The programme provides transparency and interoperability.

14.7 BLOCKCHAIN-ENABLED INTELLIGENT TRANSPORTATION SYSTEMS APPLICATIONS

Based on the literature, we draw the conclusion that blockchain technology is capable of handling BBITMS services and applications, including on-demand transportation, vehicle management, and vehicular data security. We shall examine blockchain technology in BBITMS applications in the next part.

14.8 PROTECTING AND MANAGING DATA

More automobiles will generate a lot of data as BBITMS applications expand, enhancing vehicular services and driving safety. Vehicles will store, share, manage, and use created and shared data through the use of edge computing nodes, such as RSUs. Dispersed along the roadway, edge computing nodes pose security and privacy risks. Because multiple service providers control edge nodes, regulation and trust are difficult to build. Vehicles may not transmit data for the above reasons. Vehicle data management systems now leverage blockchain technology to address security, privacy, and edge node trust. Consortium blockchain is used to create a safe and distributed data management solution for car edge computing networks. Our proposed solution benefits from smart contracts in two ways. The smart contract secures data exchange and storage in automobiles and vehicular edge computing servers like RSUs. Second, the smart contract prevents unauthorised data transfers.

To assist cars in selecting the most dependable and superior information source, this suggested system additionally makes use of a reputation-based data exchange technique. To accurately maintain vehicle reputation, a three-weight subjective logic model takes into account the number of interactions, timeliness of events, and similarity of trajectories. The suggested system detects malicious and unusual vehicles better than existing reputation algorithms. Similar to [7], DrivMan, a blockchain-based automobile solution, uses smart contracts, physically unclonable functions (PUF), and public key infrastructure to handle trust, data provenance, and privacy. DrivMan uses blockchain to distribute trust management in a non-trusted network. PUF helps DrivMan confirm data provenance by assigning a crypto fingerprint to each vehicle. PKI also registers and assigns automobile key pairs via a certificate authority. The CA can identify malevolent automobiles and cancel certifications. By severing the link between identities and public keys, the PKI protects privacy and prevents breaches. ITS vehicular data sharing is secure using blockchain. According to [8], car social networks can employ blockchain and cryptography to share multimedia data. This method addresses hazardous shared multimedia data alteration via blockchain immutability. Data tracing using blockchain detects fake user data. Cryptographic techniques safeguard the anonymity of users, cars, and RSUs when exchanging data. Identity and sharing of all entities are involved in privacy leaks. In Figure 14.1, the system model is displayed. explains a safe and effective vehicle-assisted data sharing technique based on blockchain [9]. A new key negotiation mechanism with traceability and authentication is the main contribution to this security strategy. This approach seeks to address concerns about trust, monitoring, and shared data security. The suggested method automates key exchanges using static or dynamic scripts for fast and automatic vehicle communications key negotiations. It also uses timestamps to confirm and publicise key negotiation methods to prevent decryption failure attacks. Package dropping assaults are prevented by scripts, channel availability, and negotiation timeliness.

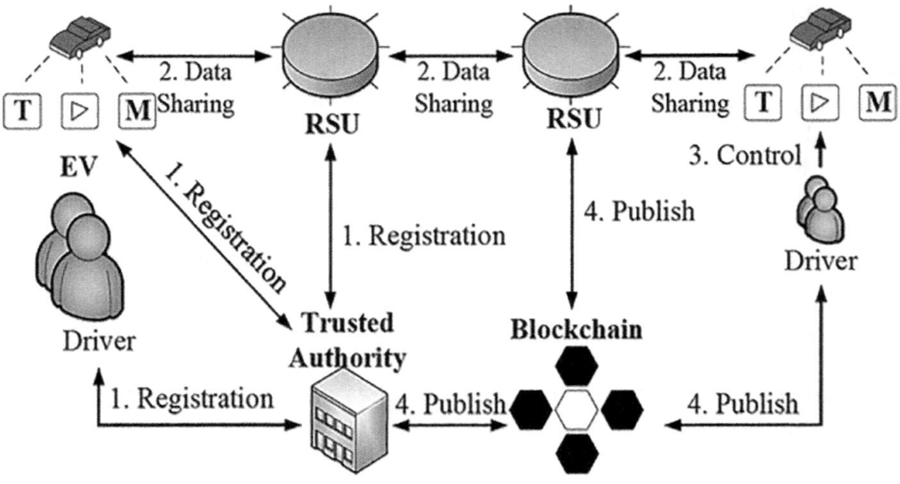

FIGURE 14.1 Blockchain-based security system concept privacy-preserving multimedia data transfer began vehicle-based social networks.

14.9 DATA AND RESOURCES

Data and resource trading in BBITMS situations expands auto and related industries. Trade in data and resources may pose security concerns, including access control and user privacy. Due to vehicle mobility and wireless links, trade scenarios may be vulnerable to DoS and jammer assaults. Indeed, unintentional attacks may occur. Another problem is avoiding harmful attacks and assuring intermittent and trustworthy trading between trading partners. Blockchain technology may solve most of the above issues, according to recent research. Blockchain could enable secure, peer-to-peer, decentralised data and resource transmission across BBITMS entities. Blockchain and vehicle data trade enable peer-to-peer trading. The article in [9] presents a blockchain-assisted BBITMS framework for secure and efficient data transmission. Blockchain technology addresses data trade difficulties such as lack of transparency, traceability, and unauthorised data tampering. The figure shows this framework's blockchain architecture. It uses a partnership of local aggregators to audit and verify transactions. The iterative double auction strategy optimises data prices, social welfare, and buyer and seller privacy, encouraging more people to trade data. System stability is improved by considering data transport costs. Vehicle resource sharing also uses blockchain.

The article in [1] discusses a blockchain-based peer-to-peer computing resource trading system. This proposal addresses edge-cloud-based resource trading challenges, such as setting a valid bid and allowing sellers and buyers to trade. This design includes a broker to maintain trading. Counting traded resources and setting a price guideline to promote honest bids can help the broker distribute resources. This approach uses iterative double-sided auctions. It emphasises maximum social welfare, individual reason, and a balanced budget. Figure 14.2 shows blockchain-based computing resource trade in detail.

14.10 RESOURCE-SHARING

BBITMS enables stationary and mobile vehicle resource sharing. Users can swap surplus processing and spectrum with nearby firms on this marketplace. This platform supports AI and latency-sensitive services. Despite the advantages, two issues remain. Because cars may not trust each other, creating and maintaining such a platform is tough. While cars share resources, blockchain technology maintains integrity. Another challenge is creating procedures that offer economic incentives to cars for resource-sharing. Blockchain can enable a decentralised infrastructure that lets cars share resources, improving efficiency and capability. Blockchain can solve resource sharing issues, including trust, security, and privacy. BBITMS resource sharing using blockchain is described in [3]. A reputation-based consensus mechanism lighter than typical PoW is detailed in this scheme to build trust and lessen reliance on computationally expensive mining procedures. Reputation scores show car reliability here. The suggested consensus process and sharing technique are combined for trust management using vehicle reputation scores. This technique preserves blockchain and sharing records via RSUs. Furthermore, in order to balance supply and demand while sharing resources, a smart contract-based resource pricing system

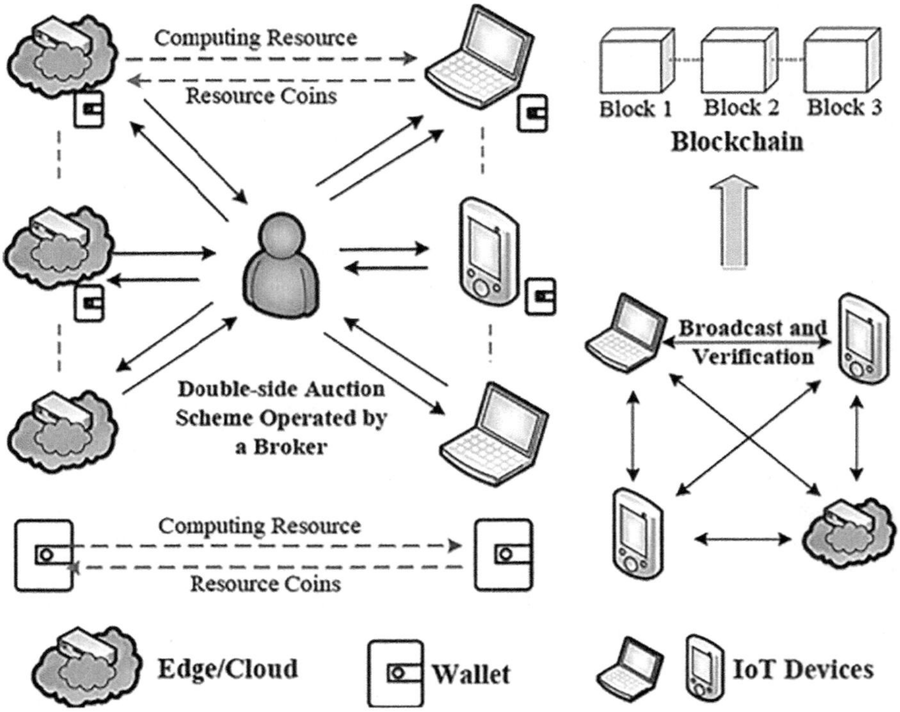

FIGURE 14.2 Blockchain-based plan workflow describes the computer resource trading platform.

makes use of deep reinforcement learning as well as vehicle mobility and position. This resource-sharing pricing model is 30% better than unified pricing. Next, this system separates resource sharing and block validator cars to safeguard their privacy and reduce communication latency when publishing new blocks.

14.11 VEHICLE MANAGEMENT

Smart parking and platooning are popular vehicle management techniques. The smart parking management system lets drivers schedule free parking places in advance. Prebooking saves drivers time and reduces traffic. However, the vehicle platoon concept groups vehicles with similar interests. A vehicle with or without a driver leads the other autonomous cars, which stay a short distance apart. The platoon head is the leading vehicle, while the others are members. As automobiles, parking spots, and roadside units proliferate, the management system will become more complex. If management uses a central system, it will struggle to secure user privacy and large-scale interaction between cars, vehicle users, and parking lot owners. Blockchain can fix these issues in vehicle management systems. Blockchain can solve the issues with centralised parking systems, such as the need to reveal private information like destination information when booking and the centralised architecture, which can lead to availability attacks and data leaks.

In [5], the authors suggest a blockchain-based scheme that lets vehicles search for and reserve parking spaces decentralised and privately. Blockchain solves centralised system issues in this design. Parking lot owners form a cooperative to administer the blockchain and share offers and information despite scepticism. Blockchain will store parking offers. Additionally, blockchain and PIR are used to secure car drivers' location privacy. Vehicles can use the PIR approach to look for parking without having to identify a location by searching the blockchain network. Drivers utilise a rapid randomisable signature to secretly confirm parking reservations with parking owners after getting blockchain offers. This quick randomisable signature provides conditional privacy, enabling legitimate authorities to identify drivers and take action against illicit activity. The proposed anonymous payment technique allows drivers to pay without disclosing sensitive information, unlike card payment methods. Openness, decentralisation, and security help blockchain speed up vehicle platooning management. To accelerate autonomous driving and intelligent transportation, for example, autonomous vehicles (AVs) can form a vehicle platoon with the help of blockchain-assisted urban BBITMS [6]. Because platooning reduces air friction, it is a fuel-efficient method of long-distance truck cargo delivery. Since the trucks are owned by the same delivery firm, no money is made. This model matches only specific AVs using path information matching to create a platoon. AV platoon heads are picked for reputation. In this concept, AVs are incentivised to become platoon heads and update platoon records. Blockchain and smart contracts protect platoon head-member automobile payments from fraud and malice. Platoon members must pay the head for contract-compliant services.

14.12 RIDESHARING

Uber and travel ease have made ride-sharing services popular. These services let users share a car to get there. Shared vehicles reduce traffic, especially during peak hours, carbon emissions, and vehicle numbers. Metropolitan vehicular mobility improves. Future driverless cars may also boost ride-sharing businesses. As cellphones and apps improve, on-demand transport services become more accessible. Despite their benefits, cloud-based ride-sharing services have two issues. Due to the centralised cloud connection, consumers may face long communication delays. Second, centralised storage exposes user privacy and raises management. A reliable, secure, and private ride-sharing service is essential to encourage car sharing. Recently, blockchain has been used here.

In [7], the writers discuss the challenges of developing a centralised ride-sharing network for AVs. Autonomous vehicles will be able to function as part of a community-driven fleet thanks to a decentralised ride-sharing system supported by blockchain technology. The suggested design provides more flexibility in transportation pricing and profit sharing by serving as a platform between passengers and autonomous cars. Through the use of blockchain, which is managed by a cooperative group of autonomous car owners, this system establishes trust amongst non-trusting nodes. The foundation of the suggested design is the chain code protocol and Hyperledger Fabric blockchain platform. Data is safeguarded by chain code while client apps are connected to the blockchain network.

14.13 CONTENT BROADCASTING

Internet-connected cars broadcast content to improve in-vehicle and safety services. These services offer advertising, internet shopping, product promotion, entertainment, and emergency announcements. RSUs and other edge computing nodes can cache popular material, broadcast it to nearby vehicles, and reduce latency to improve vehicle user experiences. Blockchain could enable V2V and V2I vehicle content exchange and streaming. A blockchain-assisted peer-to-peer paradigm can make the BBITMS efficient, cost-effective, and dependable. Blockchain also enables unique reward schemes to speed content dissemination. Recently, blockchain has been used to transmit car content. Blockchain, edge computing, and 5G technology are used to propose an event-driven message (EDM) protocol for vehicular applications [10]. EDMs are standard messages used only for emergency warning alerts, usually during accidents or emergencies. This method distributes and audits EDMs via blockchain. This idea processes EDMs locally using edge computing to increase reaction time. In addition, 5G connectivity may offer scalability and reduced latency for cars. This method uses lightweight, efficient, pairing-free multi-receiver encryption to handle problems with high processing time, security, and access control.

14.14 TRAFFIC CONTROL AND MANAGEMENT

Access to traffic management services will increase with the sharing of car accident reports and traffic data. In smart transportation systems, information can facilitate dynamic traffic control and management, traffic condition monitoring, and the reduction of traffic congestion for automobiles. Certain use cases necessitate secure administration and control. It's crucial to put security first. Vehicular traffic data storage and transfer from moving cars to roadside devices may be subject to security concerns that compromise data privacy, integrity, and availability. Another challenge is developing an automated system for traffic control and management. Blockchain might be a superior option because it offers decentralised management, availability, automaticity, and immutability. The SCTSC (semi-centralised traffic signal control) system is thus presented in [12]. This system will use autonomous traffic signalling, a BBITMS application in development, to boost traffic control efficiency. Data is gathered by this suggested system from sensors and drivers. Unlike the pretimed mode, the suggested system uses data to dynamically manage and control traffic lights per vehicle. Attribute-based encryption and blockchain are used in this system (ABE). By classifying vehicles based on their location and intended destination, ABE preserves access control in traffic-related data while increasing efficiency and surpassing pretimed vehicle passage rates. However, blockchain allows vehicles to vote on signal timing to reach an agreement. Next, blockchain will record the agreement and decision. To protect their privacy, automobiles will communicate anonymously. The paper in [13] proposes a smart transport system for intelligent traffic. This proposed solution uses blockchain and car sensor nodes connected to IoT. A credit-token system lets vehicles pay for service consumption and misuse. This initiative uses blockchain to reduce traffic and increase road safety.

14.15 APPLICATION OF FORENSICS

Digital forensics could benefit from blockchain. BBITMS is used to look into traffic incidents, particularly ones involving AVs. Blockchain can connect all parties, record vehicle-related data for autonomy, and use smart contracts to determine post-accident demurrages. Block4Forensic offers a comprehensive car forensic framework through the use of permissioned blockchain and vehicle public key infrastructure (VPKI) [14]. Car crash forensics are offered by this Block4Forensic platform. The figure illustrates how a single platform powered by the blockchain links automobiles, roadside assistance, automakers, insurance companies, and law enforcement. Evidence and other data are stored on blockchains. Systems with fragmented distributed ledgers and shared ledgers, respectively, can store hashed data and vehicle data. Shared ledgers cut down on processing and storage expenses. Membership establishment is guaranteed by VPKI. Moreover, this system uses pseudonyms to conceal the identity of cars from unauthorised users. Another study suggests a blockchain, smart contract, and SDN-based digital forensics and data tracking architecture [15]. The proposed architecture addresses centralised forensic management integrity and dependability issues. Blockchain enhances the integrity of forensic data management by storing and gathering digital evidence. Cloud computing is supported by this approach, but cloud evidence is blocked by the SDN controller. This system also makes use of sophisticated cryptography. Sensitive-aware deep ECC and secure ring verification support authentication to safeguard data. Furthermore, data provenance is tracked using a fuzzy smart contract on the blockchain.

14.16 REMARKS

In the earlier studies, we introduced eight scenarios of blockchain-assisted BBITMS applications: data management, protection, trade, resource sharing, vehicle management, ride sharing, broadcasting, traffic control, and forensics. Many applications are mentioned. The introduction of BBITMS allows many uses; however, we have only emphasised blockchain activities. The next section will present some blockchain-BBITMS designs and frameworks.

14.17 CONCLUSION

In conclusion, the blockchain-based intelligent transportation management system (BBBITMS) represents a significant advancement in addressing the challenges of modern urban mobility. BBBITMS improves transportation system efficiency and dependability by using blockchain technology's decentralisation, transparency, and security. Smart contracts automate transport procedures, minimising human error and improving efficiency. The application of advanced data analytics and machine learning within this framework further enables real-time traffic management, predictive maintenance, and rapid incident response, thereby improving overall traffic flow and safety. The successful implementation of BBBITMS has the potential to significantly reduce traffic congestion, lower emissions, and enhance the user experience for commuters and logistics providers alike. Preliminary simulations and case studies have shown promising results, indicating the feasibility and effectiveness of BBBITMS in diverse urban environments. As cities continue to grow and transportation networks become increasingly complex, the adoption of blockchain-based solutions will be crucial in creating smarter, more sustainable urban transportation systems. Overall, BBBITMS not only addresses current transportation challenges but also lays the groundwork for future innovations in intelligent transportation management, paving the way for smarter, more connected cities.

REFERENCES

1. D. S. Sarwatt, Y. Lin, J. Ding, Y. Sun and H. Ning, "Metaverse for Intelligent Transportation Systems (ITS): A Comprehensive Review of Technologies, Applications, Implications, Challenges and Future Directions," in *IEEE Transactions on Intelligent Transportation Systems*, vol. 25, no. 7, pp. 6290–6308, July 2024.
2. Y. Fu, C. Li, F. R. Yu, T. H. Luan, P. Zhao and S. Liu, "A Survey of Blockchain and Intelligent Networking for the Metaverse," in *IEEE Internet of Things Journal*, vol. 10, no. 4, pp. 3587–3610, February 2023, doi: 10.1109/JIOT.2022.3222521
3. T. Chen, H. Zhou, H. Yang and S. Liu, "A Review of Research on Metaverse Defining Taxonomy and Adaptive Architecture," 2022 5th International Conference on Pattern Recognition and Artificial Intelligence (PRAI), Chengdu, China, 2022, pp. 960–965, doi: 10.1109/PRAI55851.2022.9904076.
4. W. C. Ng, H. Du, W. Y. B. Lim, Z. Xiong, D. Niyato and C. Miao, "Stochastic Resource Allocation for Semantic Communication-Aided Virtual Transportation Networks in the Metaverse," 2024 IEEE Wireless Communications and Networking Conference (WCNC), Dubai, United Arab Emirates, 2024, pp. 1–6, doi: 10.1109/WCNC57260.2024.10570867.
5. F. Tang, X. Chen, M. Zhao and N. Kato, "The Roadmap of Communication and Networking in 6G for the Metaverse," in *IEEE Wireless Communications*, vol. 30, no. 4, pp. 72–81, August 2023, doi: 10.1109/MWC.019.2100721.
6. E. Dincelli and A. Yayla, "Immersive Virtual Reality in the Age of the Metaverse: A Hybrid-Narrative Review based on the Technology Affordance Perspective," in *The Journal of Strategic Information Systems*, vol. 31, no. 2, 2022, p. 101717, ISSN 0963-8687, https://doi.org/10.1016/j.jsis.2022.101717.
7. J. Zhang, F. -Y. Wang, K. Wang, W. -H. Lin, X. Xu and C. Chen, "Data-Driven Intelligent Transportation Systems: A Survey," in *IEEE Transactions on Intelligent Transportation Systems*, vol. 12, no. 4, pp. 1624–1639, December 2011, doi: 10.1109/TITS.2011.2158001
8. A. Siyaev, and G.-S. Jo, "Towards Aircraft Maintenance Metaverse Using Speech Interactions with Virtual Objects in Mixed Reality," *Sensors*, vol. 21, no. 6, p. 2066, 2021.
9. S. AR and B. Gupta, "A Comprehensive Study of Blockchain Services: Future of Cryptography," *International Journal of Advanced Computer Science and Applications*, vol. 11, no. 10, 2020, doi: https://doi.org/10.14569/ijacsa.2020.0111037.
10. H. Xu et al., "Smart Mobility in the Cloud: Enabling Real-Time Situational Awareness and Cyber-Physical Control Through a Digital Twin for Traffic," in *IEEE Transactions on Intelligent Transportation Systems*, vol. 24, no. 3, pp. 3145–3156, March 2023, doi: 10.1109/TITS.2022.3226746.
11. W. Huang and X. Su, "Design of a Fault Detection and Isolation System for Intelligent Vehicle Navigation System," in *International Journal of Navigation and Observation*, vol. 2015, pp. 1–19, 2015. 10.1155/2015/279086.

12. T. Huynh-The, Q.-V. Pham, X.-Q. Pham, T. T. Nguyen, Z. Han, D.-S. Kim, "Artificial Intelligence for the Metaverse: A Survey," in *Engineering Applications of Artificial Intelligence*, vol. 117, no. Part A, p. 105581, 2023, ISSN 0952-1976, https://doi.org/10.1016/j.engappai.2022.105581.
13. Panda, S.K., Elngar, A.A., Balas, V.E., & Kayed, M. (Eds.). (2020). *Bitcoin and Blockchain: History and Current Applications* (1st ed.). CRC Press. https://doi.org/10.1201/9781003032588
14. M. Aslam, R. Chaudhary, A. Bhardwaj, I. Budhiraja, N. Kumar and S. Zeadally, "Metaverse for 6G and Beyond: The Next Revolution and Deployment Challenges," in *IEEE Internet of Things Magazine*, vol. 6, no. 1, pp. 32–39, March 2023, doi: 10.1109/IOTM.001.2200248
15. M. Aloqaily, O. Bouachir, F. Karray, I. Al Ridhawi and A. E. Saddik, "Integrating Digital Twin and Advanced Intelligent Technologies to Realize the Metaverse," in *IEEE Consumer Electronics Magazine*, vol. 12, no. 6, pp. 47–55, 1 November 2023, doi: 10.1109/MCE.2022.3212570.
16. H. Jeon, H. Youn, S. Ko, and T. Kim, "Blockchain and AI Meet in the Metaverse," *Blockchain Potential in AI*. IntechOpen, Jan. 12, 2022. doi: 10.5772/intechopen.99114.
17. Sathya, A. R. (2023). Blockchain: The Foundation of Trust in Metaverse. In: Panda, S.K., Mishra, V., Dash, S.P., Pani, A.K. (eds) *Recent Advances in Blockchain Technology. Intelligent Systems Reference Library*, vol 237. Springer, Cham. https://doi.org/10.1007/978-3-031-22835-3_5
18. D. Wu, Z. Yang, P. Zhang, R. Wang, B. Yang and X. Ma, "Virtual-Reality Interpromotion Technology for Metaverse: A Survey," in *IEEE Internet of Things Journal*, vol. 10, no. 18, pp. 15788–15809, September 2023, doi: 10.1109/JIOT.2023.3265848
19. J. A. Guerrero-ibanez, S. Zeadally and J. Contreras-Castillo, "Integration Challenges of Intelligent Transportation Systems with Connected Vehicle, Cloud Computing, and Internet of Things Technologies," in *IEEE Wireless Communications*, vol. 22, no. 6, pp. 122–128, December 2015, doi: 10.1109/MWC.2015.7368833
20. Kasam, R., Sathya, A.R. (2026). Uncovering Vulnerabilities: A Comprehensive Survey of Blockchain and Smart Contract Security and Mitigation Strategies with Case Studies. In: Bhateja, V., El Barachi, M., Azar, A.T., Sharma, D.K. (eds) *Information System Design: Big Data Analytics and Data Science*. ISDIA 2025. Lecture Notes in Networks and Systems, vol 1539. Springer, Singapore. https://doi.org/10.1007/978-981-96-9248-4_22
21. A. Mahapatra, S. K. Majhi, K. Mishra, R. Pradhan, D. C. Rao and S. K. Panda, "An Energy-Aware Task Offloading and Load Balancing for Latency-Sensitive IoT Applications in the Fog-Cloud Continuum," in *IEEE Access*, vol. 12, pp. 14334–14349, 2024, doi: 10.1109/ACCESS.2024.3357122.
22. D. D. Desai et al., "Optimal Ambulance Positioning for Road Accidents with Deep Embedded Clustering," in *IEEE Access*, vol. 11, pp. 59917–59934, 2023, doi: 10.1109/ACCESS.2023.3284993.

Index

For Product Safety Concerns and Information please contact our EU representative GPSR@taylorandfrancis.com Taylor & Francis Verlag GmbH, Kaufingerstraße 24, 80331 München, Germany

Batch number: 10823957

Printed by Printforce, the Netherlands